# Economic Analysis
# of Intercity
# Freight Transportation

# Economic Analysis
# of Intercity
# Freight Transportation

GEORGE W. WILSON

Indiana University Press
Bloomington

This book was brought to publication
with the assistance of a grant from the
Indiana University School of Business.

Portions of this book originally appeared in George W. Wilson, *Essays on
Some Unsettled Questions in the Economics of Transportation,* © 1962 by
Foundation for Economic and Business Studies, Indiana University; and
in George W. Wilson, ed., *Technological Development and Economic
Growth* © 1972 by Division of Research, Indiana University.

Manufactured in the United States of America

Library of Congress Cataloging in Publication Data

Wilson, George Wilton, 1928-
Economic analysis of intercity freight transportation.

Includes index.
1.Freight and freightage—Mathematical models.
I.Title.    II.Title:Intercity freight transportation
HE199.A2W55    380.5'24    79-3131
ISBN 0-253-36915-0    1 2 3 4 5 84 83 82 81 80

*To Marie, Ron, Doug,
and Suzanne*

# Contents

# Part II:

## Efficient Expansion of Transport Capacity

# *Preface*

This book is designed to fill an apparent gap in the economic analysis of transportation problems, with special reference to intercity freight transport. Much has been written on urban and passenger transport and on transportation more generally. Yet there is a lack of careful economic analysis and attempts to assess the many empirical studies of the intercity freight market in terms of demand, supply, costs, pricing, and regulation. Part I outlines the theory of the derived demand for intercity freight transport in its several forms and examines the attempts to measure the level and elasticity of demand at various levels of aggregation. It also investigates efficient pricing criteria, with respect to the theory and measurement of transport costs by mode, and reviews what is known analytically and empirically about the economic effects of intercity transportation regulation. Part I, in essence, attempts to analyze the criteria relevant to a more efficient use of existing transport facilities. Part II takes up the problem of expanding transportation capacity using efficiency criteria.

In earlier form, this volume was used in several classes at Indiana University. To those students who suffered through it and provided useful suggestions for improvement, I am greatly indebted. My major debt, however, is to Professor L. L. Waters, who shielded and guided me over many years and provided constant support and enthusiasm for this project. I hope I have not let him down.

*Economic Analysis*
*of Intercity*
*Freight Transportation*

# PART I

# *Efficient Utilization of Existing Transport Capacity*

# The Demand for Intercity Freight Transportation

The demand for intercity commodity movement is obviously a derived demand—commodities do not receive satisfaction or utility from
being transported. Freight movements, therefore, result from decisions
made in other sections of the economy concerning production, consumption, and sales that have little to do with transport per se. Such a
derived demand for transportation can be viewed at various levels of
aggregation, ranging from that of the nation as a whole to the demand
for transport of an individual commodity between a specified pair of
points. In addition, demand for transport can refer to all modes combined at any of these levels of aggregation or for a specific mode.

For each of the above sets of demands for transportation, there are
two aspects we wish to explore: the *level* of demand and the *elasticity*
of demand. By the former we simply mean, How far from the origin
is the transportation demand curve or demand function? For any given
freight rate, are commodity movements substantial or relatively small
in terms of tonnage or ton-miles?

## The Level of Transport Demand

Other things being equal, the tonnage shipped depends on production and consumption levels. For the nation as a whole, the amount of
needed transportation in *tonnage* terms is a function of real physical-
goods production (i.e., real GNP less services). The higher the level of
goods output the higher the demand for goods movement, modified by
any change in the level of real inventories.

In terms of *ton-miles* of transport one would similarly expect in the
aggregate to find a close relationship between goods production and
ton-miles for any nation, given the geographical location of major production and consumption centers and modified by inventory changes.

In reality, the aggregate derived demand for ton-miles is closely related to real GNP or some index of real output, say, the index of indus-

3

trial production combined with an index of agricultural production. This is largely because locational patterns once established tend to be fairly stable and inventory changes are relatively small compared with total production. A simple regression between ton-miles and GNP (in constant 1958 dollars) for the United States from 1950 through 1973 yielded the following:

$$T = 224 + 2.31 \, GNP, \text{ where } T = \text{ton-miles in billions}$$
$$\text{and } GNP = \text{GNP in billions.}$$

In the regression, the coefficient of correlation is .99, which implies a coefficient of determination of a similar magnitude. Thus, the number of "needed" ton-miles is almost entirely dependent on real GNP.

Since time-series analysis is believed to represent short-run phenomena,[1] the closeness of the relationship may be somewhat less over longer periods, as industries may relocate in response to variations in locational determinants. For our purposes it is enough to note from the foregoing that the number of ton-miles in the aggregate does not appear to be sensitive in the short run to the level of freight rates or change therein. In the longer run, one would expect more sensitivity of ton-miles to freight rate changes since the latter would induce some relocation and thus alter the above relationship between real GNP and ton-miles.

One can envisage a national demand and supply schedule for transportation as shown in Figure 1.1. $D_1D_1$ and $S_1S_1$ are conventional demand and supply schedules for a factor of production, in this case "transport inputs"[2] measured by ton-miles.[3] Underlying the level and shape of the aggregate demand function is, of course, the level of GNP as noted above. The shape of the demand function also reflects the overwhelming importance of total goods production in the short run compared with the longer run. That is, the short-run aggregate demand for transport inputs is highly inelastic,[4] meaning that short-run

---

1. For a discussion of this point and of linear regression measures, see chapter 2.

2. Transport inputs are not usually viewed as one of the four basic factors of production (land, labor, capital, and entrepreneurship), and, of course, the cost of supplying transport inputs can easily be reduced to the amounts and values of the four basic factors. However, one observer has ventured the hypothesis that "had there been a certain social class which owned all transport facilities . . . , the Classicals might well have thought of transport as a (separate) factor of production. . . ." Walter Isard, *Location and Space Economy* (New York: John Wiley & Sons), p. 89.

3. Ton-miles is only one of many possible measures of transport inputs (or outputs), as examined briefly later. I have dwelt on this matter at length in G. Wilson, *Essays on Some Unsettled Questions in the Economics of Transportation* (Bloomington: Foundation for Economic and Business Studies, Indiana University, 1962), especially chaps. 1 and 2.

4. Elasticity, its meaning and measurement, is examined more fully in the next section.

changes in the freight rate[5] will not induce large changes in the quantities of ton-miles consumed or bought and sold. In the longer run, however, the demand for ton-miles of service is likely to be somewhat more sensitive to freight rate changes, say, $D_2D_2$, other things being equal. Thus, if the supply schedule were to shift to the right ($S_2S_2$) because of a technological change in the provision of freight transport services (e.g., substitution of the diesel for the steam engine), the new *short-run* equilibrium price would be $P_2$ and the increase in sales of ton-miles would be $OM_2 - OM_1$. If $D_2D_2$ represents the long-run de-

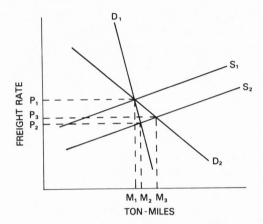

Fig. 1.1

mand, the ultimate new long-run equilibrium price would be $P_3$ and the increase in sales would be $OM_3 - OM_1$. Clearly, the elasticity of the long-run demand exceeds the short-run demand in this exhibit since by definition

$$\epsilon_T = \frac{-\%\Delta \text{ in } Q_D}{\%\Delta \text{ in } P}.$$

Along $D_2D_2$ the numerator exceeds that along $D_1D_1$ for any given shift in supply, while the denominator is less, i.e., $\dfrac{OM_3 - OM_1}{OM_1} >$ $\dfrac{OM_2 - OM_1}{OM_1}$ and $\dfrac{P_1 - P_3}{P_1} < \dfrac{P_1 - P_2}{P_1}$. It will be noted here that the extent to which the long- and short-run elasticities differ depends on the shape of the supply schedule. If the supply schedule were horizontal (i.e., if the elasticity of supply were infinite), the divergence would be greatest for a parallel shift in the supply schedule; if the

5. There is, of course, no such thing as *the* freight rate—there are thousands of freight rates. By the same token, there is no such thing as *the* interest rate, *the* wage rate, etc. Yet, conceptually, economists have found it useful to speak in such terms.

elasticity of supply were zero, both elasticities would differ solely by the percentage change in price.

The reasons why the long-run elasticity of demand exceeds the short-run are fairly obvious. A decrease in freight rates permits some combination of increased net profits to all producers and/or decreased commodity prices. The former tend to stimulate more investment expenditures while the latter stimulate consumption; either tendency will raise real GNP. However, new investment takes time, and the decrease in commodity prices may not be immediate; the speed of the decline will depend on the degree of market competition. Over longer time spans, a freight rate decrease will "transform a scattered, ubiquitous pattern of production into an increasingly concentrated one"[6] with generally longer average hauls and greater output due to increased specialization. What has happened, of course, is that transport inputs have been substituted for other inputs at higher volumes of output, as illustrated in Figure 1.2.

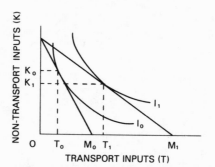

Fig. 1.2

In Figure 1.2 we have constructed two isoquants $I_0$ and $I_1$, which indicate the various combinations of transport and other inputs to produce a given output $I_0$ or $I_1$ ($I_1 > I_0$). The least-cost factor combination is determined at the point of intersection of the iso-cost line ($M_0M_0$), which indicates that $K_0$ units of other factors combined with $T_0$ units of transport inputs yield the least-cost way of producing an output of $I_0$ for given prices of other inputs and given freight rates. If freight rates decrease, the iso-cost line shifts to $M_0M_1$ and a new least-cost factor combination $K_1,T_1$ results. The total increase in transport inputs demanded can easily be decomposed into an output and substitution effect, but for present purposes it is enough to note the increase in demand for transport.

Since these adjustments take time and since substitutability among or between inputs increases with time, the divergence between long-

6. Isard, p.87.

and short-run elasticities is further rationalized. Of course, both the importance of transportation and the degree of substitutability between transport and other inputs thus tend to be overemphasized. We will stress these points later. At the moment we are interested in illustrating analytically, using well-known economic analyses, certain aspects of the demand for transportation. Precisely opposite effects occur for leftward shifts in the transport supply function and for freight rate increases and will not be spelled out here.

Similar analyses apply at lower levels of aggregation. That is, instead of referring to aggregate demand, one might apply the above to broad commodity classes or specific commodities at the national, regional, or local levels. In general, demand elasticities tend to be greater the lower the level of aggregation and the higher the ratio of freight charges to the delivered price of the commodity, as noted in the next section. However, the broad generalizations remain valid at all levels of aggregation, namely, that the *level* of the demand for transportation depends on the level of production; the rate of production is only partially responsive to freight rate changes, and the short-run responsiveness (elasticity of demand) is less than the long-run.

We turn now to a more careful elaboration of the elasticity of demand for transportation at lower levels of aggregation.

## The Elasticity of Transport Demand

In this section we explore the determinants of the elasticity of transport demand and examine various formulations and approaches to estimation. We begin with the simplest case and move on to more complex situations.

In the simplest case, we ignore considerations of supply or, more formally, assume that the supply schedule of both the transport firms and the producers of the commodity in question are perfectly elastic (i.e., horizontal in the price-output plane). Reversing the procedure of the preceding section, we consider first a single commodity without reference to space or distance and a single supplier of homogeneous transport services.

Given the level of demand for transport, we want to examine the sensitivity of sales (or purchases) of transport inputs to changes in the freight rate as far as a particular commodity is concerned. By definition, the elasticity of transport demand

$$\epsilon_T = \frac{\% \, \Delta \text{ in } Q_D}{\% \, \Delta \text{ in } P_T},\text{[7]}$$

---

7. This is equivalent to $\epsilon_T = \frac{P_T}{Q} \frac{\Delta Q}{\Delta P_T}$. In continuous form we have $\epsilon_T = \frac{P_T}{Q} \frac{dQ}{dP_T}$. These two forms will be used more extensively later.

where $P_T =$ the freight rate per unit of the commodity shipped and $Q_D =$ number of units of the commodity shipped = number of units of the commodity demanded.

To find (% $\Delta$ in $Q_D$) we need to know (1) the relative importance of the freight rate to the delivered price of the commodity ($\frac{P_T}{P_T + P_C}$, where $P_C$ is the f.o.b. price of the commodity—we will designate $\frac{P_T}{P_T + P_C}$ as $\alpha$ in what follows), which may be designated as the "price-sensitivity ratio," and (2) the elasticity of demand for the commodity in its market ($\epsilon_D$).

If it is assumed that the delivered price is always equal to $P_T + P_C$ in the market (i.e., no freight absorption or extra markup), then the percent change in delivered price will equal $\alpha$(% $\Delta$ in $P_T$). For example, if the price-sensitivity ratio ($\alpha$) is 25% and if the freight rate is raised by 10%, the delivered price of the commodity will increase by 2.5% (i.e., $25 \times .10$).[8]

More generally, assume freight rates change by $s$%. The impact on the price of the commodity being shipped is therefore $\alpha s$ in percentage terms. Since $\epsilon_D = \frac{\%\Delta Q_D}{\%\Delta P_C} = \frac{\%\Delta Q_D}{\alpha s}$, then the percent change in quantity shipped equals $\epsilon_D \alpha s$. But $\epsilon_T = \frac{\%\Delta Q_D}{\%\Delta P_T}$. Thus by substitution we have $\epsilon_T = \alpha \epsilon_D$. In the above example, if $\epsilon_D = -2$, then $\epsilon_T = -2(.25) = -.5$.

### "Critical" Elasticity of Demand ($\epsilon_D^*$)

Several studies have made use of a concept referred to as the "critical" elasticity of demand for the commodity.[9] Specifically, this is the elasticity of demand for the commodity to be shipped that makes the elasticity of transport demand equal $-1$. Thus, since $\epsilon_T = \epsilon_D \alpha$, "critical" $\epsilon_D^* = \frac{-1}{\alpha}$. The relevance of such a concept and its measurement is to obtain some notion of the pressures that might exist in the provision of transport services to *reduce* freight rates in the absence of inter-

---

8. That is, if the delivered price before the 10% rate increase was $P_T + P_C$, after the rate increase it will be $(1.10)P_T + P_C$. The percentage change in delivered price will be

$$\frac{(1.10 P_T + P_C) - (P_T + P_C)}{P_T + P_C} = .10 \frac{P_T}{P_T + P_C}.$$

But $\frac{P_T}{P_T + P_C} = \alpha = .25$.

∴. The percentage change in delivered price is $.25 \times .10 = 2.5$.

9. J. Meyer, M. Peck, J. Stenason, and C. Zwick, *The Economics of Competition in the Transportation Industries* (Cambridge: Harvard University Press, 1959), pp. 196ff.; and Ann F. Friedlaender, *The Dilemma of Freight Transport Regulation* (Washington, D. C.: The Brookings Institution, 1969), pp.50ff.

modal competition. If $\epsilon_T > 1$ (in absolute value), then a monopoly supplier of freight service would have some incentive to reduce freight rates to obtain more business, depending, of course, on the relationship of costs to traffic. Elasticities of transport demand less than 1 (in absolute value) would, on the other hand, provide incentives to increase freight rates since total revenues would rise on a slightly smaller volume of business and total costs would decrease. The reverse is true if $\epsilon_T > |1|$. The "critical" elasticity noted above thus asks the question, Are demand schedules in the commodity markets sufficiently elastic to generate downward pressures on freight rates even if the transport market is monopolistic?

For example, assume the following values for $\alpha$ for different commodities and their associated values of $\epsilon_D^*$:

| $\alpha$ | $\epsilon_D^* = \dfrac{-1}{\alpha}$ |
|---|---|
| .05 | $-20$ |
| .10 | $-10$ |
| .15 | $-6\tfrac{2}{3}$ |
| .20 | $-5$ |
| .25 | $-4$ |
| .30 | $-3\tfrac{1}{3}$ |

Thus, when $\alpha = 5\%$, the elasticity of demand for the commodity in its market must equal $-20$, whereas if $\alpha = 30\%$, the "critical" elasticity need only be $-3\tfrac{1}{3}$ to make $\epsilon_T = -1$.

What are the most typical values of $\alpha$ and $\epsilon_D$ in the real world? In general, while $\alpha$ varies substantially among commodities, it is usually much less than 10%. For example, for ferrous mining $\alpha = 9.1\%$; for chemical and fertilizer mineral mining $\alpha = 6.4\%$; for lumber and wood products $\alpha = 5.1\%$; and so on.[10] For most commodities, "transportation accounts for no more than two percent of the final-goods price."[11] These estimates refer to large commodity aggregates. However, even in disaggregation, while greater variation is evident, the size of $\alpha$ is generally far below 10%.[12] As recently noted, "the sum of the inbound and outbound relevant freight charges to value of shipments . . . is below 5 percent for 75 percent of the three-digit manufacturing industries in the study sample [some 300 commodities]."[13] These observa-

---

10. Friedlaender, p.52. See below, Table 1.6, col. 4, for estimates of $\alpha$.
11. Ibid.
12. For details at the three-digit level of industrial classification, see *Two Proposals for Rail Freight Pricing: Assessment of Their Prospective Impact*, A Report to the Federal-Provincial Committee on Western Transportation, September 30, 1974, chapter 3. See also Table 1.6 below.
13. *Two Proposals*, p.320.

tions suggest that elasticities of demand for the commodities must in general exceed $|10|$ to make $\epsilon_T > |1|$ (i.e., $\epsilon_D^* = \dfrac{-1}{.10} = -10$).

Estimates of commodity elasticities, while much more tenuous and limited, are generally believed to be less than $|5|$. For example, Table 1.1 provides some early elasticity estimates, the highest of which is 3, all others being less than 1.

TABLE 1.1

*Estimated Price Elasticities of Demand*
*for Selected Commodities ( U.S. )*

| Product | Price elasticity |
|---|---|
| 1. Beef | −0.92 |
| 2. Millinery | −3.00 |
| 3. Gasoline | −0.52 |
| 4. Sugar | −0.31 |
| 5. Corn | −0.49 |
| 6. Cotton | −0.12 |
| 7. Hay | −0.43 |
| 8. Wheat | −0.18 |
| 9. Potatoes | −0.31 |
| 10. Oats | −0.56 |
| 11. Barley | −0.39 |
| 12. Buckwheat | −0.99 |
| 13. Refrigerators | −1.07 to −2.06 |
| 14. Automobiles | −0.6 to −1.1 |
| 15. Farm Tractors | −0.5 to −1.5 |
| 16. Furniture | −1.48 |

SOURCES: H. Schultz, *The Theory and Measurement of Demand* (Chicago: University of Chicago Press, 1938), pp.551–53, for items 1–12. Estimates from data for the period 1914 or 1915 through 1929 with the years 1917–21 often eliminated. A. C. Harberger, ed., *The Demand for Durable Goods* (Chicago: University of Chicago Press, 1960), for items 13–15, where data refer to the period 1921 or 1931 to the mid-1950s. Item 16 from *U. S. Survey of Current Business*, May 1950, and refers to the period 1921–40.

To be sure, most of these estimates refer to agricultural products, which are "necessities," or nearly so, and whose prices—at least at the time most of the estimates were made (some in the 1920s or earlier and all before the mid- to late 1950s)—were already low. Thus, low elasticities might be expected. On the other hand, the range of the absolute values of more recent elasticity estimates for gasoline, refrigerators, automobiles, tractors, and furniture is not significantly higher. Richard Stone's data for England between 1920 and 1938 also indicate elasticities well below unity for a large number of food commodities. Of 22 of Stone's commodities noted in Grossack and Martin, only three had elasticities greater than $|1|$: condensed milk ($-1.23$), imported potatoes (−1.32), and home-produced apples (−1.67).[14] A somewhat later study for aluminum ingot reports an elasticity of −1.3.[15] Another study of the elasticity of demand for cigarettes indicated a range between −0.3 and −0.4.[16] More recently, concern for elasticity manifest itself in the wake of the energy crisis in late 1973. Several estimates of the elasticity of demand for oil indicated values of between −0.2 and −0.4.[17]

Two recent large-scale studies that derived a number of elasticity estimates show substantial differences. Table 1.2 presents selected commodities from the Houthakker and Taylor study in terms of consumption expenditure categories and their calculated short- and long-run elasticities. The data again indicate a pattern of relatively low magnitudes with only a few goods or services having elasticities greater than 2. In addition, it is noteworthy that, contrary to expectations, the so-called long-run elasticities are not consistently higher than the short-run. There are many problems with these estimates not least of which is the rather broad categories of the goods and services examined. In fact, the study was not mainly concerned with price elasticity. Of the 83 consumption categories examined, some of which appear in Table 1.2, 54 had price elasticities that were not significantly different from zero and, in fact, prices appear in only 45 of the "explanatory" equations.

More recently, Comanor and Wilson, using product types that are often more narrowly defined, have derived somewhat higher elasticities than any already noted (see Table 1.3). For example, the demand for apparently similar items—jewelry and watches in Houthakker and Taylor and clocks and watches in Comanor and Wilson—differ by more than a factor of 5 for short-run and even more for long-run elasticity. Large differences also appear in the computed elasticities in Table 1.2 and 1.3 for "household appliances" (−0.63 vs. −2.781 for the short run). Where comparisons are possible, the elasticities in Table 1.3 are consistently higher than other studies have indicated. Indeed, several estimates are far above the levels that seem to apply more generally. The long-run elasticity for "clocks and watches" (−9.802) is possibly the highest ever recorded, while that for millinery (−4.165) is high

---

14. Data from Richard Stone, *Measurement of Consumers' Behavior in the United Kingdom, 1920–1938* (Cambridge: Cambridge University Press, 1954), cited in I. M. Grossack and D. D. Martin, *Managerial Economics* (Boston: Little, Brown & Company, 1973), Table 8.1, p.305.

15. Meyer et al., *Competition*, p.198.

16. Cited in Edwin Mansfield, ed., *Economics, Readings, Issues and Cases* (New York: Norton, 1974), p.215. Stone's estimate for the U.K. using data from 1920–38 was within this range, namely, −0.39 ± 0.10.

17. Ibid., p.211.

but at least consistent with the relatively high −3.0 recorded in Table 1.1. Even so, the majority of items in Table 1.3 have elasticities less than unity and also exhibit some unexpected differences between short- and long-run elasticities.

TABLE 1.2

*Estimated Demand Elasticities for*
*Selected Consumer Expenditure Categories*

| Item | Relative price elasticity | |
|---|---|---|
|  | Short run | Long run |
| Purchased meals (excl. alcoholic beverages) | −2.30 | −1.18 |
| Shoes and other footwear | −0.40 | − |
| Shoe cleaning and repairs | −1.07 | +1.52 |
| Cleaning, dyeing, and pressing | −0.45 | − |
| Laundering in establishments | −1.02 |  |
| Jewelry and watches | −0.44 | −0.72 |
| Toilet articles and preparation | −0.77 | −3.14 |
| Kitchenware and other household appliances | −0.63 | − |
| China, glassware, tableware, and utensils | −1.16 | −1.31 |
| Stationery | −0.48 | −0.53 |
| Electricity (household) | −0.65 | − |
| Water | −0.68 | − |
| New cars and net purchases of used cars | −0.96 | 0.15 |
| Tires, tubes, accessories, and parts | −0.63 | −0.37 |
| Gasoline and oil | −0.16 | −0.46 |
| Street and electric railway and local bus | −1.02 | − |
| Taxicabs | −0.41 | − |
| Intercity railway | −1.21 | −2.74 |
| Airline travel | −0.06 | −2.36 |
| Nondurable toys | −0.58 | −1.72 |
| Radio and TV repair | −1.01 | − |
| Flowers, seeds, and potted plants | −0.52 | −0.62 |
| Foreign travel by U. S. residents | −0.66 | −4.06 |

SOURCE: H. S. Houthakker and Lester D. Taylor, *Consumer Demand in the United States, 1929–1970* (Cambridge: Harvard University Press, 1966).

The foregoing evidence suggests that commodity demand elasticities are typically low in absolute value and that large differences often exist in the estimates of different studies. At least the few attempts at direct estimation, dated and tenuous as many of them are, tend to confirm that most elasticities are close to or less than unity. Nor does it seem likely that elasticities have increased significantly since the time of several of these studies. Some increase in elasticity may have occurred since the availability of substitutes has increased along with discre-

TABLE 1.3

| Industry | Elasticity | |
|---|---|---|
| | Short Run | Long Run |
| Soft drinks | −1.478 | −1.540 |
| Malt liquor | −0.562 | −1.392 |
| Wine | −0.680 | −0.842 |
| Distilled liquor | −0.253 | −0.295 |
| Meat | −0.365 | −0.364 |
| Grain mill products and cereals | −1.469 | −2.099 |
| Bakery products | −0.263 | −0.313 |
| Carpets | −0.658 | −0.431 |
| Men's clothing | −0.676 | −0.276 |
| Millinery | −4.164 | −4.165 |
| Books | −0.774 | −1.078 |
| Drugs | −1.079 | −1.695 |
| Soaps | −0.758 | −0.784 |
| Footwear | −0.392 | −0.293 |
| Electrical appliances | −2.781 | −1.567 |
| Motorcycles and bicycles | −2.321 | −0.385 |
| Clocks and watches | −2.933 | −9.802 |
| Motor vehicles | −1.350 | |

SOURCE: W. S. Comanor and T. A. Wilson, *Advertising and Market Power* (Cambridge: Harvard University Press, 1974), pp.89–90.

tionary income,[18] but even if all these elasticities had doubled or even tripled by the 1970s, almost all would still be 5 or less. The more recent studies noted above on selected items provide some supporting evidence.

The available evidence thus suggests that conditions in the product markets in general are unlikely to set much of a limitation on freight rate increases and are certainly not conducive to rate *decreases* in monopolistic transport markets. If society seeks lower freight rates, either reliance on competition *within* the transportation industries or rate regulation will be required.

There is, however, an important exception to the foregoing. If a particular market has alternative sources of supply, freight rate changes that are immediately reflected in changes in the delivered price of the commodity may generate large increases (or decreases) in shipments from one of the supply sources. Thus, a railroad having a mo-

18. In fact, a rise in discretionary income may have the effect of lowering price elasticities. "Prices should be expected to exert less of an influence on consumption at high levels of income, because income becomes less of a constraining factor and because more commodities become subject to habit formation" (Houthakker and Taylor, pp.153–54).

nopoly of the shipment of widgets from supply source A to a market at B may gain a substantial volume increase by lowering rates if the buyers at B shift their purchases from other supply sources to A; the converse is true for a rail rate increase. This result occurs regardless of the magnitudes of $\alpha$ and $\epsilon_D$.

## Cross-Elasticity of Demand among Modes

The foregoing assumed a single supplier of homogeneous transport inputs. However, if there are alternative suppliers or alternative modes, demand elasticities will be greater in the absence of collusion. For example, if both rail and truck transportation are available, it is clear that changes in the rates of one mode, assuming that rates and quality of service in the other remain constant, will lead to traffic shifts between the two that will increase the elasticity of demand (absolute value) for each mode.

For example, assume the total traffic in one or many commodities between a city-pair is $T$ (in tons or ton-miles). Railroads and trucks share such traffic as follows: $\beta$ (in percent) is the present rail share; hence $1 - \beta$ is the truck share, with $0 \leq \beta \leq 1$. Thus present rail traffic is $\beta T$. Assume a rail rate decrease with no retaliation on the part of trucks. The increase in rail traffic depends on (1) the increase in total traffic due to the rail rate decrease and (2) the amount of traffic shifted from truck to rail.

The increase in *total* traffic, all of which will accrue to rail, depends on the percentage reduction in the rail rate (i.e., $\%\Delta P_R$). Thus,

$$\%\Delta T_R = \frac{T\epsilon_D(\%\Delta P_R)}{\beta T} = \frac{\epsilon_D\alpha(\%\Delta P_R)}{\beta},$$

where ($\%\Delta T_R$) represents the percentage change in rail traffic as a result of an increase in total traffic.

The amount of traffic shifted from truck depends on the cross-elasticity of demand between rail and truck service. That is,

$$\epsilon_{CROSS} = \frac{\%\Delta T_T}{\%\Delta P_R},$$

where ($\%\Delta T_T$) refers to the percentage change in truck traffic. In this example truck traffic will decrease in response to a rail rate decrease and vice versa. Hence $\epsilon_{CROSS}$ is positive. Truck traffic will decrease in amount by $(1 - \beta)T \times \epsilon_{CROSS}$ ($\%\Delta P_R$). Thus the $\%\Delta T_R = \frac{(1 - \beta)}{\beta}$ $\epsilon_{CROSS}$ ($\%\Delta P_R$). The total change in rail traffic as a result of the effects of both (1) and (2) is the sum of the two effects, in the sense of making the expression in brackets more negative. Since $\epsilon_C$ is negative, we subtract the traffic shift from truck.

Thus $\%\Delta T_R = \frac{1}{\beta}(\%\Delta P_R)[\epsilon_D\alpha - (1-\beta)\epsilon_{(CROSS)}]$.

Since $\epsilon_{RT} = \frac{\%\Delta T_R}{\%\Delta P_R}$, under the present assumptions we have

$\epsilon_{RT} = \frac{1}{\beta}[\epsilon_D\alpha - (1-\beta)\epsilon_{CROSS}]$.

If there was no previous truck traffic (i.e., $\beta = 1$), this equation reduces to the monopoly situation noted earlier, namely, $\epsilon_{RT} = \epsilon_D\alpha$. The smaller the $\beta$ and the larger the $\epsilon_{CROSS}$, the larger the $\epsilon_{RT}$ will be compared with the monopoly rail situation, both because there is a larger amount of traffic potentially shiftable to rails (small initial $\beta$) and because the truck traffic is highly sensitive to rail rate reductions (high $\epsilon_{CROSS}$). The magnitude of the traffic shifts, of course, is dependent on truck rate (and quality of service)[19] responses. The "pure" effect noted above assumed no response, which would be unlikely if $\beta$ was small and especially if $\epsilon_{CROSS}$ was large.

Since few estimates exist of $\epsilon_{CROSS}$[20] and response patterns are generally nonpredictable or at least dependent on the reaction of the transport suppliers, we need pursue this issue no further here. Suffice it to note, however, that the very low elasticities (in absolute values) deduced for the monopolistic transport firm may quickly become very large if there is competition or if there is freedom of entry into the transport business. In the above illustration, for example, even if $\beta = 1$ and $\epsilon_{RT}$ is very low (because $\alpha$ and $\epsilon_D$ are both low), a rail monopoly might hesitate to raise rates if there were freedom of entry. Indeed, a rail rate increase might invite new entry or induce shippers to provide their own transportation.

### Direct Empirical Estimates of Elasticity by Mode

We have already noted the very low $\epsilon_T$ for all modes combined since total demand for goods movement depends on aggregate output. How-

---

19. Service quality is an important determinant of demand, not only among modes but also among firms of the same mode. A discussion of service quality follows below.

20. Equations 1, 3, 4, 5, 6 ,7, 8, 11, 12, and 14 in Table 1.4 provide some cross-elasticity estimates. However, a large number of them have a negative sign and are statistically insignificant. Only equations 7, 11, and 14 have "reasonable" and statistically significant cross-elasticities. These relate to rail demand for all agricultural products and for forest products, both of which vary positively with truck rates. The aggregate truck demand (equation 14) also varies positively with the rail rate.

ever, demand relationships by mode would not be expected to follow real GNP or some other index of goods production so closely.

Several studies using linear, multivariate analysis have been made. One using data from 1946 through 1961 yielded results as follows:

%$\Delta$ *Rail* Ton-Miles/capita = .103 − .842($\%\Delta P_{TR}$) + .976(%$\Delta$ Index of Industrial Production) − 54.153(%$\Delta$ Percent of Population Urban). ($R^2$ = .912)

%$\Delta$ *Truck* Ton-Miles/capita = 5.964 − 1.873($\%\Delta P_{TT}$) + .342 (%$\Delta$ Index of Industrial Production) − 247.064 (%$\Delta$ Percent of Population Urban). ($R^2$ = .460)

%$\Delta$ *Water* Ton-Miles/capita = .751 − .264 ($\%\Delta P_{TW}$) + 1.305 (%$\Delta$ Index of Industrial Production) − 318.170(%$\Delta$ Percent of Population Urban). ($R^2$ = .807)[21]

The analysis, despite severe data problems, implies that, in the aggregate:

$$\epsilon_{RTD} = -.842; \; \epsilon_{TTD} = -1.873; \; \epsilon_{WTD} = -.264.$$

More recently and using data from 1945 to 1968, Morton has derived the demand relationships shown in Table 1.4, using equations of the type

$$T = a_1 R_1{}^{a_2}(\text{GNP})^{a_3} R_2{}^{a_4},$$

where $T$ refers to volume of traffic (usually) by rail for all commodities or one commodity class, $R_1$ refers to the rail rate, GNP is gross national product in real terms, and $R_2$ is (usually) the truck rate. Data on each of these variables (or proxies thereof) are developed for each year 1945–1968 and values for the $a_i$'s are deduced using standard regression techniques. Since the variables are in logarithmic form, the cofficients are elasticities, i.e., log $T$ = log $a_1$ + $a_2$ log $R_1$ + $a_3$ log GNP + $a_4$ log $R_2$. Let us examine Morton's results.

The price or rate elasticities all have the expected (or "correct") sign, although there are wide variations in the magnitudes for different regions and different products. For example, rail price elasticities in absolute value vary from a low of −.136 in the southern region (equation 5) to a high of −.964 in the Pocahontas region (equation 4). There is no obvious rationale for such large differences other than the probability that intermodal competition is greater in the latter region than in the former. Even this is largely a guess. Note also that the cross-elasticities in both equations have negative signs, whereas the theory requires positive cross-elasticities.[22] This makes it even more difficult

21. H. Benishay and E. Whitaker, "Demand and Supply in Freight Transportation," *Journal of Industrial Economics,* July 1966, pp.243–62.

22. See also note 20 above.

TABLE 1.4

*The Prime Demand Equations*

*Aggregate rail demand:*

1. RR VOL = −.537 RR RATE +.628 GNP −.730 TK RATE          $R^2$ = .79
   ton-miles          (.202)          (.241)          (.549)          $F$ = 8.9

2. RR VOL
   ton-miles = −.696 RR RATE +.322 GNP          $R^2$ = .76
                    (.166)          (.074)          $F$ = 11.9

*Rail demand—Eastern District:*

3. RR VOL = −.317 RR RATE +.425 GRP −1.786 TK RATE          $R^2$ = .88
   tons          (.267)          (.391)          (.786)          $F$ = 18.0

*Rail demand—Pocahontas region:*

4. RR VOL = −.964 RR RATE +.925 GRP −.749 TK RATE          $R^2$ = .77
   tons          (.368)          (.374)          (.829)          $F$ = 7.9

*Rail demand—Southern region:*

5. RR VOL = −.136 RR RATE +.576 GRP −.521 TK RATE          $R^2$ = .92
   tons          (.181)          (.175)          (.444)          $F$ = 28.3

*Rail demand—Western district:*

6. RR VOL = −.684 AV RATE +.074 RT RATIO +.213 GRP          $R^2$ = .58
   tons          (.478)          (.352)          (.221)          $F$ = 2.7

*Rail demand—agriculture:*

7. RR VOL =
   tons −.837 RR RATE +.370 CROP INDEX +.661 TK RATE          $R^2$ = .94
              (.118)          (.203)          (.208)          $F$ = 42.1

*Rail demand—animals:*

8. RR VOL = −.207 RR RATE −.997 LIVESTK INDEX −1.115 TK RT     $R^2$ = .95
   tons          (.221)          (.556)          (.589)     $F$ = 50.9

*Rail demand—mines:*

9. RR VOL = −.819 RR RATE +.012 MINERAL PROD.          $R^2$ = .67
   tons          (.262)          (.181)          $F$ = 6.9

*Rail demand—coal:*

10. RR VOL = −.128 RR RATE +.953 COAL PROD.          $R^2$ = .93
    tons          (.268)          (.167)          $F$ = 53.6

*Rail demand—forests:*

11. RR VOL = −.366 RR RATE +.762 LUMBER PROD. +.410 TK RATE $R^2$ = .82
    tons          (.143)          (.165)          (.161)

*Rail demand—manufactures:*

12. RR VOL = −.391 RR RATE +.682 MANUF. −1.105 TK RATE          $R^2$ = .82
    tons          (.208)          (.205)          (.552)          $F$ = 11.2

13. RR VOL = −.670 RR RATE +.289 MANUF.          $R^2$ = .77
    tons          (.167)          (.066)          $F$ = 12.6

*Aggregate truck demand:*

14. TK VOL = −1.841 TK RATE +2.323 GNP +.932 RR RATE          $R^2$ = .996
    ton-miles          (.343)          (.151)          (.126)          $F$ = 678.1

N.B. All variables are in logarithmic form—coefficients are elasticities.

SOURCE: A. L. Morton, "A Statistical Sketch of Intercity Freight Demand," *Highway Research Record,* No. 296 (Washington, D.C.: Highway Research Board, 1969).

to interpret the results. If we look at particular commodity groups similar differences arise. It is hard to believe, for example, that the absolute value of the rail transport elasticity of demand for coal ($-.128$ in equation 10) is much smaller than that for manufactures ($-.670$ in equation 13), because the $\alpha$ for coal is much higher than the $\alpha$ for manufactured commodities. However, several of these estimates can be compared directly with estimates by Perle, Benishay and Whitaker, and, more recently, the ICC.

|  | Morton | Perle[23] | B. & W. | ICC[24] |
|---|---|---|---|---|
| Agg. $\epsilon_{RTD}$ | $-.696$ | $-.7226$ | $-.842$ | $-.232$ |
| Agg. $\epsilon_{TTD}$ | $-1.841$ | $-2.0230$ | $-1.873$ | $-.861$ |

Given serious data deficiencies, the different time periods involved in the four studies, and different variables used in the regression equations, these results are surprisingly close, except for those of the ICC, which employed Morton's technique but used data for 1955–1974.

A study by Felton has the following comment on other elasticity findings in transportation:

Berger and Nelson sought to measure the price elasticity of demand for the transportation of hard red spring wheat from country elevators in North Dakota and portions of Minnesota and South Dakota to markets in the Duluth-Superior and Minneapolis-St. Paul area for the years 1965, 1966, and 1967. Employing multiple regression analysis in which rail rates, truck rates, and the total marketable hard red spring wheat available at individual elevators were regressed on the quantity of such wheat shipped by rail cars from these elevators, Berger and Nelson found mean point elasticities from various origins to the Duluth-Superior and Minneapolis-St. Paul markets to be as follows: North Dakota ($-2.42$), western Minnesota ($-7.53$), North Dakota-western Minnesota ($-2.08$), and North Dakota-western Minnesota, northern South Dakota ($-2.09$).

All of the foregoing rail price elasticity coefficients are substantially higher than those computed by Perle, Benishay and Whitaker, and Morton. One possible explanation for this divergence is that the latter studies all employed time-series while Berger and Nelson utilized cross-sectional methods. Therefore, it may be that Perle, Benishay and Whitaker, and Morton were measuring short-run demand elasticities while Berger and Nelson were computing long-run elasticities.

A second possible explanation is that elasticity of demand increases as the commodity is more narrowly defined and the origin and destination are more specifically identified. Thus, variations in the relative rates of alternative

23. E. D. Perle, *The Demand for Transportation: Regional and Commodity Studies in the United States* (Chicago: University of Chicago Press, 1964), p.43.

24. ICC, *A Cost and Benefit Evaluation of Surface Transport Regulation*, Statement No. 76-1 (Washington, D.C., 1976), pp.4–5.

modes as between a particular origin and various possible destinations may affect the specific destination of a particular commodity much more than it affects the intermodal, or even the intramodal, distribution of traffic. If so, the railroad system as a whole and even an individual railroad may find the demand for the transportation of grain to be of less than unitary elasticity even though the demand for the transportation of a particular grain from a particular origin to a particular destination is highly elastic. Furthermore, even if the long-run demand for the transportation of grain should prove to be of greater than unit elasticity, this does not demonstrate that railroads, individually or collectively, will profit from rate reductions. For one thing, the addition to total costs may be greater than the addition to total revenues. Secondly, any prospective long-run additions to net revenue need both to be discounted and to be offset by interim discounted reductions in net revenue attributable to the apparent inelasticity of short-run demand for rail transport.[25]

## An Alternative Approach

Using ICC data for railways that show the ratio of revenues to out-of-pocket costs for broad commodity groups, we can crudely deduce the elasticity of rail transport demand for each group under some fairly restrictive assumptions. Let us construce $\frac{P}{MC}$ as the ratio of rail revenues to out-of-pocket costs, and assume that rails maximize profits such that $MC = MR$. Then since $MR = P(1 - \frac{1}{\epsilon})$[26] we obtain $\frac{P}{MC} = \frac{\epsilon}{\epsilon - 1}$. Using the ICC ratios that are proxies for $\frac{P}{MC}$, we can compute $\epsilon$ as shown in Table 1.5.

The estimated elasticities are very high compared with many of the others given before. In view of the large number of assumptions, the crudeness of the data, and their questionable interpretation as $\frac{P}{MC}$, too much weight should not be given to the actual magnitudes. It is worth noting, however, that the estimated elasticities are roughly consistent with $\alpha$ (i.e., the higher the $\alpha$ the higher the elasticity) and with the value per ton. One may also note that if regulation holds rates at levels lower than a profit-maximizer would, then $\frac{P}{MC}$ is lower and the estimated elasticity is higher than would otherwise be the case since the

---

25. J. R. Felton, "Freight Car Shortages in Grain Transport: An Institutionalized Disequilibrium," mimeographed (Lincoln, Nebraska, May 1974).

26. Note that $MR = \frac{dTR}{dQ} = \frac{dPQ}{dQ} = P + Q\frac{dP}{dQ}$. But $\epsilon = -\frac{P}{Q}\frac{dQ}{dP}$. $\therefore MR = P - \frac{P}{\epsilon} = P\left(1 - \frac{1}{\epsilon}\right)$.

TABLE 1.5

| Commodity Group | Ratio of Rail Revenues to Out-of-Pocket Costs $\left(\dfrac{P}{MC}\right)$ | Estimated $\epsilon_{RTD}$ | Ratio of Freight Rate to Delivered Price $(\alpha)$ | Value of the Commodity ($/Ton) |
|---|---|---|---|---|
| Products of agriculture | 1.18 | −6.6 | 8.2% | 101 |
| Animals and products | 1.11 | −10.1 | 3.7 | 601 |
| Products of mines | 1.06 | −17.7 | 28.1 | 11 |
| Products of forests | 1.17 | −6.9 | 14.2 | 58 |
| Manufactures and miscellaneous | 1.48 | −3.1 | 4.1 | 281 |
| All commodities | 1.27 | −4.7 | 5.8 | − |

SOURCE: Friedlaender, Table 3.6. More detailed data at the five-digit *STCC* code level are provided in ICC, *Rail Revenue Contribution by Commodity and Territory for the Year 1972*, Statement No. 153-72 (Washington, D.C., April 1975).

estimated elasticities in Table 1.4 vary inversely with the ICC's ratio.[27] How much non-profit-maximizing prices deviate from profit-maximizing prices is unknown. Note, however, that it seems reasonable to infer that without regulation the ratios would be higher and the apparent elasticities would be lower in absolute value.

A more recent set of estimates of rail demand elasticities has been made using several of the empirical studies noted above but mainly using indirect estimation techniques involving the formulae and the variables $\alpha$, $\epsilon_D$, $\beta$, and so on, which are presented in Table 1.6. Of the 95 commodity groups for which the elasticity is given in the table, only 20 have elasticities $\geq |1|$ at the lower end of the range, although 62 have elasticities $\geq |1|$ at the upper level of the calculated range. Not much can be read into these observations since for a large number of commodities (groups 46–66) the same (lower) estimate made by Morton for the aggregate "forests"[28] was applied to every one. However, it is noteworthy that, consistent with the above analysis, the higher elasticities are invariably associated with low rail shares $(\beta)$. In particular, all elasticities above $|3|$ have an estimated rail share of about 25% or less, usually less. For example, the high elasticity of rail transport demand for fresh vegetables is −12.0 while the estimated rail modal share is 15%; for textile products, the elasticity is −13.5

27. That is, the estimated elasticity $\epsilon = \dfrac{-k}{k-1}$, where $k$ is the ratio of rail revenues to out-of-pocket cost.

28. See Table 1.4 above, where the rail elasticity of demand for products of "forests" is −.366. This was applied in Table 1.6 as the lower rail elasticity estimate for such things as newsprint, plywood and veneer, and pulpwood chips.

and the share 5%. There is a less systematic relationship between the freight rate ratio ($\alpha$) and the resultant elasticities, which indicates the overwhelming importance of $\beta$. Overall, the estimates are consistent with the foregoing analytical and empirical results but the range between the high and low estimates in most cases indicates the crudity of the art of elasticity calculation. Nevertheless, the attempt to get more disaggregative is worthwhile—indeed, indispensable—and the results are at least marginally encouraging. In the next section we examine further analytical extensions of the elasticity of the demand for transport but with considerably less empirical content.

### Further Extensions of the Elasticity of Transport Demand

The foregoing has ignored considerations of the supply curve for the commodity. Yet, as noted earlier, conditions of supply can, and do, influence the elasticity of demand for transportation. This section examines some of these relationships. In essence, we drop the assumption that the supply curve for the commodity being shipped is perfectly elastic, i.e., parallel to the abscissa ($x$-axis) in the price–output plane.

### *Case I. Rising Supply Curves and $\epsilon_T$*

Assume linear supply and demand functions for a given commodity, as in Figure 1.3, in which $S_0$ refers to the supply in some origin and

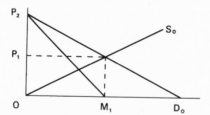

Fig. 1.3

$D_D$ refers to the demand in some destination a given distance away. If transport costs are zero, equilibrium price and quantity at the market would be $OP_1$ and $OM_1$, respectively. If delivered price equals the *supply price* plus a freight rate per unit of sales equal to the vertical distance between the supply and demand functions, then the derived demand for transportation can readily be deduced.[29] Thus, if the freight rate per unit is $OP_2$, quantity demanded is zero; as the freight rate drops, the quantity demanded at the destination increases linearly, approaching $OM_1$ as the freight rate declines to zero.

---

29. That is, $P_T = P_D - P_S$, where $P_T =$ the freight rate, $P_D =$ demand price, and $P_S =$ supply price.

TABLE 1.6

*Interstate Commerce Commission*
*Estimates of Rail Demand Elasticities*

| Commodity Group Number | Commodity Description | 1975 Estimated Supply Price per Short Ton | 1975(2) Freight Rate Ratio | 1972(5) Estimated Rail Modal Share | Range of Estimated Rail Demand Elasticities | |
|---|---|---|---|---|---|---|
| | | | | | Less Elastic | More Elastic |
| 1 | Cotton | $1,002.30 | 0.022 | 90.0%(6) | -0.11 | -0.837(M) |
| 2 | Wheat | 117.10 | 0.081 | 73.6(3) | -0.38 | -0.837(M) |
| 3 | Corn and Sorghum | 87.50 | 0.087 | 45.1(3) | -0.837(M) | -1.32 |
| 4 | Barley | 99.50 | 0.117 | 52.5(6) | -0.38 | -0.95 |
| 5 | All Other Grain | — | — | — | -0.5(E) | -1.0(E) |
| 6 | Soybeans | 153.40 | 0.041 | 34.6(3) | -0.837(M) | -1.95 |
| 7 | Rice | 174.80 | 0.058 | 20.0(6) | -0.5(E) | -2.5 |
| 8 | Potatoes, Other Than Sweet | 96.30 | 0.306 | 15.0(6) | -1.0(E) | -2.05 |
| 9 | Sugar Beets | 27.40 | 0.098 | 32.5(6) | -1.10 | -2.20 |
| 10 | Citrus Fruit | 62.60 | 0.480 | — | -0.63 | -10.0(E) |
| 11 | Apples | 128.00 | 0.346 | 10.0(6) | -0.45 | -13.0 |
| 12 | Deciduous Fruits | — | — | — | -0.50(E) | -10.0(E) |
| 13 | Fresh Vegetables | 124.00 | 0.331 | 15.0(6) | -1.0 | -12.0 |
| 14 | Melons | 80.00 | 0.441 | 5.0(6) | -1.3 | -10.0(E) |
| 15 | Iron Ore | 19.10 | 0.132 | 63.9(3) | -0.39 | -0.819(M) |
| 16 | Nonferrous Concentrates | 1,284.00 | 0.007 | 100.0(3) | -0.05 | -0.819(M) |
| 17 | Calcined or Activated Bauxite Ores | 20.67 | 0.299 | 30.0(6) | -0.819(M) | -2.6 |
| 18 | Anthracite Coal | 32.45 | 0.214 | 74.2(3) | -0.128(M) | -0.38 |
| 19 | Coking Coal | 36.50(1) | 0.133 | — | -0.128(M) | -0.37 |
| 20 | Steam Bituminous Coal | — | 0.180 | 73.9(3) | -0.128(M) | -0.38 |

Estimates of Rail Demand Elasticities (continued)

| Commodity Group Number | Commodity Description | 1975 Estimated Supply Price per Short Ton | 1975(2) Freight Rate Ratio | 1972(5) Estimated Rail Modal Share | Range of Estimated Rail Demand Elasticities | |
|---|---|---|---|---|---|---|
| | | | | | Less Elastic | More Elastic |
| 21 | Lignite | 18.75 | 0.141 | — | −0.128(M) | −0.37 |
| 22 | Fluxing Limestone and Dolomite | 2.15 | 0.649 | 50.0(6) | −0.32 | −1.65 |
| 23 | Aggregates | 1.48(1) | 0.692 | 24.9(3) | −0.35 | −4.40 |
| 24 | Sand | — | 0.828 | — | −0.41 | −4.70 |
| 25 | Clays | 6.95(1) | 0.701 | 15.0(6) | −0.35 | −8.0 |
| 26 | Feldspar | 17.00(1) | 0.482 | 40.0(6) | −0.24 | −2.1 |
| 27 | Potash Fertilizers | 49.25 | 0.167 | 90.0(6) | −0.20 | −0.56 |
| 28 | Phosphate Rock | 23.00 | 0.048 | 76.9(3) | −0.33 | −0.65 |
| 29 | Fresh Meats | 1,500.00 | 0.026 | 18.7(4) | −2.67 | −4.42 |
| 30 | Canned Fruits and Vegetables | 579.00(8) | 0.041 | — | −1.0 | −1.9 |
| 31 | Other Foodstuffs | — | — | 35.2(4) | −1.0(E) | −1.9(E) |
| 32 | Frozen Fruits and Vegetables | 447.00(8) | 0.079 | — | −1.0 | −1.9 |
| 33 | Wheat Flour Milling Products | 211.00 | 0.053 | — | −0.74 | −2.37 |
| 34 | Dry Corn Milling Products | 200.00(8) | 0.065 | — | −0.77 | −2.37 |
| 35 | Other Grain Mill Products | — | — | 61.9(4) | −0.80(E) | −2.37 |
| 36 | Wet Corn Mill Products | 142.00(8) | 0.124 | — | −0.91 | −2.37 |
| 37 | Cereal Preparations (Cooked) | 1,450.00(8) | 0.020 | — | −0.66 | −2.37 |
| 38 | Sugar | 622.00 | 0.026 | 44.4(4) | −2.11 | −3.31 |
| 39 | Malt Liquors | 297.00(8) | 0.059 | — | −3.50 | −5.5 |
| 40 | Wine and Brandy | 556.00(8) | 0.073 | 15.9(4) | −4.28 | −5.6 |
| 41 | Alcoholic Liquors | 557.00(8) | 0.047 | — | −1.57 | −5.36 |
| 42 | Fats and Oils | 325.00(8) | 0.055 | 46.9(4) | −0.73 | −1.17 |
| 43 | Seed, Nut and Vegetable Cake or Meal | 123.65 | 0.067 | 46.9(4) | −0.75 | −1.18 |

*Estimates of Rail Demand Elasticities* (continued)

| Commodity Group Number | Commodity Description | 1975 Estimated Supply Price per Short Ton | 1975(2) Freight Rate Ratio | 1972(5) Estimated Rail Modal Share | Range of Estimated Rail Demand Elasticities | |
|---|---|---|---|---|---|---|
| | | | | | Less Elastic | More Elastic |
| 44 | Cigars, Cigarettes and Manufactured Tobacco | — | — | 51.3(4) | −0.5(E) | −1.0(E) |
| 45 | Textile Products | 2,950.00(8) | 0.012 | 5.0(4) | −5.0 | −13.5 |
| 46 | Pulpwood Logs | — | — | 61.4(3) | −0.366(M) | −0.814 |
| 47 | Pulpwood Chips | — | — | — | −0.366(M) | −0.814 |
| 48 | Lumber | — | 0.025 | 45.4(4) | −0.366(M) | −1.23 |
| 49 | Treated Wood Products | 125.00(8) | 0.102 | 38.4(4) | −0.366(M) | −1.74 |
| 50 | Wood Posts, Poles and Piling | — | 0.108 | 38.4(4) | −0.366(M) | −1.75 |
| 51 | Millwork and Other Lumber Products | 220.00(8) | 0.086 | 50.2(4) | −0.366(M) | −1.08 |
| 52 | Plywood and Veneer | — | 0.113 | 50.2(4) | −0.366(M) | −1.10 |
| 53 | Hardwood Stock and Flooring | 125.00(8) | 0.186 | 45.4(4) | −0.366(M) | −1.41 |
| 54 | Wood Particle Board | 154.00(8) | 0.148 | 38.4(4) | −0.366(M) | −1.80 |
| 55 | Furniture | 1,262.00(8) | 0.051 | 26.9(4) | −3.0 | −5.5 |
| 56 | Woodpulp and Other Pulps | 364.00 | 0.041 | 78.0(4) | −0.366(M) | −0.64 |
| 57 | Newsprint | — | 0.037 | 58.7(4) | −0.366(M) | −0.85 |
| 58 | Ground Wood Paper | 485.00(8) | 0.039 | 58.7(4) | −0.366(M) | −0.85 |
| 59 | Printing Paper | — | 0.043 | — | −0.366(M) | −0.85 |
| 60 | Wrapping Paper and Paper Bags | — | 0.050 | — | −0.366(M) | −0.85 |
| 61 | Pulpboard | 814.00(8) | 0.021 | 71.9(4) | −0.366(M) | −0.70 |
| 62 | Corrugated Pulpboard | — | 0.023 | — | −0.366(M) | −0.70 |
| 63 | Sanitary Paper Products | — | 0.333 | 51.3(4) | −0.366(M) | −0.98 |
| 64 | Paperboard Boxes and Containers | — | 0.046 | 7.2(4) | −0.366(M) | −6.9 |
| 65 | Food Containers and Fibre Cans, Drums and Tubes | 518.00(8) | 0.069 | 7.2(4) | −0.366(M) | −6.9 |

*Estimates of Rail Demand Elasticities* (continued)

| Commodity Group Number | Commodity Description | 1975 Estimated Supply Price per Short Ton | 1975(2) Freight Rate Ratio | 1972(5) Estimated Rail Modal Share | Range of Estimated Rail Demand Elasticities | |
|---|---|---|---|---|---|---|
| | | | | | Less Elastic | More Elastic |
| 66 | Building Paper and Board | 146.00(8) | 0.134 | 71.9(4) | −0.366(M) | −0.70 |
| 67 | Inorganic Chemicals | 530.00(9) | 0.038 | — | — | — |
| 68 | Barium and Calcium Compounds | 225.00(9) | 0.084 | — | — | — |
| 69 | Sodium Alkalies | 170.00 | 0.061 | — | — | — |
| 70 | Soda Ash | 57.00(9) | 0.277 | 45.3(4) | −0.4(E) | −0.7(E) |
| 71 | Industrial Gases | 135.00 | 0.104 | — | — | — |
| 72 | Organic Chemicals | 290.00(9) | 0.066 | — | — | — |
| 73 | Sulphuric Acid | 48.00 | 0.152 | — | — | — |
| 74 | Anhydrous Ammonia | 180.00(9) | 0.068 | — | — | — |
| 75 | Superphosphate | 240.00(9) | 0.042 | 56.0(4) | −0.05(E) | −0.3(E) |
| 76 | Agricultural Chemicals, Including Fertilizers | 160.00(9) | 0.075 | — | — | — |
| 77 | Plastic Materials | 670.00 | 0.035 | 44.5(4) | — | — |
| 78 | Rubber | 598.00 | 0.035 | 44.5(4) | −0.5(E) | −1.5(E) |
| 79 | Detergents and Other Cleaning Chemicals | 680.00 | 0.039 | 21.1(4) | — | — |
| 80 | Salt | 9.00 | 0.482 | 30.1(4) | −0.75(E) | −1.5(E) |
| 81 | Carbon Black | — | — | 30.1(4) | −0.5(E) | −1.5(E) |
| 82 | Petroleum Products | — | — | 8.3(4) | −0.5(E) | −1.5(E) |
| 83 | Petroleum, Lube Oils and Greases | — | — | 8.3(4) | — | — |
| 84 | Asphalt and Tars | — | — | 8.3(4) | −0.5(E) | −1.5(E) |
| 85 | Liquified Gases | — | — | 8.3(4) | — | — |
| 86 | Construction Material, Asphalt or Asbestos | — | — | 20.8(4) | — | — |

*Estimates of Rail Demand Elasticities (continued)*

| Commodity Group Number | Commodity Description | 1975 Estimated Supply Price per Short Ton | 1975(2) Freight Rate Ratio | 1972(5) Estimated Rail Modal Share | Range of Estimated Rail Demand Elasticities Less Elastic | More Elastic |
|---|---|---|---|---|---|---|
| 87 | Petroleum Coke | – | – | 70.1(4) | –0.5(E) | –1.5(E) |
| 88 | Coal Coke | 73.25(1) | 0.103 | – | – | – |
| 89 | Tires and Tubes | 1,097.00(8) | 0.031 | 40.9(4) | –0.5(E) | –1.60 |
| 90 | Plastic Products | 1,366.00(8) | 0.038 | 16.0 | –0.5(E) | –1.5(E) |
| 91 | Glass Containers | 250.00(8) | 0.097 | 10.8(4) | – | – |
| 92 | Hydraulic Cement | 26.79(1) | 0.197 | 15.1(4) | – | –1.5(E) |
| 93 | Brick and Blocks | – | – | 24.0(4) | – | – |
| 94 | Clay Refractories | – | – | 24.0(4) | –0.75(E) | – |
| 95 | Lime | 21.92(1) | 0.232 | 16.8(4) | – | – |
| 96 | Gypsum Building Materials | – | – | 16.8(4) | – | – |
| 97 | Mineral Wool | – | – | 53.9(4) | – | – |
| 98 | Pig Iron | 181.76 | 0.038 | – | – | – |
| 99 | Semifinished Steel | 195.00 | 0.040 | – | – | – |
| 100 | Manufactured Iron or Steel | 319.00 | 0.048 | – | –0.1(E) | –0.3(E) |
| 101 | Iron and Steel Pipe | 507.00 | 0.052 | 43.7(4) | – | – |
| 102 | Railway Track Material | 254.40 | 0.072 | – | – | – |
| 103 | Ferroalloys | – | – | – | – | – |
| 104 | Primary Copper Products | 1,286.00 | 0.017 | 67.2(4) | –0.2(E) | –0.6(E) |
| 105 | Primary Zinc Products | 780.00 | 0.031 | – | –0.56 | –1.93 |
| 106 | Primary Aluminum Products | 796.00 | 0.036 | 35.4(4) | –0.2(E) | –0.6(E) |
| 107 | Brass, Bronze and Copper Shapes | 1,300.00 | 0.020 | – | – | – |
| 108 | Aluminum Shapes | 1,280.00 | 0.023 | – | – | – |
| 109 | Metal Containers | – | – | 18.9(4) | –1.0(E) | –2.5(E) |
| 110 | Farm Machinery | 1,455.00(8) | 0.037 | 24.8(4) | –3.18 | –4.0 |

*Estimates of Rail Demand Elasticities* (continued)

| Commodity Group Number | Commodity Description | 1975 Estimated Supply Price per Short Ton | 1975(2) Freight Rate Ratio | 1972(5) Estimated Rail Modal Share | Range of Estimated Rail Demand Elasticities | |
|---|---|---|---|---|---|---|
| | | | | | Less Elastic | More Elastic |
| 111 | Heavy Machinery | – | 0.033 | 20.4(4) | -3.16 | -4.0 |
| 112 | Household Appliances | 1,285.00(8) | 0.047 | 58.3(4) | -0.84 | -2.7 |
| 113 | Radios and Television Sets | – | 0.037 | 18.7(4) | -4.66 | -8.38 |
| 114 | Automobiles | – | 0.009 | – | -0.76 | -1.68 |
| 115 | Other Motor Vehicles | 7,400.00(8) | 0.010 | 57.3(4) | -0.76 | -1.75 |
| 116 | Motor Vehicle Parts | – | 0.005 | – | -0.75 | -1.68 |
| 117 | Locomotive and Railway Car Parts | – | 0.004 | 79.9(4) | -0.75 | -1.75 |
| 118 | Iron and Steel Scrap | 63.00 | 0.112 | – | -0.05 | -0.14 |
| 119 | Nonferrous Scrap | – | – | 87.9(3) | -0.05(E) | -0.14(E) |
| 120 | Textile Scrap | – | – | – | – | – |
| 121 | Waste Paper | – | – | 32.5(6) | -0.1(E) | -0.7(E) |
| 122 | Chemical and Petroleum Waste | 282.00 | 0.029 | 50.0(6) | – | – |
| 123 | Empty Shipping Containers | – | – | 100.0 | 0.0 | 0.0 |
| 124 | Freight Forwarder Traffic | – | – | 100.0 | – | – |
| 125 | Shipper Association Traffic | – | – | 100.0 | -2.50(E) | -3.0(E) |
| 126 | Miscellaneous Mixed Shipments | – | – | 30.0(7) | – | – |
| 127 | All Other, NEC | – | – | 30.0(7) | -1.0(E) | -1.5(E) |
| | TOTAL | – | – | 30.0(7) | – | – |

NOTES:

(1) Value per ton in 1974.
(2) Rail revenue per ton calculated from 1975 1% Waybill Sample.
(3) Source is the bulk commodity data base from the Transportation Systems Center.
(4) Source is the 1972 Census of Transportation.
(5) Percent of tons.
(6) A. T. Kearney, Inc. estimate based on production levels, 1% Waybill Information and Annual Rail Freight Commodity Statistics.
(7) Source is TAA. In ton-miles, nearly 38% moved by rail in 1972.
(8) Value per ton in 1972 inflated to 1975 levels using wholesale price indices.
(9) February 6, 1976 prices, Chemical Marketing Reporter.
(10) Indicative rates for elasticity estimates: (E) = Estimate, (M) = Morton study, op. cit.
SOURCE: ICC, *The Impact of the 4-R Act, Railroad Ratemaking Provisions* (Washington, D.C.: October 5, 1977), Exhibit 27, p.E-37.

Notice that as the supply curve pivots about the origin in the direction of the abscissa, the derived demand for transport approaches the demand for the commodity. In general, as the elasticity of supply $\left( \epsilon_s = \dfrac{P\,dQ}{Q\,dP} \right)$ approaches zero, the elasticity of the derived demand for transportation gets smaller, and vice versa. In the limit, when $S_0$ coincides with $OD_D$ (i.e., zero production costs), the demand curve for the commodity is identical with the demand for transportation and has the same elasticity because $P_T = P_D$ and thus $\alpha = 1$.

The derived demand for transport deviates from the demand for the commodity as $S_0$ pivots away from the abscissa toward the ordinate or, what is the same thing, as the elasticity of supply moves from infinity toward zero. Figure 1.4 indicates three positions of a supply function and the associated transport demand function for a given demand curve.

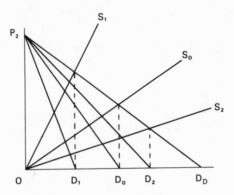

Fig. 1.4

$P_2D_1$ is the derived demand for transportation with $OS_1$; $P_2D_0$ is the derived transport demand for $OS_0$ and $P_2D_2$ with supply curve $OS_2$. The elasticity of supply for these three supply functions differs in the sense that at any common price $P_1$, the change in quantity supplied is least along $OS_1$ and greatest along $OS_2$ for any given percentage change in price. In a similar vein it is obvious that the elasticity of the demand for transport varies directly with the elasticity of supply.

### The Special Case When $OS_0$ Bisects the Demand Curve

If $S_0$ bisects $P_2D_D$, the derived demand for transportation coincides with the $MR$ curve associated with the commodity demand curve.

Proof:

Assume the situation as shown in Figure 1.5, where $P_2K = KD_D$. $P_2M_1$ is the $MR$ associated with $P_2D_D$. It can be shown that for linear demand curves the $MR$ curve bisects any line drawn perpendicularly from the ordinate (or parallel to the abscissa) to the demand curve.[30] It follows, then, that for any increase (or decrease) in commodity price, the decrease (or increase) in quantity demanded will equal twice the decrease (or increase) along $P_2M_1$.[31]

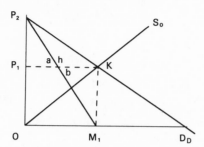

Fig. 1.5

Thus, the rate of change in quantity demanded in response to a change in price is twice as great along the demand curve as it is along the $MR$ curve, or, by the same token, the decrease in "price" required to generate an equal increase in quantity demanded along both the demand and $MR$ curves will be twice as great along $MR$ as along the demand curve.

It is this necessary property of linear demand and supply curves that has led some to assert that "such a marginal revenue curve will have an elasticity equal to one-half that of the demand curve from which it is derived. . . ."[32] While it is true that the *slope* of the $MR$ curve is

---

30. A geometric proof is as follows: Since the area of the triangle $P_2OM_1$ = the area $OM_1KP_1$, it follows that the area of $P_2P_1L$ = the area of $M_1KL$. Since angle $a$ = angle $b$, and both triangles are right triangles, their corresponding angles are equal. For triangles of equal area, the sides opposite equal angles are also equal. Thus $P_1L = LK$. It can similarly be shown for any line parallel to $P_1K$ that the $MR$ curve ($P_2M_1$) bisects it. Thus $OM_1 = M_1D_D$.

31. Proof: In the accompanying figure, a shift from $F$ to $A$ increases the variable along the abscissa by $DE$ along $P_2D_D$ and by $BC$ along $P_2M_1$. We know that $AB + BC = CD + DE$.
$\therefore FG + BC = CD + DE$
$\therefore FG + BC = BD - BC + DE$
$\therefore FG + 2BC = GH + DE$
But $GH = FG$, $FG + 2BC = FG + DE$
$\therefore DE = 2BC$.

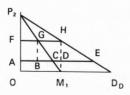

32. Felton, p.16.

twice the *slope* of the demand curve, elasticity does not refer to the slope of the demand curve. The ratio of the elasticity of demand for the commodity to be transported to the elasticity of demand for transportation is

$$\frac{\epsilon_T}{\epsilon_D} = \frac{\dfrac{P_T}{Q_T}\dfrac{dQ_T}{dP_T}}{\dfrac{P_D}{Q_D}\dfrac{dQ_D}{dP}}.$$

Thus, any given change in $P_T$ ($\Delta P_T$) will lead to a ($\frac{1}{2}\Delta P_T$) change in $P_D$ in order to have the change in $Q_T = Q_D$. Alternatively, it follows from the fact that $\dfrac{dQ_T}{dP_T} = \dfrac{1}{2}\dfrac{dQ_D}{dP_D}$ for linear demand curves that

$$\frac{\epsilon_T}{\epsilon_D} = \frac{1}{2}\frac{P_T}{P_D}.$$

But $\dfrac{P_T}{P_D}$ is the freight rate ratio, or what we have previously designated as $\alpha$. Thus for linear demand curves the elasticity of the derived demand for transportation is $\epsilon_T = \dfrac{1}{2}\alpha\epsilon_D$ for the situation where the $MR$ curve defines the demand schedule for transportation. Note that $0 < \alpha < 1$ and thus $\epsilon_T \to \dfrac{1}{2}\epsilon_D$ as $\alpha \to 1$ and $\epsilon_T \to 0$ as $\alpha \to 0$.

## Transport Demand and Elasticity of Supply

We have already noted that the elasticity of demand for transport depends not only on the elasticity of demand for the commodity but also on the elasticity of supply of the commodity (see Figure 1.2). The relationship can be spelled out more formally and precisely.

Assume linear demand and supply functions as follows:

$$Q_D = a - bP$$
$$Q_s = -c + dP.$$

The associated inverse demand and supply functions are

$$P_D = \frac{1}{b}(a - Q)$$
$$P_s = \frac{1}{d}(c + Q).$$

We define the freight rate $P_T$ as the vertical distance between the two functions or as the difference between the demand price $P_D$ and the supply price $P_s$. Thus $P_T = P_D - P_s = \dfrac{1}{b}(a - Q) - \dfrac{1}{d}(c + Q)$. Or

$P_T = \left(\dfrac{a}{b} - \dfrac{c}{d}\right) - Q\left(\dfrac{1}{b} + \dfrac{1}{d}\right)$. Relating the quantity bought and sold to $P_T$ we have:

$$Q = \frac{\left(\dfrac{a}{b} - \dfrac{c}{d}\right)}{\left(\dfrac{1}{b} + \dfrac{1}{d}\right)} - \left(\frac{1}{\dfrac{1}{b} + \dfrac{1}{d}}\right) P_T.$$

The elasticity of the demand for transport is

$$\epsilon_T = \frac{P_T}{Q}\frac{dQ}{dP_T} = \frac{-P_T}{Q}\left(\frac{1}{\dfrac{1}{b} + \dfrac{1}{d}}\right).$$

However, $b = \dfrac{-\epsilon_D Q}{P_D}$ and $d = \dfrac{\epsilon_S Q}{P_S}$.

$$\therefore \epsilon_T = \frac{-P_T}{Q}\left(\frac{Q\epsilon_D\epsilon_S}{P_D\epsilon_S - P_S\epsilon_D}\right) = \frac{P_T}{P_D}\left(\frac{\epsilon_D\epsilon_S}{\epsilon_S - \dfrac{P_S}{P_D}\epsilon_D}\right).$$

However, $P_S = P_D - P_T$, and $\dfrac{P_T}{P_D} = \alpha$. $\therefore \epsilon_T = \alpha\,\dfrac{\epsilon_D\epsilon_S}{\epsilon_S - \epsilon_D(1-\alpha)}$.

Note that as $\epsilon_S \to \infty$, the expression $\dfrac{\epsilon_S}{\epsilon_S - \epsilon_D(1-\alpha)} \to 1$. Thus when $\epsilon_S$ is infinite, $\epsilon_T = \alpha\epsilon_D$, as derived before.

Note also that the expression $\dfrac{\epsilon_S}{\epsilon_S - \epsilon_D(1-\alpha)}$ is positive (since $\epsilon_D$ is negative and $\alpha$ lies between 0 and 1) and less than 1 (i.e., $0 < \dfrac{\epsilon_S}{\epsilon_S - \epsilon_D(1-\alpha)} < 1$) except when $\epsilon_D = 0$. Thus the influence of $\epsilon_S$, except when it is infinite, is, in essence, to "scale down" the previous elasticity of demand for transportation. For $\epsilon_S <$ infinity, the $\epsilon_T$ will be consistently less than $\alpha\epsilon_D$.

This result is not confined to linear supply and demand curves. A more general formulation is as follows:

Assume the following inverse demand and supply functions:

$$P_D = f(Q) \text{ and } P_S = g(Q).$$

Also, $P_D = P_S + P_T$, or $f(Q) = g(Q) + P_T$.        (1)

Taking derivatives of (1) with respect to $P_T$ we have:

$$\frac{df(Q)}{dQ}\frac{dQ}{dP_T} = \frac{dg(Q)}{dQ}\frac{dQ}{dP_T} + 1.$$

$$\therefore \frac{dQ}{dP_T} = \left[\frac{df(Q)}{dQ} - \frac{dg(Q)}{d(Q)}\right]^{-1}.$$

Now $\epsilon_T = \dfrac{P_T}{Q} \dfrac{dQ}{dP_T} = \dfrac{P_T}{Q} \left[ \dfrac{df(Q)}{dQ} - \dfrac{dg(Q)}{dQ} \right]^{-1}$ .

But $\epsilon_D = \dfrac{P_D}{Q} \dfrac{dQ}{dP_D} = \dfrac{P_D}{Q} \dfrac{dQ}{df(Q)}$ .

$\therefore \dfrac{df(Q)}{dQ} = \dfrac{P_D}{\epsilon_D Q}$ .

Similarly, $\dfrac{dg(Q)}{d(Q)} = \dfrac{P_S}{\epsilon_S Q}$

$\therefore \epsilon_T = \dfrac{P_T}{Q} \left( \dfrac{P_D}{\epsilon_D Q} - \dfrac{P_S}{\epsilon_S Q} \right)^{-1}$

$\qquad = \dfrac{P_T}{Q} \left( \dfrac{\epsilon_S P_D - \epsilon_D P_S}{Q \epsilon_S \epsilon_D} \right)^{-1}$

$\qquad = P_T \dfrac{\epsilon_S \epsilon_D}{(P_D \epsilon_S - P_S \epsilon_D)}$ .

But $P_S + P_T = P_D$.

$\therefore \epsilon_T = P_T \dfrac{\epsilon_S \epsilon_D}{P_D \epsilon_S - (P_D - P_T) \epsilon_D}$

$\qquad = \dfrac{P_T}{P_D} \left( \dfrac{\epsilon_S \epsilon_D}{\epsilon_S - \epsilon_D + \dfrac{P_T}{P_D} \epsilon_D} \right)$ .

Defining $\dfrac{P_T}{P_D} = \alpha$, as before, we have

$$\epsilon_T = \dfrac{\alpha \epsilon_S \epsilon_D}{\epsilon_S - \epsilon_D (1 - \alpha)} \, . [33]$$

Thus the elasticity of demand for transportation varies directly with the products of $\epsilon_S$ and $\epsilon_D$, directly with $\alpha$, and inversely with the *sum* of the elasticities since $\epsilon_S \geqq 0$ and $\epsilon_D \leqq 0$.

Few studies of supply elasticity exist other than for agricultural products. Table 1.7 gives the results of one such study.

The data indicate extremely low short-run elasticity of supply, doubtless because of the dominant influence of weather on supply. A study relating the output of all crops in the United States to price and weather variables indicated very low elasticity of supply with respect to price (only .152) and a much higher elasticity with respect to weather (.428).[34] Over longer periods, the supply response to price

33. Walters, who first derived this expression, uses a slightly different approach. See A. Walters and E. Bennathan, *The Economics of Ocean Freight Rates* (New York: Praeger, 1969), Technical Appendix.

34. Z. Griliches, "Estimates of the Aggregate U.S. Farm Supply Function," *Journal of Farm Economics*, May 1960.

TABLE 1.7

*Supply–Price Elasticities*

| Commodity | Short-Run | Long-Run |
|---|---|---|
| Green lima beans | 0.10 | 1.70 |
| Cabbage | 0.36 | 1.20 |
| Carrots | 0.14 | 1.00 |
| Cucumbers | 0.29 | 2.20 |
| Lettuce | 0.03 | 0.16 |
| Onions | 0.34 | 1.00 |
| Green peas | 0.31 | 4.40 |
| Tomatoes | 0.16 | 0.90 |
| Watermelons | 0.23 | 0.48 |
| Beets | 0.13 | 1.00 |
| Cantaloupes | 0.02 | 0.04 |
| Spinach | 0.20 | 4.70 |

SOURCE: M. Nerlove and W. Addison, "Statistical Estimation of Long-Run Elasticities of Supply and Demand," *Journal of Farm Economics,* November 1958. Data estimates derived from data pertaining to 1919–1955.

changes is much greater, as would be expected. Even in the long run, however, most supply elasticities do not exceed unity, and some are surprisingly low.

A third study of a supply function for milk in New Hampshire and Maine also implied a supply elasticity of less than one,[35] although it is not strictly comparable to the above. More recently, agricultural supply elasticities have been estimated to fall within the range of zero to 2, although the authors note that "the disparity in estimates does require considerable interpretation."[36]

Thus, the empirical content of transport demand elasticity related to $\epsilon_D$, $\epsilon_S$, and $\alpha$ is even more elusive than suggested earlier. However, if we equate the behavior of supply with the behavior of marginal cost, some empirical generalizations are possible; they will be investigated more fully later. At this point, it is worth noting that many cost studies indicate constancy of unit average or marginal costs over a wide range of output. That is, unit costs tend to be constant (after a relatively small volume of output) with given plant capacity as output per time period expands until capacity constraints become operative.[37]

35. G. Frick and R. Andrews, "Aggregation Bias and Four Methods of Summing Farm Supply Functions," *Journal of Farm Economics,* August 1965.

36. L. Tweeten and C. Quance, "Positivistic Measures of Aggregate Supply Elasticities: Some New Approaches," *American Economic Review,* May 1969, p.182.

37. J. Johnston, *Statistical Cost Analyses* (New York: McGraw-Hill, 1960), p.168. Long-run cost behavior (i.e., variable plant capacity) also appears to be linear over a wide range of output. See L. Scherer, *Industrial Market Structure and Economic Performance* (Chicago: Rand McNally, 1970), pp.74–93.

If this principle is true of most goods-producing processes, the assumption of infinite elasticity of supply becomes more reasonable, although, strictly speaking, in industries that are not perfectly competitive a supply curve does not relate uniquely to cost functions. To this extent we are justified in using the simpler expression for $\epsilon_T$ (namely, $\alpha\epsilon_D$) in most instances.

A simple linear example may help clarify the above. Assume the following demand and supply schedules:

$$Q_D = 100 - P \quad \text{or} \quad P_D = 100 - Q$$
$$Q_S = -5 + P \quad\quad\quad P_S = 5 + Q$$

$$P_T = P_D - P_S = 95 - 2Q, \text{ or } Q = \frac{1}{2}(95 - P_T).$$

If $P_T = 0$, $Q = 47\frac{1}{2}$, which is the equilibrium quantity bought and sold at a price $P_C = 52\frac{1}{2}$.

If $P_T = 95$, $Q_D = 0$, and no goods are transported.

Then $\epsilon_T = \dfrac{-P_T}{Q}\left(\dfrac{1}{2}\right)$.

Using the formula $\epsilon_T = \alpha \dfrac{\epsilon_D\epsilon_S}{\epsilon_S - \epsilon_D(1-\alpha)}$ and substituting the values of $\epsilon_D$, $\epsilon_S$ from the linear functions, namely, $\dfrac{-P_D}{Q}$ and $\dfrac{P_S}{Q}$, respectively, and recognizing that $\alpha = \dfrac{P_T}{P_D}$ we obtain

$$\epsilon_T = \frac{-P_T}{P_D}\frac{P_D P_S}{Q^2}\left(\frac{Q}{P_S + P_D - P_T}\right).$$

But $P_D - P_T = P_S$.

$$\therefore \epsilon_T = -\frac{1}{2}\frac{P_T}{Q}.$$

### Production Costs and Elasticity of Transport Demand

If we refer to costs of production of the commodity to be shipped rather than to the supply schedule, since the two are only uniquely linked under perfectly competitive conditions, some simple and intuitively plausible results emerge.

Assume that the delivered price of the commodity is always equal to the freight charge per unit plus the marginal production costs per unit, i.e., $P_D = P_T + MC$. This means that $\Delta P_D = \Delta P_T + \Delta MC$. Thus if a change in the freight rate is to induce more sales, it must lead to a change in the price of the commodity. However, if $\Delta MC$ is positive (i.e., rising marginal cost), the freight rate reduction must exceed $\Delta MC$ to induce a reduction in price. In short, rising marginal production costs partly offset any decrease in the freight rate as far as $P_D$ is concerned. On the other hand, if $\Delta MC$ is negative (i.e., decreasing marginal cost), the resultant change in $P_D$ will be greater than the decrease in the freight rate.

It is possible to derive an expression showing these relationships in terms of elasticities. For example, the ratio of $\epsilon_T$ to $\epsilon_D$ is

$$\frac{\epsilon_T}{\epsilon_D} = \frac{\dfrac{P_T}{Q_T}\dfrac{\Delta Q_T}{\Delta P_T}}{\dfrac{P_D}{Q_D}\dfrac{\Delta Q_D}{\Delta P_D}}.$$

But $Q_T = Q_D$ and $\Delta Q_T = \Delta Q_D$ since all production is assumed to be shipped to the market.

$$\therefore \frac{\epsilon_T}{\epsilon_D} = \frac{P_T}{P_D}\frac{\Delta P_D}{\Delta P_T}.$$

Since $\Delta P_D = \Delta P_T + \Delta MC$ and $\dfrac{P_T}{P_D} = \alpha$, by substitution we obtain

$$\frac{\epsilon_T}{\epsilon_D} = \alpha \frac{\Delta P_T + \Delta MC}{\Delta P_T}$$

or $\epsilon_T = \alpha\epsilon_D\left(1 + \dfrac{\Delta MC}{\Delta P_T}\right)$.

If $MC$ is constant (i.e., $\Delta MC = 0$), the last equation reduces to our earlier relationship. Where $\Delta MC$ is *rising* with respect to output in response to a *decrease* in $P_T$, the $\epsilon_T$ is "scaled down" because $\dfrac{\Delta MC}{\Delta P_T}$ is negative and less than 1. When $\Delta MC$ is *falling* in response to a *decrease* in $P_T$, the expression in parentheses is greater than 1 and increases $\epsilon_T$. The converse is true for increases in $P_T$. Since the expression in parentheses is always $<1$ and negative, it represents a "scaling down" factor for $\epsilon_T$ whenever $\Delta MC > 0$, analogous to our findings in terms of $\epsilon_S$. Note that when $\Delta MC = 0$ (i.e., constant costs per unit of output), the expression collapses to our old rule that $\epsilon_T = \alpha\epsilon_D$. Some simple illustrations are shown in the table below.

| | | Case 1 | | Case 2 | | Case 3 | |
|---|---|---|---|---|---|---|---|
| $Q_D$ | $P_c$ | $MC_1$ | $P_{T_1}$ | $MC_2$ | $P_{T_2}$ | $MC_3$ | $P_{T_3}$ |
| 1 | 20 | 4 | 16 | 4 | 16 | 4 | 16 |
| 2 | 18 | 4 | 14 | 5 | 13 | 4.2 | 13.8 |
| 3 | 16 | 4 | 12 | 6 | 10 | 4.4 | 11.6 |
| 4 | 14 | 4 | 10 | 7 | 7 | 4.6 | 9.4 |
| 5 | 12 | 4 | 8 | 8 | 4 | 4.8 | 7.2 |
| 6 | 10 | 4 | 6 | 9 | 1 | 4.0 | 5.0 |

For the change in $Q_D$ from 4 to 5 in Case 1, we have $\epsilon_D = \dfrac{14}{-4} \times \dfrac{1}{2}$
$= \dfrac{-7}{4}$ and $\epsilon_T = \dfrac{-10}{4} \times \dfrac{1}{2} = \dfrac{-5}{4}$, computed directly. Note that in this case $MC_1$ is constant, so $\Delta MC = 0$. Using the above formula, $\epsilon_T = \alpha\epsilon_D$
$= \dfrac{-10}{14} \times \dfrac{7}{4} = \dfrac{-5}{4}$ .

However, for Case 2, $MC_2$ is rising as output increases. A direct calculation yields $\epsilon_T = \dfrac{-7}{4} \times \dfrac{1}{3} = \dfrac{-7}{12}$. According to our generalization

above, $\epsilon_T = \alpha\epsilon_D\left(1 - \dfrac{\Delta MC}{\Delta P_T}\right) = \dfrac{7}{14}\left(\dfrac{-7}{4}\right)\left(1 - \dfrac{1}{3}\right) = \dfrac{-7}{12}$ .

Finally, for Case 3, $MC_3$ is rising by 0.2. A direct calculation of $\epsilon_T$

for a change in $Q_D$ from 4 to 5 is $\epsilon_T = \dfrac{9.4}{4}\left(\dfrac{1}{-2.2}\right) = \dfrac{-9.4}{8.8}$. From the

formula, $\epsilon_T = \dfrac{9.4}{14}\left(\dfrac{-7}{4}\right)\left(1 - \dfrac{0.2}{2.2}\right) = \dfrac{-9.4}{8.8}$ .

In short, when the shipper–producer faces rising per-unit production costs, the elasticity of transport demand is further reduced in the sense that for any increase in sales in the market, the proportionate reduction needed in freight rates is greater. In fact, the necessary proportionate reduction in freight rates varies directly with the magnitude of the increases in cost of production or the elasticity of costs with respect to output, a conclusion formally identical to that derived with respect to elasticity of supply.

### A More General Formulation

Removing both assumptions simultaneously, namely, an infinitely elastic supply curve and a single monopoly supplier of transport, we may deduce a more general expression for elasticity facing a single mode or firm. For example, with rail in competition with, say, truck, the *diverted* traffic with respect to, say, a rail rate reduction of $s$ $(= \%\Delta P_R)$ will be $\dfrac{1}{\beta}[(1 - \beta)\epsilon_{CROSS}]s$ (see p.14). The *generated* traffic will be $\dfrac{1}{\beta}[\alpha\epsilon_D(1 + \dfrac{\Delta MC}{\Delta P_R})]s$. Hence total elasticity is the sum of the two divided by $s$, or $\epsilon_{RT} = \dfrac{1}{\beta}[\alpha\epsilon_c(1 + \dfrac{\Delta MC}{\Delta P_R}) - (1 - \beta)\ \epsilon_{CROSS}]$. Note that when $\Delta MC = 0$ and $\beta = 1$, this equation boils down to the simple relationship first derived on p.8.

### Case II. Supply and Demand in Each of Two Regions

Instead of assuming a different supply origin and demand destination for a single commodity, as in Case I, we can assume two (or more) regions each having a separate supply and demand schedule for a single commodity, and then investigate the trade possibilities between the two regions in this commodity at alternative freight rates. The only difference between this situation and Case I is that in the "destination" region the commodity can be produced while in the "origination" region there is some demand for the commodity. Figure 1.6 illustrates this for the two-region case.

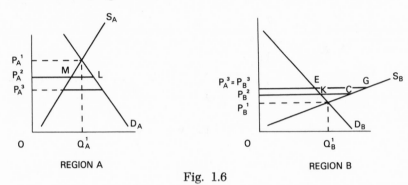

Fig. 1.6

If there is no trade between A and B, the prices and quantities bought and sold will be $P_A^1$, $Q_A^1$ in A and $P_B^1$, $Q_B^1$ in B. As long as the freight rate equals or exceeds $P_A^1 - P_B^1$ this situation will persist. If the freight rate falls below $P_A^1 - P_B^1$ producers in B will find it profitable to expand output in B but export some to A. Assume $P_T < P_A^1 - P_B^1$ and that producers in B expand output to point $C$ along the supply schedule $S_B$. Now there will be an excess in $B(= KC)$, which will be exported to A. The price in Region B will rise to $P_B^2$, reflecting the reduced quantity remaining in Region B. Analogously, in Region A, the increased supply $ML$ $(= KC)$ will reduce the price to $P_A^2$. A new equilibrium will occur when $P_T = P_A^2 - P_B^2$. In the extreme, when $P_T = 0$ then $P_A^3 = P_B^3$. When the freight rate declines from $P_A^1 - P_B^1$ to zero, there will be increasing amounts exported from Region B to Region A. We can, therefore, trace out a derived demand curve for transportation.

More formally, we may designate linear supply and demand schedules for each region as follows:

$$D_A = A - a_1 P_A$$
$$S_A = a_2 P_A - M$$
$$D_B = B - b_1 P_B$$
$$S_B = b_2 P_B - N$$

Assume that initially without trade $P_A > P_B$, or from a transportation viewpoint $P_T \geqq P_A - P_B$, then equilibrium prices in the two regions will be

$$P_A = \frac{A + M^{38}}{a_1 + a_2} \text{ and } P_B = \frac{B + N}{b_1 + b_2}.$$

In essence $P_T \gtreqqless \dfrac{A + M}{a_1 + a_2} - \dfrac{B + N}{b_1 + b_2}$, and the quantity demanded of transport services is zero. As $P_T$ decreases, however, suppliers in Region B will receive higher net prices, i.e., $(P_A - P_T) > P_B$, and will produce more in B and ship more of it to A. In the extreme, when $P_T = 0$ and $P_A = P_B$, we can treat the two regions as one. Thus $D_A + D_B = S_A + S_B$ in equilibrium when $P_T = 0$.

$$\therefore P_A = \frac{(A + B) + (M + N)}{a_1 + a_2 + b_1 + b_2} = P_B.$$

Similarly $D_A = A - a_1 P_A$ and $S_A = -M + a_2 P_A$. The difference between $D_A$ and $S_A$ represents the quantity of the commodity shipped from B to A. Thus, $D_A - S_A = A + M - (a_1 + a_2) P_A$. Substituting the value of $P_A$ noted above, we obtain the following result:

$$D_A - S_A = \frac{(b_1 + b_2)(A + M) - (a_1 + a_2)(B + N)}{a_1 + a_2 + b_1 + b_2}.$$

We now have two points on the linear derived demand for transport: $\left(0, \dfrac{A + M}{a_1 + a_2} - \dfrac{B + N}{b_1 + b_2}\right)$ and $\left(\dfrac{(b_1 + b_2)(A + M) - (a_1 + a_2)(B + N)}{a_1 + a_2 + b_1 + b_2}, 0\right)$.
Thus the equation of the demand schedule for transportation is

$$P_T = \frac{(b_1 + b_2)(A + M) - (a_1 + a_2)(B + N)}{(a_1 + a_2)(b_1 + b_2)} - \frac{a_1 + a_2 + b_1 + b_2}{(a_1 + a_2)(b_1 + b_2)} Q_T \tag{1}$$

or

$$Q_T = \frac{(b_1 + b_2)(A + M) - (a_1 + a_2)(B + N)}{a_1 + a_2 + b_1 + b_2} - \frac{(a_1 + a_2)(b_1 + b_2)}{a_1 + a_2 + b_1 + b_2} P_T \tag{2}$$

Notice that $a_1 + a_2$ is the *difference* between the slopes of the demand and supply schedules in A, and $b_1 + b_2$ is the *difference* between the slopes in B since one is positive and the other negative. The greater these slopes, the greater is the slope of the derived demand for transport. The elasticity of the demand for transportation is therefore

$$\epsilon_T = \frac{P_T}{Q_T} \left[ \frac{(a_1 + a_2)(b_1 + b_2)}{a_1 + a_2 + b_1 + b_2} \right], \text{ using equation (2)}.$$

Since the $a$'s and $b$'s can be expressed in terms of elasticities of supply or demand,[39] the elasticity of the demand for transport depends solely

---

38. That is $D_A = S_A$. Thus $A - a_1 P_A = -M + a_2 P_A$, or $P_A = \dfrac{A + M}{a_1 + a_2}$.

39. For example, $a_1 = \dfrac{Q_A}{P_A} \epsilon_{DA}$, $a_2 = \dfrac{Q_A}{P_A} \epsilon_{SA}$, $b_1 = \dfrac{Q_B}{P_B} \epsilon_{DB}$, and $b_2 = \dfrac{Q_B}{P_B} \epsilon_{SB}$.

on these elasticities. The resultant expression is rather messy and difficult to interpret and will not be included here.[40]

For a simple illustration of the foregoing, assume supply and demand relations in Regions A and B as follows:

$$D_A = 30 - P_A, \; S_A = P_A - 10$$
$$D_B = 21 - P_B, \; S_B = P_B - 5.$$

Without trade equilibrium, prices and quantities in each region are:

$$P_A = 20, \; D_A = S_A = 10$$
$$P_B = 13, \; D_B = S_B = 8.$$

Other things being equal, if the freight rate between A and B $\geqq 7$, no trade will take place. If the freight rate drops below $7, producers in B can obtain a net price in A $= \$20 - P_T$, which is greater than the price in B. As a consequence, they will expand output and export from B to A until the *net* price in $A = P_B$. As $P_T \to 0$, $P_A - P_T = P_B$, or when $P_T = 0$ and $P_A = P_B$, the two regions can be treated as one. The new equilibrium can be determined by summing the demand and supply relationships, respectively, and equating them. Thus, we obtain

$$51 - 2P_A = 2P_A - 15$$
$$\therefore P_A = 16\tfrac{1}{2}.$$

At this price $D_A = 13\tfrac{1}{2}$ (i.e., 30-16½) and $D_B = 4\tfrac{1}{2}$. $S_A = 6\tfrac{1}{2}$ (i.e., 16½ − 10), and the imports into A will be 7 units. Similarly, $S_B = 11\tfrac{1}{2}$, and exports, of course, are 7 units (i.e., 11½ − 4½). Thus when $P_T = 0$, the demand for transport is 7 units and when $P_T = 7$, the demand is zero—the demand schedule for transportation is therefore

$$Q_T = 7 - P_T,$$

which can be obtained by substituting in the several formulae noted above.

### Case III. The Case of Regional Development

An alternative approach to the estimation of elasticity of demand for transportation relates to what may be termed the "developmental" case. Assume a region where the land is equally fertile throughout and where the productivity of a given commodity is one ton per acre per year. Suppose the commodity can be sold at a given fixed price $k$ per ton at a port P or market located at one edge of the region. Assume that the original cost of transport is constant at $a$ per ton-mile shipped to the market or port and is the only cost involved.

40. For details, see H. van der Tak and A. Ray, "The Economic Benefits of Road Transport Projects," World Bank Report EC-160, March 18, 1968, and their more extensive treatment in World Bank Staff Occasional Papers, no.13, IBRD, 1971.

Assume further that transport can take place only in a north–south or east–west direction—not diagonally. The total cost per ton from any point in the region to the port or market is therefore $ax + ay$. As long as $ax + ay \leqq k$, the producers will produce and transport one ton per acre. The limits of cultivation are given by $a(x + y) = k$, or when $x + y = \dfrac{k}{a}$. If we always refer to N–S movements in absolute values, we determine a triangular region of cultivation with base $\dfrac{2k}{a}$ and

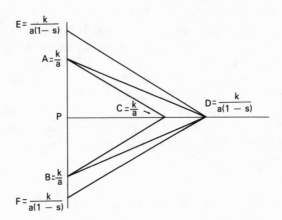

Fig. 1.7

"height" $\dfrac{k}{a}$ (see Figure 1.7) and hence area $ABC = \dfrac{1}{2}\left(\dfrac{2k}{a}\right)\dfrac{k}{a} = \left(\dfrac{k}{a}\right)^2$, which also represents the number of acres cultivated and the number of tons produced.

Assume now a transport improvement along the east–west axis, but only beyond point $C$, which reduces transport costs by a given amount, say $s\%$. With $0 < s < 1$, the new transport cost per ton-mile is therefore $a(1 - s)$. The new area of cultivation and production will now expand to $ABD$, or $\dfrac{k^2}{(a^2 - a^2 s)}$. The proportional change in output is $\left(\dfrac{k^2}{a^2 - a^2 s} - \dfrac{k^2}{a^2}\right) \div \dfrac{k^2}{a^2} = \dfrac{s}{1 - s}$. Since $\epsilon_T = \dfrac{-\%\Delta Q_D}{\%\Delta P_T}$, then $\epsilon_T = -\left(\dfrac{s}{1 - s}\right) \dfrac{1}{s} = \dfrac{-1}{1 - s}$. For small values of $s$ (.01, .02, .05, or .10), $\epsilon_T$ is close to $-1$, and in the limit as $s \to 0$, $\epsilon_T \to -1$.

On the other hand, if transport improvements take place throughout the whole system and extend both N–S as well as E–W, so that the new area of cultivation is $EFD$, $\epsilon_T$ will obviously rise. The new area of cultivation will become $\dfrac{1}{2}\left[\dfrac{2k}{a(1 - s)}\right]\dfrac{k}{a(1 - s)} = \dfrac{k^2}{(a - as)^2}$. The proportional change in area (or output) $= \dfrac{1 - (1 - s)^2}{(1 - s)^2}$. Thus $\epsilon_T =$

$-\left(\dfrac{1-(1-s)^2}{(1-s)^2}\times\dfrac{1}{s}\right)=\dfrac{s-2}{(1-s)^2}.$ Again in the limit as $s\to 0$, $\epsilon_T\to$ $-2.$[41]

The foregoing referred to tons transported rather than ton-miles. Since the latter was the unit in which the freight rate was expressed, it is important to assess elasticity in these terms as well. The average distance hauled per ton is given by $\dfrac{1}{2}\dfrac{k}{a}$ prior to the transport improvement. After the improvement the average haul per ton is $\dfrac{1}{2}\dfrac{k}{a(1-s)}$.

Ton-miles before and after a ubiquitous improvement leading to a rate reduction of $s$ are, respectively, $\dfrac{1}{2}\left(\dfrac{k}{a}\right)^2\dfrac{k}{a}$ and $\dfrac{1}{2}\left[\dfrac{k}{a(1-s)}\right]^2\dfrac{k}{a(1-s)}$, or $\dfrac{1}{2}\dfrac{k^3}{a^3}$ and $\dfrac{1}{2}\dfrac{k^3}{a^3(1-s)^3}$. Thus, the proportionate change in ton-miles is $\dfrac{1}{(1-s)^3}-1$ and $\epsilon_T=\dfrac{-1}{s}\left[\dfrac{1}{(1-s)^3}-1\right]=\dfrac{-3+s(3-s)}{(1-s)^3}$. As $s\to 0$, $\epsilon_T\to -3$. This is, of course, the maximum and assumes that $a$ declines throughout the region. Confining the reduction in $a$ by $s\%$ to a "lengthening" only of the E–W road, elasticity in terms of ton-miles becomes $-2.$[42]

These elasticities are large in absolute value compared with those deduced earlier because we have assumed infinite elasticity of supply and demand. In the case of poor countries supplying a relatively homogeneous commodity (e.g., rubber) for the world market, the assumptions may be realistic.[43] The results are not affected if costs other than transport are included, assuming them to be constant per unit of output, because this only affects the "net" price received by producers. The proportionate change in tons or ton-miles resulting from a change

---

41. Alternatively, this can be derived by determining the rate of change of the original area $\left(\dfrac{k}{a}\right)^2$ with respect to a change in $a$, i.e., $\dfrac{d\left(\dfrac{k}{a}\right)^2}{da}=\dfrac{-2k^2}{a^3}$. But $\epsilon_T=$ $\dfrac{P}{Q}\dfrac{dq}{dp}$, or in the above terms, $\epsilon^T=\left(\dfrac{a}{\dfrac{k^2}{a^2}}\right)\dfrac{-2k^2}{a^3}=-2.$

42. The proportionate change in ton-miles is $\dfrac{1}{(1-s)^2}-1$. For a given change in $a$ of $s\%$, elasticity in terms of ton-miles is $\dfrac{1}{s}\left[\dfrac{1}{(1-s)^2}-1\right]$. Since $0<s<1$, as $s\to 0$, the elasticity $\to -2$. This result is identical with that of A. A. Walters, who first drew attention to this form of discussion in terms of demand elasticities in transportation. See *The Economics of Road User Charges*, World Bank Staff Occasional Papers, no.5, 1968, chap. 5, and "A Development Model of Transport," *American Economic Review*, May 1968.

43. Walters, *The Economics of Road User Charges*, has analyzed the impact of altering the assumptions in this case. Since the results are analogous to what we have already derived, we will not examine the various consequences here.

in freight costs or rates would thus not be influenced by inclusion of nontransport costs assumed to be constant. Thus $\alpha = \dfrac{P_T}{P_D}$, which loomed so large before, is not a determinant of $\epsilon_T$ in the case envisaged here.

The applicability of the several cases clearly depends on the circumstances being investigated. In the latter case, some of the above results have been partially verified in a Central American study by Churchill.[44]

## Conclusion

We have concluded our analysis of the price elasticity of transport demand. Obviously, many further extensions, modifications of assumptions, and so on, are possible. However, for present purposes the foregoing should suffice to convey a sense of the interrelations among the prices of transport, prices of commodities, production costs, and the resultant estimates of $\epsilon_T$. As complex and difficult to quantify as many of these relationships and variables appear, the reality is even more so. Here we have vastly simplified the problems by assuming a constant *quality* of transport service and have concentrated solely on price. Yet more and more shippers view the quality of transport service as more significant than the freight rate in choice of mode and even in choice of firm. Indeed, if rate competition is impeded by regulation, differences in quality of service become critical in determining transport demand by mode or firm. We turn therefore to a discussion of service quality.

## Quality of Service

In examining the demand for a particular mode of transport, we need to consider more than the freight rate—we need to consider service *quality*. If the quality of one mode of transport is distinctly superior to a competing mode, it can charge a higher *rate* and still retain the traffic—in short, the *net* cost of transportation to the shipper for a particular mode = rate ± the value of the quality differences where two or more modes exist.

This can be illustrated as follows: Assume five shippers ($S_1$, $S_2$, . . . , $S_5$) who value the service of one type of transport (say truck) over another (say rail) as follows:

---

44. Anthony Churchill, *Road User Charges in Central America*, World Bank Staff Occasional Papers, no.15, 1972, pp.96–101.

Superior *Value of*
*Truck over Rail*
*Service to the Shipper*
($)

| | |
|---|---|
| $S_1$ | 0 |
| $S_2$ | 2 |
| $S_3$ | 4 |
| $S_4$ | 6 |
| $S_5$ | 8 |

This is interpreted to mean that the superior speed, dependability, etc., of truck over rail service confers different nontransport cost savings to different shippers. If both rail and truck costs are linear at $C_R =$ \$10/ton and $C_T =$ \$15/ton, then several cases can be examined.

*Case I.* If rail and truck rates are equal, $S_1$ would be indifferent as to mode, and the probability is that half the shipments by $S_1$ would be by rail and half by truck. On the average, then, society incurs \$12½ in costs when freight rates are equal [i.e., ½(10) + ½(15)]. All other shippers who prefer truck over rail would use truck. The economic cost when $S_2$ uses truck is the truck cost (\$15) less nontransport cost savings by virtue of the superior truck service (\$2), or \$13/ton. Similarly for $S_3$, $S_4$, and $S_5$, the net economic costs are \$11, \$9, and \$7, for a total of \$52½.

*Case II.* If the relative rail/truck rates differ by the same amount as their cost differences (namely, \$15 − \$10 = \$5/ton), then the *net* economic cost for $S_1$, $S_2$, and $S_3$ is \$10/ton each (equal to rail cost per ton) because when the truck rate exceeds the rail rate by \$5 (equal to the cost differences), the nontransport cost savings are less and each shipper has lower net costs by using rail. On the other hand, $S_4$ and $S_5$ would use truck since the value to them of the service quality differences exceeds \$5. Their net costs are \$9 and \$7, respectively, per ton. Thus, total economic costs to society are \$46, compared with \$52½. For rate differences that are unequal to cost differences, it can easily be shown that total costs exceed \$46. Thus efficient pricing combined with freedom of shipper (modal) choice requires freight rate differences that reflect transport cost differences.

In general, the *quality* of service (for freight) among modes may be ranked as follows: air (highest), truck, rail, water. The dimensions of service quality are:

1. Minimum size of shipments offered or accepted
2. Speed of delivery
3. Susceptibility of goods to loss and damage
4. Dependability of service
5. Flexibility of service

All of these relate to the differences among modal technologies and/or the quality of transport management, which may also differ among modes as well as within a particular mode.

Any quality difference, whether rooted in the technology or related to managerial qualities, in any of these dimensions will be evaluated differently by shippers of different commodities and according to particular shipper circumstances. It is possible, however, to specify in a general way the conditions under which the qualitative differences between any pair of modes will be valued more or less highly. For expository purposes only, we will concentrate on quality differences between rail and truck. A comparable analysis can be made for any other pair of modes. We will also ignore the cost impact on the transport supplier of attempts to improve the service quality[45] and concentrate only on the value to the shipper (i.e., the demand aspect of quality).

## Speed of Service[46]

It is generally acknowledged that truck transport is more rapid than rail. The diverse rail consignments that necessitate spotting, switching, makeup, and breakup of trains cause sufficient delays to offset the faster track speed so that the amount of time elapsed is generally greater by rail than by truck.[47] Improved efficiency in yard service and the ability to handle boxcars in blocks offset this speed disadvantage. Indeed, in some instances rail transport may be speedier, but generally truck transport has the advantage.

However, the value of the speed element is highly variable, although we can suggest two circumstances in which speed takes on greater importance: when items are perishable, and when there are incentives to reduce the ratio of inventory to sales. The former affects a rough category of commodities that is fairly stable. The latter varies with the phase of the business cycle; that is, during the contraction phase, the inventory/sales ratio tends to be too high and efforts are made to reduce it. Hence, rapidity of supply is of less consequence.

---

45. For an analysis of the cost impact and potential adjustments among quality, costs, and rates, see Wilson, *Essays*, pp.101–108.

46. The material on pp.44–48 is taken directly from Wilson, *Essays*, pp.108–12, with minor amendments.

47. This elapsed time differential is generally admitted by the railroads. Indeed, it has been suggested that "to expect railroads to meet truck transit time on single carloads—is like asking a ready-to-wear clothier to match the service of a custom tailor . . . (T)he railroad is not economically justified in trying to meet truck speed at an equal or lower charge because, in meeting truck speed (shipper to consignee) on single carload shipments, the railroad would probably incur excessive switching costs which would destroy its 'inherent advantage.'" ("How to Get 'Quality Control,'" *Railway Age*, Sept. 1, 1958, p.34.)

During the expansion phase, when demand is outstripping current supply, the value of increased delivery speed is much greater. This would seem to give the greater advantage to truck transport during expansion and to rail transport during contraction. However, it has often been observed that during contraction the relative decline in rail transport is far greater than that of truck. The reason for this is that the smaller unit of truck output permits more "hand-to-mouth" buying, which, coupled with faster delivery, also gives the relative advantage to trucks during contraction.

On the other hand, during expansion (if entrepreneurs envisage a relatively long period of rising sales) output commitments tend to be longer-run in nature, thereby offsetting to some extent the importance of speed for any particular consignment. Thus, the rail disadvantage is somewhat minimized during expansion if entrepreneurs are optimistic and have a long-run viewpoint. This permits longer-run planning, which, in turn, offsets the special advantage of speed for any particular shipment.

The significance of speed therefore depends on: (1) the perishability of the commodity; (2) the phase of the business cycle; (3) the entrepreneurial time horizon; and (4) the general state of entrepreneurial confidence. Variations in any of these will alter the value of the speed differential, and therefore the inherent truck advantage with respect to speed will fluctuate in the fashion indicated above.

### Flexibility of Service

Flexibility is closely tied to the time-in-transit (or speed) factor. The ability of trucks to load at the shipper's door and unload at the customer's door reduces the amount of handling required and hence saves on transit time. Of course, the less-complete rail service depends on the location of the shippers and their customers. If both are located along the rail line, much of the relative superiority of trucks with respect to flexibility disappears. However, the general advantage of trucks in door-to-door service takes on more importance as industrial location patterns become less and less tied to the rail network.

In addition, trucks can handle smaller lots more expeditiously than can railroads. Admittedly, the reduced size of consignment permitted is an advantage only to those enterprises geared to relatively small individual shipments, and it is a definite disadvantage to firms requiring mass transportation at specific times. As the ICC has pointed out:

Railroads appear to be making some headway in and may have an inherent advantage in the large-scale transportation of special bulk commodities, such as those which are adaptable to transportation in covered hopper cars but which would otherwise be moved only in packages. Thus, there has developed in the last few years a significant trend toward the hopper-car transportation of such commodities as sugar, flour and dry chemicals. At equal rates and rail and motor minima of 80,000 and 20,000 pounds, respectively, on trisodium phosphate from Joliet, Illinois, to Ivorydale, Ohio, shippers made use of the rail rate. The rail movement was in paper-covered open-hopper cars and certain consignees were able to receive loadings per car which averaged 104,000 pounds. Movement by motor carrier was in bags, which presumably involved expense for filling, handling and emptying greater than the unit expense of loading and unloading railroad cars. . . (ICC, *Administration of the Motor Carrier Act*, pp.322–23. Sodium Products, Ready Truck Lines, 53 M.C.C. 63, 1951).

On the other hand, the smaller truck capacity permits less expensive packaging for shipments that constitute a truckload but are less than a carload. Indeed the commission once concluded that "the transportation at carload rates of much smaller lots than are possible by railroad, and elimination of costly railroad packing requirements" constitute an advantage of truck service.[48]

The advantage, then, of the differing capacities of a boxcar and a truck depends on the relative size of consignments made by any shipper, which in turn is partly a function of inventory policy. We can, however, generally conclude that for any firm whose typical consignment is at or below truckload capacity, motor transport will be relatively more advantageous, while the reverse is true for firms with consignments typically in excess of truck capacity.

## Dependability of Service

In addition to average speed or average transit time for any shipment, shippers are interested in the *variability* about the average. As has been noted,

the ability to offer second morning service to a shipper 95% of the time is more desirable from the shipper's viewpoint than the ability to offer first morning service 50% of the time, second morning service 25% of the time, and third morning service 25% of the time. The desire for consistency stems from the opportunity this gives the shipper and his customer to reduce inventories . . . and enable them to plan their own operations more effectively.[49]

Because the greater complexity of rail operations means more opportunity for delays on any particular shipment, dependability is gen-

---

48. *Fifteen Percent Case, 1931* (1931), 178 ICC 539, 574.
49. F. Saleh et al., *Creative Selling and the Systems Concept: The Motor Carrier Selection Process* (Washington, D.C.: American Trucking Association, Inc., 1971), chap. 5, p.3.

erally less for rails than for trucks. Essentially, however, the difference in the degree of dependability is a function of management. The problem rests largely on establishing reasonable schedules and then making actual performance meet such schedules. Even though the elapsed time of any schedule will normally be less for truck than for rail, rail service is not less dependable as long as the rails meet their announced schedules. There is some evidence that railways are rather slack in this respect, but this is not inevitably an inherent disadvantage. As a result, though the greater complexity of rail operations makes scheduling less assured, the degree of dependability difference appears to be mainly due to different degrees of managerial interest in and emphasis on punctuality.

### Safety of Service

The safety of service depends on the susceptibility of a commodity to damage, the packaging and storage of the commodity, the "roughness" of the ride, and the susceptibility of the carrying unit to accidents. Because of all these factors, it would seem that no significant inherent advantage or disadvantage accrues to either rail or truck. Rather, the care taken in handling particular consignments would seem to be most important with respect to safety, and the quality of care is not indigenous to any carrier type.

In summing up the quality features, it is evident that they are highly variable among shippers. An advantage to some shippers (say, the smaller truck capacity) may be a disadvantage to others. The importance of speed is subject to extreme variations both among shippers and over time. As a consequence, it is not surprising that the ICC confines any mention of inherent advantages to specific cases and has not generally defined the term. Indeed, the commission has held that "in view of these considerations it is not always easy or safe to generalize about inherent advantages. The commission has not made over-all generalizations of this kind in its decisions" (ICC, *Administration of the Motor Carrier Act*, p.321). In individual cases, relative service advantages, like relative costs, tend to be *sui generis* and give support to the commission's case-by-case approach. Since the importance and value of the qualitative elements are so dependent on the circumstances of particular shippers as well as on the nature of the commodity, it follows that shippers must be left free to assess the value of the different qualities of transport service. Only the shippers themselves are in a position to know the nontransport savings that accrue from different qualities of transport service. This implies freedom of shipper choice (that is, no arbitrary allocation of traffic among the various media), and this, if (but only if) coupled with rates based on relative costs, will ensure an efficient allocation of traffic among modes.

The important point to stress is that for different shippers these quality differences involve different costs in *addition* to the freight rate when lower-quality modes (or firms) are being considered or costs *less* than the freight rates when higher-quality modes are compared. For example, the cost of truck transport to any shipper is $P_T$ — (value of service differential rail vs. truck); while the cost of rail transport to any shipper is $P_R$ + (value of service differential rail vs. truck). We need to analyze and attempt to measure the expression in parentheses. For two quality dimensions—shipment size and speed of delivery—estimates have been made for rail vs. truck quality differences.

*Shipment Size.* There are three types of inventory costs that vary with size of shipment for a manufacturer: (1) storage (warehousing); (2) risk, interest, and obsolescence; and (3) cost per order. The larger the minimum size of shipment, the larger the inventory costs and the smaller the number of orders, and vice versa.

$$TCI = \left(\frac{QC}{2}\right) I + \left(\frac{Q}{2}\right) K + \left(\frac{Y}{Q}\right) S,^{50}$$

where $TCI$ = total costs of inventory holding
$\quad\quad Y$ = expected sales in physical units/year
$\quad\quad C$ = value of the goods per ton
$\quad\quad I$ = cost of interest, risk, and obsolescence as a % of value
$\quad\quad K$ = storage charge per unit
$\quad\quad S$ = costs of a single order
$\quad\quad Q$ = minimum size of order

The first term is the *average* amount of money tied up in inventory per year.[51]

---

50. See Meyer et al., *Competition,* p.350.

51. The division by 2 means that for steady and equal rates of production and sales, a unit of inventory is held for half a year.

E.g., divide the year into five periods. One unit of the commodity enters inventory now and will stay in inventory five periods; a unit that entered one period earlier will be held for four more periods, and so on.

∴ On the average, one unit is held in inventory

$$\frac{5 + 4 + 3 + 2 + 1}{5} = \frac{15}{5} = 3 \text{ periods or } \frac{3}{5} \text{ time.}$$

Divide the year into ten periods; then average detention time is

$$\frac{10 + 9 + \ldots + 3 + 2 + 1}{10} = 5.5.$$

Divide the year into 20 periods to get $\frac{210}{20} = 10.5$, and so on. Notice that as the number of periods gets larger, the average time of detention approaches ½ (i.e.,

∴ The interest foregone $= \left(\dfrac{QC}{2}\right) I.$

The second term is the average amount of inventory stored per year multiplied by the unit cost of storage.

The third term is the number of times transport must be ordered, i.e., (annual sales ÷ minimum order) × cost of ordering.

∴ The total inventory cost of using rail service is:

$$\frac{Q_R C}{2} I + \frac{Q_R}{2} K + \frac{Y}{Q_R} S = \frac{Q_R}{2}(CI + K) + \frac{Y}{Q_R} S.$$

Similarly, the total inventory cost of using truck service is:

$$\frac{Q_T}{2}(CI + K) + \frac{YS}{Q_T}.$$

Since $Q_R > Q_T$, the *difference* in inventory cost *per unit* (dividing by $Y$) is:

$$\frac{CI + K}{2Y}(Q_R - Q_T) + S\left(\frac{1}{Q_R} - \frac{1}{Q_T}\right).$$

To illustrate, take some estimates of the variables and compute the difference in inventory costs for goods of different values. For example, assume:

$Y = 5{,}000$ tons, $Q_R = 20$, $Q_T = 10$, $K = 30$, $I = 10\%$, $S = \$1$.

Let us examine two commodities, using the values given in Table 1.6:

tires and tubes at \$1097/ton
iron and steel pipe at \$507/ton

The rail-truck difference in inventory costs for tires and tubes is:

$$\frac{1097\,(.10) + 30}{10{,}000}(20 - 10) + \$1\left(\frac{1}{20} - \frac{1}{10}\right)$$
$$= \$.0897/\text{ton or } 8.97 \text{ cents/ton}$$

∴ The truck rate could exceed the rail rate by amounts up to 8.97

---

0.6, 0.55, 0.525, . . .). Recall that the sum of the first $n$ digits $= \dfrac{n(n+1)}{2}$. Thus for n $= 300$, average detention time is

$$\frac{300(301)}{2} \times \frac{1}{300} \times \frac{1}{300} = \frac{301}{600} \cong .5017$$

∴ In general, average detention time $= \dfrac{n(n+1)}{2}\left(\dfrac{1}{n}\right)^2 = \dfrac{n}{2n} + \dfrac{1}{2n} = \dfrac{1}{2} + \dfrac{1}{2n}$. The limit of $\left[\dfrac{1}{2} + \dfrac{1}{2n}\right]$ as $n \to \infty = \dfrac{1}{2}$.

cents/ton and trucks would get all the business, other things being equal.

For iron and steel pipe, the difference = 3.07 cents/ton.

In general, the indifference rail rate/ton $R_R = R_T$ − the inventory difference. In the case of tires and tubes $R_R = R_T - 8.97$, while for iron and steel pipe, $R_R = R_T - 3.07$.

*Time in Transit Analysis.*[52] The basic equation is

$$T = \left(\frac{m}{18.7} - \frac{m}{29.9}\right) + 0.1\left(\frac{m}{18.7}\right) + \frac{m}{228.5}(6-3) + \frac{m}{140}(8) + 49,$$

where $T$ = time difference between rail and truck in hours and $m$ = miles of haul. The numbers (now out of date) are as follows:

18.7 mph = average speed of freight trains
29.9 mph = average speed of common carrier truck

The second term assumes that 10% of time is spent on sidings for rail.

The third term is the number of interchanges. The average distance between interchanges is 228.5 miles; rails take 6 hours on the average while trucks take 3 hours on the average at each interchange.

The fourth term is average time spent switching at rail terminals (8 hours), with terminals on the average 140 miles apart.

The fifth term is the average time difference between origin and destination.

Thus, for any distance $m$, a time differential can be computed, which the authors value at 68.5¢/day. This figure is the average value per ton of commodities presumed to be rail-truck competitive ($2,500) divided by 365 days at 10% to reflect risk, obsolescence, and interest per unit of time (year). Then they divide $T\left(\frac{68.5}{24 \text{ hrs.}}\right)$ by ton-miles to get the ton-mile figures in Table 1.8.

Notice that for the nation as a whole this figure or the figures so computed are averages of averages of averages. The authors do not indicate where or how such figures were determined. We are therefore entitled to dismiss the evidence as totally irrelevant in specific situations and probably irrelevant in the aggregate. However, for any shipper, the *method* is appropriate and permits a shipper to deduce the rail rate for these two quality differences that would make rail and truck transport equally attractive; and similarly for each pair of modes or even firms within the same mode.

Thus the indifference rail rate $R_R = R_T$ − (value to the shipper of minimum shipment difference between rail and truck) − (value to the shipper of time in transit difference between rail and truck).

---

52. From Meyer et al.; and Friedlaender, *Dilemma.*

TABLE 1.8

*Time in Transit Differential*
*Truck vs. Rail*
*Cents/Ton-Mile*

| Distance (miles) | Differential |
|---|---|
| 50 | 2.99 |
| 100 | 1.66 |
| 200 | .95 |
| 400 | .61 |
| 600 | .52 |
| 800 | .43 |
| 1,000 | .39 |

SOURCE: Meyer et al., Table 39, p.190.

It is also apparent that the last two terms and the value of the other qualitative differences have been rising over time and may be expected to continue to rise in the future. The reasons are as follows:

There is a trend toward higher quality goods *within* product classes.

On the average, products are increasing in value per unit of weight, placing an increasing premium on all aspects of service quality.

There is an increasing proliferation of brands, styles, models, etc. in many products. This increases the premium on transport speed, reliability, and small shipment size.

Increasing emphasis on service competition and an avoidance of price competition among manufacturers have increased the premium on the quality of transport service.

Improved technology has led to increasing specialization in producers' goods, placing a premium on higher quality transport.

Improved management systems and procedures have led to more carefully controlled distribution systems, which require higher quality transport.

An increase in interest rates has increased inventory carrying costs, and, again, put an increasing premium on higher quality transport.[53]

Thus, as far as rail–truck competition is concerned (or any intermodal competition), the "inherently" lower-quality mode must be far more careful in pricing than has been the case in the past. If we add to this the general belief that the quality of management seems to correlate roughly with the inherent technological difference in modal quality, the dilemma of the railroads is compounded. Far more concern over pricing policy and its relationship to both quality of service and the costs of providing the service is clearly dictated.

How much more are shippers generally willing to pay for superior truck service? We have noted above some differences in absolute terms

---

53. Unpublished document from Association of American Railroads, 1973.

but not as a proportion of the rail or truck rate. Indeed, while the above savings are relatively small as far as the value per ton is concerned, the differential as a percent of the freight rate is much more significant.

Morton[54] has examined the situation from this latter point of view as far as all manufactured commodities are concerned. He notes three dimensions of a shipment relevant to modal split: length of haul, shipment size and nature of the commodity.

*Length of Haul.* For all manufacturing, the rail share falls slightly below 20% on only the shortest of hauls, while the truck (private and common carriers) share falls below 20% only on hauls > 1200 mi. While in general the rail share increases with length of haul, both rail and truck appear to "compete" (i.e., each has a "not insignificant" share) for all distances.

*Shipment Size.* Rails carry less than 6% of all tonnage moving in shipments < 10,000 lbs., while trucks carry only 6% of shipments > 90,000 lbs. Both modes, however, participate substantially in all intermediate blocks.

*Commodity Characteristics.* Taking commodities from the 24 Shipper Groups in the 1967 Census of Transportation, Morton finds that the share of either mode drops below 20% on only five groups and that these groups account for only 9% of the total tonnage of manufactured goods other than petroleum and coal products. Thus, rails and trucks "compete" across most of the commodity spectrum.

Combining the three characteristics to obtain the percent of traffic that is competitive in all three dimensions, Morton estimates that between 32% and 78% of the manufacturing tonnage (excluding petroleum products) is so competitive. "Competitive" traffic is defined as "any block of traffic in which both rail and for-hire trucks carry 10% or more of the traffic" (p.159), i.e., both modes have a demonstrated capacity to compete successfully for the traffic.[55]

Morton then turns to *rate* differentials (average revenue/ton-mile) on the competitive and noncompetitive traffic (see Table 1.9). Note

54. A. L. Morton, "Truck-Rail Competition for Traffic in Manufactures," *Proceedings—Twelfth Annual Meeting, Transportation Research Forum, 1971* (Oxford, Ind.: Richard B. Cross, 1971), pp.151–68.

55. This finding of a high range of competitive traffic is, however, inconsistent with more recent evidence. Using the 1972 Census of Transportation, Roth determines that only about 27% of manufactured goods are rail–truck competitive, using the same 10% criterion of competitiveness as does Morton. Roth, however, used only two shipment characteristics, weight (six weight brackets) and distance (seven mileage blocks), and omitted "nature of the commodity," although he examined 89 product categories. (R. D. Roth, "Approach to Measurement of Modal Advantage," Transportation Research Record, #637 [Washington, D.C.: National Academy of Sciences, 1977], pp.62–70.)

TABLE 1.9

Ratio of Truck Rates to Rail Rates by Weight and Mileage-Block
Using 1967 Truck Waybills and 1965 Rail Waybills
Weight-Block (tons)

| Mileage-Block (miles) | 5-7.5 tons | 7.5-10 tons | 10-12.5 tons | 12.5-15 tons | 15-20 tons | 20-25 tons | Mileage-Block Average |
|---|---|---|---|---|---|---|---|
| 0– 24 | .544 | .446 | .435 | .103 | .435 | .179 | .312 |
| 25– 49 | 1.027 | 1.315 | 1.202 | 1.209 | 1.414 | 2.209 | 1.448 |
| 50– 74 | 1.328 | 1.428 | 1.040 | 1.267 | 1.543 | 1.914 | 1.420 |
| 75– 99 | 1.158 | 1.176 | 1.201 | 1.087 | 1.324 | 1.780 | 1.288 |
| 100– 124 | 1.189 | 1.201 | 1.153 | 1.354 | 1.241 | 1.818 | 1.326 |
| 125– 149 | 1.272 | 1.240 | 1.024 | 1.081 | 1.379 | 2.236 | 1.372 |
| 150– 174 | 1.297 | 1.191 | 1.157 | 1.110 | 1.298 | 1.818 | 1.312 |
| 175– 199 | 1.220 | 1.140 | 1.133 | 1.170 | 1.355 | 1.760 | 1.296 |
| 200– 224 | 1.030 | .862 | 1.060 | 1.160 | 1.229 | 1.372 | 1.119 |
| 225– 249 | 1.412 | 1.182 | 1.082 | 1.388 | 1.444 | 1.521 | 1.338 |
| 250– 274 | 1.150 | 1.283 | 1.148 | 1.138 | 1.268 | 1.312 | 1.217 |
| 275– 299 | .910 | 1.031 | 1.023 | 1.102 | 1.228 | 1.316 | 1.102 |
| 300– 349 | 1.067 | 1.162 | 1.079 | 1.056 | 1.278 | 1.321 | 1.161 |
| 350– 399 | 1.287 | 1.156 | 1.118 | 1.171 | 1.226 | 1.362 | 1.220 |
| 400– 449 | 1.262 | 1.068 | 1.125 | 1.066 | 1.185 | 1.145 | 1.142 |
| 450– 499 | 1.025 | 1.226 | 1.094 | 1.173 | 1.174 | 1.323 | 1.169 |
| 500– 599 | 1.190 | 1.170 | 1.084 | 1.086 | 1.216 | 1.257 | 1.167 |
| 600– 699 | 1.208 | 1.112 | 1.038 | 1.066 | 1.103 | 1.156 | 1.114 |
| 700– 799 | 1.188 | 1.027 | .988 | 1.102 | 1.120 | 1.267 | 1.115 |
| 800– 899 | 1.211 | 1.073 | 1.165 | 1.370 | 1.307 | 1.363 | 1.248 |
| 900– 999 | 1.069 | 1.198 | 1.223 | 1.096 | 1.213 | 1.500 | 1.217 |
| 1000–1199 | 1.273 | 1.054 | 1.129 | 1.232 | 1.272 | 1.248 | 1.201 |
| Weight Block Average* | 1.180 | 1.157 | 1.108 | 1.166 | 1.277 | 1.524 | 1.235 |

*Weight-block averages exclude first row.
SOURCES: 1967 MAC Continuing Traffic Study; 1965 ICC Rail Carload Waybill
Study.

that the ratio of truck to rail rates for varying mileage and weight
blocks does not appear to change much as either mileage or weight
increases. In general, as of 1965–67, "shippers pay less than a 20%
premium to ship a similar shipment by motor carrier rather than by
rail." Morton refers to this as a "very low premium that shippers pay
for the service advantages of truck delivery" (p.167). If, however, a
shipper buys a large number of ton-miles, a 20% differential might
well be "significant," certainly relative to net profit. Furthermore, over
the past decade, as noted above, the value of the quality elements
of transportation has been rising. It is likely therefore that a replication of the above procedures would now produce more than a 20%

differential. This is further reinforced by the general deterioration of rail service as a consequence of undermaintenance and inability to acquire improved rolling stock due to low earnings.

More recently, attempts have been made to estimate quality variables other than time-in-transit and shipment size as well as to improve on the above estimates. In general, such studies conclude (1) that the above estimates of time-in-transit and shipment size understate the values to shippers from such intermodal differences and (2) that omitted variables such as *variance* in transit time, loss and damage claims including the speed with which the modes process such claims, demurrage penalties that apply only to rail, different dunnage requirements, and flexibility between any pair of modes significantly increase the value of the service differentials, possibly by several orders of magnitude.[56]

If this is the case, such intermodal quality differences may be far more significant than price or cost differentials. Levin finds, for example, that modal share is more sensitive to (one) quality variable than to price.[57] Indeed, he concludes, subject to several caveats, "the expected benefits from deregulation of freight rates are small."[58] Moreover, since $\epsilon_{CROSS}$ varies inversely with the value of the service differential, where truck alternatives exist $\epsilon_{RT}$ may be closer to $\frac{1}{\beta}\alpha\epsilon_D$ than to the larger negative value $\frac{1}{\beta}[\alpha\epsilon_D - (1-\beta)\epsilon_{CROSS}]$ except for very large reductions in specific railway rates.[59]

## Conclusion

The foregoing has presented some of the pertinent analysis of the determinants of the level and elasticity of demand for intercity freight transportation at various levels of aggregation, along with considerations of service quality. In addition, we have examined some of the more or less heroic efforts at measuring some of the concepts. Very few firm conclusions emerge. Although the analytical conclusions are fairly rigorous, there are several approaches that can be taken, especially with respect to elasticity analysis. The rigorous results from each

56. See K. D. Boyer, "Intermodal Competition and the Measurement of Service Differentials," in *Motor Carrier Economic Regulation,* Proceedings of a Workshop (Washington, D.C.: National Academy of Sciences, 1978), pp.449–69.

57. R. C. Levin, "Allocation in Surface Freight Transportation: Does Rate Regulation Matter?" *Bell Journal of Economics,* Spring 1978, p.32.

58. Ibid., p.42.

59. See G. Wilson, "Notes on the Elasticity of Demand for Freight Transportation," *Transportation Journal,* Spring 1978, p.11.

approach, however, arise from a prior set of assumptions that may or may not be "realistic" or that are at best approximations of the "real" world. Attempts to put some empirical flesh on the analytical bones leave much to be desired because of inadequate data and dubious specifications of relationships, such as the heavy reliance on assumptions of linearity.

It is apparent that our knowledge of the demand side of the markets for transportation is woefully incomplete and uncertain even in areas where empirical estimates have been made. In general, this is true of demand analysis regardless of area of application—be it household behavior, demand for any product, service, or factor of production—possibly because of the subjective aspect of demand interpreted as the amounts of anything buyers *choose* to purchase at alternative prices. There are too many *ceteris paribus* assumptions; the ultimate basis of demands and, hence, derived demands, is consumer preferences (or utilities), and these are not readily observable or analyzed except under strict assumptions concerning rational behavior involving maximizing satisfactions or profits.

It is therefore easy to believe that the state of demand theory and measurement must inevitably be mushy and inconclusive, as the present chapter indicates, except under such a restrictive set of assumptions as to render the analysis irrelevant even though occasionally elegant. There is then a disposition to turn to the supply side of the market as a more promising arena for meaningful analysis and measurement. Indeed, there are far more studies pertaining to supply than to demand in virtually all aspects of microeconomic theory and measurement. After all, is not supply related to technology and costs that are clearly more tangible and "real" than preferences or utilities? Technology is related to engineering, costs to accounting. What more precise and matter-of-fact disciplines exist, certainly as compared to disciplines purporting to analyze human behavior? And, of course, engineering and accounting have numbers and, more important, relationships among numbers, some of which are even testable under controlled conditions. Little wonder that those interested in transport problems quickly flee from the murky, ephemeral arena of demand to the presumptively solid and objective realm of supply where numbers abound and an infinite set of testable interrelationships is possible.

Indeed in this volume we follow the same path, although our retreat from demand to supply has not been quick, or quick enough for some readers. Yet even *a priori*, supply, defined as the amount of output producers are willing to offer at alternative prices, has the same degree of subjectivity as demand. Supply schedules only reflect marginal costs directly under perfectly competitive conditions, which, of course, do not generally prevail. Under less than perfectly competitive conditions (i.e., everywhere in the economy), even an enterpreneur who maximizes short-run profits will have to be concerned with marginal revenue as with marginal cost. The amount such a producer is willing to supply is therefore dependent not only on costs but also on demands, and we are thus forced back into the subjective area of the latter. Even ignoring such esoteric considerations, the supply side must concern itself with the nature of the product (i.e., the output unit) and its quality, which influences not only the choice of shipper, as just examined, but costs as well. In transportation these pose extremely vexing analytical and empirical problems.[60] Although in the next chapter we turn to questions of costs, cost functions, and supply in transportation without having cleared up much in the domain of demand, the reader should not venture further in the belief that, at last, firmer ground has been reached. For, in fact, the conclusions regarding costs are not much different from those regarding demands.

---

60. See Wilson, *Essays*.

# The Supply of Intercity Freight Transportation

## The Interrelatedness of Rates and Costs

The twin determinants of price in a "relatively" free market are, of course, supply and demand. Supply bears a one-to-one relation to costs only under conditions of perfect competition. Under competitive conditions, where all suppliers can sell all they choose at a given market price without affecting that price, each seller, seeking to maximize profits, will produce an output such that $P = MC$. If the behavior of $MC$ is "reasonable" (i.e., rising with output), then the $MC$ will determine the amounts supplied at alternative prices. Under less than perfectly competitive circumstances, the amount supplied at alternative prices will also depend on the level and elasticity of the demand schedule, since profit-maximizing behavior requires that $MR = MC$ and $MR < P$ except under perfect competition. Thus conditions on the demand side will also influence the optimal profit output. The level and elasticity, or behavior, of costs with respect to output is the subject of the present chapter.

Costs and prices (freight rates) are interrelated except for those cases where the cost function is perfectly elastic. For example, if total traffic depends on the freight rate (at all or any levels of aggregation by mode) and if per-unit cost depends on volume, then per-unit cost depends on the freight rate.

More formally, if $Q_T = f(P_T)$ and if total cost, $C = g(Q_T)$, then $C = g[f(P_T)]$. For example, if $Q_T = 55 - \frac{P_T}{10}$ and $C = 20 + \frac{Q_T}{2}$, then $C = 20 + \frac{55}{2} - \frac{P_T}{20}$, and $C = h(P_T)$. Thus, costs depend on prices, since prices determine volume and volume determines per-unit costs, as long as costs are not constant per unit of production. If costs are constant, then for any $Q_T$ (as a function of $P_T$), costs will not vary. Only in this case are costs independent of prices.

This has some bearing on an old dispute, namely, that the ICC should not substitute its judgment regarding the effects of any proposed rate change on the volume of traffic ($\epsilon_T$) for that of the proponent, nor in some cases even consider the effects of any rate change on volume. The ICC is, however, required by law to ensure that no rates are below *MC* (i.e., noncompensatory). Thus it has an obligation to examine estimates of $\epsilon_T$ as long as *MC* is not deemed to be constant.

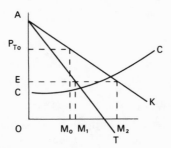

Fig. 2.1

Graphically (see Figure 2.1), suppose that the proponent carrier assumes its demand curve is *AK* and its marginal cost is *CC*, and that the present rate is $P_T$. Suppose further that the ICC views the demand as *AT*. If the commission allows a rate decrease down to *OE* and the traffic generated is $OM_2$, the rate is noncompensatory (i.e., $P_T < M_C$). The reverse is true for opposite interpretations of demand. Similarly, if costs are decreasing with volume, different interpretations of $\epsilon_T$ can lead to $P < MC$. If *MC* is constant with volume, then different interpretations of $\epsilon_T$ will make no difference as far as rates $\geqq MC$.

Thus, efficient pricing can no more ignore demand than it can ignore supply. Transport supply, like the supply of any other service or commodity in a predominantly free enterprise economy, is closely related to production costs. We need therefore to examine what is meant by "costs" in transportation, various cost concepts, cost behavior as volume changes, and, finally, cost measurement.

## Cost Concepts

*Marginal costs* (*MC*). The increase (decrease) in total costs occasioned by an increase (decrease) in traffic is $MC = \dfrac{\Delta C}{\Delta \text{Traffic}}$. The change in output (traffic) can be measured in terms of ton-miles (gross or revenue), car-miles, or some other proxy of whatever it is transport firms produce. *MC* may be rising, falling, or constant with respect to output. In a linear cost function of the form $C = a + bT$, $MC = b$ and is constant.

Nonlinear cost functions of the U-shaped type postulated in economic analysis may take the form

$$C = a_1T^3 - a_2T^2 + a_3T + a_4, \text{ where } 3a_1a_3 > a_2{}^2.$$

In this case for small changes in $T$, $MC = 3a_1T^2 - 2a_2T + a_3$, which obviously varies with $T$. The particular way it varies with $T$ depends on the value of the constants. For values of the constants restrained as noted above, as $T$ increases from 0, this $MC$ function will decrease initially, reach a minimum, and then rise. We will not make much use of nonlinear cost functions in what follows and thus need not explore this further at this point.

*Average costs* ($AC$). There are two averages that should be noted: average variable cost $AVC$ and average total cost $ATC$. In general, total cost ($C$) is composed of two parts in the *short run* (i.e., the length of time in which plant and equipment are deemed to be fixed): fixed costs ($FC$), which do not change as output changes; and variable costs ($VC$), which do change as output changes. Therefore $ATC = \frac{C}{T}$. For linear cost functions of the form $C = a + bT$, $ATC = \frac{a + bT}{T} = \frac{a}{T} + b$, whereas $AVC = \frac{bT}{T} = b$. Thus for linear cost functions $MC = AVC = b$.

For nonlinear functions this is not true. In the previous nonlinear function we found that $MC = \frac{dc}{dt} = 3a_1T^2 - 2a_2T + a_3$, whereas $AVC = \frac{C'}{T} = \frac{1}{T}(a_1T^3 - a_2T^2 + a_3T) = a_1T^2 - a_2T + a_3$.

In this function, $AVC = MC$ at only one volume of output, namely at $T = \frac{a_2}{2a_1}$, which also coincides with the minimum point of the U-shaped $AVC$ curve.

$ATC$ is similar to $AVC$ except that the fixed cost $a_4$ is added. $ATC = AVC + \frac{a_4}{T}$. $\therefore ATC = a_1T^2 - a_2T + a_3 + \frac{a_4}{T}$. $MC$ also equals $ATC$ at the minimum point of the latter, but only when the output is greater than $\frac{a_2}{2a_1}$.

*Long- and short-run costs.* In the long run all costs are variable. Hence a *linear* long-run cost function would drop the constant and $LRMC = LRAC = b$. In the nonlinear case noted above, $LRMC$ would remain the same and $LRAVC = LRATC$. More intuitively we may construe long-run cost behavior in terms of a series of short-run cost functions as noted in Figure 2.2. Figure 2a shows that as volume increases, it becomes more efficient to increase plant size to obtain lower unit costs $CC$, or, alternatively, the larger the plant size, the more efficient the production in terms of unit cost (as well as $MC$). If plant size is infinitely divisible, the "curve" $CC$ results. This is the case of

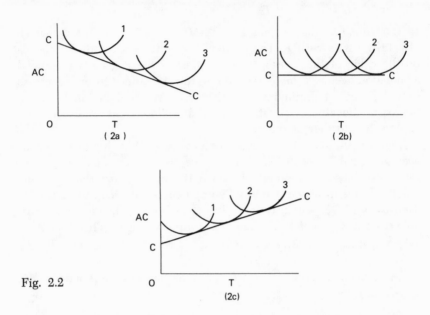

Fig. 2.2

economies of scale. Figure 2b shows that as volume increases, the minimum achievable unit costs do not change. If plant size is infinitely divisible, the "curve" *CC* in Figure 2b results. This is referred to as constant returns to scale. Finally, in Figure 2c, as plant size grows, the minimum achievable unit costs also rise: hence we have diseconomies of scale. The long-run "curves" are drawn as straight lines for convenience only.

## The Importance of Marginal Cost in Transportation

It has often been demonstrated that efficient pricing requires prices to equal *MC:* hence in transportation, freight rates should closely reflect or equal *MC.* Beyond this, under regulation it is illegal to set any rate below *MC,* variously designated by the ICC as "variable cost" or "out-of-pocket" cost, that at least approximates what is meant by *MC* in economics.

Now the logic of the *MC* criterion requires that the costs involved include more than simply the costs actually incurred by those who provide the service, to the extent that these do not include certain "social" or external costs. In transportation the difference between private and social costs includes the following:

1. Some carriers may pay or be charged less than the costs they oc-

casion by use of publicly provided rights of way (e.g., waterways, airways, and highways).

2. Carriers contribute to air and noise pollution and are not (yet) specifically charged for such costs.

3. There may be certain "congestion" costs occasioned by carriers using publicly provided facilities at peak periods for which specific incremental charges are *not* made (e.g., delays at airports because carriers schedule too many arrivals at preferred hours: delays at peak hours in urban transport because some trucks add to congestion).

There may be certain offsetting benefits not considered by the suppliers of transport services, but we will not concern ourselves with them.[1] The main point is that if the carriers are not correctly charged for these external costs, they will not consider these costs in their pricing and output decisions. Simply equating *private MC* with freight rates will not lead to efficiency from the point of view of society if such costs are above, or more likely below, *social MC*. One of the aims of transport policy, to the extent it is or should be based on efficiency criteria, must be to implement appropriate charging schemes to internalize these external costs. Until this is done, and it is no easy task, the $P = MC$ rule will not lead to the results postulated in economic analysis.

A second point in the interpretation of the $P = MC$ criterion involves the issue of "second best." This asserts that if efficiency criteria are not followed everywhere in the economy, it is not necessarily true that fulfilling them in one industry, say, transportation, will provide a net improvement in overall efficiency. Thus, for example, if certain trucks, competitive with rail, pay more than they should for use of the highways, it may be better to require the railways to charge rates higher than $MC$ to enable shippers to make efficient choices of mode. Since marginal cost pricing is conspicuous by its absence in the U.S. economy, it cannot be proven that insistence on marginal cost pricing in transportation will provide net social benefits. It might even lead to an excessive amount of resources devoted to transportation if $P_T = MC_T$ when most other prices in the economy exceed $MC$. In practical terms there is little that can be done about this situation. Furthermore, even if insistence on $MC$ pricing in transportation would lead to too many, or too few, resources being devoted to the transport industry (or industries), there is still legitimate concern for efficient

---

1. For a brief outline of some such benefits, see G. W. Wilson, "The Logic of Economic Regulation: The Case of Transportation" in D. McConaughy and C. J. Clawson, eds., *Business Logistics—Policies and Decisions* (Los Angeles: University of Southern California, 1968), pp.37–38.

allocation *within* transport as a whole, and this requires $P_T = MC_T$ to enable shippers to make "optimal" choices among modes and carriers. However, it is true that over the whole discussion of optimality, "there looms most menacingly the injunction of the theorem of the second best: Thou shalt not optimize piece-meal."[2]

A third issue involving the $P = MC$ rule or criterion is whether *short-run MC (SRMC)* or *long-run MC (LRMC)* is the appropriate criterion. Short- and long-run cost behavior and cost levels may, and normally would, be quite different. There are, however, several divergent views on the issue of whether *SRMC* or *LRMC* is relevant. Kahn, for instance, argues that "it is short-run marginal cost to which price should at any given time—*hence always*—be equated, because it is short-run marginal cost that reflects the social opportunity cost of providing the additional unit that buyers are at any given time trying to decide whether to buy."[3] Walters asserts that "the short-run marginal cost is *always* the appropriate value."[4] On the other hand, Friedlaender argues that "in assessing the relative costs of the various modes, it seems to be generally agreed that long-run marginal costs are the relevant carrier costs."[5] Another set of transport economist viewers proclaim that "neither extremely short-run nor extremely long-run incremental cost is an economic concept of general applicability. . . ."[6]

In principle it is easy to specify which "run" is appropriate, but in practice serious problems emerge. If an increment of traffic represents a once for all shipment and if the carrier has adequate capacity, then the relevant costs are those that would be immediately escapable were the shipment not moved. These costs would doubtless be very low, possibly only the added fuel, labor, and depreciation (i.e., more wear and tear on equipment and right-of-way) associated with the ship-

2. W. J. Baumol, *Welfare Economics and the Theory of the State*, 2d ed. (Cambridge: Harvard University Press, 1965), p.30.

3. A. E. Kahn, *The Economics of Regulation*, vol.1 (New York: Wiley, 1970), p.71.

4. A. A. Walters, *The Economics of Road User Charges*, World Bank Staff Occasional Papers, no.5, 1968, p.61.

5. Ann F. Friedlaender, *The Dilemma of Freight Transport Regulation* (Washington, D.C.: The Brookings Institution, 1969), p.31. J. Meyer, M. Peck, J. Stenason, and C. Zwick, *The Economics of Competition in the Transportation Industries* (Cambridge: Harvard University Press, 1959), after explicitly developing what are to be regarded as *long-run MC*, note that these are "useful for rate-making and revenue comparisons" although certain modifications are necessary (p.61). The stress is clearly on *LRMC*.

6. W. J. Baumol et al., "The Role of Cost in the Minimum Pricing of Railroad Services," *Journal of Business*, October 1968, reprinted in *A Guide to Railroad Cost Analysis* (Washington, D.C.: American Association of Railroads, December 1964), p.92. See also A. A. Walters, "The Long and Short of Transport," *Bulletin of the Oxford Institute of Statistics and Economics*, May 1965.

ment. If no excess capacity existed and new equipment was needed, the *SRMC* would, of course, be much higher. On the other hand, if the shipment was expected to be repeated in the future, the costs associated with it would encompass more than those immediately escapable to the extent that such future movement required more resources of some kind. Kahn is therefore correct as long as we remember that economic costs are prospective, not historical, and that if a shipment is to be repeated, all future costs associated with the prospective traffic need to be added. These costs include not only variable labor, fuel, etc., but also the variable capital inputs associated with the traffic.

However, in practice, various compromises are essential because *SRMC* are extremely variable in transport. Specifically, *SRMC* varies with "(1) the different elasticities of transport demand; (2) the degree of temporal and spatial excess capacity; (3) geographical cost differences; (4) the time span and contractual arrangements of the various suppliers of transport; (5) the relative importance of the particular traffic; (6) whether the additional traffic helps to balance the movement or not; and (7) whether the traffic is offered sporadically or regularly."[7] Note that not only does each of these factors vary over time—often over very short periods—but also many of them vary for each commodity and for different suppliers of transport. For example, since $\epsilon_T = \alpha \dfrac{\epsilon_D \epsilon_S}{\epsilon_S - \epsilon_D (1 - \alpha)}$, $\epsilon_D$, $\epsilon_S$, and $\alpha$ vary among commodities, $MC = \dfrac{\Delta C}{\Delta \text{Traffic}}$, and the change in traffic for any rate change depends on $\epsilon_T$, *SRMC* will vary across commodities and doubtless over time as well; it will behave similarly for each of the other variables noted above.

In addition, use of the ton-mile as an output unit in transportation (gross, revenue, or net) introduces additional complications since weight and distance are independent as well as interdependent sources of cost. Costs also vary with velocity of movement. Thus any given number of ton-miles composed of different proportions of weight and distance will yield different costs. As noted elsewhere, "One hundred ton-miles may be one ton moved 100 miles, 4 tons moved 25 miles, 100 tons moved one mile, and so on. Since each of these would involve varying proportions of terminal and line-haul costs . . . it follows that both the *level* and *variability* of costs per ton-mile depend upon the proportion of tons and miles even where the product of the

7. G. Wilson, *Essays on Some Unsettled Questions in the Economics of Transportation* (Bloomington: Foundation for Economic and Business Studies, Indiana University, 1962), p.40. Detailed explanation of each of these factors is given on pp.32–40.

two is identical."[8] The variability of costs with velocity (or average speed) and other qualitative aspects of transport, as noted in chapter 1, further adds to the variability and elusiveness of SRMC.

To allow rates to change with every alteration of these circumstances would be totally impractical and confusing. Thus rates are set and held in effect for a period of time even though costs may vary substantially during the interval. In addition, the costs that can be causally identified with particular shipments or outputs in a multi-product enterprise would normally add up to a sum less than the total costs of maintaining the enterprise over time. This is independent of whether or not scale economies exist—of course, if there are scale economies such that $MC < AC$ and $P = MC$, revenues will fall short of total costs, requiring either a subsidy or a "permission" (or toleration) of prices that deviate from $MC$ (more on this later). In transportation the costs that can be causally associated with sales units (construed as revenue ton-miles) are relatively small because of the divergence between sales and output units, the existence of large amounts of joint cost (the back haul, for example), and the existence of extremely long-lived assets (e.g., railroad track, if properly maintained!).

Thus, in transportation there is no such thing as *the MC* of output—there are a vast number of "marginal costs." Nor is the output unit homogeneous in the sense required by production theory in economic analysis. Indeed, the output unit is multi-dimensional in terms of weight, distance, and velocity, each one of which is an independent source of cost, to say nothing of the other quality aspects of particular movements (dependability, safety, flexibility, etc.).

In short, while the logic of the rule $P = MC$ is by and large impeccable, its application in transportation as well as in many other industries is exceedingly difficult. In later sections we will examine various approaches and attempts at pinpointing that elusive animal, "marginal cost in transportation."

In addition to marginal cost, however, it is important to attempt to obtain some knowledge of the shape of the cost function for each of

---

8. Ibid., p.41. These and other shortcomings of the ton-mile as a sales or production unit have long been recognized. See A. Flott, L. Batts, and R. Roth, "The Ton-Mile: Does It Properly Measure Transportation Output," *Transportation Research Record #577*, Transportation Research Board, Washington, D.C., 1975. However, no generally accepted substitute has appeared. Data and research continue to be oriented around the ton-mile measure even though "U.S. transportation policies have been hampered for too long by faulty analyses based on the inappropriate use of ton-miles" (ibid., p.25).

See also A. R. Ferguson, "Empirical Determination of a Multidimensional Marginal Cost Function," *Econometrica*, July 1950, especially pp.228–29, for an early and explicit statement of the issues involved. Later in this chapter we note the spurious conclusions with regard to economies of scale in the motor carrier industry that emerge from regressing costs against ton-miles.

the various modes. For obvious reasons it is important for each carrier to know its own costs, but knowledge of costs is also important for public policy considerations. In general, if a particular industry is characterized by firms whose unit costs ($AVC$ and/or $MC$) begin to rise more or less sharply at levels of output that are small relative to the total industry output and if there are no economies of scale, that industry has most of the technical features required for a competitive market. Such an industry should not, on economic grounds at least, be subjected to any form of regulation other than that specified generally under the antitrust laws. On the other hand, if an industry is characterized by firms whose unit costs decline up to levels of output that are large relative to total industry output, this implies an oligopolistic market structure or, in the extreme, single-firm monopoly. Since the forces of competition cannot therefore be expected to be effective, the industry *may* be subjected to some nonmarket (i.e., regulatory) constraint[9] to protect consumers from excessive prices and discrimination and perhaps even for efficiency considerations. This does not mean that the industry *should* be regulated: rather, given these *cost* characteristics *one* of the conditions leading to the possibility of economically successful regulation will be fulfilled.[10]

In the intermediate case, where unit costs do not change or do not change much with a firm's volume of output or with the size of the firm, the situation with respect to reliance on competitive forces or regulation is somewhat ambiguous on *a priori* grounds. Such a situation means that the total industry output could be efficiently supplied by one or many firms. If entry to the industry is fairly easy (i.e., if the initial costs of the minimum efficient-sized plant is low), then on technical grounds, competitive forces would provide for least-cost production: even if the market structure were less than required for competitive results, ease of entry and awareness thereof would induce a set of prices that did not deviate much from $MC$ or $AVC$. If each firm's cost function were strictly horizontal (i.e., in the linear case, $C = a + bT$, then $a = 0$), then $MC = AVC$ and no economies of scale would exist in the long run. While in principle in the strict case of long-run cost linearity, the "natural" market structure is indeterminate, in practice it does not matter much if there is freedom of entry and exit and product homogeneity at least in the sense that the *quality* of the output does not relate positively to the size of the firm. Thus, important issues concerning regulation, deregulation, and greater or less reliance on competitive forces depend critically on the way unit costs

9. The various forms of constraint and their possible consequences will be examined in chap. 4.
10. A further discussion of this and the other conditions appears in chap. 4.

behave or vary as output changes (i.e., on the shape of the cost function).

In addition, important public policy considerations revolve around the *structure* of costs. If joint, fixed, and other indivisible costs (i.e., costs that cannot be assigned to particular sales units on a strictly cost-occasioned basis) are large, then the firm must inevitably charge prices that exceed the directly assignable costs if the firm is to be financially viable. Under these circumstances, efficient pricing (which we will examine later) requires a systematic pattern of discrimination often referred to in the transportation literature as "value-of-service" pricing. Such pricing may, however, violate certain standards of equity, such as higher rates on grain following the grain harvest each year, when the farmers' needs for transportation increase sharply (i.e., the inelasticity of grain transport demand increases) or higher fares on the public transit system during peak hours, which may more adversely affect the poor, who have fewer alternative modes of transport. Thus, in situations where the magnitude of nonassignable costs is large, price discrimination is inevitable for an economically viable operation. It *may* take a socially undesirable form and so justify some form of social limitation or control. On the other hand, if such costs are small, the issue of regulation or not reverts to questions already noted regarding the shape of the cost curve.

One more aspect of "costs" needs to be noted in transport. All transport markets are capable of being supplied by more than one transport technology or mode. Each mode has varying quality characteristics, as noted earlier, and each mode has different cost *levels,* as well as different structure and behavior. For particular commodities moving between particular pairs of cities, the *level* of costs will normally differ among the modes. Knowledge of such levels and especially their differences is important for the (potentially) competing modes as well as for regulatory purposes. Society is interested not only in efficient pricing and production by mode but also in an efficient division of traffic among modes and this requires information on relative cost levels.

In short, improved knowledge regarding the level, structure, and behavior of costs of transportation enterprises is a prerequisite both for the broad issues of regulation or not and for sensible regulatory or antitrust decisions in particular cases. As ICC Commissioner Charles A. Webb once put it:

No transportation enterprise can afford to disregard either its own costs or those of its competition. For the Commission, costs represent an indispensable guide in determining what is a just and reasonable level of rates. . . . Consideration must be given to the practical problems involved in tailoring the economic concept of variable costs to the experience of an individual carrier. And finally, considerably more thought must be given to the development of appropriate and commensurable cost standards for use in intermodal competitive rate cases.[11]

## Cost Measurement

Insights into transport costs can be gained by examining data produced by the carriers themselves. All carriers keep accounts, mostly for financial purposes but increasingly for control purposes. Any attempt to measure costs must cope with the problem that data in the form necessary for measuring the kinds of things noted above are seldom available. The cost analyst is therefore often required to use proxy variables, inference, or judgment.

The simplest approach to cost finding is to take a carrier's or group of carriers' total operating costs and divide them by some measure of output or sales during a particular period. The result, of course, is average cost and is more or less meaningful depending on the composition of the traffic. If the composition is relatively uniform (e.g., all steel shipments moving a given distance over similar terrain at regular intervals), the use of such an average as a pricing floor is reasonable. If, however, the traffic is highly diverse and includes many commodities of different density, moving different distances in different-sized shipments and requiring varying amounts of terminal, switching, or other (specialized) services, such an average is not merely meaningless but dangerously misleading as an indicator for pricing or of cost levels. Certainly no single average gives a reliable indication of cost behavior or structure.

A somewhat better way to measure the economic cost concepts noted above is to use linear regression analysis. The simplest form is univariate linear regression, where $C = a + bT$, $C$ = total costs, and $T$ is some measure of transport output. The approach is to obtain a series of observations of $C$ and $T$ (the more the better) and find the equation that minimizes the sum of the squares of the distances between every point of observation in the $C$-$T$ plane: the so-called line of best fit.[12]

The data may be obtained from a single carrier over a period of time, from a group of carriers for a single time period, or from a group of carriers for several time periods over which the $C$'s and $T$'s

11. Charles A. Webb, "Costs for Rate Making Purposes," remarks before the annual meeting of the National Accounting and Finance Council of the American Trucking Association, Washington, D.C., May 13, 1963, mimeographed, pp.3 and 6.

12. Formulae for this and other linear regression techniques are available in most statistics textbooks and need not be repeated here.

are averaged to prevent "peculiar" results because of the choice of a particular year. "Time-series analysis," as the former is called, is presumed to represent the short run. One observes period-to-period changes in $C$ and $T$ while plant and equipment are not adjusted to varying levels of output in each period and are thereby assumed to be fixed. This situation coincides with the economist's definition of short run. It is clear, however, that if enough periods are chosen, say, years to offset seasonal variations within the year, there will be time enough to adjust plant and equipment. Thus, a time-series analysis may be something of a hybrid involving short-run as well as long-run considerations. In specific analyses the researcher would want to know whether, when, and to what extent the capital stock of the enterprise changed and would interpret the results accordingly. Two other well-known problems of time-series analysis are the question of deflating cost measures in periods when prices are changing and the changing character of the traffic over time, both of which would distort the so-called true technical relationship between costs and traffic. Deflation procedures inevitably involve judgment, especially in transportation, where cost and price indexes are either nonexistent for some modes or seriously deficient when they do exist. These problems, of course, are over and above the obvious "index number problem." All involve judgment and a certain degree of arbitrariness in deciding which proxy index to use. Similar, but more serious, problems arise in trying to account for changing output characteristics since no index exists to account for changes in traffic type (weight, density, distance, commodity). Thus, for example, rail output has shifted from $LCL$ to $CL$ and from short to longer distance, yet none of the changes are adequately captured in a single measure of gross, net, or revenue ton-miles.

Cross-section analysis of many firms avoids these problems but introduces a new difficulty, namely, the homogeneity of the sample. If the firms have different traffic compositions (some short-haul traffic, others mostly long-haul; some with mostly $LTL$, others with mostly $TL$ traffic; some operating in rugged terrain, others in flat), the results will be difficult to interpret at best and meaningless at worst. The choice of time period for the observation may also distort the results if exceptional circumstances prevailed during that period. A researcher would not want to pick a wartime period, a period of labor strife in transportation, or a period when natural disaster disrupted service. However, finding a single year that represents a "normal" period is subjective. Most researchers select a three- to five-year span over which data on $C$ and $T$ are averaged in order to reduce the possibility of unusual events in a particular year distorting the true relationship between $C$ and $T$. Finally, it should be mentioned that cross-section cost analysis is often believed to yield results that represent the long-run cost function. The reason is that the firms are assumed to have optimally adjusted their plant and equipment to the level of traffic prevailing in the period of observation. This is more likely to be true in cross-section analysis than for the single firm on a year-to-year basis in time-series analysis. However, it is unlikely that all carriers observed will have so adjusted during the observation period. Indeed, it is possible that none of them have, since "optimal plant size" in the real world is not something readily observable or possibly even achievable in a dynamic environment.[13] Thus it is more in the nature of wishful thinking to argue that cross-section analysis yields what the economist means by a long-run cost function. Like the so-called short-run cost function of time-series analysis, the long-run cost function of cross-section analysis is a hybrid. Some firms may have fully adjusted, but many, perhaps most in the sample, have not. It may well be that cross-section analysis yields a "longer" run than time-series but there can be no valid inference that the "runs" involved correspond very closely with the economic conception of long run and short run.

### Illustration of Simple Regression Analysis

Suppose we obtain the information shown in Table 2.1. Column 1 refers to *time-series* analysis if one or a homogeneous group of carriers is involved over 10 time periods (years); it refers to *cross-section*

TABLE 2.1

*Hypothetical Data for Cost Regression*

| Year or Carrier | Total Operating Cost ($) | Total Traffic |
|---|---|---|
| 1 | 30 | 200 |
| 2 | 80 | 400 |
| 3 | 30 | 100 |
| 4 | 50 | 300 |
| 5 | 50 | 200 |
| 6 | 60 | 350 |
| 7 | 30 | 250 |
| 8 | 20 | 150 |
| 9 | 70 | 300 |
| 10 | 40 | 300 |

13. As Salter notes, "best practice" techniques never prevail among all firms in any industry, especially when technology is changing. Some firms are always hostage to earlier and less efficient techniques because they built their plants earlier. (W. E. G. Salter, *Productivity and Technical Change*, 2d ed. [London: Cambridge University Press, 1969)], Part I.)

analysis if the data are from different carriers for one year or are averages for each carrier for several years. Column 2 refers to all costs associated with the provision of the service designated in Column 3. There may be problems for some transport firms because they may also be engaged in nontransport business and some of the costs may have to be arbitrarily allocated to one set of activities or another. For carriers providing both passenger and freight service certain cost categories are truly common and need to be separated somehow (more on this later) if we are to ascertain, say, *MC* of freight transport. Finally, the costs in Column 2 may refer to tens, hundreds, thousands, etc., of dollars of operating costs. Column 3 refers to traffic units deemed to be homogeneous—it is usual in transportation to talk in terms of revenue or gross ton-miles; vehicle-miles; truck, car, or train miles; and so on.

Regardless of the specific interpretation, when plotted these data generate the scatter diagram shown in Figure 2.3, in which the linear

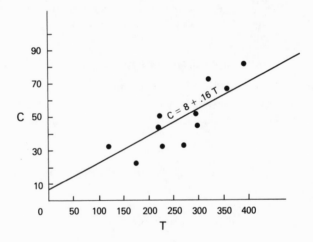

Fig. 2.3

regression (i.e., line of best fit) has been drawn by inspection. A more precise regression function is easily derived. But assume that the equation is $C = 8 + .16T$. This means that $MC = .16$ in the sense that for every increase (or decrease) in $T$ ($\Delta T$) total cost increases (or decreases) by $.16\Delta T$. Since we defined $MC = \dfrac{\Delta C}{\Delta T}$, it is clear that .16 is to be interpreted as *MC* in this regression. It is also constant and equal to the slope of the line, as is implicit in the definition of a straight line.

Average cost $AC = \dfrac{8}{T} + .16$ (short run or long run, depending on whether the data are interpreted as cross-section or time-series and whether one wishes to believe these correspond to long run and short run, respectively). AC clearly declines as $T$ increases, thus implying economies of scale if the data are interpreted as long-run or implying merely lower unit costs as fuller utilization of existing plant and equipment occurs. Note that AC is constant only if the $y$-intercept is zero— then $AC = MC$, implying LRMC (or SRMC) constancy. In this case the regression would go through the origin and would imply either no economies of scale or movement along the flat portion of a short-run cost function. Finally, if the intercept were negative (i.e., $a < 1$ in the general equation), AC would increase as $T$ increased, and this could be interpreted as diseconomies of scale or as movement along the rising portion of the short-run cost function.

### The Concept of "Percent Variable"

Concern with the proportion of railway expenses that varied with changes in traffic has had a long history. From an early view that rail costs were 50% variable with traffic and 50% fixed, the ICC developed figures of 80% variable and 20% fixed, which more recently have been revised to 100% variable by another author. We discuss some of these calculations below. At this point we wish to note the meaning of "percent variable" since it relates directly to the previous regression function. The percent variable expenses is simply the ratio of the variable costs $(.16T)$ to total costs $(C)$: thus % variable $= \dfrac{.16T}{C}$.

But since $C = 8 + .16T$, % variable $= \dfrac{.16T}{8 + .16T} = \dfrac{.16}{\dfrac{8}{T} + .16}$. Note that

$.16 = MC$ and that $\dfrac{8}{T} + .16 = AC$. Thus, % variable $= \dfrac{MC}{AC}$.

Since for linear cost functions, AC depends on $T$, % variable depends on $T$. Thus in the above example if $T = 50$ units, % variable $= \dfrac{.16}{.16 + .16} = 50\%$; if $T = 100$ units, % variable $= \dfrac{.16}{.08 + .16}$
$= 66\frac{2}{3}\%$; if $T = 200$ units, % variable $= \dfrac{.16}{.04 + .16} = 80\%$, and so on. Thus any single % variable figure assumes a given traffic volume or density, usually the average for the carriers observed, at least as far as the ICC cost studies are concerned.

More generally, given a linear cost function $C = a + bT$, the % variable $= \dfrac{bT}{a + bT}$ and the behavior of the % variable with respect to changes in $T$ depends on the magnitude and sign of $a$ as follows:

If $a > 0$, then the % variable varies directly with $T$, as noted in the above example, and approaches 100 as $T$ becomes large.

If $a = 0$, then the % variable equals 100 and is invariant with respect to changes in $T$.

If $a < 0$, the % variable exceeds 100 and approaches 100 as $T$ increases (i.e., varies inversely with $T$).

An interpretation often made is that if $a$ is positive, relatively large, and statistically significant, then economies of scale are said to exist. This simply means that $MC < AC$, or % variable $< 100$. Similarly, if $a$ is close to zero, $MC = AC$ and constant returns to scale exist. Finally, if $a$ is negative, relatively large, and statistically significant, decreasing returns to scale exist, $MC > AC$. This interpretation requires the set of assumptions noted above.

We turn now to some empirical estimates of transportation cost functions beginning with railroads.

## Railroad Cost Functions

The ICC's Cost Finding Section, using linear regression analysis of gross ton-miles (assumed to be the output unit) against a number of separate expense categories, not total costs as we have used above, for all U.S. railroads for the years 1939–46 (note the wartime period and thus an unusual sample) obtained the following results:

| Account Group | % Variable (All U.S.) |
|---|---|
| I. Maintenance of Way | 108 |
| II. Maintenance of Equipment | 79 |
| III. Traffic Expenses | 32 |
| IV. Transportation Expenses (linehaul) | 123 |
| V. General Expenses | 74 |

SOURCE: ICC Statement No. 4-54.

The commission noted that the median % variable was 79 (the average is 83) and thus concluded that railway expenses are about 80% variable with traffic and 20% fixed. In other words, if traffic of every kind over every railroad increased by the same percentage, say, 10%, operating costs would increase by less than this, or 8% for a 10% traffic increase but only for *the type specified above.*

Note that if this is true, railroads are subject to economies of scale, since $MC < AC$. However, much confusion surrounds this conclusion and serious questions can be raised about the ICC's approach. For one thing, the account groups in the table are not equally important in terms of proportions of total operating costs—Group III constitutes about 1% of total cost and Group IV about 50%. A weighted average yields a % variable estimate of about 100; that is, if we multiply the % variable figure for each account group by the relative importance of each group and add the products, we obtain a figure close to 100 for the % variable. If this is the case, then railroads are subject to constant returns to scale, and $MC = AC$, under one interpretation.[14]

Of course, none of this necessarily applies to any individual carrier. As Commissioner Webb long ago noted, "In the past, the 80 percent and 90 percent (for motor carriers) variable have been widely accepted and used. But . . . they have become controversial to the extent that some consider them not applicable to a specific carrier—not even over the long run."[15] Thus its utility is open to question even when one ignores the conceptual issues (such as using GTM as an output measure for all expense groups, the items included in each expense group) and the statistical issues (such as use of weighted vs. unweighted averages).

## Griliches's Rail Cost Functions

More recently, Griliches[16] has taken the ICC to task and reappraised some of the findings using the same data as the commission did. He has two main criticisms of the ICC approach. First, there is the weighting problem. Since the percent variable depends on the level of output (or the average level of output), it is "crucial to specify what one means by this average."[17] In 1958 the ICC estimated by regression methods that the marginal cost per ton-mile was about 6.64 mills, the average cost was 8.56 mills, and thus the percent variable is 77.6 $\left( \text{i.e.,} \frac{6.64}{8.56} \right)$. But this "average" cost was computed by taking the average cost per ton-mile for each of the approximately 100 railroads in the sample and averaging them. This calculation gives equal importance to each railroad, regardless of size. For example, suppose we have three railroads—A, B, and C—whose traffic and cost experience are as follows:

| Railroad | Total Operating Costs ($) | Traffic Ton-Miles |
|:---:|:---:|:---:|
| A | 10 | 50 |
| B | 100 | 600 |
| C | 1,000 | 7,000 |

The unit operating costs are $\frac{10}{50} = .20$ for A, $\frac{100}{600} = .167$ for B, and $\frac{1000}{7000} = .143$ for C. The average of these averages is .17. But this clearly is

---

14. A discussion of the issue of returns to scale and several conflicting views are given in Wilson, *Essays*, pp.48–51.

15. Webb, p.6.

16. Z. Griliches, "Railroad Cost Analysis," *Bell Journal of Economics and Management Science*, Spring 1972, pp.26ff.

17. Ibid., p.28.

*not* the average cost experience of the "average ton-mile" because most of the ton-miles are generated by railroad C. If we weighted the unit costs by the relative importance of the total traffic a more "representative" average, in the sense of more closely approximating the performance of the average ton-mile, would be obtained. Thus we might weight the average cost per ton-mile per firm by the relative importance of the ton-miles generated per firm to the total ton-miles (7650 ton-miles). Performing this exercise we obtain a weighted average as follows: $.20\left(\frac{50}{7650}\right) + .167\left(\frac{600}{7650}\right) + .143\left(\frac{7000}{7650}\right) = .145.$ This is equivalent to dividing total operating costs (all three railroads = \$1110) by total ton-miles (7650).[18] Performing such a calculation, Griliches obtains an average cost per ton-mile of 6.64 mills, which makes the percent variable equal 100, a radically different figure from the ICC measure.

Friedlaender also notes that the commission fails to weight its results appropriately and points out that by "applying a figure of 80 percent variable to all railroads, the ICC is, in effect, assuming that all railroads are producing under identical increasing returns to scale."[19] Such criticisms have some validity. The main point, however, is that either approach to weighting is valid depending on the purpose. If one wishes to obtain an average cost experience *per carrier*, the commission's approach is correct. If one wishes to obtain an average cost experience per ton or per ton-mile, the latter approach is correct. Average cost experience per carrier may be useful to indicate the cost experience of carriers of different sizes or traffic composition characteristics. An average of such averages standing alone is, however, pretty meaningless and downright misleading if the single figure is interpreted to mean the average cost of moving a ton-mile by rail. For this interpretation, Griliches and Friedlaender are correct in criticizing the ICC's approach.

---

18. For example, let $C_1$, $C_2$, etc., represent total operating cost for railroads 1, 2, etc., and $T_1$, $T_2$, etc., represent ton-miles. We can weight each railroad in terms of its relative ton-mile importance and multiply each railroad's average cost per ton-mile by this factor, as done above. Thus we obtain

$$\frac{C_1}{T_1}\left(\frac{T_1}{T_1 + T_2 + T_3 + \ldots + T_n}\right) + \frac{C_2}{T_2}\left(\frac{T_2}{T_1 + T_2 + T_3 + \ldots + T_n}\right)$$
$$+ \ldots + \frac{C_n}{T_n}\left(\frac{T_n}{T_1 + T_2 + T_3 + \ldots + T_n}\right).$$

This reduces to $\left(\frac{1}{T_1 + T_2 + T_3 + \ldots + T_n}\right)(C_1 + C_2 + C_3 + \ldots + C_n)$, or total operating costs of the whole system of railroads divided by total system ton-miles.

19. Friedlaender, p.33. In fact, other studies of scale economies (e.g., G. H. Borts, "The Estimation of Rail Cost Functions," *Econometrica*, vol.28, January 1960) concluded that scale economies differ by region. As we note below, they also differ by size of carrier as well as among carriers of similar size.

The second major point made by Griliches involves several recomputations using the ICC data and definitions of cost and output. Given the same data, one can regress costs against ton-miles in several ways: (1) One may "deflate" the data by dividing by some size variable, say, miles of track; (2) one can regress the logarithms of the data; and (3) one can regress the data as they stand.

Some of the alternative results are as follows:

$$\text{Costs/mile} = \$13,010 + 6.43 \text{ mills} \left(\frac{\text{ton-miles}}{\text{mile}}\right);$$
$$R^2 = .365, \% \text{ variable} = 74.6.$$
$$\text{Log costs} = \log a + 82.3 \, (\log \text{ton-miles});$$
$$R^2 = .944, \% \text{ variable} = 82.3.$$
$$\text{Costs} = \$2,811 + 6.39 \text{ mills} \, (\text{ton-miles});$$
$$R^2 = .944, \% \text{ variable} = 97.0.$$

Notice the variation in the % variable figures, which depend entirely on which way one chooses to construe the data. It is also noteworthy but not surprising that estimated $MC$ are close in all three calculations.[20]

Griliches also noted that the average costs per railroad appeared to differ between the very small and large roads. When he split the sample of 97 roads on the basis of miles of track operated (over or under 500 miles) and performed exercises similar to those above, rather different behavior patterns were observed. Using only undeflated units, the regressions were as follows:

$$\text{Small roads: Costs} = \$3,197 + 6.84 \text{ mills} \, (\text{ton-miles});$$
$$R^2 = .434, \% \text{ variable} = 70.3.$$
$$\text{Large roads: Costs} = \$1,473 + 6.42 \text{ mills} \, (\text{ton-miles});$$
$$R^2 = .929, \% \text{ variable} = 99.1.$$

Ignoring small roads, which in the aggregate accounted for only about 5% of total railway costs, and for which the $R^2$ is small, Griliches concludes that there is "little or almost no evidence of economies of scale in the railroad industry."[21]

Again, we note that the $MC$ estimate is close to 6.5 mills, as in the other regressions. What relevance such a figure may have in specific situations (i.e., movement of commodity X between points A and B) is, of course, totally ambiguous for reasons already pointed out. As Friedlaender cautiously suggests, "ICC estimates of out-of-pocket costs are often meaningless for specific point-to-point movements."[22]

---

20. In the second equation, the coefficient of the log of ton-miles is the elasticity of costs with respect to output and comes from an equation of the form $C = aT^b$. If average costs are around 8 mills, then $\frac{MC}{8} = .823$. Thus $MC = 6.58$ mills.

21. Griliches, p.36.

22. Friedlaender, p.33. I would omit the word "often" and would include other measures as well.

From the foregoing, and as noted earlier, the attempt to derive quantitatively meaningful estimates of MC in the economists' sense is exceedingly difficult. As Griliches admits, the results just shown "are based on very questionable definitions of cost and output, and on a very gross aggregation of types of traffic, dimensions of output, regions of the country and sizes of railroads."[23] He thereupon calls for more ad hoc, detailed investigations.

### An Alternative Approach

Another way to estimate economies of scale is to use a production function. The most common is the Cobb-Douglas, which has the form

$$Q = AK^{\alpha}L^{\beta} \text{ (linear, homogeneous)}$$

where $Q$ is output, $A$ is a parameter, $K$ and $L$ are usually interpreted as "capital and labor," and $\alpha$ and $\beta$ are the change in output with respect to a change in $K$ and $L$.

If $\alpha + \beta > 1$, economies of scale exist.
If $\alpha + \beta < 1$, diseconomies of scale exist.
If $\alpha + \beta = 1$, there are constant returns to scale.

Indeed, if $\alpha + \beta = 1$, this production function gives rise to a cost function of the form $C = aQ$, where $a = rK + wL$, $r =$ per-unit cost of capital $= MP_K$, and $w =$ wage rate $= MP_L$. $MP_K =$ marginal product of capital, and $MP_L =$ marginal product of labor.

Hence $MC = AC = a$, and % variable $= 100$.

If one could obtain data and determine $\alpha$ and $\beta$, one could estimate whether or not economies of scale exist. A recent study of five railroads yielded the following data using time-series analysis for the period 1962–72:

| | $Q$ | $R^2$ | $\alpha + \beta$ |
|---|---|---|---|
| Southern Railway System | $AK^{.29} L^{1.07}$ | .92 | 1.36 |
| L & N | $AK^{.25} L^{1.08}$ | .92 | 1.33 |
| Seaboard Coast Line | $AK^{.21} L^{.87}$ | .89 | 1.08 |
| Illinois Central | $AK^{.15} L^{.91}$ | .73 | 1.06 |
| Gulf, Mobile & Ohio | $AK^{.16} L^{.77}$ | .60 | 0.93 |

where $Q =$ GTM, $K =$ investment in plant and equipment, $L =$ number of crews.

SOURCE: J. T. Kneafsey, *Studies in Railroad Operations and Economics*, vol.13, *Costing in Railroad Operations*, prepared for the Federal Railroad Administration, March 1975, p.30.

Over the period of the observations, a 10% change in inputs generated a 13.6% change in output, as defined here for the Southern

---

23. Griliches, p.39.

Railway, but only a 9.3% change for the GMO. This result partially confirms several previous observations to the effect that economies of scale may or may not typify the railroad industry as a whole but only certain lines in certain regions. Again, it is hazardous to interpret these results strictly in terms of $(\alpha + \beta)$ since to an unknown extent the differences may reflect such things as managerial talents and different input and output mixes.

An earlier study of the U.S. railway system deduced the production function

$$Q = AL^{.89} K^{.12} M^{.28},{}^{24}$$

where $Q$ refers to ton-miles, $L$ and $K$ are interpreted as labor and capital, and $M$ is materials (i.e., fuel). The sum of the exponents is 1.3, indicating economies of scale—i.e., a doubling of all inputs increases output 2.6 times. Note the inclusion of an additional variable, which indicates that the results for the several railroads noted above would be different if a variable representing "materials" is included. It is not clear how the distinction between freight ton-miles and passenger miles is made. One way is to convert passenger miles into ton-miles by assuming a certain weight per passenger. Another way is to recognize that railroads used to produce different outputs—freight and passenger service, for example—most of the costs of which are common. One could then regress the combined output against various inputs. Indeed, the *final* equation of the regression just noted is

$$L^{1.0} K^{.135} M^{.312} = AX_1^{1.22} X_2^{.181},$$

where $X_1$ is net freight ton-miles and $X_2$ is net passenger miles.[25] Without appropriate weights for $X_1$ vis-a-vis $X_2$ and so on, it is difficult to interpret this equation as representing economies of scale. Griliches[26] has reconstructed it as

$$[L^{.69} K^{.09} M^{.22}] = k[X_1^{.86} X_2^{.14}] \, .90$$

and asserts that the estimates in brackets may be interpreted as input and output indexes. He then suggests that this equation indicates a % variable of 90, i.e., small economies of scale.[27]

---

24. Cited in Irvin M. Grossack and David D. Martin, *Managerial Economics* (Boston: Little, Brown, 1973), pp.405–406.
25. L. Klein, *A Textbook of Econometrics* (Evanston: Row Peterson, 1953), p.234.
26. Griliches, p.38, *n*21.
27. That is, designate the index of output as $Q$ and the index of input as $K$. The above equation asserts that $kQ^{.9} = K$. In log form we have $\log k + .9 \log Q = \log K$.

$$\therefore \log Q = \frac{\log K - \log k}{.9} = 1.11 \, [\log K - \log k].$$

Thus any increment in the index of inputs will lead to a greater increase in output.

The foregoing approaches to the issue of rail economies of scale indicate that much confusion exists about levels of aggregation, appropriate indicators of output, appropriate indicators of input, and appropriate measures of size. The results are likewise influenced by the form of the production function, whether the data are "deflated" or not, whether they are used in "raw" or logarithmic form, and the composition of output and input.[28] Since there is little compelling justification for selecting any of the many possible indicators for most of the variables used or the way in which they are used, the question of whether railroads are subject to economies of scale remains an empty economic box. Indeed, it may not even be a very interesting or relevant question, as is suggested by note 28. Some railroads may well experience decreasing costs with increasing size; others may not. Much of the observed variation in costs may be due to a host of factors only peripherally related to size, such as management, the changing nature of the shipments (longer hauls, heavier densities), technological changes, or the extent of excess capacity in one or all of the line haul, terminal, and rolling stock dimensions. No research to date has been able to disentangle all these aspects of rail cost behavior. Certainly, no research that relates in a linear fashion an aggregate of operating costs to a single arbitrary output unit, whether in a cross-section or time-series regression, is capable of shedding much light on the issue of economies of scale. At the very least, we need more than two sets of observations.

### Multivariate Linear Regression

The foregoing analysis was primarily concerned with a single variable. Cost was assumed to depend on a single measure of output, except in the production function approach, which had at least two input variables. We must now turn to the more realistic situation, where cost depends on several outputs as well as on other variables. The most obvious case is that of a transportation firm that provides both freight and passenger services, which most railroads used to do. Alternatively, costs may depend on the size of the firm. Thus, multivariate linear regression analysis involves regressing some figure of

---

28. As Griliches puts it, the various studies he examines (whether using national or regional aggregates) all ask the question, What will happen to average costs if total traffic is expanded on the average in the same proportions and having exactly the same distribution over the various commodities, types, routes, and seasons as the previously handled traffic? (p.40). That such circumstances are unusual in transport means that most of the regressions are asking a question that has little relevance. Railroads have regularly shifted their output away from passenger to freight service, away from *LCL* to *CL,* away from light to heavy density commodities, away from short- to long-haul traffic, away from branch lines to main lines.

total costs against more than one particular variable. It takes the form $C = a_1 + a_2 T_1 + a_3 T_2 + a_4 S + \ldots$, where the $T_i$ are some output measures and $S$ is a size measure. In principle, we fit a plane or hyperplane of dimension $N - 1$ in $N$-space, and the regression finds the plane that minimizes the sum of the squares of the distances from the point in $N$-space to the plane of dimension $N - 1$. Thus, univariate analysis finds a line (Dimension 1 in 2-space). If there are two variables on the righthand side of the equation, we would fit a regression plane in 3-space, and so on. The mathematics is the same as regression analysis in 2-space that we have already examined. The analogy is complete, although much more complex and tedious—especially using manual methods. Fortunately, there are computer programs that permit one to perform these operations fairly easily. Graphically, regression analysis in 3-space may be shown as in Figure 2.4, in which total costs depend

**MULTIVARIATE COST FUNCTION IN THREE DIMENSIONS**

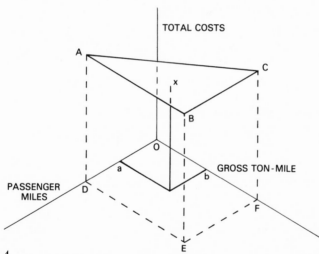

Fig. 2.4

on the combination of passenger miles and gross ton-miles. Every point on plane $ABC$ indicates the total costs for any given combination of the two outputs. Thus, for a passenger output of $a$ and a freight output of $b$, total costs would be $x$, a point on the plane.

An early approach to railway costing using multivariate linear regression analysis was done by Meyer et al.[29] In general, this technique requires defining various expense categories, such as general expenses, traffic expenses, yard expenses, and train expenses, and finding the

---

29. *Economics of Competition.* . . .

output unit that is most appropriate to each expense category. With the available information, either from cross-section or time-series analysis, one can then regress each expense category against its most appropriate output unit or, in some cases, units. For example, suppose there are three expense categories that differ in the sense that the units that occasion the expenses are different. Suppose we have expense categories $E_1$, $E_2$, $E_3$ and that an observer concludes that category $E_1$ is related to both gross ton-miles of freight and revenue passenger miles of traffic; that category $E_2$ depends on weight and distance separately; and that category $E_3$ depends on the number of pieces of paper (bills of lading, etc.) required to process the particular traffic. If regressions are run, we may obtain the following:

$$E_1 \text{ (in \$)} = 20 + .005 \, GTM + .006 \, RPM$$
$$E_2 \text{ (in \$)} = 1,000 + .6W + .02D$$
$$E_3 \text{ (in \$)} = 5 + .1 \text{ (No. of bills)},$$

where $GTM$ = gross ton-miles, $RPM$ = revenue passenger miles, $W$ = weight per shipment, and $D$ = distance per shipment. For shipments having specific characteristics in the above variables, marginal cost can be readily calculated. Assume a shipment requires 5 pieces of paper for processing, weighs 20 tons, and moves 500 miles. This shipment involves 10,000 $RTM$. If on the average $\dfrac{RTM}{GTM} = .4$, then the shipment involves 25,000 $GTM$. Thus,

$$
\begin{aligned}
E_1 &= .005 \, (25,000) & &= \$125.0 \\
E_2 &= .6(20) + .02(500) &= &\ \ \$22.0 \\
E_3 &= .1(5) & &= \ \ \$ \ 0.5 \\
\hline
&\quad Total & &\quad \$147.5
\end{aligned}
$$

One may therefore infer that the marginal cost of shipments having these characteristics is \$147.5.

More generally, if

$$E_1 = a_1 + b_1 GTM + c_1 RPM$$
$$E_2 = a_2 + b_2 W + c_2 D$$
$$E_3 = a_3 + b_3 N,$$

then the $MC$ of any shipment with known $GTM$, $W$, $D$, and $N$ is simply $b_1(GTM) + b_2 W + c_2 D + b_3 N$.

Specifically, the procedure of Meyer et al. was as follows: a sample of 25 of the largest Class I railway systems (excluding the New York Central and the Pennsylvania System) was selected. Data on various expense categories and traffic were averaged for each of the 25 railroads for the period 1947–50. The expense categories regressed against specific outputs yielded the results in Table 2.2. We are interested

## TABLE 2.2

### *Operating Costs, 1947–1950, Regression Results*

General Expenses $(E_g)$ = \$1.4 million + $0.00012\ Q_f$ + \$4.844 $\sqrt{Q_p}$
Traffic Expenses $(E_t)$ = 0.7 million + $0.0000709\ Q_f$ + $0.0001457\ Q_p$
Station Expenses $(E_s)$ = 1.2 million + $0.000212\ Q_p$ + $0.0000018\ Q_f$
$\qquad\qquad$ + $944.96\ S_m$
Yard Expenses $(E_y)$ = 1.2 million + $9.21\ Q_{yhd}$ + $16.03\ Q_{yhs}$
Train Expenses $(E_t)$ = 10.3 + $0.000622\ Q_{fd}$ + $0.000411\ Q_{fs}$
$\qquad\qquad$ + $0.003451\ Q_{ps}$ + $0.001519\ Q_{pd}$.

$Q_f$ = gross ton-miles of freight traffic
$Q_p$ = gross ton-miles of passenger traffic
$Q_{yhd}$ = number of yard hours of diesel engines
$Q_{yhs}$ = number of yard hours of steam engines
$S_m$ = miles of track

SOURCE: Meyer et al., Appendix B.

only in determining the marginal cost of freight traffic, and hence we can ignore $Q_p$ and $S_m$. From Table 2.2 one can determine the marginal operating costs $(MOC)$ per gross ton-mile of freight $(GTM)$ by simply adding the coefficients of $Q_f$ in each equation:

$$MOC = E_g + E_t + E_s + E_y + E_t = \$0.0006037 \text{ per } GTM + 9.21\ Q_{yhd}.$$

A single figure cannot be derived without converting $Q_{yhd}$ into $GTM$. Experience at the C&O during the period indicated that a "typical" merchandise car travels 400 miles with an average load of 25 tons and is therefore the "equivalent" of 10,000 $GTMs$. The C&O also reported that such a car takes "approximately 24 minutes to originate, classify, and terminate. . . ."[30] The cost per typical merchandise car of, say, yard diesel service is \$9.21 (from $E_y$ in Table 2.2) multiplied by $\dfrac{24}{60}$ = \$3.684. Since each typical car "contains" 10,000 $GTMs$, the cost of yard hour service in terms of $GTMs$ = \$0.0003684. Thus, total $MOC$ = 0.9721 mills per $GTM$.[31]

The authors then deduce, in similar fashion, so-called long-run marginal maintenance, depreciation, and variable capital expenses. Various adjustments are made in these estimates such as the conversion of yard hour coefficients into $GTMs$ for yard engine maintenance and the conversion of the coefficient of road engine miles into $GTMs$ by a process similar to that noted above, except that averages for the entire sample, not only for the C&O, were used. Marginal depreciation and variable capital expenses were obtained only for regressions covering 1952–1955, rather than 1947–1950, and thus were "price-cor-

---

30. Ibid., p.48.
31. Meyer et al. report 0.8721 as the figure, which is an error of addition.

rected" (by an unspecified index). The cost of money was assumed to be 6½%. The results of these manipulations yielded an estimate of total "long-run marginal costs" (*LRMC*) per *GTM* of 2.2752 mills.

For pricing purposes costs need to be obtained in terms of revenue ton-miles (*RTM*) since *GTM*s are not priced. The study asserts that a "generous" estimate of the rate of *RTM* to *GTM* is .4. If so, *LRMC* per *RTM* may be estimated as $\frac{2.2752}{.4} \cong 5.69$ mills/*RTM*.

There are many problems and ambiguities in the above methodology that seriously affect the meaningfulness of the results. We have already noted that *GTM* is only one of many possible output measures. Regardless of which measure is used, *MC* (long or short run) is highly variable, and for costing and pricing purposes the determination of a single estimate evades all the complexities that exist in rail transport. To be sure, Meyer et al. reiterate on several occasions that "certain normative assumptions" were made, that the results apply to railroad operations conducted under "average or median operating conditions," that the estimates "are based on a sort of central tendency . . . that will apply to freight movements only of a very average or ordinary kind."[32]

Nevertheless, for the pricing of any shipment between any pair of points, the single estimate of *LRMC* per *RTM* is likely to be far from the mark. Nor can "price-correcting" the figure by some index render it any more useful even as a guide to regulatory policy. From an analytical point of view, the method suffers from all the defects we have noted before—assumptions of linearity, arbitrary but not unreasonable specifications of costing units, and arbitrary but not unreasonable sample selection of carriers and years of observation. The use of C&O data to convert yard hours to *GTM*s is highly questionable, as is the conversion process itself, since the desire to obtain a single figure hides the diversity of cost characteristics among shipments and adds another element of arbitrary averaging.

For its time, this approach was something of an advance over Rail Form A, accounting allocations, rules of thumb, or simple averages.[33] The basic method of segregating accounts according to the "output" units that seem to occasion the particular costs and running some kind of statistical regression on each can lead one closer to that elusive animal, marginal costs, to the extent that shipments containing vari-

---

32. Meyer et al., chap. 3, pp.43, 61, 63.

33. It is interesting to note that a simple average for 1947 yields a "cost" per *RTM* of 5.3 mills. That is, total "transportation expenses" per revenue ton-mile for all Class 1 railroads for 1947 is 5.3 mills, a figure close to that derived above. It excludes maintenance and some other expenses included in the 5.69 mills/*RTM* estimated by regression techniques and, of course, is not directly comparable in other respects. (The 5.3 mills figure is from AAR, *Yearbook of Railroad Facts*, 1969 edition [Washington, D.C.] April 1969.)

ous combinations and amounts of specified output units can be assigned the apparent $MC$ of each such unit. Indeed, the two major Canadian railroads have adopted this approach to costing and pricing.[34] More detailed methods have been applied to costing by many railroads in the United States—notably, the Southern Pacific.

A recent study done for the U.S. Department of Transportation has attempted to determine the short- and long-run marginal cost for Class I railroads for 1972 by using a methodology similar to that noted above at pp.79–80.[35] Roughly 120 separate accounts for all Class I railroads were grouped into 31 cost categories, each of which was believed to be related to one or more distinct service variables. "The strategy is to group accounts that are related to common transportation outputs and activities or are in some way related to each other."[36] The relationships were determined by using a cost function for each cost and service variable of the form

$$C_i = A_i S_i{}^{B_1} Q_i{}^{B_2},$$

where $S_i$ = size of the railroad, $Q_i$ = some output variable, $A_i$ = a constant, and $B_1$ and $B_2$ represent the elasticity of costs with respect to $S_i$ and $Q_i$, respectively.[37]

For example, the cost category "Locomotive repairs—yard" was regressed against the freight service unit "per yard switch locomotive miles" to yield a $B_2$ for this category of $0.404 for Western Territory. Similar coefficients of the $Q_i$ were determined for each of the 31 cost categories for the short-run analysis.

For specific shipments (e.g., Iron ore Western—Western territory—within Western Territory), the number of service units were determined. When these are multiplied by the $B_i$ and summed, the total variable operating cost for that shipment can be estimated. In the case of iron ore shipped within Western Territory, the number of "yard switch locomotive miles" was estimated to be 1.128, and thus the variable "locomotive repairs—yard" costs attributable to such a shipment is $0.456 (i.e., 1.128 × 0.404). Such figures are summed for each cost category to obtain total operating (variable) costs for the typical iron

34. W. J. Stenason and R. A. Bandeedn, "Transportation Costs and Their Implications: An Empirical Study of Railway Costs in Canada," in *Transportation Economics*, edited by J. R. Meyer (New York: Columbia University Press, 1965), pp.121–39.

35. A. Lago, D. Flynn, E. Battison, and R. Price, *Short- and-Long-Run Cost Models of U.S. Class I Railroads*, RMC Report UR-283, prepared for Transportation Systems Center, U. S. Department of Transportation, Cambridge, Mass., March 26, 1976.

36. Ibid., p.27.

37. Note that this form of the cost function has constant % variable with respect to $Q_i$ equal to $B_2$ for each cost category $\left( \text{i.e., } \dfrac{MC_i}{AC_i} = B_2 \right)$.

ore shipment within Western Territory. In this instance, the cost was estimated as $61.722. Data problems abound and many adjustments had to be made, but as an application of a reasonable method of obtaining estimates of $MC$, this approach has considerable merit.

From this study and that of Meyer et al. it is not clear whether economies of scale exist in rail transportation. Meyer et al. assert, however, that "substantial indivisibilities and scale economies . . . are almost solely limited to the railroads."[38] The Lago et al. study did attempt a limited analysis of $LRMC$ and tentatively concluded that "the methodology for the estimation of long-run marginal operating costs is promising and results in estimates of long-run variability of close to 1.0 and in long-run marginal costs exceeding the short-run marginal costs for all accounts (10) investigated."[39] A long-run cost elasticity of 1.0 implies the absence of scale economies, while $LRMC > SRMC$ implies excess capacity.

Another attempt to determine whether railways are subject to economies of scale employed regression techniques similar to those of Meyer et al., but used mostly $RTMs$ rather than $GTMs$ (somewhat different cost categories—most on a per-mile basis) and a cross-section analysis of all Class I railways for 1968.[40] A large number of separate regressions were run on particular expense categories, such as general expenses, freight traffic expenses, transportation expenses, train fuel and related expenses, station expenses, yard expenses, and maintenance of way expenses. The results cannot be compared with those of Meyer et al. because different explanatory variables were used. The main conclusion is that "the evidence shows that for a wide variety of railroad operating accounts the cost per mile increases less than proportionately to the traffic. This indicates that there are economies of scale in railroading."[41]

Unfortunately, Miller's results do *not* indicate scale economies in railroading. Economies of scale relate decreasing unit cost to size of firm, however the latter is defined (in terms of assets, employees, miles of track, etc.). Miller's results do, however, indicate economies of *density* of traffic. Harris has explicitly attempted some estimates of costs relative to traffic density, using the following cost model:

$$TC = B_0 RTM + B_1 RFT + B_2 MR,$$

where $TC$ = total operating plus capital cost (the latter is omitted in

38. Meyer et al., p.146.
39. Lago et al., p.106.
40. Edward Miller, "Economies of Scale in Railroading," *Proceedings, Fourteenth Annual Meeting, Transportation Research Forum, 1973* (Oxford, Ind.: Richard B. Cross, 1973), pp.683–701.
41. Ibid., p.701.

the studies noted above), $RTM$ = revenue ton-miles (not gross ton-miles), $RFT$ = revenue freight tons, and $MR$ = miles of road.

Using a variant of the above (i.e., dividing by $RTM$), he obtains

$$AC = \frac{TC}{RTM} = B_0 + B_1 \frac{1}{ALH} + B_2 \frac{1}{\text{Density}},$$

where $AC$ = average cost, $ALH$ = average length of haul $\left(\text{i.e.,} \frac{RFT}{RTM}\right)$, and Density = revenue ton-miles per mile of road $\left(\text{i.e.,} \frac{RTM}{MR}\right)$. Harris uses as his sample 55 Class I railroads in 1972 and 1973 with revenues over \$5 million and passenger revenues less than one percent of total revenues (to avoid any arbitrary allocation of costs between freight and passengers or an arbitrary combination of freight and passengers into a single output unit). He solves for the $Bs$ and concludes that "there are very significant economies of traffic density in the rail freight industry."[42]

Other findings regarding cost indivisibilities and the influence of average length of haul[43] are consistent with our previous analytical discussion and will not be further elaborated here.

The distinction between economies of density and economies of scale should now be apparent. Small firms with high densities and longer average hauls may "very well have lower average costs than a large firm with low density."[44] Hence the scale economy issue remains unresolved. Many of the empirical studies noted above fail to adjust for shipment characteristics and density to which average cost is very sensitive regardless of the size of the firm.

A more elaborate model using a production function approach likewise finds "substantial unexploited economies of traffic density for most railroads, but constant long-run returns to scale."[45] Of some interest in the light of our previous discussion of % variable is the enormous range of this measure among the 51 railroads examined. The % variable ranges from a low of 7.2(!) to a high of 78.7. Consistent with

---

42. R. G. Harris, "Economies of Traffic Density in the Rail Freight Industry," *Bell Journal of Economics*, Autumn 1977, p.561.

43. The latter is extremely important, as we note in the section dealing with motor carrier costs below.

44. Ibid., p.557.

45. T. E. Keeler, "Railroad Costs, Returns to Scale, and Excess Capacity," *Review of Economics and Statistics*, May 1974, p.207. The production function was of the form $Q_i = A_i T_i{}^{\alpha_i} R_i{}^{\beta_i} F_i{}^{\gamma_i} L_i{}^{\delta_i}$, where $Q$ = thousands of *gross* ton-miles, $T$ = track miles, $R$ = rolling stock investment, $F$ = fuel consumed, and $L$ = labor used per unit of time. The subscripts ($i = 1, 2$) refer to freight and passenger service, respectively. Data from 51 selected railroads for the years 1969 through 1971 were used.

our earlier discussion of marginal cost pricing Keeler finds that "for the great majority of firms, short-run marginal cost pricing would recover less than 70% of total costs."[46]

Two earlier studies partially confirm the above. Healy examined 37 independent Class I railways using data averaged over 1954–1956 and concluded that "increasing scale for railroads beyond some 10,000 employees leads to poorer performance."[47] He did, however, note some *regional* differences related to *density* (revenues per mile of track or net ton-miles per mile of track) that do not relate to scale but that are partially consistent with a prior study by Borts.[48] Both studies found decreasing per-unit costs as density increases in the West and, less clearly, in the South. Borts, however, found increasing costs in the East, while Healy found little relationship between density and any of his measures of performance. Sidhu and Due studied 209 Class II railroads using cross-section linear regression analysis for 1968. They regressed costs against weight and distance separately and found that average costs decrease as either weight or distance or both increase and that "costs of Eastern railroads are higher than those of the Southern and Western railroads."[49] These results are consistent with Borts's findings regarding Class I roads.

These studies, like Miller's noted above, may refer more to economies of density than of scale. Indeed, one might rationalize the higher or increasing costs in the East and the lower or decreasing costs in the West and South as evidence of the persistence of excess capacity in the latter two regions compared with the North. The "overbuilding" of the railroads in the South and the West[50] could very well lead to lower or decreasing costs as volume grows. This says nothing whatsoever about economies of scale. It does, however, imply certain relationships between volume of traffic and "capacity." The notion and measurement of capacity in transportation are extremely important, but they pose formidable conceptual and empirical problems, some of which are discussed in the following section.

### The Concept of Rail Capacity

Decreasing unit costs related to increased density implies excess

46. Ibid. For the pricing implications, see below, chap. 3. This is also consistent with the findings of Lago et al.

47. Kent T. Healy, *The Effects of Scale in the Railroad Industry* (New Haven: Yale University Press, 1961), p.4.

48. George H. Borts, "The Estimation of Rail Cost Functions," *Econometrica*, January 1960.

49. N. Sidhu and J. Due, "Cost Functions of Class II Railroads and the Question of Railway Abandonment," Transportation Research Paper #4 (Urbana: University of Illinois, September 5, 1974), p.12.

50. See Borts, p.128.

capacity in one or all of a railroad's dimensions—terminals, yards, right-of-way, shops. If a railroad has excess capacity in all these areas, unit costs will decrease as volume of traffic increases. Indeed, the economic definition of full capacity utilization is the volume of traffic beyond which unit costs begin to rise more or less rapidly. However, since a railroad operation, like many others, consists of an interrelated series of steps or processes to produce the "final" product (marshalling, line-haul movement, repairs, etc.), and since each of these processes normally has a different capacity, increased traffic can be expected to create rising unit costs in some processes before others. Terminal congesion may occur long before line-haul congestion, for example, and thus unit *terminal* costs may begin to rise well before unit *line-haul* costs. It is therefore possible to have excess capacity in some processes and no excess (or inadequate) capacity in others. However, as long as excess capacity exists in some areas, there are possibilities of reduced unit costs.

The problem may be generalized as follows: Assume a production process consisting of three interrelated processes—A, B, and C—with daily capacities per process unit of 10, 25, and 65 components, respectively. If total demand per day is 65 completed products, the firm would have to employ 7 units of process A, 3 units of B, and one unit of C. It would therefore have excess capacity of 5 components in process A and 10 in process B. To eliminate excess capacity in every process one would need a demand of 650 products per day[51] or some multiple thereof. To say that a firm or a whole industry has "excess" capacity is therefore a very simplistic statement and one easily subject to misinterpretation.

However, the "economies of density" referred to in the studies noted above relate to *line-haul* capacity, because density has been defined as revenue or gross ton-miles per mile of track. Even if we confine ourselves to this single "process," there are many variables that determine the capacity of a rail line. For example, various "rough guides" concerning the number of "trains per day" are often cited, but they depend on the gauge, the number of tracks, and the type of signaling.[52] For example, the DOT study (n.52) provides *engineering* estimates of capacity as follows:

51. The number 650 is the least common multiple of 10, 25, and 65. See also H. Mohring, *Transportation Economics* (Cambridge, Mass.: Ballinger, 1976), p.136.

52. See, for example, ECAFE, *Introduction to Transport Planning* (New York: United Nations, 1967), p.9, and an example from Taiwan in Appendix VII, p.75. A more recent study showing similar data is A Report by the Secretary of Transportation, *Rail Service in the Midwest and Northeast Region*, vol. 2 (Washington, D.C.: Department of Transportation, February 1, 1974), p.5.

| Type of Line | Trains per Day | Gross Tons per Year per Route Mile (Millions) |
|---|---|---|
| Single track, automatic block signal | 40 | 62 |
| Double track, automatic block signal | 120 | 186 |
| Single track, CTC | 60 | 93 |
| Double track, CTC | 160 | 250 |

These figures show a 50% increase in single-line capacity can be achieved by moving to Centralized Traffic Control (CTC), and that capacity triples when double tracking occurs with automatic block signaling. But the volume of freight and passenger traffic that can be moved per train per period also depends on train size (i.e., number of cars per train) and load per car, both of which vary with the commodities to be moved and the time of day, week, etc. As the DOT study puts it, the figures on trains per day for varying numbers of tracks and types of signaling represent "the engineering capacity. *Practical* capacity will be affected by terrain, train size, tonnage, operating procedures, etc."[53] Note that practical capacity need not relate closely to economic capacity as we have defined it. The Interstate Commerce Commission stresses that

the capacity of a rail line is not readily subject to generalization. Numerous factors affect the practical capacity of a given section of track, and this is true whether or not a signal system is present. Capacity depends on grades, curves, clearances, track conditions, location and length of sidings, local switching performed, the requirement to slow down through certain populated areas, and the mix of trains operating at different speeds. Additional considerations include the need to make allowances for equipment breakdowns, delays and necessary out-of-service periods for maintenance activities, particularly those involving the use of on-track maintenance equipment.

It must be realized . . . that line capacity is more dependent upon the number of trains operated over a segment than on the accumulated gross tonnage on the line. Congestion, a limiting factor of capacity, occurs as a result of the numbers of trains and the mix of train speeds rather than the gross weight of the trains.[54]

We have not exhausted all the factors that influence capacity:

In addition to the general findings concerning key variables, a potentially significant phenomenon concerning line capacity evolved from these simulations. It was found that as the capacity of a given line is approached, train delays increase very rapidly and become asymptotic. Adding double track

---

53. Ibid.
54. ICC, *Evaluation of the Secretary of Transportation's Rail Service Report* (Washington, D.C.: Government Printing Office, May 2, 1974), p.23.

in high volume sections or on line segments with significant grades can materially increase line capacity, but the phenomenon of asymptotic delays is repeated; however, at a higher volume level.

This delay phenomenon has significant implications for those planning to add more trains to a given rail line. The line may be nearer to capacity than it appears.

Likewise, policy changes, such as reduced train speeds due to slow orders for fuel conservation, priorities for AMTRAK trains, operation of smaller, but more frequent freight service, stepped-up track maintenance, deferral of locomotive maintenance with a resulting increase in road train breakdown, could have a sudden, unanticipated and unacceptable impact on line capacity and delays.

Many railroads may be nearer to capacity than is generally believed, especially on single-tracked lines. The asymptotic delay phenomenon lulls one into a feeling that there is ample reserve capacity; yet a small change in policy and the addition of a few trains may cause the line to break down. A similar phenomenon has been observed in yard operations as yard facilities approach their practical and economic capacity.[55]

The meaning and usefulness of capacity measures become all the more suspect and subjective when consideration is given to an "acceptable" level of service.

These caveats concerning the meaning and measurement of capacity tend to be forgotten when specific calculations of capacity are presented, even when they have significant implications for new investment. Yet all capacity estimates depend on a large variety of factors; some are inherently subjective, while others depend in a critical way on operating procedures and practices not subject to unique quantification. Furthermore, none of these factors have much bearing on the *economics* of capacity and its utilization. Economic capacity is not a strictly physical concept dictating that traffic volume or throughput cannot exceed a certain fixed amount. Rather, there are trade-offs, which become increasingly important as the volume rises beyond some point on an hourly, daily, weekly, etc., basis. Such trade-offs include slower average speeds, longer delays at particular points, or more accidents, which can be translated into higher operating, maintenance, administrative, and inventory costs, as well as into the private and social costs of congestion and pollution. Thus, for any given right-of-way or line-haul, as the volume of traffic rises, at some point unit costs begin to rise—often quite sharply. At this point economic capacity may be said to have been reached.

Of course, the calculation of this critical point and, indeed, the relationship between costs and volume are exceedingly complex. Not

55. Charles W. Hoppe, "Volume Spells Profits—Or Does It?" *Modern Railroads*, March 1974, p.59.

only is the measurement of the appropriate traffic or output units conceptually ambiguous, but equally serious problems exist with respect to the amount and nature of the private and social costs to be considered and the overall impact on service quality. As has aptly been said, "the capacity of a specific railroad line is not easily subject to generalization."[56]

In Part II we will return to the concept of capacity with reference to benefit-cost analysis where the point or traffic volume beyond which unit costs begin to rise (i.e., economic capacity) is crucial for benefit estimation. In the present connection, the various studies purporting to examine economies of scale may have confused them with economies of density. However, the way the latter relate to capacity (namely, excess capacity) is also somewhat ambiguous to the extent that the notion of capacity and its measurement are ambiguous.

## Conclusion

In the study of cost concepts and rail cost functions very few firm conclusions are possible regarding such important notions as short-run or long-run costs, economies of scale or density, or railway capacity. The realm of cost, at least as far as railway costs are concerned, is as nebulous (or concrete) as the realm of demand. Despite the vastly greater quantity of data available on costs as compared with demand, considerable dispute remains regarding these issues. From the various studies noted in this chapter, as well as others, one can conclude that railway cost behavior is not very well understood. For *some* railways, in *some* parts of the country, over *some* periods of time, both short- and long-run costs appear to decline as size and/or density increase. But this is not universally true. Much depends on what data were used and how they were used. The railway cost function, if one exists, remains a puzzle, perhaps because the industry is subject to large costs that are fixed, joint, and otherwise indivisible. These costs in turn relate to the enormous discrepancy between a reasonable conception of an output unit (e.g., train-journey) and a pricing or sales unit in terms of hundredweight, tons, or ton-miles. Perhaps an examination of a transport mode having few of these characteristics, or having them to a smaller degree, will lead to less ambiguous results. In anticipation, we turn next to the motor carrier industry (or industries). Once again, however, the reader needs to be forewarned that although certain aspects of trucking costs are basically different from those of rail, other problems make it difficult to determine motor carrier cost functions. Indeed, if anything, there

---

56. Ibid., p.60.

is more vigorous dispute over the economies-of-scale issue in trucking than in rail.

## Motor Carrier Cost Functions

One of the reasons that railway costs per shipment or per unit of output are so complex and difficult to pinpoint is that railroads provide and maintain their own right-of-way. Allocating right-of-way costs to any particular output or sales unit inevitably involves a good deal of arbitrary averaging regardless of cost-finding technique. The motor carriers are luckier in this connection. Their right-of-way is publicly provided and financed largely by "user" charges. Thus what is essentially an "indivisible" or quasi-fixed cost for the railroads, in the sense that maintenance of the right-of-way is largely independent of changes in traffic volume in the short run,[57] is converted by the circumstances of ownership into a variable cost for motor carriers. The issue of whether commercial motor carriers, or at least those competing with railroads, pay the "correct" amount for their use of publicly provided highways is extremely complex, for precisely the same reasons that the costs of a railway right-of-way is difficult to assign to any particular use of that right-of-way. However, even more complex problems emerge in connection with the motor carriers' right-of-way. Highways are multipurpose facilities built by public authorities for various reasons, including the needs of commerce, private travel or transport, national or regional development, national defense, and the creation of jobs when large-scale unemployment exists. The motor carrier right-of-way does not exist solely for the private profit of the motor carriers. Thus, the proportion of highway costs that *should* on either efficiency or equity criteria be collected from particular user and non-user groups becomes a critical problem. Indeed, the whole problem of how much particular users and non-users *should* pay has normally been approached in terms of equity rather than efficiency. In the subsequent discussion we first seek to establish efficiency criteria for highway user charges and then examine some allocative techniques that have been developed and used in the past.

### The Economics of Highway User Charges

The *efficiency* criterion for highway pricing requires setting a "price" per vehicle journey for use of an existing highway segment

---

57. The idea of indivisible cost "permits" railways to defer certain maintenance expenditures. However, if they are deferred too long, the quality of service will deteriorate, and the vicious circle of reduced quality, reduced business, reduced profits, reduced maintenance, and reduced quality will begin or continue, as is typical of much recent railroad experience.

equal to the short-run marginal social cost occasioned by the particular vehicle journey. If excess capacity exists, as would normally be the case with respect to intercity highways and rural roads (except near urban centers), short-run marginal cost boils down to the variable portion of maintenance, supervision, and administrative expenses. This analysis is, of course, extremely simple and straightforward conceptually but raises a host of problems in practice. Conceptually, we can envisage a demand schedule for vehicle journeys related to the cost per vehicle journey or trip over a particular highway segment. For any highway segment, there exists a sort of demand for its services (e.g., access between or past two points) that is a function of the nature of the activity or economic attraction of the two points or in the region. Similarly, one can envisage travel costs that depend on the nature of the highway in terms of width, surface, gradients, curvature, etc. Assume that these features of the highway are given and that all vehicles are the same and all drivers perform equally, so that each vehicle trip occasions the same costs per mile of travel for any given level of traffic. We can then determine the cost behavior related to the number of vehicle trips per time period (hour, day, week, year, etc.) for the highway segment under consideration. Such costs are assumed to behave roughly as indicated in Figure 2.5.

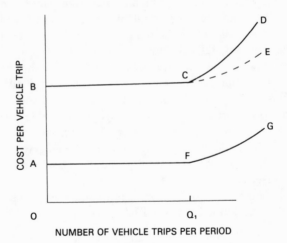

Fig. 2.5            NUMBER OF VEHICLE TRIPS PER PERIOD

For an existing highway there are two sets of costs: those associated with the vehicle itself—such as the driver's time, wages, or opportunity costs of time spent traveling on his own account; the gas and oil consumed; wear and tear on tires; and physical deterioration of the vehicle, which are usually borne by the vehicle owner but which represent resources used up for each vehicle journey; and those associated with the highway itself—damage to the road and administrative costs (such as for policing), which are usually borne by some public authority.

The first set of costs (expressed in pecuniary terms) per vehicle trip is usually regarded as being constant up to some point short of "capacity" as the number of vehicle trips per unit of time (commonly referred to as average daily traffic, *ADT*) increases over any given highway segment. They are pictured initially as an amount *AB* along *BCE* up to a level of highway use or highway density $OQ_1$. This representation implies that as long as an extra vehicle trip does not impede the existing traffic flow by reducing average speed or by increasing the amount of maneuvering necessary or the number of stops and starts, unit operating costs are constant for each vehicle trip. Similarly, the wear and tear on the highway and administrative costs are believed to be constant up to, and often beyond, $Q_1$. These costs are represented by *OA* in Figure 2.5. The total social costs are the sum of the two sets of costs up to $Q_1$ trips.

However, beyond a certain point, in this case $Q_1$, both sets of costs per vehicle trip tend to rise. Both need not begin to increase at the same traffic density, but for simplicity of exposition let us assume they do. Thus total social cost per vehicle journey begins to rise along *CD*, which exceeds the sum of the average operating costs along *CE* and the wear and tear plus administrative costs along *FG* because the extra or marginal cost per vehicle trip beyond $Q_1$ is imposed on *all* users—hence $MC > AC$.

*Vehicle Operating Costs.* As speeds drop below a certain average, often around 30–40 mph, depending on vehicle type and road conditions, fuel consumption in terms of gallons per mile begins to rise, and thus fuel consumption per vehicle trip will rise. On the other hand, if average speed decreases from levels well above 40 mph, fuel consumption will decline per vehicle trip. However, in either case, travel time per vehicle trip rises as average speed declines, and that, combined with the behavior of other operating costs, usually means that for higher densities there are higher operating costs per vehicle trip. This is all the more apparent when one considers that beyond $Q_1$ each additional vehicle trip adds not only to its own costs via reduced average speed but to all others as well. Thus, the total amount of resources used up by the addition of extra trips beyond $Q_1$ may be far in excess of that for a single vehicle.[58]

---

58. Vehicle cost behavior is in reality much more complex than is implied here. For some engineering details and the behavior of the separate components of motor vehicle running costs, see R. Winfrey, *Economic Analysis for Highways* (Scranton: International Textbook Co., 1969), chaps. 13 and 14. A simplified but more economically oriented discussion of the above, although mainly relevant to urban travel, is given in Mohring, chaps. 3 and 4.

*Highway Costs.* As density along a highway increases beyond a certain point, say, $Q_1$, it is probable that the wear and tear on the highway surface per vehicle trip does not increase much. Indeed, some linear regressions of maintenance expenditures against average daily traffic yield reasonably high coefficients of correlation.[59] On the other hand, others report sharply rising maintenance costs after ADT reaches some critical level.[60] One of the many problems in this connection is the definition of "maintenance" expenditures. Indeed, the distinction between maintenance and capital outlays is inherently arbitrary. Maintenance expenditures can often be deferred for longish periods of time in response to financial constraints of the highway department; or they can be accelerated if the financial situation improves. Thus, year-to-year variations of such expenditures may reflect the particular financial condition of the highway department rather than variation in ADT.

On the other hand, as traffic density rises, despite lower average speeds, more careful policing is needed and accidents tend to increase, adding to the costs, not all of which are borne directly by vehicle owners. It is probable that the costs for police and accidents per vehicle trip also rise after point $Q_1$ in Figure 2.5.

Let us add to Figure 2.5 the *demand* for vehicle trips, which is related more or less inversely to the cost or price of highway use. It is believed to be decreasing because of the diminishing evaluation of the "worth" of successive vehicle trips per unit of time. Now it is possible to specify an "efficient user charge." Two "demands for vehicle trips per unit of time" are shown in Figure 2.6. Let us examine $D_1$ first. At the point where the valuation that generators of vehicle trips place on each trip equals the marginal social cost of providing the extra trip, we have a condition of optimal efficiency: the valuation of one or more fewer trips exceeds the cost of making them, and, conversely, the valuation of additional vehicle trips is less than the costs of making them.[61] This point is clearly $OQ^*$, which implies an efficient user charge of $Q^*H + JK$. The highway administrator should collect not only the *highway* costs occasioned by the additional vehicle

59. Regressions of the form $M = a + b(ADT)$, where $M$ = maintenance expenditures, are often made. High correlation coefficients imply constancy of variable maintenance costs $b$. See R. M. Soberman, "Economic Analysis of Highway Design in Developing Countries," Highway Research Record No. 115, Highway Research Board, Washington, D.C., 1966.

60. Above 1,000 ADT, according to an early report (Highway Research Board Bulletin 155, Highway Research Board, Washington, D.C., 1957).

61. We will discuss this idea more fully later, when examining optimal pricing and transport investment criteria. The reader may recognize it as maximizing the sum of producers' plus consumers' surplus.

trips but an additional amount *JK* which is needed to ration the demand to *OQ\**. The amount *JK* is often referred to as a "congestion-cost" levy.

On the other hand, if the demand for trips is at a lower level, such as $D_2$, the optimal user charge is simply the incremental cost of an additional trip, which is constant at *OA* and which, combined with the incremental vehicle operating cost, will just ration the demand to *OQ\*\**.

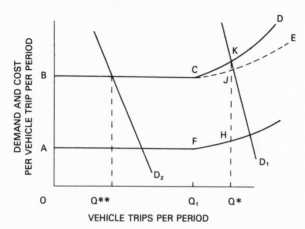

Fig. 2.6                     VEHICLE TRIPS PER PERIOD

Since this book is concerned with *intercity* freight transport, and since intercity and rural highways are seldom congested to the extent that urban roads are, except as the vehicles approach urban areas or along circumferential highways, efficient user charges will normally not be expected to cover more than the short-run variable costs associated with vehicle trips; i.e., in most cases, the demand for trips will intersect the linear portion of operating and highway costs. The need to calculate the required additional congestion cost is thus vastly reduced. While this simplifies our task, there remain many formidable conceptual problems, especially in terms of quantifying and applying efficient user charges.

### Conceptual and Practical Problems of Implementation of Efficient User Charges

The foregoing, though correct in principle, made several simplifying assumptions, including the following:

homogeneous vehicles and drivers
fixed demand per unit of time
the notion of highway capacity

a given highway type in terms of number of lanes, curvature, nature of the surface, rise and fall, roadside obstructions, and the like.

Let us explore the analytical and empirical difficulties that result from modifying these assumptions and coming closer to reality.

*Homogeneous Vehicles and Drivers.* The vehicle fleet of all nations is exceedingly heterogeneous and ranges from animal-drawn carts in the poorer countries (including Amish horse-drawn carts in the United States) to double- and even triple-bottom trucks. Obviously, vehicles of different size, weight, and speed capability will affect the number of vehicles that may pass a given point on a given highway per unit of time. Even the passenger car classification hides a wide variety of weights, sizes, and speeds; as do light trucks, heavy trucks, buses, and campers. To speak, then, of a single homogeneous vehicle type is an enormous abstraction. It is, of course, possible to pretend that there are "passenger car equivalents," and that all vehicles can be translated into some basic vehicle type chosen as the standard.[62] For example, a standard-sized truck may be construed as the equivalent of three or four passenger cars when estimating total number of vehicles. Similar "equivalents" may be established for as many vehicle-type classifications as is deemed reasonable to make. For the economics of the case, the purpose is to determine such equivalents in a manner that represents the differential costs, especially with respect to highway costs, including congestion as well as wear and tear and administration. Thus, to determine the truck-passenger-car equivalent (*pce*) one needs to be able to ascertain the differential highway costs of "standard" trucks vis-à-vis cars. If this can be done, then the meaning to be attached to any statement is that if the truck *pce* is said to be 3, the standard truck occasions three times the highway costs (wear and tear, etc., plus congestion) that a standard passenger car does.

Conceptually, then, each vehicle can be translated into some standard (say, smallest passenger car) in terms of highway-cost occasioning equivalents,[63] but we must also consider the fact that *pce*s (in whatever terms one chooses as a kind of Walrasian "numeraire")

---

62. See D. Winch, *The Economics of Highway Planning* (Toronto: University of Toronto Press, 1963), p.21.

63. Indeed, this procedure has long historical precedents in economic analysis, especially with respect to the labor theory of value. Both Ricardo and Marx reduced different qualities of labor into equivalent quantities by admittedly crude, circular, and/or arbitrary notions. Similarly, economists have treated "capital" in the abstract, even though it is a vast heterogeneous amalgam, and attempted to render it homogeneous in terms of "vintage" capital or in terms of "degrees of productiveness." Analytically, this is the same as talking about a "homogeneous vehicle stock" and homogeneous rates of flow per unit of time along a given length of highway.

vary among every highway type. For example, a truck *pce* of 3 determined along a straight, flat stretch of four-lane interstate highway cannot be applied to a narrow, two-lane road through mountainous terrain with many curves even if the distance is the same. We must note that for different sets of highway specifications as well as varying weather there are systematic variations among *pces*.

If we then note varying driver capabilities and desires with respect to average speed at varying times and under differing circumstances, the probable combinations of *pces* and the very concept of *the* vehicle fleet in homogeneous terms lose much in the way of relevance or even meaning. This is especially true if *pces* are viewed in economic terms as representing the differential costs occasioned under all possible combinations of vehicle types, highway, weather, and driver conditions.

Finally, we may note the implicit assumption underlying the efficient user-charge analysis that for each highway segment each vehicle trip is of equivalent length. That is, for the marginal social cost to behave in the manner portrayed in figures 2.5 and 2.6, each vehicle trip must cover the same distance so that a single congestion-plus-cost-occasioned tax or price can be established for our homogeneous (in terms of *pces*) vehicles. This is clearly not the case even conceptually unless one is willing to argue that there are mileage-equivalent vehicle trips or that the costs occasioned are strictly proportional to mileage for each *pce*.

Yet for any given road connecting two urban centers, there is a general pattern of heavy utilization close to each center, which consistently tapers off as one approaches the midway point. The level of traffic volume also depends on whether the segment in question is part of a through route connecting two or more other, presumably larger, in the traffic-generating sense, centers. One needs, therefore, to define the relevant highway segment to ascertain the number of vehicle trips and costs pertaining to it. Thus, for interurban links, one needs to determine which segments are "congested" and which are "free flowing" in terms of $D_1$ and $D_2$ of Figure 2.6. In addition, particular segments may have different characteristics that influence maintenance costs or travel behavior related to subsoil characteristics or other phenomena, such as rise and fall, number of curves. Delineating the "relevant" segment becomes a practical matter in specific situations.

*Fixed Demand Per Unit of Time.* However one defines *pce* or the "relevant" length of highway, there is a problem of demand shifts within the unit of time being considered. There are clearly seasonal variations within the year related to weather and local, regional, or national vacation periods; weekly variations reflecting workday and weekend activities; and daily variations reflecting the normal hours of beginning and ending work and, to a lesser extent, hourly variations. Traffic density and therefore costs of travel vary according to each of these kinds of variation. Congestion at one time of the day, week, month, or year will be matched by no congestion at most times of the day, week, month, or year; hence, $D_1$ shifts to $D_2$ and back, depending on "time." This gives rise to the questions, problems, and/or possibilities of "peak/off-peak" pricing to ration traffic.[64] But it also means that no single, optimally efficient user charge is possible for each vehicle journey since the time of day, week, month, etc., makes an enormous difference between congestion and noncongestion, between circumstances envisioned as $D_1$ and as $D_2$ in Figure 2.6.

*The Notion of Highway Capacity.* As noted with respect to rail right-of-way and implicit in the discussion of user charges, the concept of "capacity" is extremely elusive. On the one hand, capacity of any given right-of-way may be construed in terms of the total possible physical vehicular movements along it (or, more correctly, the number of vehicles passing by a fixed point) during an interval of time, regardless of cost. This "conveyor-belt" approach asserts that at any fixed speed for each (homogeneous) vehicle, a determinate number of vehicles *can* pass a given point per time period if in a continuous flow. It assumes that at all points along the right-of-way, or relevant road segment, the traffic level is constant, contrary to observed differences near urban centers or intersections. The maximum number of vehicles that is technologically possible depends on the coordination of all the vehicles so that they travel at the same speed without breakdown; the conditions of the right-of-way; the average, coordinated speed that is possible to avoid breakdown or interference with the traffic flow. On the other hand, capacity can refer to the economical or efficient number of vehicles that can traverse a given right-of-way during a period of time.

That an enormous gap between these two concepts of capacity exists cannot be doubted. Indeed, a classic study of highway capacity defines it as "the maximum number of vehicles which has a reasonable expectation of passing over a given section of a lane or a roadway in one direction (or in both directions for a two-lane or three-lane highway) during a given time period under prevailing roadway and traffic conditions."[65] Prevailing "roadway" conditions are those "that are established by the physical features of the roadway," while "traffic"

64. This pricing problem is discussed in chap. 3.
65. Highway Research Board, *Highway Capacity Manual*, Special Report 87 (Washington, D.C., 1965), p.5.

conditions depend on the nature of the traffic (in terms of volume and composition), which may be "changed from hour to hour" or over any other time period."[66] But even when such "prevailing conditions" are fixed, any roadway can and normally will accommodate a wide variety of traffic volumes at *varying levels of service,* which is a "qualitative measure of the effect of a number of factors which include speed and travel time, traffic interruption, freedom to maneuver, safety, driving comfort and convenience and operations costs."[67] In short, for any given highway segment, "capacity" depends on the traffic composition; the variation of total traffic and its composition hourly, daily, weekly, monthly, and annually; and some notion of minimally acceptable service levels for a variety of users.

At the moment, we are taking the existing right-of-way as given (expansions or contractions thereof are considered in Part II under efficient *investment* criteria) and seeking to ascertain efficient user charges regardless of whether the present system is efficient; regardless of whether in particular regions it is excessive or deficient. An *economic* conception of "capacity" therefore depends on the demand for trip journeys along the existing rights-of-way. As Walters notes, "there are as many definitions of . . . capacity as there are demand curves."[68] Conceptually, therefore, the degree of excess road capacity is extremely elusive, and thus the point at which unit costs begin to rise ($Q_1$ in Figures 2.5 and 2.6) is even more so in any practical sense.

*A Given Highway Type.* Highways obviously differ radically in width, number of lanes, shoulder width, surface type, gradients, roadside obstructions, and so on. For each variation, highway costs (operating plus maintenance) will differ for each vehicle trip. When these costs are combined with the variety of vehicles and shifting demands during different periods, we have a seemingly infinite number of efficient user charges. While it is conceptually possible to envisage such a system of charges (i.e., a separate charge for every vehicle trip, which varies among vehicles, highway types, time of journey, weather conditions, and extent of capacity utilization), the principle can only be applied in an extremely broad fashion. Ingenious schemes have been proposed involving sensors at many points in the right-of-way and meters under each vehicle showing the time of day the vehicle passes over the sensor. These schemes would make a separate charge at each point depending on some or all of the characteristics noted above. Their practicability is highly questionable, but even if they were practicable, the establishment of an efficient charging schedule

66. Ibid, pp.6–7.
67. Ibid., p.7.
68. *The Economics of Road User Charges,* p.26.

for each characteristic cannot be done unambiguously. Thus, while the principle underlying the efficient user charge is correct, it is exceedingly difficult to implement even if the basic information on costs and cost behavior is available. Innumerable compromises between the theory and its application are obviously inevitable.

It is largely for these reasons that highway-user-charging schemes rely more on what each vehicle type *should* pay rather than on what efficiency considerations dictate. The present state of the actual analysis and implementation of user charges is thus based more on considerations of equity, reasonableness, and administrative tractability. Strenuous efforts have been devoted to finding plausible justifications for charging particular users and non-users particular amounts. Often they result in charging schemes that seriously violate efficiency criteria and thus lead to economic waste. But the problems of attempting to measure efficient user charges, with their enormous variability over time, space, and highway types, suggest that the benefits from such a charging scheme may not be worth the costs of measuring, administering, and policing a pricing system based on such elusive criteria. As Walters notes, "our [empirical] knowledge of [efficient user charges] is so scant and approximate that they can be described only in the most general terms."[69]

We turn now to an examination of attempts to determine "equitable" user and non-user charges, or, as it is more often referred to, the "highway cost allocation problem."

## The Highway Cost Allocation Problem

The practical difficulties of determining an *efficient* user charge and applying it to specific vehicle journeys have led to a shift of emphasis from efficiency to equity criteria. This trend, however, raises more complex and even philosophical issues concerning what is meant by "equity" in the context of highway finance. Simply stated, we seek a method of allocating to highway users and non-user beneficiaries a share of annual highway expenditures that is broadly deemed to be "fair" or "equitable" on some basis, usually assumed or asserted to be in terms of relative costs occasioned or relative benefits received—the well-known principle of cost vis-à-vis value of service, except in this instance it is applied to a publicly provided facility.

At the start there are difficulties concerning two main issues: How much of the total annual expenditures on highways should be in-

---

69. Ibid., p.191. See also H. Mohring and M. Harwitz, *Highway Benefits* (Evanston: Northwestern University Press, 1962), chap. 2, for an early discussion of the equity vis-à-vis efficiency criteria for pricing highway services.

cluded in the annual amounts to be collected? How shall we distinguish between general taxes and those taxes or charges specifically designed on efficiency or equity terms to ration highway use or equitably spread the annual costs among those directly affected by highways?

*The Annual Expenditures to be Recouped.* Highway cost allocation schemes in the United States have generally used estimates of *total* highway expenditures for one year (or averaged over several years) as the proper amounts that need to be collected and allocated. Such totals include capital improvements as well as maintenance, administration, policing, and debt expenditures[70]—a sort of total cash-flow approach on an annual basis. The assumption is that all highway costs (including capital costs) are to be covered by receipts derived from users of the highways and other direct beneficiaries or cost-occasioners. However, for an existing highway system it is not evident that efficient user charges will, in fact, lead to revenues just sufficient to cover costs. In areas where congestion costs are imposed revenues may exceed costs, depending on how much in the way of capital expenditures is made; in areas of excess capacity, revenues will fall short of costs by amounts related to the capital expenditures. This would imply reducing user charges in congested areas and raising them in uncongested areas—a policy that would lead to further economic waste. Since the overall deficit or surplus for any highway system or segment would depend largely on the extent of capital outlays and since these should be determined by principles of benefit-cost analyses (to be examined later), efficient charging for highways has nothing to do with whether or not the highway authority covers its costs with receipts.

On the other hand, if the highway system as a whole is extensively subsidized, the gap between private and social costs is widened with attendant economic waste. For example, if the actual maintenance costs of a highway are $OA$ but the charge to users is only $OB$, with a subsidy paid from general tax receipts of $AB$, for any demand $DD$ (assume for simplicity that all other costs of using the highway are zero), the number of vehicle trips will be $OQ_1$. But at $OQ_1$, the total (social plus private) cost is $OA$, whereas the marginal valuation of the $Q_1$th trip is only $Q_1B$ (or $OB$). Indeed, for all vehicle trips beyond $OQ_2$, there is economic waste equal to the difference between the demand $DD$ and the total cost per trip $OA$. The total waste is the triangle $CBD$

70. See, for example, *Allocation of Highway Cost Responsibility and Tax Payments, 1969*, prepared for U.S. Department of Transportation, Federal Highway Administration and Bureau of Public Roads, May 1970, pp.14–20, for a discussion of each of these spending categories.

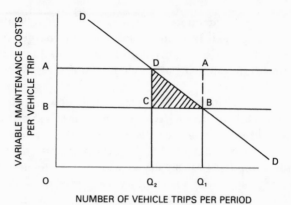

Fig. 2.7                    NUMBER OF VEHICLE TRIPS PER PERIOD

$= \frac{1}{2}(Q_1 - Q_2)(OA - OB)$.[71] Thus subsidy will lead to inefficient use of existing facilities. This implies that all variable maintenance, administrative, etc., costs should on efficiency grounds be covered by appropriate charges—in this case $OA$—per vehicle trip.

Since it appears that intercity highways are generally uncongested and that the variable costs are mostly linear, the case for covering at least the variable costs with receipts is especially compelling. This will lead to revenue surpluses if such costs are rising and deficits if costs are falling, as noted earlier. What to do with the surpluses or how to finance the deficits are secondary problems. However, the main point is that surpluses should not suggest lower charges, for they would accentuate congestion; nor should deficits lead to higher charges, for they would increase excess capacity. Rather, if the efficient user charge has been imposed, it should not be altered—the deficits or surpluses that may result give rise to investment or disinvestment decisions requiring a different form of analysis than that relevant to efficient pricing of existing facilities. Thus the amount of expenditures to be recouped need not be determined by the total highway expenditures actually made during a particular time period on grounds of efficiency.

On grounds of *equity*, the problem is more complex and arbitrary. The argument is often heard that since railways must cover their right-of-way costs from users, highways should do the same. The extent to which motor carriers pay the efficient user charge for their use of the highways should provide competitive equality with respect to rail-truck competition, and that will happen whether or not the highway authority's budget is in balance.

However, the argument is often extended to mean that the right-of-way costs should be financed *on the same basis* by each mode, espe-

---

71. This is the familiar "welfare" triangle, and will be discussed in chap. 3.

cially in situations where they are in direct competition. The rail right-of-way is not deemed to be fundamentally different from a highway. The fact that highways are owned and maintained by governmental bodies but used by others whereas railways and rolling stock are under common ownership should not, it is alleged, change their basic similarity. Thus, as noted earlier, what is largely an indivisible cost for the railroads is converted by the circumstances of ownership into a variable cost for motor carriers. Because of this difference, it is frequently suggested that the government buy the rail right-of-way and provide it on a user basis to rail companies. Then both truck and rail companies would be financing the indivisible costs associated with use of the right-of-way in the same fashion. If each paid the variable costs of a noncongested way, greater competitive equality would result since both modes would be operating under similar rules and handicaps.

While it is the railway interests who usually advance this proposal, presumably in the belief that it would benefit their net revenue position, in reality it is the trucking interests who are disadvantaged by the present situation.[72] The disadvantage arises because truck marginal cost for a particular movement inevitably includes a portion of what is an indivisible cost to the railway ( e.g., maintenance of the highway is paid largely by the gas tax, which is a variable cost to the motor carrier). Rails could quote a rate in specific competitive situations down to directly variable cost, which would not contribute to the indivisible costs associated with right-of-way ownership, and make it up on other, less competitive traffic. Other things being equal, this puts trucks at a disadvantage.

The basic issue is whether the present differences in right-of-way ownership are in some sense inherent in the two technologies or more in the nature of an historical accident that leads to different techniques of financing right-of-way costs. In short, is rail technology sufficiently distinct from that of truck to require joint ownership, or at least control, of *both* the rolling stock and the right-of-way?

A railway has been defined as "merely a specialized road,"[73] but one so highly specialized that the flow of vehicles must be exactly con-

---

72. This assumes, of course, that trucks are now paying an efficient or equitable user charge and that the railways would, too, under a track nationalization scheme. Part of the rail argument is that trucks now do not pay a "fair share" for publicly provided facilities. We will investigate this below. The other part of the rail argument is that the "fixed charges" associated with debt payment on the right-of-way; property taxes; and maintenance, often on little-used trackage, mainly branch lines, would be avoided under track nationalization.

73. Sir Reginald Wilson, "Technical Modernization and New Freight Charges on British Railways," paper read at the National Conference of the British Institute of Management, November 28, 1958, p.3.

trolled, a condition that implies joint operation under common or single control but does not necessarily mean common ownership. Indeed, there are many industrially owned rail cars that use the rail company's right-of-way, and in the early days of railroading the initial intent was to have separate companies own the right-of-way and lease or rent it to anyone possessing appropriately designed vehicles. All such attempts failed.[74] In practice, joint ownership appeared to provide a better mechanism for close control than did the alternative, although in theory this need not be the case. In fact, "there are no valid precedents for suggesting that separation of ownership and control of fixed plant from train operations is operationally feasible. To the contrary, in the past, substantial practical problems inherent in such separation have resulted in its rejection whenever the matter was considered."[75]

Motor transport does not have the problem of exact control because it is not subject to the discipline of a fixed track. Its vehicles can maneuver on a paved surface to pass slower-moving traffic. This situation permits, but does not in principle require, separate ownership by myriad shippers and travelers of vehicles and by-and-large unrestricted use of the right-of-way, certainly along uncongested interurban roads. While tandem trailers are becoming more common and hence more "railroad-like," it is difficult to envision much more than triple-bottoms on the highway and certainly nothing comparable to trains of 50 to 80 boxcars. Nor with the ubiquitous and highly diverse automotive fleet is it easy to conceive of the sort of close control of access of the kind required to run frequent trains at high speed.[76]

In short, the different technologies create the possibilities for differing ownership, and historical evidence may suggest that the type of

---

74. For details in various countries, see Richardson Associates' (New York) report to the Association of American Railroads, *Operating and Financial Implications of Government Takeover of the U.S. Railroad Industry's Fixed Plant,* May 1975, Appendix.

75. Ibid., pp.11–12.

76. "In order to understand the fundamental differences between a train running on a track and a truck running on a highway, it is necessary to appreciate the fact that train routing and direction are carried out not by 'steering' the engine, but rather by switching track connections. Hence, while a motor vehicle can simply enter, move upon, and exit more or less at will from the highway system . . . a train must await clearances from a central coordinator to enter, move upon, and exit from main line track. . . . [This] requires close coordination of train crews and dispatching forces.

Moreover, ability to provide reliable and dependable rail . . . service requires effective coordination and scheduling of the use of the track network, which can only be achieved when the rail operator retains integrated control of track and train operations.

It is not surprising, therefore, that historically no serious attempts have been made to separate these two closely related functions or otherwise deprive the rail operator of the ability to control the use of fixed rail plant" (Ibid., pp.3–4).

ownership represents an inherent difference.[77] Thus suggestions for a nationalized rail right-of-way are in essence thinly veiled plans for subsidy to relieve the railways of most or all of the financial costs of track ownership. Such a subsidy could be provided directly without the sort of (probably) unworkable institutional shake-up implicit in separating track ownership from rolling stock.

While the matter of subsidy is not directly related to the amount of highway expenditures that should be recouped from users and non-user beneficiaries, it does suggest that the amount and the share allocated to motor carriers has wide ramifications for intercarrier competition as well as for financing the indivisible costs.

*General Taxes vs. Special Charges for Highways.* Highway services are not sold in the same fashion as most other goods and services because, inter alia, it is not possible to price each vehicle trip in the same way as one monitors and prices each kilowatt-hour of electricity or the sale of each television set. If we agree that for efficiency or equity considerations users and non-user beneficiaries should pay a price for highways and their use (just as rail and air users pay, via rates and fares, for use of rights-of-way), what is the best way to price highway services? The only feasible way is to institute some special tax, toll, or other charge over and above the level of general taxation that would otherwise prevail and specifically relate it to highway costs and/or benefits. In short, it is necessary to "synthesize" a market.[78]

The problem is to decide which taxes or charges to construe as highway user charges or as appropriate charges for non-user beneficiaries. There already exist property, sales, income, and other sorts of taxes, as well as import duties that inevitably fall on vehicles, parts, and fuel. Given a general sales tax of X% applicable to purchases of all goods and services, it is difficult to argue that a certain proportion of that represents a user charge simply because it is applicable to vehicles, parts, and fuel. A similar situation exists with respect to import duties. A specific highway-related user charge must refer to a *differentially* higher tax, duty, toll, etc., than would otherwise exist and that is especially designed to finance the costs of the highway system. For example, if a state sales tax of 6% is applicable to a wide variety of goods and services, the 6% paid for purchase of a new

---

77. A somewhat more sympathetic approach to nationalized track is presented in R. L. Banks & Associates, *Roadbed Costs and Cost Relief for Canada's Contiguous Railways,* Report to the Federal-Provincial Committee on Western Transportation, March 14, 1975. However, chaps. 14 and 15 highlight the enormous complexities and problems involved, thereby implying conclusions similar to those of Richardson Associates cited above.

78. D. Winch, p.7.

truck cannot logically be construed as a user charge. If a special surcharge were placed on trucks or other vehicle purchases so that the total tax amounted to 10%, then 4% may be viewed as a user charge.

In practice, most taxes on vehicles and fuel existed before any intent to simulate a special price for highway use. The proceeds went to the general fund in the same manner as did income taxes and other general taxes. There was never any intent at either the state or the federal level to allocate all such taxes on vehicles and fuel or certain property taxes exclusively to highways. Indeed, there has seldom been any attempt to link taxes paid by any industry to public expenditures on behalf of that industry. Even the special excise taxes on cigarettes and whiskey are levied with no presumption that the proceeds are to be spent for research on lung cancer or alcoholism.

In 1956 the federal Highway Trust Fund was created. All or some of the proceeds of federal excise taxes on motor fuel, tires, tubes, retread rubber, trucks, buses, trailers, and heavy vehicles were henceforth automatically allocated to the Fund and presumed to be *user* charges. Some of them were specifically changed or added at the time, but many were originally enacted for quite different purposes[79] and explicitly regarded more as sources of general revenues than as special imposts on highway users. Nor was there any attempt to determine "the amount which should be raised for highway expenditures and the amount of pure taxation which should be imposed on highway users to raise revenues for non-highway purposes."[80] Linking previous taxes to highway expenditures or earmarking a portion of them does not constitute a "user charge" in any meaningful sense of that term. Present federal highway user taxation is thus a hodgepodge of pure taxation and user charge. We have no inkling of the proportions represented by either. It is totally inadequate as a synthesized "price" in terms of either equity or efficiency. The same is even more apparent at the state level, where large-scale "diversions" regularly occur even in states where funds are earmarked.[81]

Thus, the "price" currently paid by highway users, even if (inappropriately) called a user charge and even if earmarked for a specific highway trust fund, is a far cry from a synthetic market price. This makes it all the more difficult to determine whether motor carriers are paying the "correct" amounts for their use of the highways, espe-

---

79. For some illustrative examples see J. Munro and G. W. Wilson, *Road Transportation: History and Economics*, Indiana Readings in Business, no.35 (Bloomington: Indiana University, October 1962), pp.115–16.
80. Winch, p.146.
81. For some examples, see ibid., pp.106ff.

cially when combined with the ambiguity with respect to the "correct" total amount to be allocated among all users and non-user beneficiaries.

## The Basic Logic of Equitable Highway Cost Allocation

Let us *assume* that the problems of the correct total expenditures to be allocated and the correct version of what constitutes a user charge can be or have been solved. We are still left with the problem of equity of highway allocation. The problem is usually approached in two stages: the first involves the amounts that should be paid by users and non-user beneficiaries in the aggregate; the second involves the amounts that should be paid by specifically identified users and non-users; among the former are, of course, motor carriers.

### STAGE 1: THE APPROPRIATE USER AND NON-USER SHARE

Assume the annual expenditures for a particular highway system are estimated at $X billion. These expenditures include all maintenance, administrative, and operating expenses deemed essential for safe, economical highway use and capital outlays. The precise estimation of what amount is really "essential" and the inclusion of capital expenses are troublesome. But let us assume that the estimate of $X billion is reasonably representative of reality—at least for determining the amount that needs to be allocated on equity, not efficiency, grounds. Let us assume further that only three types of highways are involved in this system: main intercity highways, local and county roads, and city streets. Assume further that each type is homogeneous within each classification and that "essential" annual expenditures are $A, $B, and $C billion, respectively, where $X = $A +$B + $C.

The essence of the problem at this stage is to determine what proportion of A, B, and C should be paid by users and non-users. Let the user shares be represented by $U_A$, $U_B$, and $U_C$, where the Us are expressed as percentages. Let the non-user share be expressed by $N_A$, $N_B$, and $N_C$. In each case the comparable Ns and Us add up to 100 percent. That is, $U_A + N_A = U_B + N_B = U_C + N_C = 100$ percent. Inserting these into the previous equation we have

$$\$X = \$A(U_A + N_A) + \$B(U_B + N_B) + \$C(U_C + N_C).$$

This equation tells us that the amount users should pay toward the $X billion is $(AU_A + BU_B + CU_C)$, while the non-users should pay $(AN_A + BN_B + CN_C)$. The objective of public policy would then be to ensure that each group was taxed the appropriate amount.

It is no simple task to estimate the various Us and Ns. If we look at some of the "non-users," such as the military, property owners, the outdoor advertising industry, and perhaps even "the general public," it is clear that each receives a variety of benefits from the existence and adequate upkeep of the highway system and each "occasions" some amount of the highway expenditures. For example, the Department of Defense needs some excess highway capacity in the event of an enemy attack and thereby derives some benefit from such capacity independently of actual use. Likewise, to the extent that highways lead to more efficient transportation, they widen the market, increase the ability to specialize, and thus contribute to higher productivity in the economy as a whole—to this extent the general public receives benefits. Property owners obtain access to their homes or businesses, which yields benefits greater than their relative use thereof. At the same time, each of these groups is responsible to some degree for the annual costs. For example, bridges must be built of better design to accommodate some heavy military vehicles, and the excess highway capacity that might be needed in case of war or emergency imposes additional costs.

For users a similar pattern of "benefits" and costs exists. Some of the benefits may be psychological, as when a passenger car drives along a smooth, scenic, well-constructed, limited-access highway, or some may represent cost savings to the driver or firm incidental to such a highway. Constructing highways of various types for direct use thereof obviously occasions substantial costs. So there is again a large variety of costs and benefits. It is impossible to aggregate and compare them among users and non-users in a scientific way. It is not therefore surprising that a variety of techniques have provided widely divergent estimates of the $Us$ and $Ns$, varying between 10 and 90 percent for users for secondary and local roads and zero to 20 percent for users for primary highways.[82]

Both the great divergence in assigned responsibility to motor vehicle users for the highway system and the many different techniques used to arrive at these figures illustrate the morass one encounters in the murky arena of "equity." All that seems to be generally conceded is that the user share of highway costs *should* be greatest on primary highways, less on secondary highways, and smallest on local roads.

Two general methods—"relative use" and "earnings credit"—are used in making this division. They indicate the complexities involved and the essential arbitrariness implicit in any particular set of "fair-share" estimates.

---

82. C. Taff, *Commercial Motor Transportation* (Homewood, Ill.: Irwin, 1955), p.64.

*The Relative Use Technique.* The relative use technique seeks to assign the cost responsibility for each road and street system to two main kinds of "users" in proportion to which each system renders different kinds of service. That is, we could assume that strictly neighborhood travel (e.g., going to and from the grocery store, elementary school, and, in towns and smaller cities, place of work) within a relatively confined area is mainly an activity undertaken for other than travel purposes, whereas through travel between cities or origins and destinations extending beyond a neighborhood involves much more of a strictly travel component. Thus, it may be considered appropriate to finance highways and city streets from user taxes and other (non-user) revenue sources in proportion to the relative number of vehicle-miles associated with neighborhood (or access) service on the one hand and through travel on the other.

There is no compelling logic behind this assumption other than the view that travel *within* a narrowly confined area is different in character from travel *between* two such regions and thus represents a different kind of product or service rendered by the highway system involved. This is a form of value-of-service pricing in which costs are allocated in proportion to the relative importance of the different services yielded by a given highway system.[83]

To clarify what is involved in this technique, we shall summarize an early analysis. Two main difficulties in using this method are obtaining data in appropriate form and making workable definitions of what constitutes neighborhood as opposed to through travel. The *Final Report of the Highway Cost Allocation Study* made a threefold distinction in type of highway service and defined through traffic, access, and neighborhood service. The *access* portion of a trip was taken as "the distance in the direction of travel along the road or street serving the point of origin to the first intersection, plus the distance from the last intersection to the destination."[84] As is so often the case in empirical analyses, data limitations forced adoption of a rigid and partially arbitrary standard. The average length of a city block or street was taken to be about .08 miles, which means that the average access portion of a trip is .04 miles (half the length of an average city block).

To calculate the *neighborhood* portion of a trip it was assumed that a neighborhood consisted of a "uniform distance of one mile . . . around

83. *Final Report of the Highway Cost Allocation Study,* House Document no.54, 87th Cong., 1st sess. (Washington, D.C.: Government Printing Office, 1961), pp.111–22.
84. Ibid., p.113.

all origins and destinations," except in central business districts of towns over 5,000 population, where a uniform distance of one-half mile was used.[85]

*Through travel* was then construed as that portion of a trip (in vehicle-miles) *not* accounted for by access or neighborhood mileages.

The problem was to obtain data on the number and characteristics of individual trips to permit an evaluation of the relative number of vehicle-miles generated for each of the three types of highway service. We shall not dwell on the problems of data collection here. The results of detailed questionnaires were used to derive the percentages in Table 2.3 for 1957 for the various types of highway systems.

TABLE 2.3

*Travel According to Highway System*

| Highway System | Access Travel % | Neighbor- hood Travel % | Total % | Through Travel % |
|---|---|---|---|---|
| Interstate | | | | |
| Rural | 1.21 | 2.63 | 3.84 | 96.16 |
| Urban | .48 | 13.49 | 13.97 | 86.03 |
| Other federal aid primary | | | | |
| Rural | .76 | 3.15 | 3.91 | 96.06 |
| Urban | .65 | 22.48 | 23.13 | 76.87 |
| Federal aid secondary | | | | |
| Rural | 2.09 | 8.49 | 10.58 | 89.42 |
| Urban | .69 | 31.07 | 31.76 | 68.24 |
| Nonfederal aid | | | | |
| Rural | 16.30 | 20.26 | 36.56 | 63.44 |
| Urban | 4.90 | 62.29 | 67.19 | 32.81 |

SOURCE: *Final Report,* Table III-F-2, p.117.

The data generally conform to expectations. For example, regardless of the highway system, the travel on urban highways is relatively less of the through-travel variety than over rural routes. Furthermore, the proportion of through travel diminishes as one moves from the Interstate System to nonfederal aid highways. From the percentages in the table one can easily calculate the amount to be collected by user taxes on the one hand and other revenue sources on the other. For each highway system, simply compute the weighted average of rural and urban through travel to represent the proportion of total costs for that system that "should" be financed by user taxes. After

---

85. *Ibid.,* p.114. An alternative assumption was also utilized, but since we are merely interested in showing one way of arriving at answers in this area, we shall not introduce the second alternative.

a variety of adjustments, the *Final Report* summarized the percentage cost allocations for federal aid systems as shown in Table 2.4.

TABLE 2.4

*Cost Allocations for Federal Aid Systems*

|  | Percent Chargeable to Motor Vehicle User Taxes | Percent Chargeable to Other Revenue Sources |
|---|---|---|
| Interstate system | 94.8 | 5.2 |
| Other federal aid primary highways | 90.4 | 9.6 |
| Federal aid secondary systems | 86.0 | 14.0 |
| All federal aid systems | 93.0 | 7.0 |

SOURCE: *Final Report,* p.119.

It is worth reiterating that this system of allocation is essentially a modified version of value-of-service pricing in the sense that payment for highway costs is related to relative benefits received as measured by the different types of service—access, neighborhood, and through travel. It is not a system of pricing related to costs occasioned and hence does not conform to the economic criterion discussed earlier. It may be defended on other grounds, such as equity, fairness, or "reasonableness," but on strict economic grounds a noncost-oriented pricing policy is difficult to defend *unless it is found to be impossible to set prices on a cost-occasioned basis.* In this respect, there is an alternate way—the earnings-credit method—of making the user–non-user allocation, which bears some resemblance (albeit slight) to cost.

*The Earnings-Credit Method.* The two approaches to this technique are referred to as the "top-drawer" solution and the "bottom-drawer" solution. The first involves computing the annual average total cost per vehicle-mile ($ATC/VM$) for the "top" highway system (where the top system is defined in terms of the quality of the highway, i.e., type of surface, thickness of base, width) and then applying it to the number of vehicle-miles on all other systems. For example, assume three highway systems with total annual costs estimated as $5 billion for the top system, $3 billion for the intermediate system, and $4 billion for the bottom system. If vehicle-miles are 800 billion, 400 billion, and 300 billion, respectively, then $ATC/VM$ for the top system is 6¼ mills. When this figure is applied to each road system, the contribution to the top system is, of course, 6¼ mills × 800 billion = $5 billion; in essence the top-drawer solution requires users to pay 100 percent of the costs of the top-drawer highway. But if we apply the 6¼ mills per vehicle-mile to the number of vehicle-miles generated by the other two systems, the amounts obtained are $2.5 billion and $1.875 billion, respectively. For the intermediate and bottom systems, revenues collected via the flat 6¼ mills per vehicle-mile would fall short of costs by $0.5 billion and $2.125 billion, respectively. These differences would be made up by non-user charges.

The bottom-drawer solution requires computation of average total costs per *mile* ($ATC/M$) (*not* per vehicle-mile) of a designated bottom system, which is then applied to the mileage of the other systems to obtain the non-user share. The amounts determined for each system are then deducted from the total costs of each to obtain the user share. The total user charges for all systems are then aggregated and divided by the total vehicle-miles to obtain a single average cost per vehicle-mile.

Using the same example as for the top-drawer solution, let us assume the mileages to be 300,000 miles for the top system, 900,000 miles for the intermediate system, and 2,000,000 miles for the bottom system. Since the cost of the bottom system has been assumed to be $4 billion per year, the cost per mile is $2,000 per year. When this rate is applied to the other systems, we get a non-user charge of $600 million for the top system and $1.8 billion for the intermediate system. When these are deducted from the total costs for each system the user charges are $4.4 billion for the top system, $1.2 billion for the intermediate system, and none for the bottom system, for a total of $5.6 billion. Since assumed annual travel on all three systems is 1,500 billion vehicle-miles, the average cost per vehicle-mile using the bottom-drawer technique is 3.73 mills per vehicle-mile. The average of the top-drawer and bottom-drawer costs per vehicle-mile is ½ (6.25 + 3.73) = 4.99 mills per vehicle-mile. The "final" estimates are computed by applying the 4.99 mills figure to the number of vehicle-miles generated on each system. The results are summarized in Table 2.5. It cannot be stressed too much that these figures are purely illustrative. The actual results of the earlier study are summarized in Table 2.6.

We now have two sets of results that may be used in determining the user–non-user proportional cost assignment. Neither approach is especially "scientific"; both are based upon certain assumptions that one either accepts or rejects. Despite their "reasonable" appearance, the data employed consist of broad averages that hide substantial differences in highway systems in various regions. But on purely theoretical grounds it is evident that no single technique can be shown to be better than any other. This opens the door to those with vested interests to select whichever analysis technique yields results most

TABLE 2.5

| (1) System | (2) Annual total costs ($ billions) | (3) Vehicle-miles (billions) | (4) User Charge* ($ billions) | (5) Non-user Charge** ($ billions) | (6) User Share (%) | (7) Non-user Share (%) |
|---|---|---|---|---|---|---|
| Top | 5.0 | 800 | 3.992 | 1.008 | 79.9 | 20.1 |
| Intermediate | 3.0 | 400 | 1.996 | 1.004 | 66.5 | 33.5 |
| Bottom | 4.0 | 300 | 1.497 | 2.503 | 37.4 | 62.6 |
| Total | 12.0 | 1,500 | 7.485 | 4.515 | 62.4 | 37.6 |

* Number of vehicle-miles multiplied by 4.99 mills.
** Difference between column (2) and column (4).

TABLE 2.6

Distribution of Highway Costs between
Users and Non-users

|  | Motor Vehicle Share (%) | Nonmotor Vehicle Share (%) |
|---|---|---|
| Interstate and other federal aid primary | 98.6 | 1.4 |
| Federal aid secondary | 60.0 | 40.0 |
| All federal aid systems | 85.7 | 14.3 |
| Other state highways | 48.0 | 52.0 |
| Other local roads and streets | 60.0 | 40.0 |
| All nonfederal aid systems | 58.4 | 41.6 |
| All roads and streets | 74.9 | 25.1 |

SOURCE: *Final Report,* p.140.

favorable to them. Thus, the railways argue that non-user charges should be zero, while various motor vehicle groups argue for much higher non-user charges.

The *Final Report* chose to resolve the conflicting results obtained by the relative-use and earnings-credit techniques by arithmetically averaging the two figures to obtain what the researchers called a "mediation" between the two methods. The results are shown in Table 2.7. It is interesting to compare this "ideal" allocation with the

TABLE 2.7

Averaging of Relative-Use and Earnings-Credit Study Findings,
to Determine Final Values of General Allocation between
Motor-Vehicle-User Taxes and Other Revenue Sources.

|  | General Allocation | |
|---|---|---|
|  | To motor vehicle users (%) | To other revenue sources (%) |
| Interstate system | 96.7 | 3.3 |
| Other federal aid primary | 94.5 | 5.5 |
| Federal aid secondary | 73.0 | 27.0 |
| Weighted average | 92.29 | 7.71 |

SOURCE: *Final Report,* p.147.

actual allocation in 1961. In that year, highway users provided only 72.05 percent of total highway receipts. Even if we neglect receipts from investments and the sale of bonds, the percentage is still only

83.04.[86] We may conclude, then, that on the basis of this information and crude allocative techniques, our highway and street costs were not being properly apportioned between users and non-users. User groups as a whole were not paying their "rightful" share. With this disquieting conclusion, we now consider the equally difficult problem of identifying various user and non-user groups and allocating road costs among them in as equitable a manner as possible.

The public policy implications are clear: user taxes should be raised relative to those of non-users. However, it cannot be emphasized too much that this conclusion emanates from techniques that leave much to be desired. Nor are the available data sufficiently accurate and extensive to support the accuracy of such a conclusion even if the concepts were clear and the assessment of what constitutes a fair share unambiguous. The above computations are presented mainly to illustrate the inherent weaknesses of present allocative techniques and concepts. There can be no presumption that the derived figures represent the final word in the split-up between users and non-users. Other techniques, assumptions, and data can be employed to deduce varying allocations, all of which would appear to the disinterested observer to be equally reasonable.

However, for the sake of argument, let us assume that a change in the proportions of total highway receipts collected from users and non-users would be economically desirable. Since there are a variety of both user and non-user taxes, which particular tax or set of taxes should be changed and by how much? In other words we must now go beneath the broad categories of "user" and "non-user" and try to determine whether particular user and non-user groups are paying their "fair" share.

STAGE 2: THE APPROPRIATE SHARE FOR DIFFERENT USERS

Since we are concerned with intercity freight transportation and its associated demands and costs, it is not necessary to concern ourselves with a further analysis of specific *non-user* "equitable" shares, fascinating as an examination of this issue is. Rather, we will concentrate on the estimation of the appropriate user share, with special attention to various categories of trucks.

Once the "sum of money" to be allocated to users has been ascertained, along the lines noted above or by alternative means, there must be a determination of the "fair share" that should be allocated to various user types. Users are normally identified by vehicle type.

---

86. U.S. Department of Commerce, *Estimate of Receipts and Disbursements for Highways, 1959–62*, Press release BPR 62-1, January 7, 1962.

Three kinds of basic information are required: identification of as many vehicle classes as seem reasonable in terms of costs occasioned or benefits received; estimation of the actual or expected number of vehicles in each class so identified, usually from vehicle registration data; and estimation of travel characteristics for each class in terms of vehicle-miles traveled or ton-miles generated per year and other relevant information, all of which will be averaged for each vehicle classification.

This basic information can be used in four different methods for determining "fair shares": the *incremental* method, the *cost-function* method, the *gross ton-mile* method, and the *differential-benefits* method.

*The Incremental Method.* User charge responsibility is assigned on the basis of the incremental cost of highway construction and maintenance occasioned by the different vehicle classes or types. The logic of this approach is that the strength and thickness of highway pavement increase as vehicle size and weight or weight per axle increase. The cost of a "basic" road (the first increment) suitable to the "smallest" vehicle class, in terms of weight or weight per axle, would be shared by all vehicle classes on the basis of some use factor (vehicle-miles, ton-miles, etc.), whereas the extra cost of a road suitable for the next highest (or heaviest) vehicle class would be shared by vehicles in all subsequent classes but not by those vehicles in the "lowest" class, and so on for all further increments. As the most recent "incremental" cost study for the United States D.O.T. puts it, "the cost of each successive increment is . . . distributed among the progressively smaller number of increasingly heavy axles that require it."[87] In short, the vehicle types or classes that require more expensive construction and maintenance will share the extra cost while those that do not need such high quality highways will not.

*The Cost-Function Method.* The annual costs to be allocated are divided into those that (1) vary with some measure of weight or size of vehicle, (2) vary with some measure of use of the highway, and (3) are independent of either weight or traffic volume. The usual procedure is to divide the first set of costs by gross ton-miles (*GTM*), the second set of costs by vehicle-miles, and the third by the number of vehicles in each class.

*The Gross Ton-Mile Method.* This method is the simplest in terms of availability of data and technique. It merely involves obtaining estimates of the total *GTM* generated by each vehicle class, which data are regularly reported, and assessing the cost responsibility for

---

87. *Allocation of Highway Cost Responsibility and Tax Payments, 1969*, p.10.

any given expenditure level on the basis of the ratio of the *GTM* of each class to the total *GTM* for all classes. That is, if the annual expenditure on highways to be collected from users is deemed to be $K, and if the relative *GTM* for each class of vehicles are $GTM_1$, $GTM_2, \ldots, GTM_n$, for user classes 1 through $n$, then each class "should" pay an amount equal to $\$K \left( \dfrac{GTM_i}{\sum\limits_{i=1}^{n} GTM_i} \right)$.

*The Differential-Benefits Method.* This method is the most difficult of all in terms of data requirements. It is a value-of-service approach and allocates cost responsibility among vehicle classes on the basis of the relative benefits each class of vehicles receives from a "unit" improvement in the highway system. If total benefits from any given highway improvement are deemed to be $R_1$, $R_2, \ldots, R_n$ for the various classes 1 through $n$, then if total user charges to be financed per year are $K, each class "should" pay an amount equal to $\$K \left( \dfrac{R_i}{\sum\limits_{i=1}^{n} R_i} \right)$. This method is precisely analogous to the *GTM* method, but it uses totally different data to obtain the respective ratios.

*A Simplified Numerical Illustration of the Four Methods.* The following examples will show the host of data problems and latent assumptions underlying each of the above methods. The purpose of these examples is not only to illustrate each method but also to indicate the wide variation that results even when we use the same basic data with some selected additional data unique to each method.

Assume four vehicle classes with the characteristics shown in Table 2.8. Class I might refer to the average private automobile, Class II to light trucks, and the other classes to heavier trucks or vehicles.[88]

TABLE 2.8

| Class | Miles/ Gallon | Miles Traveled per Year per Vehicle | Average Gross Weight per Vehicle (tons) | Number of Vehicles |
|-------|-------|-------|-------|-------|
| I | 20 | 10,000 | 2 | 50,000 |
| II | 15 | 15,000 | 6 | 20,000 |
| III | 10 | 20,000 | 10 | 15,000 |
| IV | 5 | 30,000 | 20 | 15,000 |

88. A more detailed breakdown of vehicle types is preferable. *Allocation of Highway Cost Responsibility and Tax Payments, 1969* used 65 separate vehicle classes.

The data refer to a single highway system, although in practice various highway types are usually distinguished, such as the Interstate System, Federal Aid-Primary and Secondary, and Other State and Local Highways. To begin the incremental analysis additional information is required. Assume that the annual aggregate cost of this hypothetical highway system is $110 million and that the user share, determined by the methods just examined, is 90.95%. Thus the amount to be assigned to and hence collected from users in the aggregate is $100 million. All methods seek to decide how much each class should pay.

(a) The Incremental Method. Assume further that the costs attributable solely to a basic road suitable only for Class I vehicles amount to $30 million, and that the incremental costs for successively "higher" vehicle classes are $25 million for Class II, $25 million for Class III, and $20 million for Class IV. Even if these incremental cost estimates were reasonably accurate (and in general they are not since they rely on a variety of assumptions, regressions, and allocations, each of which is suspect), there would be difficult problems in making appropriate (i.e., "equitable") cost assignments. For example, how should the assignment of the costs of a "basic" road be made? Even if it is agreed that *all* users should be assessed some portion of the basic road, the question remains on what basis? The $30 million could be allocated according to the relative number of vehicles, vehicle-miles, axle-miles, ton-miles, or some other proxy for "cost-occasioned" not routinely collected. Clearly, the results will differ with the choice of units.

Eschewing such problems for the moment, assume that $GTM$ is the most appropriate unit for assigning cost responsibility. The incremental method then assigns the costs of the "basic" road proportionally to all vehicle classes on the basis of $GTM$. (= total vehicle-miles × average gross weight, where total vehicle-miles = number of vehicles × miles traveled per year.) The $GTM$ for Class I vehicles is one billion; the total $GTM$ for all vehicles is 14.8 billion. If all vehicle classes are to share the basic road costs of $30 million and $GTM$ is deemed an appropriate indicator of cost responsibility, then each vehicle class is responsible for $0.002 per $GTM$ of total highway expenditures (i.e., $30 million ÷ 14.8 billion $GTM$).

Only Classes II through IV "share" in the second increment in costs ($25 million). Since the total $GTM$ for all classes subsequent to Class I is 13.8 billion, the cost responsibility is $0.0018 per $GTM$ for Class II and above. Thus, the *total* cost responsibility for Class I vehicles is $2 million (i.e., $0.002 multiplied by $GTM_I$), while for Class II it is $6.84 million (i.e., $0.002 + $0.0018 multiplied by $GTM_{II}$).

On the other hand, the analyst may conclude that vehicle-miles is a better indicator of cost responsibility, or what is more likely, weight per axle-mile. For illustrative purposes only, assume allocation on the basis of vehicle-miles. Although the procedures are comparable, this apparently simple change in measurement unit yields the cost-assignments per vehicle in each class as indicated in column (3) of Table 2.9. Assumptions using axle-mile units would give somewhat

TABLE 2.9

| | Incremental | | | |
|---|---|---|---|---|
| (1) | (2)<br>GTM<br>$/Vehicle | (3)<br>VM<br>$/Vehicle | (4)<br>Cost Function<br>$/Vehicle | (5)<br>GTM<br>$/Vehicle |
| Class I | 40 | 194 | 340 | 135 |
| Class II | 342 | 648 | 738 | 608 |
| Class III | 1,160 | 1,531 | 1,301 | 1,351 |
| Class IV | 4,860 | 3,629 | 3,219 | 4,054 |

different results, even though the same basic method was used. Note that the Class I assignment changes by a factor close to five merely by altering the units chosen for allocative purposes.

(b) The Cost-Function Method. Let us use the same basic data and assume that costs can be distinguished by valid empirical techniques such that of the $100 million to be collected from users, 10% represents vehicle function costs (e.g., administrative and police), 25% travel function costs (e.g., maintenance, etc.) and 65% costs that vary with weight-distance factors (e.g., construction). Then the allocation on the basis of number of vehicles, vehicle-miles, and *GTM*, respectively, for each class yields the cost assignments per vehicle shown in column (4) of Table 2.9.

(c) The *GTM* Method. The relative *GTM* per class multiplied by the amount to be collected from users in the aggregate yields the amount assigned per vehicle in column (5) of Table 2.9.

We will not outline here the differential-benefits method since it requires an entirely new set of information, which is not readily obtainable. It is obvious that the results would not, except by accident, coincide with any of the others.

There are serious logical difficulties connected with each method of assigning cost responsibility. Of course, they are implicit in the concept of "equity" which has little or no empirical content. All the methods seem plausible and none is inherently unreasonable. Yet the varying results using the same basic information, itself a product of judgment (i.e., the number of classes and the averaging of characteristics within each class), plus the additional data requirements for the incremental, differential-benefits, and cost-function methods (themselves subject to judgment and ambiguity), indicate that there is no single correct approach even if one could agree on what constitutes equity. Thus assertions to the effect that "highway user taxes on truck operations appear reasonably equitable . . ."[89] lack credibility even if each vehicle paid via an exclusive user charge any of the amounts per year shown in Table 2.9.

To complete this illustration of the problems of highway cost allocation, let us assume, arbitrarily, that the equitable amounts to be collected are those shown in column (2) of Table 2.9. How shall we collect such sums? At one extreme, each vehicle could simply pay an annual tax equal to the amount indicated. At the other extreme, to account partly for relative differences in the use of the highway system by vehicles in the same class, a fuel tax could be employed. To use the latter approach, which is basically the one now in operation in most Western countries (although without explicit reference to the questions considered here), one would need to determine what tax rate for each fuel type would just cover the estimated cost responsibility for one of the vehicle classes without exceeding that of the other classes. The fuel consumption per year (i.e., miles per gallon divided into total mileage) for Class I vehicles is 500 gallons of fuel per vehicle. Dividing the assigned cost per vehicle ($40) by 500 gallons yields a fuel tax of 8 cents. Such a tax would collect the precise amount allocated to Class I vehicles, if the averages remain the same, but would yield insufficient revenues for each of the other classes. The differential amounts for these classes could be collected by levies such as differential license fees. In this way each class and each vehicle in each class may be construed to be paying its "fair share" of the annual highway costs.

Given the arbitrary calculations and judgments involved at every stage of the calculation process, no conclusion that these charges represent either equity or efficiency is warranted. For example, the question of whether trucks pay the correct price for their use of the publicly provided right-of-way is unanswerable on equity grounds. Whatever amounts they pay are a hodgepodge of user taxes and pure taxation, which were decided on other than equity or efficiency grounds and bear no necessary relation to the amounts they *should* pay on either basis. The sticker on the rear of many trucks proclaiming "This vehicle pays $X per year in taxes" has no normative significance whatsoever.

---

89. Meyer et al., p.85.

## Motor Carrier Cost Functions

We now examine the private costs of over-the-road trucking with the realization that there is no evidence that they represent the social costs occasioned or even an equitable portion of the costs of the highway system.

There have been many studies of the behavior and level of the (private) costs of motor carriers. They have used a variety of techniques but mainly in the form of regression analysis of the kind noted earlier with respect to railroad cost functions. The early studies by the ICC, Roberts, and Nelson[90] all indicated either limited or no economies of scale and generally concluded that the long-run marginal cost of truck transport was constant.

These findings became predominant in the analysis of the trucking industry and, indeed, became part of the conventional wisdom—especially among academics. Before proceeding with a critique of these studies and more recent ones, let us outline the implications that were regularly drawn from them. Long-run cost linearity was taken to mean that "small" firms *could* be as efficient, in terms of achievable unit cost of production, as "large" firms, and thus no competitive advantage because of size existed. The industry was therefore portrayed as one that had most of the features of a highly competitive market, and hence there were no economic grounds for subjecting it to regulation. "Naturally operative" economic forces would ensure "cheapness and plenty." This statement is a misinterpretation of the probable consequences of constant returns to scale. If there is no economic penalty to being small, there is equally no economic penalty to being large. Under production conditions described as having no economies (or diseconomies) of scale, the "natural" market structure is indeterminate. The inference that the absence of scale economies meant workable competition was erroneous although other "structural" features of the motor carrier industry in general, such as low entry costs, were also involved. (Questions of economic regulation will be discussed in chapter 4, which deals with policy matters.)

Later studies yielded conflicting results on the issue of scale economies in the motor carrier industry. Table 2.10 summarizes the more familiar studies and indicates the basic methodology, the nature of the sample, the variables employed, and the "representative" conclusion.

---

90. M. J. Roberts, "Some Aspects of Motor Carrier Costs: Firm Size, Efficiency and Financial Health," *Land Economics*, August 1956, pp.228–38; R. A. Nelson, *The Economic Structure of the Highway Carrier Industry in New England*, submitted to the New England Governors' Committee on Public Transportation, Boston, July 1956.

TABLE 2.10

## Summary of Existing Economic Studies of Motor Freight Economies of Scale in the U.S.

| Author | Type of Study | Data Used, Population Size & Geographic Territory Considered | Additional Homogeneity Properties of Sample |
|---|---|---|---|
| Roberts 1956 | Approximation of long run average cost curve relationship by size groups. | 1952 cross section of 114 Class I motor carriers operating in Central Territory for primary analysis. 1952 cross section of 92 Class I transcontinental carriers for supplementary analysis. | General Freight, Regular route, intercity assumed (criteria not specified). |
| Nelson 1956 | Approximation of long run average cost curve relationship by size groups using rank correlation. | 1954 cross section of 102 Class I motor carriers domiciled in New England and 65 Class I carriers but domiciled outside of New England. | General Freight Intercity (criteria specified). |
| Emery 1965 | Approximation of long run average variable cost curve relationship by size groups. | 1960 cross section of 233 Class I and 11 motor carriers operating in Middle Atlantic territory. | General Freight, intercity. Intercity carrier must receive at least 70% of revenue from intercity service. |
| Warner 1965 | Log linear long run total cost function estimated. | 1953–1960 pooled cross section—time series of 72 Class I motor carriers operating in the U.S. | General Freight, intercity (criteria not specified), no ownership entanglements and continuous data available from 1953–1960. |
| Dailey 1973 | Log linear long run average cost function estimated. | 1968 cross section of 69, 85, 62 and 32 Class I and II motor carriers operating in TRINCS regions: New England, Pacific-Southern, Central States, and Southwest, respectively. | General Freight, Intercity (criteria not specified). |
| Ladenson and Stoga 1974 | Log linear Cobb-Douglas production function estimated. | 1971 cross section of 116 randomly picked motor carriers in the U.S. | General Freight, intercity. Intercity carrier must receive at least 50% revenue from intercity service. |
| Lawrence 1976 | Log linear long run average cost estimated. | 1973 cross section of 124 Class I motor carriers. | General freight carriers subgrouped by revenue size and length of haul. |

| Author | Measure of Scale and Approximate Range of Scale (1) Largest (2) Smallest | Dependent Variable | Independent Variables | Representative Conclusion |
|---|---|---|---|---|
| Roberts 1956 | Tangible Assets—Central Territory Sample: (1) about $2,000,000 (2) less than $350,000 Interterritorial Sample: (1) greater than $8,000,000 (2) not given | Average cost per vehicle mile (excluding terminal expenses). | Average length of haul. Percent of truckload freight to total freight. Route to average haul. Vehicle mile per route mile. | "...small companies who were not disadvantaged in utilization and haul characteristics performed as efficiently as bigger ones." |
| Nelson 1956 | Revenue—New England Sample (1) $9,480,000 (2) not given Non-New England Sample (1) $47,820,000 (2) not given | Average cost per vehicle mile. Average cost per ton-mile. | Average length of haul. Average load. | "... size of firm bears little relation to operating cost." |
| Emery 1965 | Revenue (1) greater than $12,401,300 (2) averaged $226,000 | Average cost per ton-mile. | Percent of truckload freight. | "Relating the carriers total expenses to their ton-miles of output a perfect progressively declining expense per ton-mile from 21.67¢ for the smallest to 8.98¢ for the largest carrier size group was found." |
| Warner 1965 | Number of shipments, statistics not given; however largest carrier by revenue was about $14,000,000 and by assets $10,000,000 | Total Operating Cost. | Average length of haul. Average weight of shipment. | "... the results clearly suggested economies of scale.... the economies suggested are not overpowering in the sense that such differences as there are cannot be overcome by a favorably situated small firm." |
| Dailey 1973 | Revenue—New England (1) $9,551,000 (2) $374,000 Pacific-Southern (1) $59,902,000 (2) $374,000 Southwest (1) $45,385,000 (2) $351,000 Central States (1) $262,662,000 (2) $320,000 | Average cost per ton-mile. | Average length of haul. Average load. Annual miles per power unit. | "Our results for our cost function suggest that the primary determinants of variations in motor common carrier costs are average length of haul, average load per vehicle, and, to a lesser degree, size of firm... there are actually diseconomies of scale once route structure is held constant." |

## TABLE 2.10 (*cont.*)

| | | | | |
|---|---|---|---|---|
| Ladenson and Stoga 1974 | Number of employees (1) greater than 2,000 employees (2) 1–50 employees | Ton-miles per unit of labor input. Ton-miles per unit of capital input. | Labor—Ratio of total wages and salaries to average hourly wage of drivers and platform workers, or ratio of the sum of total workers to their average wage ratio. Capital—Net Carrier Operating Property or the sum of depreciation and amortization, road and property taxes paid and 5 percent of net worth. Ratio of labor to capital. | "With one exception, our estimates . . . indicate that once the firm has attained a size of fifty employees or more it is subject to increasing returns to scale." |
| Lawrence 1976 | Total tonnage, statistics not given but revenue sizes were: Group 1 – (1) $10,000,000 (2) $1,000,000 Group 2 (1) $50,000,000 (2) $10,000,000 Group 3 & 4 (1) not given (2) $50,000,000 Group 5 (1) not given (2) $10,000,000 | Total Operating Cost. | Average length of haul. Average load. Ratio of less-than-truck-load (LTL) tonnage to total tonnage. Average tons per LTL shipment. Percent of business in large metropolitan areas. | "The research reported here generally reveals the same type of results reported by Warner . . . these same regression coefficients for output, if valid, generally reflect highly significant economies of scale." |

NOTES

Roberts, M. J. "Some Aspects of Motor Carrier Costs: Firm Size, Efficiency and Financial Health." *Land Economics*, August 1956, pp.228–38.

Nelson, R. A. *The Economic Structure of the Highway Carrier Industry in New England*. Submitted to the New England Governors' Committee on Public Transportation, Boston, July 20, 1956.

Emery, P. W. "An Empirical Approach to the Motor Carrier Scale Economies Controversy." *Land Economics*, August 1965, pp.285–89.

Warner, S. L. "Cost Models, Measurement Errors, and Economies of Scale in Trucking." In M. L. Burstein, *The Cost of Trucking: Econometric Analysis*, pp.1–46. Dubuque: Wm. C. Brown, 1965.

Dailey, V. A. "The Certificate Effect: The Impact of Federal Entry Controls on the Growth of the Motor Carrier Firm," pp.78–98. Ph.D. dissertation, University of Virginia, 1973.

Ladenson, M. L., and Stoga, J. "Returns to Scale in the U. S. Trucking Industry." *Southern Economic Journal*, January 1974, pp.390–96.

Lawrence, M. L. "Economies of Scale in the General Freight Motor Common Carrier Industry: Additional Evidence." *Proceedings—Seventeenth Annual Meeting of the Transportation Research Forum*, pp.169–76. Oxford, Ind. Richard B. Cross, 1976.

In part, the conflicting results emerge from differences in all of these aspects.

But more fundamentally, the studies are flawed by assuming all carriers in the sample are homogeneous and produce a homogeneous product. All general freight intercity carriers designated as Class I do not produce identical services, nor are they using the same technology (e.g., those emphasizing less than truckload [LTL] vs. truckload [TL] service and long- vs. short-haul carriers). In addition, even the carriers in such an apparently homogeneous classification have widely differing geographical coverage, which influences the quality of the service and may involve geographical cost differences.

Garland Chow seeks to reduce this heterogeneity by classifying carriers by whether they are predominantly long or short haul, LTL or TL, and by size. Significant scale economies are found in the short-haul LTL classifications while constant (or slightly) decreasing economies of scale are found in the long-haul LTL and, to a lesser extent, TL classifications. The relationship tested for each group of carriers was derived from Warner's and took the following form:[91]

$$\log TC = b_0 + b_1 \log S + b_2 \log W + b_3 \log H,$$

where $TC$ = total operating cost, $S$ = total number of shipments, $W$ = average weight per shipment, and $H$ = average length of haul per ton. The data employed referred to a single year, 1973, and involved 538 carriers. Arbitrary but not unreasonable distinctions between short and long haul (less or greater than an average haul of 400 miles) and TL, LTL (average shipment weight less or greater than 5,000 pounds) as well as carrier size were necessary, and, of course, influenced the results.

Yet this study, by distinguishing among the various sub-industries within the broad "intercity motor carrier" umbrella, in the sense of different types of service and hence different production functions and cost behavior (and service in different regions), is an improvement over the previous studies, which lumped together or ignored most of these varying characteristics. Even so, the results are far from conclusive, although they are consistent with *a priori* reasoning.

For example, a predominantly LTL carrier incurs relatively more terminal expenses than a predominantly TL carrier. If there are economies of scale in terminals, a point not yet thoroughly investigated, they would account for the economies of scale in this segment of the trucking industry. Certainly the fact of large terminal expenses suggests that entry costs for such a carrier are much higher than the

---

91. The model also incorporated dummy variables for different regions.

"single vehicle and rented office" so often referred to in discussions seeking to verify the alleged ease of entry that exists in the absence of economic regulation featuring entry restrictions.

However, the elusive nature of motor carrier cost behavior is further indicated in a study by Friedlaender that appeared concurrently with Chow's.[92] Friedlaender likewise acknowledged and sought to account for the different quality of service inherent in differing average shipment sizes, average lengths of haul, and TL or LTL traffic. Each of these service types influences the costs of providing the same number of ton-miles. In general, as earlier studies implied and these later ones explicitly show, LTL shipments, short average hauls, and light average loads cost more to produce than TL shipments, long average hauls, and heavy average loads even for the identical number of ton-miles generated during any period. To examine the economies of scale it is necessary to account for these factors separately. Small carriers, by some size measure, may be confined to inherently more costly activities than larger firms. Thus in simple regressions of costs against a ton-mile variable, there would appear to be economies of scale. However, if small carriers could, in the absence of regulation, achieve longer average hauls and heavier average loads (these two variables are likewise correlated), they could then achieve the efficiency levels per ton-mile of large carriers and no economies of scale would exist.[93]

Friedlaender used a sample of 171 firms located in the Central, Middle Atlantic, and New England regions in 1972 and a hedonic cost function of the form

$$\text{Cost} = C[\psi(y_1, q_1, q_2, q_3); W_1, W_2, W_3, W_4],$$

where $\psi(y, q_1, q_2, q_3)$ is a function that measures "output" with $y$ = ton-miles; $q_1$ = either average size of shipment or average load (tons per truck); $q_2$ = average length of haul; $q_3$ = percentage of tons shipped in LTL lots; and $W_1$, $W_2$, $W_3$, and $W_4$ represent the prices of labor, fuel, capital, and purchased transportation.

Friedlaender concludes that "evidence of increasing returns to scale exists when ton-miles are used as an output measure, but fails to exist when output is adjusted for length of haul and other quality differentials," and "since there is little reason to believe that these economies of haul or service are related to the technological structures of the industry, it is likely that any observed economies of scale are" due to regulation. Indeed, she even finds significant diseconomies for

---

92 A. Friedlaender, "Hedonic Costs and Economies of Scale in the Regulated Trucking Industry," in *Motor Carrier Economic Regulation*, Proceedings of a Workshop (Washington, D.C.: National Academy of Sciences, 1978), pp.33–56.

93. Indeed Roberts's early study found that the observed average cost differences were largely related to average length of haul—not to carrier size.

large levels of output and U-shaped marginal and average cost curves "when measured in terms of quality-adjusted output."[94] These findings are the opposite of Chow's.

We may conclude, therefore, that motor carrier cost behavior is no more clearly defined than that of rail. Some types of carriers may be subject to economies of scale, but others may not. Chow has indicated, holding shipment size and length of haul constant, some of the characteristics leading to economies of scale (LTL, long distance) but even this finding leaves much to be desired, especially when various dimensions of service quality are included.[95] Indeed, as was long ago argued, even if there are constant returns to scale, if service quality in terms of speed, dependability, and safety relates positively to size (as it appears to), then the "natural" market structure of the various segments of the motor carrier industry will tend toward more concentration and probably oligopoly, certainly between specific pairs of cities.[96]

Friedlaender's findings to the contrary do not, of course, include these kinds of service quality. Neither Friedlaender's nor Chow's "quality" measures reflect shipper preferences for one line service (hence larger firms) as well as the qualities of speed, dependability, and safety.[97]

It is apparent that even if there are no economies of scale or even diseconomies, the implications with respect to the market structure that would result from deregulation are more complex than is usually implied. We will examine this issue in more detail in chapter 4.

Some research on the costs of the less-regulated segment of the motor carrier industry supports the findings that shipment characteristics rather than firm size and the type of operation are most important in determining cost levels and behavior. For irregular route, exempt, or owner-operated trucks, the costs per ton-mile, even for distances over 1,000 miles per shipment, are below rail revenues per ton-mile on such "rail-captive" traffic as coal, steel, canned goods, and grain.[98] The reasons for such low-cost levels in this segment of

---

94. Friedlaender, p.52.

95. See Chow, "The Cost of Trucking Revisited."

96. G. W. Wilson, "The Nature of Competition in the Motor Transport Industry," *Land Economics*, November 1960, pp.387–91. More recently, similar observations have been made with special reference to the Australian and British experience, where increasing concentration occurred following substantial deregulation. Shipper preferences for larger firms were also revealed. D. Wyckoff, "Factors Promoting Concentration of Motor Carriers under Deregulation," *Proceedings of the Transportation Research Forum—Fifteenth Annual Meeting, 1974* (Oxford, Ind.: Richard B. Cross, 1974), pp.1–7.

97. These qualitative elements are elaborated on in the latter part of chapter 1, above.

98. D. Wyckoff and D. Maister, *The Owner-Operator: Independent Trucker* (Toronto: Lexington Books, 1975), p.37.

the trucking industry are the absence of terminal costs, better possibility of back-haul traffic, very heavy equipment utilization, heavy average loads, long average hauls, and, in the case of owner-operators, an apparent willingness to accept lower average earnings in preference to the "way of life"[99]—further evidence that unit costs depend largely on the type of operation and other variables. The multidimensional nature of the output unit is now belatedly being recognized in recent empirical research. Though far from having resolved or even considered all the associated problems, the more recent studies represent a substantial advance over previous work.

In addition, while the issue of economies of scale remains unresolved, the behavior of unit costs with respect to certain shipment characteristics is well known. Indeed, many of the previously noted studies clearly delineated cost behavior *per shipment* on the basis of such characteristics as density, length of haul, TL or LTL. In terminal costs, the categories usually distinguished are billing and collecting, pickup and delivery, platform costs, and overhead such as property taxes and terminal management costs. Whatever output unit we use— tons, miles, ton-miles, or vehicle-miles—it is obvious that each of these cost categories does not vary directly or proportionately with any of them. Clearly, billing and collecting and terminal overhead are independent of weight or distance; pickup and delivery costs vary mostly with *running time,* which is largely independent of any weight or distance factor; and platform handling costs are independent of distance and more variable with density than with weight. Thus terminal costs per ton decrease sharply as the number of tons per shipment increase, and decrease even more sharply with regard to a ton-mile or vehicle-mile unit.

Similarly, line-haul costs per shipment decrease with weight and distance. Certain fixed expenses per vehicle per year, such as depreciation or insurance and license fees, are largely or totally independent of any weight or distance factor. Running costs are largely independent of weight. Indeed, the observed positive relationship between average load and distance[100] suggests that line-haul costs per ton or per ton-mile vary inversely with weight. Vehicle-mile costs do, however, vary with distance, although not proportionately because of the fixed component noted above. However, while line-haul costs per shipment vary inversely with weight and/or distance such costs are completely variable with respect to *total* volume of business in terms of tons, miles, or even shipments tendered because the number of vehicles can readily be adjusted to total traffic demand.

---

99. Ibid.
100. Nelson, p.38, notes that "the carriers get larger average loads as the length of haul increases."

The foregoing suggests that unit costs per shipment overall decrease sharply with weight and distance factors. For any particular trucking firm, the actual cost behavior will depend on the type of operation—especially the relative significance of terminal costs, since these are the costs that are most invariant with respect to weight and distance factors. It is not surprising, therefore, that Nelson found that the cost per ton-mile decreases as both the average haul and the average load increase.[101]

Thus, we may conclude that the cost per shipment varies inversely with all the usual output measures. This conclusion may partially account for the so-called small shipments problem. That is, according to the conventional wisdom there are no economies of scale in the motor carrier industry, various studies to the contrary notwithstanding. Thus *LRMC* (long-run marginal cost) is constant with respect to size of firm and is often interpreted to mean that total costs vary in proportion to ton-miles, as noted by *AA* in Figure 2.8. If this interpretation

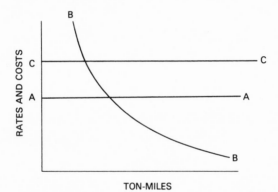

Fig. 2.8           TON-MILES

has led to a rate structure without much taper as ton-miles increases, we have rates that in the extreme appear as *CC*. However, if the cost per shipment varies inversely with ton-miles, as noted above, it may look like *BB*. Thus it is extremely profitable to concentrate on heavy, long-haul shipments and to avoid light, short-haul traffic. The rate structure, in short, may not adequately reflect the cost behavior *per shipment*. Since it is the individual shipment that is being priced, incentives are provided for presently regulated carriers to stress long hauls and heavy loadings. This may partially explain why some of the largest and most profitable trucking firms are predominantly long

---

101. Ibid. Roberts's and Warner's findings are similar. The more recent studies by Chow and Friedlaender more formally seek to "correct" or at least adjust for these considerations in attempting to determine scale economies (i.e., costs related to number of shipments as distinct from shipment characteristics).

haul and typically have heavier average loads per vehicle than do smaller carriers.

## Cost Functions of Other Modes

### Inland Waterway Cost Functions

Inland waterways are the third most important mode of intercity freight transportation within the United States. (We will omit consideration of coastal and intercoastal shipping.) The treatment here will be brief because the cost and demand situation with respect to the waterways has been less extensively analyzed, but mainly because the types of problems facing cost analysis are comparable to those already examined for rail and truck intercity transport.

The users of the inland waterways do not own their rights-of-way. Consequently, we are faced with the user-charge problem analogous to highways, since improvements in and maintenance of the waterways are performed by the federal and, to a lesser extent, by state and local governments. To date, however, no waterway user charges have been imposed in the United States, although they have been proposed by the federal government from time to time. The issue of how much users *should* pay is identical to the issue with respect to highway users. Let us turn directly to the *private* costs of waterway users, with full knowledge that they are below the social costs by some unknown amount and that the difference confers a competitive advantage via implicit subsidy in those situations where rail and/or highway service provide alternatives.

Two recent studies of inland waterway cost functions have been made.[102] The first used quarterly data for five barge operators for the period 1962–66, defined an output unit in terms of "equivalent barge mile" ($EBM$),[103] defined the size of firm by four proxy variables, and made other seasonality and firm characteristic adjustments. It ran regression analyses of the following form against various cost categories:

$$\log \frac{\text{Cost}}{EBM} = a_0 + a_1 \log E_{ijt} + a_2 \log S_{ijt} + a_3 C_i + a_7 t + a_8 Q_j,$$

102. R. Case and L. Lave, "Cost Functions for Inland Waterways Transport in the United States," *Journal of Transport Economics and Policy*, May 1970; and G. Polak and R. K. Koshal, "Cost Functions and Changing Technology for Water Transport: Some Empirical Results," presented at the Eastern Economic Association, April 17, 1976, mimeographed.
103. An *EBM* is the movement of a fully loaded jumbo barge one mile, equal to 1,350 cargo ton-miles.

where $E_{ijt}$ = output in *EBMs* for the $i$th firm during the $j$th quarter of the $t$th year; $S_{ijt}$ = a measure of firm size (in terms of total towboat horsepower, number of towboats, net tons of cargo capacity, or number of barges) for the $i$th firm during the $j$th quarter of the $t$th year; $C_i$ = a dummy variable for the different firms; $t$ = annual time trend $(1962 = 1, \ldots, 1966 = 5)$ and $Q_j$ = quarterly dummy variables, fourth quarter omitted.

The results of the regressions indicated that "the slopes of both short and long-run cost functions were negative and significant. . . . [A] 10 per cent increase in output would raise indirect costs by 2.3 per cent, direct costs by 4 per cent and total costs by 3.7 per cent. A 10 per cent increase in firm size (together with an equal increase in output) would raise . . . total costs by 3.0 per cent."[104] This is taken to mean that there are increasing returns to scale in the inland waterway cargo industry even though by one size measure the regression coefficient is positive "for some reason."[105]

The second study divides costs for the entire "shallow draft" U. S. industry into 11 categories and uses the following relationship in the regression exercise:

$$C_{it} = a + bQ_t + cT_{47\text{-}49} + dT_{50\text{-}57} + eT_{58\text{-}63} + fT_{64\text{-}69} + gD_{58\text{-}60},$$

where $C_{it}$ represents the cost for the $i$th cost category (e.g., wages, fuel, etc.) in year $t$ and $Q_t$ is the output measured in ton-miles of revenue freight. The other variables seek to account for technological change during the years indicated as subscripts, which had previously been identified by "non-statistical" interpretations as, in a sense, distinct periods of technological change that would alter the cost functions and, if not accounted for, distort the measure of the economies of scale. The results of the regression analysis indicate "the presence of economies of scale in the shallow-draft water transport industry."[106]

*Oil Pipelines Cost Functions*

The usual approach to measuring oil pipeline cost curves is to derive a production function combining various engineering parameters or relationships. The earliest study along these lines was done by L. Cookenboo.[107] Starting with a hydraulic formula relating to typical crude oil movements (60 SUS viscosity, 34° API gravity) in

---

104. Case and Lave, p.190.
105. Ibid., p.188.
106. Polak and Koshal, p.19.
107. L. Cookenboo, Jr., *Crude Oil Pipe Lines and Competition in the Oil Industry* (Cambridge: Harvard University Press, 1955), p.17.

the mid-continent, for different diameter pipes, he obtained the following formula:

$$T^{2.735} = \frac{HD^{4.135}}{0.01046},$$

where $T$ = throughput (in barrels per day), $H$ = horsepower, and $D$ = inside diameter of pipe.

In terms of economies of scale, output, defined as barrels of throughput per day, increases more slowly than horsepower, other things being equal. Thus, if cost per unit of horsepower is given, unit costs of producing a unit of throughput will rise sharply. On the other hand, if diameter of pipe is increased, there are sharply decreased unit costs as throughput rises.[108] Since size of enterprise does not inherently relate to pipeline diameter, the issue of economies of scale for oil pipelines is moot. We do, however, observe that for given diameters unit costs behave in the familiar U-shaped pattern of short-run costs in competitive industries. But when diameters are allowed to vary, the situation is the reverse. We may thus conclude that there are economies to diameter of pipe, which may or may not relate to size of enterprise, although for any given pipeline system, the larger the diameter the greater the initial capital costs and hence the size of the firm, other things being equal. Capital costs, of course, also vary with the terrain, but for any given pipeline between a pair of points, the bigger the diameter the larger the initial investment costs and, depending on throughput volume, the smaller the unit costs per barrel of throughput. In this sense, economies of scale exist for crude oil pipelines.

### Conclusion

Frequently in the literature references are made to such cost differentials among the modes as are shown in Table 2.11. The meaning to be attached to such numbers is somewhat ambiguous. They do, however, imply that for *average* types of traffic for *each* of the modes, the cost differences may be roughly as noted. Another interpretation would be that the cost differences for a *given* shipment, in terms of weight, density, and distance, are those noted in the table. This is obviously the most relevant comparison, especially if rates reflect costs, since individual shippers making modal choices care little about any mode's *average* costs unless their shipments reflect the average. Yet it

---

108. Ibid., p.26. See also John Hazard, *Transportation: Management, Economics, Policy* (Cambridge, Md.: Cornell Maritime Press, 1977), p.188.

TABLE 2.11

*Modal Cost Differentials*

| Mode | Marginal Cost in Mills per Ton-Mile |
|---|---|
| Rail: | |
| Bulk, boxcar | 7.0 |
| High-valued commodities | 15.6 |
| Motor carriers | 21.7 |
| Inland waterways: | |
| Manufactured commodities | 4.0–5.0 |
| Bulk commodities | 1.0–2.0 |
| Oil pipelines | 1.0 |

SOURCE: Friedlaender, p.51. Data refer to costs in 1963.

is not clear that this is the correct interpretation of such cost comparisons. For each mode the costs were computed from an analysis (of some kind) that necessarily reflected the shipment characteristics of each mode separately. These differ widely on the average among modes as shown in Table 2.12. Thus, the costs do *not* refer to shipments having similar characteristics. They may therefore be seriously misleading if interpreted in this way. For example, the great discrepancy between regulated motor carrier and railway costs indicated may shrink considerably as weight, distance, and density of any shipment rise—at least up to certain limits. The costs, as we have already indicated, of an owner-operator, independent trucker may approximate those of a railroad for hauls up to 1,000 miles of high-density material (e.g., steel). Furthermore, there is substantial variation in costs for different shipment characteristics and types of service, as we have repeatedly stressed. Finally, the figure for motor carriers is rendered more suspect because of the variation in back-haul traffic, especially when measured in terms of revenue ton-miles.

To ensure an efficient allocation of traffic among modes, the relevant cost comparisons must refer to the *same* movement and make some

TABLE 2.12

| | Average Weight per Shipment (lbs.) | Average Haul per Ton (miles) |
|---|---|---|
| Rail | 140,000 | 551 |
| Motor (common carriers) | 900–1,000 | 264 |
| Inland waterways | 120,000 | 330 |
| Oil pipelines (crude) | | 300 |
| Air Cargo | < 500 | 1,100 |

provision for the kinds of quality distinctions noted at the end of chapter 1. None of this is easy, as we have emphasized throughout. Indeed, the complexities are such that the issue arises whether efficient traffic allocation requires more (or less) economic regulation or more (or less) reliance on interfirm and/or intermodal rivalry among those supplying freight service. In chapter 4 we will examine the issues involved in the economic regulation of transportation.

# Efficiency Criteria
# for Pricing

## Introduction

In a market-oriented economy, the theory of economic regulation is rooted in "market failure"—those conditions in the market that lead to results deemed "undesirable" by firms seeking to maximize private profits. Where such conditions exist, the industry or industries in question may be subjected to some form of regulatory constraint that seeks to redress "market failure" and that often takes, as a point of departure, the competitive model.

The competitive model leads to results in which the (single) market price per period just equals the $MC$ of each firm in the market. Thus $P = MC$ for society as a whole, assuming no externalities. Deviations of $P$ from $MC$ over extended periods of time represent evidence that competitive forces are not "working." This may provide justification for public actions that will stimulate or create conditions that will ensure an equivalence between $P$ and $MC$ in each market under consideration.

Conceptually, the "waste" associated with prices that deviate from $MC$ are easily illustrated. Suppose cost and demand conditions in a particular market are as shown in Figure 3.1. The demand curve is to be construed as the amounts consumers are willing to pay for alternative quantities of the good in question, presumably representing the "benefits" or "satisfactions" derived. Assuming diminishing satisfactions from increasing quantities consumed per period of time, the social evaluation decreases as more of the good is offered for sale per period. If the supply curve reflects marginal production costs, it is then evident that maximum *net* satisfaction (i.e., the greatest amount of benefits over costs) is given at an output of $Q_0$ at which point $P_0 = MC$. Each unit of output up to $Q_0$ confers more total benefits than it occasions costs to society, and each unit of output beyond $Q_0$ costs more than the benefits derived. The triangle $P_1AP_2$ then represents the maximum net benefits that can be reaped per period with the assumed demand and production conditions. This area is clearly

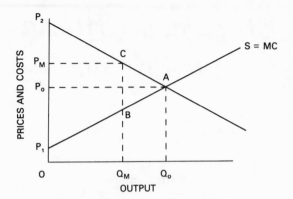

Fig. 3.1

the sum of producers' plus consumers' surpluses. The consumers' surplus is the triangle $P_0AP_2$ (i.e., the difference between the price $P_0$ and the amounts consumers would be willing to pay if they had to). The producers' surplus is the triangle $P_1AP_0$ (i.e., the difference between the price $P_0$ per unit and the marginal costs of producing successive increments of output).

Assume now that some market imperfection resulted in a price greater than $P_0$, say $P_M$. The welfare or net loss in satisfactions or benefits is the triangle $BCA$, in the sense that at a price equal to $P_M$ consumers evaluate the output from $Q_M$ to $Q_0$ as greater than the costs. The welfare *loss* is thus equal to $BAC$. This triangle is in turn equal to one-half the deviation of price from $MC$ ($= Q_MB$ at output $Q_M$) multiplied by the deviation of quantity purchased $OQ_0 - OQ_M$, or $\frac{1}{2}\Delta P\Delta Q$, where the $\Delta$s indicate the above deviations from the optimal outcome, *given the cost and demand relationships* postulated.

There are many analytical and philosophical problems associated with this theory. Yet, crude and simple as it is, it represents the basis not only for much of the transport investment analysis carried out around the world but also for the evaluation of part of the "costs" of economic regulation of transportation in the United States. The triangle is often referred to as "deadweight loss," and, in transportation, it is deemed to be inherent in any attempt to set freight rates on any basis other than $MC$. The difficulties in finding $MC$ ($SR$ or $LR$) have already been elaborated in chapter 2. Yet despite—or perhaps because of—these difficulties, more careful cost research remains to be done. Even though it is difficult to pinpoint $MC$ in transportation, and this concept is only remotely approximated in practice, this theory remains for many people the basic starting point for efficiency purposes, especially under any regulatory scheme. Indeed, one of the functions or purposes of economic regulation is to attempt to establish freight rates and other prices as close to $MC$ as possible. In essence, the purpose is to replicate the competitive market results under conditions where the impersonal market mechanism is inoperable or at least deemed to be so. There are, of course, other reasons for regulating an industry, but basically the economic rationale resides in the above manifestations of market failure.

### Density-Based Rate Structure

The application of marginal cost pricing to particular shipments is most complex, as we have noted. For transport modes whose unit of capacity creation is relatively small, a rate structure based on the density (weight per cubic foot) has often been recommended as a more practical way to implement cost-based rate making than costs per ton-mile or per ton.[1]

Let us examine this structure with respect to motor carrier rate making. Assume the capacity of a given truck is $C^*$ (in cubic feet) and the maximum load is $W^*$ (in tons). One could then define a "normal" density as $\dfrac{W^*}{C^*}$ in pounds per cubic foot—"normal" in the sense that a truck loaded with shipments having such a density would be "full" in both its cubic and its weight capacity—"full and down," as is said in the ocean shipping industry.

Assume now that the cost of operating a round trip truck journey of any given total distance is estimated as $\$K$, including "normal" rate of return on capital invested as well as operating costs, maintenance, and depreciation. For all shipments in this type of vehicle over the specified distance, the firm wants at least to recover $\$K$ per round trip. If so, for any commodity whose actual density, $\dfrac{W}{C} \geqq \dfrac{W^*}{C^*}$, the rate per pound should be $\dfrac{\$K}{W^*}$. For commodities whose density is less than $\dfrac{W^*}{C^*}$, the rate should be $\dfrac{\$K}{C^*\left(\dfrac{W}{C}\right)}$ per pound.

According to an ICC survey, the average volume, or space capacity, of truck trailers in 1971 was 2,512 cubic feet, and the average payload capacity was 42,500 pounds. Thus the average normal density is 16.9 pounds per cubic foot.[2] If we assume a round trip truck journey, with

---

1. A. White, "Can Rates Be Raised on Density, Load Units?" *Railway Age,* February 24, 1964, pp.29–31.
2. Data cited in R. A. Mays and M. P. Miller, "Intercity Freight Fuel Utilization at Low Package Densities—Airplanes, Express Trains and Trucks," Office of Energy and Emissions, BCAC, July 10, 1975, mimeographed.

TABLE 3.1

| Density (lbs./cu. ft.) | Actual Rate (assume mid-point density) |
|---|---|
| 3 | 26.54 cents/lb. |
| 4–6 | 7.96 cents/lb. |
| 7–10 | 4.68 cents/lb. |
| 11–17 | 2.84 cents/lb. |
| 17 and over | 2.35 cents/lb. |

no back-haul, for a given distance costs $1,000, any commodity with a density of 16.9 or above should therefore pay 2.35 cents per lb. Commodities with lower densities would pay proportionately greater amounts in terms of cents per pound. Thus one could construct a schedule of rates for various density brackets as given in Table 3.1.

Since the truck journey costs vary with distance, one could specify an analogous rate scale for various distance blocks. Because rates vary inversely with density, up to normal density, the rate structure permits recouping the costs per truck journey plus whatever markup represents "normal" profits. Competitive conditions could well call for modifications of this scheme, and, of course, we have ignored back-haul possibilities. However, as a point of departure for orienting rates more toward costs than toward value, this scheme has much to commend it. It is less applicable to rail and barge since the incremental costs of an additional rail car (or barge) to a train (or tow) destined to be dispatched in any event are negligible. One could revert to averages, but they would approximate the economic meaning of MC far less than for truck transport, thus necessitating departures from strict marginal cost pricing—namely, value-of-service pricing.

## Value-of-Service Pricing

The principle that $P$ should be brought into equality with $MC$ has been questioned in recent years by analysts. Indeed for decades, many transportation economists and the ICC have held that value-of-service pricing, especially for railroads, may be indispensable—at least as a pricing technique designed to recoup the fixed, joint, and indivisible costs on an "equitable" basis. As the ICC noted in its first annual report: "It was seen not to be *unjust* to apportion the whole cost of service among all the articles transported upon a basis that should consider the relative value of the service more than the relative cost."[3] Note that this relative downplaying of cost, presumably $MC$, emphasizes "justice"—not efficiency—as the overriding criterion. Indeed, the

3. *Annual Report of the Interstate Commerce Commission, 1887* (Washington, D.C., 1888), pp.30–31 (emphasis supplied).

commission has seldom stressed the latter. It is this failure plus the persistent support of a non-cost-oriented rate structure that has resulted in generations of economists disparaging ICC regulation. More recently, however, the case for value-of-service pricing, even on efficiency grounds, has been rendered more convincing. We will therefore outline the concept of the value of the service and develop its contemporary rationale.[4]

Since value-of-service pricing is a form of price discrimination, the theory of price discrimination is therefore uniquely relevant to understanding the concept. Briefly, for any firm to practice price discrimination requires that it have some degree of monopoly power, that it have the ability to segregate markets at costs less than the increased revenues derivable from discriminating, and that there be differing elasticities of demand in each of the markets so segregated.[5] The object of the firm is to charge the maximum profit price in each submarket. That requires setting $MR_i = MC_i$ in each of the $i$ submarkets. Since $MR_i = P_i \left( 1 - \dfrac{1}{\epsilon_i} \right)$, then for each differing $\epsilon_i$, there will be a different ratio of $P_i$ to $MC_i$ whenever $MR_i = MC_i$ in each market.

Assume a single-firm monopolist with constant unit costs at \$25 and the demand schedule facing the firm as shown in Table 3.2. For every dollar reduction in price, two more units will be sold. Thus the $MR/$ unit can be calculated as shown in column (3), assuming no fractional prices or quantities. The maximum profit situation obviously occurs under a single price at a price of \$56 with quantity bought and sold equal to 64 because every unit produced up to 64 units contributes more to total revenue than it does to total cost (i.e., $MR > MC$), whereas beyond 64 units sold the opposite is the case.[6]

---

4. It is true, however, that earlier writers concerned with railway pricing stressed prices that varied inversely with demand elasticities and that this *could* lead to lower rates for everyone if profits are limited to some reasonable amount. If so, this would augment consumers' (i.e., shippers') surplus and thus be *efficient* as well as equitable. (See W. M. Ackworth, *The Railways and the Traders* [London, 1891]; A. F. Hadley, *Railroad Transportation* [New York and London, 1886]; and others. W. A. Lewis, as is so often the case, perceived the issue early and clearly in *Overhead Costs* [London, 1949], especially pp.20–21.)
   See also the references cited in W. J. Baumol and D. F. Bradford, "Optimal Departures from Marginal Cost Pricing," *American Economic Review*, June 1970, for earlier formulations relative to the *efficiency* as distinct from the equity of value-of-service pricing.
5. More elaborate treatments are given in most contemporary intermediate economic theory texts.
6. If we acknowledge that the equation of the inverse demand curve is $P = 88 - \dfrac{1}{2} Q$, then profit $\pi = PQ - 25Q = 88Q - \dfrac{1}{2} Q^2 - 25Q.$
   $\therefore \dfrac{d\pi}{dQ} = 63 - Q = 0$
   $\therefore$ Optimal $Q = 63$ and optimal $P = 56.5$ if we allow fractions of dollars.

TABLE 3.2

| (1)<br>P | (2)<br>Q | (3)<br>MR/unit |
|---|---|---|
| 65 | 46 | |
| 64 | 48 | 41 |
| 63 | 50 | 39 |
| 62 | 52 | 37 |
| 61 | 54 | 35 |
| 60 | 56 | 33 |
| 59 | 58 | 31 |
| 58 | 60 | 29 |
| 57 | 62 | 27 |
| 56 | 64 | 25 |
| 55 | 66 | 23 |
| 54 | 68 | 21 |
| 53 | 70 | 19 |
| 52 | 72 | 17 |
| 51 | 74 | 15 |
| 50 | 76 | 13 |

Assume now that the firm can segregate the market into two separate groups and can keep the groups from trading with each other. The previous total demand can be split up as shown in Table 3.3. At a price of 65, the members of Group 1 will purchase 15 units, while the members of Group 2 will purchase 31 units, a total of 46 units at the price as noted in the single aggregate demand for this product. The marginal revenue, however, differs between the two submarkets for any given single price because the demand elasticities differ at each

TABLE 3.3

| (1)<br>P | (2)<br>$Q_1$ | (3)<br>$MR_1$ | (4)<br>$Q_2$ | (5)<br>$MR_2$ |
|---|---|---|---|---|
| 65 | 15 | | 31 | |
| 64 | 16 | 49 | 32 | 33 |
| 63 | 17 | 47 | 33 | 31 |
| 62 | 18 | 45 | 34 | 29 |
| 61 | 19 | 43 | 35 | 27 |
| 60 | 20 | 41 | 36 | 25 |
| 59 | 21 | 39 | 37 | 23 |
| 58 | 22 | 37 | 38 | 21 |
| 57 | 23 | 35 | 39 | 19 |
| 56 | 24 | 33 | 40 | 17 |
| 55 | 25 | 31 | 41 | 15 |
| 54 | 26 | 29 | 42 | 13 |
| 53 | 27 | 27 | 43 | 11 |
| 52 | 28 | 25 | 44 | 9 |
| 51 | 29 | 23 | 45 | 7 |
| 50 | 30 | 21 | 46 | 5 |

price. In general, given the above information, $|\epsilon_1| > |\epsilon_2|$. Note also that at the single price of \$56, $MR_1 = 33$ and $MR_2 = 17$. If a unit of sales could be shifted from the second submarket and sold in the first, there would be a net gain of $31 - 17 = \$14$. If a second unit could be shifted, the net gain would be $29 - 19 = \$10$, and so on. Units would continue to be shifted until no further net gain was possible, when $MR_1 = MR_2 = MC$. To accomplish that, the firm would reduce its price in the more-elastic submarket from the single price prevailing before and raise it in the less-elastic submarket. The maximum-profit set of prices would be $P_1 = \$52$ and $P_2 = \$60$, with profit rising by \$32 above the level prevailing at the single price of \$56 in each submarket.[7]

In highly simplified form, the basis for value-of-service pricing in transportation is: Transport suppliers seek to segregate markets in order to enhance their net profitability by charging the maximum-profit rate in each submarket subject only to competitive pressures and legal constraints. Conceptually at least, for any commodity, the precise meaning to be attached to the value of the service is very clear; namely, given the cost and demand characteristics for a particular commodity, *the* value of the service is the maximum-profit rate. In Figure 3.2, *the* value of the service is simply $OP_0$.

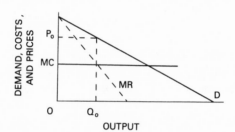

Fig. 3.2

While this theory is very easy and straightforward, in practice there are severe problems, as the discussion in chapters 1 and 2 indicated. Costs are not known with much accuracy; nor are the demand level and elasticity much clearer. However, most commercial transport firms search out a series of prices like $OP_0$ for a wide variety of commodities and city-pairs. The fact that they cannot do it with much accuracy should lead to considerable experimentation, but the present pattern of U.S. transport regulation has long inhibited such experimentation. That may be one reason why some of the values are so conjectural—more on this later! What should be emphasized at this point is that if the demand should drop because of intensified

7. For example, the increment of \$32 is made up of \$14 for the first unit shifted, \$10 for the second, \$6 for the third, and \$2 for the last.

intermodal competition but the carrier(s) retain the former rate, $OP_0$ no longer represents the value of the service as described above. Rather, it would be foolish pricing or misapplication of value-of-service pricing, assuming that the cost and demand functions were known. One of the reasons for disparaging value of service as a pricing principle is its frequent misapplication, which is associated with the rigidity of the rate structure in the face of altered costs and demands. Yet for conceptual clarity, the profit-maximizing criterion seems preferable to the earlier confusion surrounding the meaning of value-of-service pricing.[8] Any other conception really boils down to "stupid" pricing, or at least pricing behavior inconsistent with maximization principles.[9]

It may well be, however, that in transport markets not workably competitive, the rigorous application of value-of-service pricing could lead to excess profits. At the same time, rates that reflected *SRMC* would doubtless fail to generate revenues adequate to cover the fixed, joint, and indivisible costs. Finally, if some modes are subject to economies of scale—possibly rail, barge, and pipelines—rigorous application of marginal cost pricing will lead to revenue deficiencies. In all three of these situations, it may prove desirable that revenues cover costs plus some amount ensuring a "normal" or "reasonable" rate of return. Certainly, this would be essential if private ownership and operation of the transportation systems were deemed desirable. In the first instance, where monopoly power was ubiquitous, limitation of profit would be called for. In the latter two situations, where revenue deficiencies would occur, some deviation from marginal cost pricing or some subsidy arrangement would be necessary to sustain a private operation. In all three cases, additional costs to society would be incurred. In the monopoly case, some agency would have to determine what a "fair return" or "fair" level of profits would be and monitor it on a continuing basis. In the case of revenue deficiency, a subsidy would cause higher taxes and/or higher public deficits, both of which lead to other cost-occasioning distortions in the economy. Clearly, prices that deviate from *MC* lead to welfare losses, as noted earlier in this chapter, but in considering the alternatives, especially a subsidy, it is not clear that there are net losses for society as a whole.

---

8. See G. Wilson, *Essays on Some Unsettled Questions in the Economics of Transportation* (Bloomington: Foundation for Economic and Business Studies, Indiana University, 1962), pp.150ff.

9. In some cases, the regulated carriers may be forced by the ICC for equity or other considerations to set rates different from $OP_0$. They would not do so voluntarily if they had the requisite knowledge of demand and cost functions.

## Optimal Prices Subject to Revenue Constraint

Let us examine the issue of a revenue constraint on a firm being regulated either because as a monopoly it would make too much profit or because systematic application of *MC* pricing would lead to revenue deficiencies that would require subsidy or deviation from *MC* pricing—i.e., some form of value-of-service pricing.

Assume an even flow of demand per unit of time[10] and an enterprise that produces a variety of outputs $(q_i)$. The objective is to determine an efficient set of prices $(P_i)$. In the unconstrained case, as previously noted, from the point of view of maximizing the difference between benefits *B* and costs *C* to society as a whole, $P_i = MC_i$ is the pricing rule. More formally, and to note explicitly the difference a revenue constraint makes, the earlier rule may be derived as follows: To find Max. $(B - C)$ with respect to $P_i$ (or $Q_i$), assuming the appropriate second-order conditions of production and demand,[11] take the partial derivative of $(B - C)$ and set it equal to zero.

$$\frac{\partial(B - C)}{\partial Q_i} = \frac{\partial B}{\partial Q_i} - \frac{\partial C}{\partial Q_i} = 0.$$

If all publicly and privately provided goods are priced properly, then $\frac{\partial B}{\partial Q_i} = P_i$. Similarly, $\frac{\partial C}{\partial Q_i} = MC_i$. Optimality then requires that $P_i = MC_i$.

Now suppose we insist, for reasons noted briefly above and to be examined more fully later, that the railway, highway, port, or airport authority is required to price its services such that total revenue *R* $= P_i q_i$ equals or exceeds total costs *C*, i.e., that $R = \alpha C$ where $\alpha \geq 1$. In this case we seek to maximize $(B - C)$ subject to $C = \alpha \Sigma_i P_i Q_i$. For simplicity assume $\alpha = 1$; no difference in principle results.

Formally, this operation is simply maximization subject to a constraint. We therefore set up the Lagrangian function

$$\text{Max. (Net Benefits)} = (B - C) + \lambda(\Sigma P_i Q_i - C)$$

and proceed as before:

---

10. "Uneven" flows will be discussed below under "peak/off-peak" pricing. The contemporary impetus to this analysis was given by Baumol and Bradford, "Optimal Departures. . . ." A. A. Walters had earlier derived the same theorem in about the same way in his *The Economics of Road User Charges* (World Bank Staff Occasional Papers, no.5, 1968), pp.115–17. A variant of Walters's version is used here.

11. See J. M. Henderson and R. E. Quandt, *Microeconomic Theory* (New York: McGraw-Hill, 1958), chap. 3.

$$\frac{\partial(B - C)}{\partial Q_i} = \frac{\partial B}{\partial Q_i} - \frac{\partial C}{\partial Q_i} + \lambda \left( P_i + Q_i \frac{\partial P_i}{\partial Q_i} - \frac{\partial C}{\partial Q_i} \right) = 0.$$

Recall that $\frac{\partial B}{\partial Q_i} = P_i$, $\frac{\partial C}{\partial Q_i} = MC_i$, and $Q_i \frac{\partial P_i}{\partial Q_i} = \frac{-P_i}{\epsilon_i}$. By substitution, we set

$$\frac{P_i - MC_i}{P_i} = \left( \frac{\lambda}{\lambda + 1} \right) \frac{1}{\epsilon_i}.$$

This means that for optimal pricing, $P_i$ should *not* equal $MC_i$. Indeed, optimality, under a revenue constraint, *requires* that prices should systematically deviate from $MC_i$ inversely and proportionately on the basis of the elasticity of demand.

Pricing on the basis of demand elasticity is what we previously defined as value-of-service pricing. The foregoing thus appears to conflict with efficiency criteria requiring $P_i = MC_i$. The difference, of course, lies in the existence of the revenue constraint. Under what circumstances would a revenue constraint appear to be "efficient"?

A revenue constraint can either seek to *prevent* excess profits or to *ensure* normal profits for any desired level of capacity. In the former, we have the situation of "natural" monopoly, which in the absence of regulation would lead to "excessive" profits by equating $MR_i = MC_i$ in every submarket. In the latter, there may be such a combination of competitive pressures and cost indivisibilities that normal rates of return for large segments of the industry are unachievable. If significant capacity reductions are not desirable, society has three main choices: direct subsidy to sustain a private operation, nationalization and indirect subsidy, or systematic deviations from marginal cost pricing tolerated or supported by a system of economic regulation.

In the first case, we have the classical situation of economies of scale, in which in a given, relevant market no more than one firm can supply the output at efficient prices. The profit-maximizing firm without regulation would discriminate among users to the extent possible and develop a pattern of prices among different users that deviated from $MC_i$ on the basis of relative elasticities. If unit costs are decreasing, this would lead to expanded output and probably excess profits. Regulation of such situations, as in the case of local public utilities, is designed to eliminate excess profits and establish a rate or price structure that is deemed to be "equitable" rather than efficient. However, if efficiency criteria prevail, the previous theorem argues that in the excess profits case, the rate structure should be based on relative $\epsilon_i$'s while the rate level should be based on revenues covering receipts. That is, the weighted average of the prices should provide revenues equivalent to the weighted average of the costs, including a "fair return."

In practice, this can become most complicated because there are many sets of prices capable of yielding adequate revenues. For example, assume three submarkets, which, at the single price of $\$P^*$, yield quantities bought and sold of $q_1$, $q_2$, and $q_3$ and whose elasticities at that price are $\epsilon_1$, $\epsilon_2$, and $\epsilon_3$. For simplicity, assume $MC_i$ is constant for each volume of output. Thus at $P^*$, total revenues equal $P^*(q_1 + q_2 + q_3)$. If $MC_i$ is constant and equals $LRMC$, then for a revenue constraint equal to total costs we require that $P^*(q_1 + q_2 + q_3) = MC_i (q_1 + q_2 + q_3)$. If discrimination is not possible, then we revert to $P^* = MC_i$. But for a multiservice or multiproduct endeavor, with price discrimination possible, there are various alternatives. In each submarket the price could just as well be raised as lowered from the profit-maximizing level. Various sets of higher prices in each submarket could sufficiently reduce net receipts to satisfy the revenue constraint at lower output levels. Alternatively, various combinations of price increases and decreases in specific submarkets relative to the profit-maximizing price would produce the situation in which revenues equalled costs. In principle there are an infinite set of prices that can meet any predetermined revenue constraint when discrimination among various submarkets is possible.

The question in practice (and theory) is, Which set of prices is "efficient," in the sense of maximizing the consumer plus producer "surplus" criterion?[12] Assume three separable, linear, inverse demand functions for a presumptively homogeneous product, as follows:

$$P_1 = a_1 - b_1q_1; P_2 = a_2 - b_2q_2; P_3 = a_3 - b_3q_3.$$

Marginal costs are assumed to be constant at $k$. Each separable sub-

---

12. Even in the single-price situation, there may be two (or more) alternative prices that satisfy the constraint if the demand curve intersects the *ATC* curve at two (or more!) points. If *ATC* is declining at least up to a point and the demand curve intersects it as shown below, then either $P_1$ or $P_2$ satisfies the constraint. While in theory the preferred solution is obvious ($P_2$), in practice if a firm is just "breaking even," a regulatory agency will be reluctant to order a rate reduction, especially since the underlying demand and cost relationships are so uncertain and even their general shapes, let alone levels, are not known with much accuracy. See A. E. Kahn, *The Economics of Regulation*, vol.II (New York: Wiley, 1970), p.107–36.

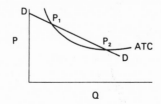

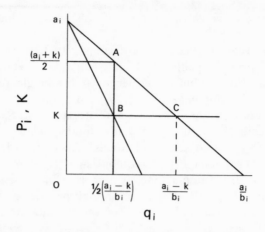

Fig. 3.3

market can be portrayed as shown in Figure 3.3. Maximum consumer surplus is given when $P_i = k$ and output in each of the three submarkets $q_i = \dfrac{a_i - k}{b_i}$. Maximum consumer surplus can be calculated as follows:[13]

$$\text{Max. } S = \sum_{i=1}^{3} \frac{1}{2b_i}(a_i - k)^2,$$

which occurs when $P_i = k$, the perfectly competitive outcome.

Assume now a single-firm, profit-maximizing monopolist. The maximum-profit price in each submarket, assuming $MC = k$ and is constant, is: $P_1 = \frac{1}{2}(k + a_1)$; $P_2 = \frac{1}{2}(k + a_2)$; and $P_3 = \frac{1}{2}(k + a_3)$.[14] At such prices the *producer* surplus is $\pi = \sum_{i=1}^{3} \dfrac{1}{4b_i}(a_i - k)^2$, the rectangle $\left(k, B, A, \dfrac{a_i + k}{2}\right)$.

However, the consumer surplus at such prices is reduced to $\sum_{i=1}^{3} \dfrac{1}{8b_i}(a_i - k)^2$. The sum of the new producer plus consumer surplus is therefore $\sum_{i=1}^{3} \dfrac{3}{8b_i}(a_i - k)^2$ under the profit-maximizing, discriminating monopoly situation. This is obviously less than the

---

13. Note that with constant $k$ there is no producer surplus, a point to which we return later.

14. These prices are derived by differentiating the profit function

$$\pi = P_1 Q_1 + P_2 Q_2 + P_3 Q_3 - k(Q_1 + Q_2 + Q_3)$$

using the above demand functions. Clearly, if the $MC$ of supplying in each separate submarket differs, the above maximum-profit rate or price structure would be $P_i = \frac{1}{2}(k_i + a_i)$, where $k_i$ represents $MC_i$ and need not be the same in all three markets. For simplicity of exposition we have assumed $k_1 = k_2 = k_3 = MC$.

Max. $S = \sum_{i=1}^{3} \dfrac{1}{2b_i} (a_i - k)^2$ possible under marginal cost pricing. In-

deed, the so-called welfare loss $= \sum_{i=1}^{3} \dfrac{1}{8b_i} (a_i - k)^2$, the area of the

triangle $ABC$ in Figure 3.3.[15]

From a transportation point of view, the application of value-of-service (i.e., maximum-profit) pricing in each submarket, under monopolistic conditions, leads to reduced efficiency in the sense of reduced surplus (consumer plus producer). Under such circumstances, regulatory or competitive pressures are needed to push prices or rates in each submarket closer to $MC_i$.

Suppose, however, that $\sum_{i=1}^{3} kQ_i$ in each submarket, with $P_i = k$

$= MC_i$, yielded insufficient revenues to cover total costs because of cost indivisibilities or other costs not directly assignable to specific sales units on a cost-occasioned basis. There are several alternatives as previously noted: (1) allow the firm to shrink investment so that rising $MC_i$ will occur, in which case $P_i = MC_i$ would yield positive profits; (2) provide a subsidy; (3) permit deviations from $MC$ pricing.

Let us examine the last in the light of the above demand and marginal cost situation. We seek then to determine an optimal rate structure such that $\Sigma P_i Q_i = \Sigma k Q_i + M$, where $M$ is the amount of costs not assignable to specific sales units on a cost-occasional basis, but which is necessary for continued operation at the existing or optimal level of capacity. In short, we seek to maximize net consumer surplus subject to $\Sigma P_i Q_i - \Sigma k Q_i - M = 0$, or

$$\text{Max. } S = \sum_{i=1}^{3} \int_{0}^{Q_i} (a_i - b_i Q_i) dQ_i - \sum_{i=1}^{3} k Q_i,$$

subject to the above constraint. We form the Lagrangian function

$$\pounds = \sum_{i=1}^{3} \int_{0}^{Q_i} (a_i - b_i Q_i) dQ_i - k \sum_{i=1}^{3} Q_i + \lambda \left( a_i Q_i - b_i Q_i^2 - k \sum_{i=1}^{3} Q_i - M \right).$$

$$\frac{\partial \pounds}{\partial Q_i} = a_i - b_i Q_i - k + \lambda a_i - 2 b_i Q_i \lambda - \lambda k = 0$$

But $a_i - b_i Q_i = P_i$, and $\lambda(a_i - 2b_i Q_i) = \lambda MR_i$. Thus by substitution

---

15. Directly computed, the triangular welfare loss $= \dfrac{1}{2} \left( \dfrac{a_i + k}{2} - k \right) \left( \dfrac{a_i - k}{b_i} \right.$

$\left. - \dfrac{a_i - k}{2b_i} \right)$ for the $i$th submarket, or $\dfrac{1}{8b_i} (a_i - k)^2$.

we have $P_i + \lambda MR_i = k(1 + \lambda)$. Recall that $MR_i = P_i \left(1 - \dfrac{1}{\epsilon_i}\right)$; then

$$P_i = \frac{k(1 + \lambda)}{1 + \lambda\left(1 - \dfrac{1}{\epsilon_i}\right)}.^{16}$$

Note that the larger $\epsilon_i$ is in absolute value, the closer the expression $\dfrac{(1 + \lambda)}{1 + \lambda\left(1 - \dfrac{1}{\epsilon_i}\right)}$ approaches unity and the closer $P_i$ is to $k = MC_i$. Conversely, the smaller $|\epsilon_i|$, the greater the gap between $P_i$ and $k$. When $\epsilon_i = 1$, $P_i = k(1 + \lambda)$.

To illustrate, assume three specific (inverse and linear) demand functions for the homogeneous transport service

$$P_1 = \$50 - 2Q_1; \quad P_2 = \$40 - 3Q_2; \quad P_3 = \$30 - Q_1$$

in each of three submarkets. If $k = \$10$ and is assumed constant for all volumes of output, the *net* consumer surplus in the submarkets can be calculated as follows:

$$S_1 = \int_{10}^{50} \frac{1}{2}(50 - P_1)dP_1; \quad S_2 = \int_{10}^{40} \frac{1}{3}(40 - P_2)dP_2; \quad S_3 = \int_{10}^{30} (30 - P_3)dP_3.$$

The results are $S_1 = 400$, $S_2 = 150$, $S_3 = 200$, and thus maximum surplus $= \$750$.

Fig. 3.4

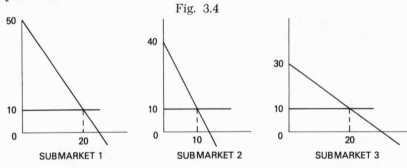

SUBMARKET 1    SUBMARKET 2    SUBMARKET 3

The three demand and cost situations are portrayed in Figure 3.4. In submarket 1, the maximum net surplus is the triangle above the $10 unit cost level whose "area" and value is $\tfrac{1}{2}(50 - 10)(20) = 400$,

---

16. This solution is not confined to linear demand or to any given number of submarkets. Indeed, the identical expression emerges for $P_i = f(Q_i)$ with constant $MC$.

and similarly for the other submarkets. If a single firm supplies the three submarkets and seeks to maximize profits, the respective prices and quantities will be:

$$P_1 = 30, \; Q_1 = 10; \; P_2 = 25, \; Q_2 = 5; \; P_3 = 20, \; Q_3 = 10.[17]$$

Note that at these prices and quantities, the higher the elasticity the lower the prices, as our previous analysis indicated.[18] However, at these discriminatory prices the net producer-plus-consumer surplus is reduced below the maximum. Thus, the process of converting consumer into producer surplus, given the usually assumed slopes of cost and demand formations, inevitably leads to greater losses in consumer surplus than gains to producer surplus. In short, as soon as prices deviate from $MC$, the losses exceed the gains and there is net social waste. The allowance of value-of-service pricing in this example, therefore, leads to waste.[19]

### Reconsideration of Pricing Principles

Optimal pricing requires that $P_i = MC_i$ in each submarket. However, if the firms are subjected to a revenue constraint, optimal pricing requires a rate structure that systematically deviates from $MC_i$. The difference in conclusions depends entirely on the existence of the revenue constraint. Under what conditions "should" society impose a revenue constraint in the transportation industries? A revenue constraint may be justified in a monopolistic industry when, over a reasonable time period, total receipts exceed total costs by excessive amounts for which no automatically corrective forces, such as new entry and/or automatic capacity expansion, would bring the revenue/cost relationship closer to "normality." Total revenues may fall below total costs through $MC$ pricing by amounts leading either to significant reductions in capacity (or what is often the same thing, sharp reductions in service quality—e.g., railroads) or total service aban-

---

17. These figures can be determined in a variety of ways. The simplest is to take the equation for the maximum-profit price or rate in each submarket, noted in an earlier section in general terms, and substitute. Thus $P_1 = \dfrac{k_1 + a_1}{2}$, which becomes $P_1 = \dfrac{10 + 50}{2} = 30$, and so on.

18. That is, in submarket 1 with $P_1 = 30$ and $Q_1 = 10$, $\epsilon_1 = -1.5$; similarly, $\epsilon_2 = -1.67$ and $\epsilon_3 = -2.0$. Prices vary inversely with elasticities.

19. In submarket 1, with a maximum profit $P_1 = 30$ and $Q_1 = 10$, the welfare loss is $\frac{1}{2}(30 - 10)(20 - 10) = \$100$. By similar calculations the triangular welfare losses are $\$37\frac{1}{2}$, in submarket 2, and $\$50$ in submarket 3, for a total of $\$187\frac{1}{2}$.

donment and bankruptcy.[20] Assuming that demand conditions warrant the existing capacity and service quality (i.e., the net consumer surplus *could* be positive), the two options in the second case, previously noted, need to be examined.

But even in the first case, where the objective is to reduce total revenues, problems of an optimal rate structure emerge. Clearly, rates should be reduced from the maximum-profit level in the submarkets with the greater elasticities down to $MC$ until total revenues are brought into consistency with total costs, including normal profits. However, we can be more precise. As the price is reduced in the more elastic submarkets toward $MC_i$, the elasticity is progressively reduced. In the case of linear demand functions with constant slope, the elasticity declines directly as $P_i$ falls. Thus the price reductions in the most elastic submarket should continue to the point at which the elasticity of demand in that submarket first falls below the elasticity in the next most elastic submarket. If excess profits still exist, price reductions in that submarket should be made until its elasticity just falls below that of any other submarket, and so on. Depending on the extent of excess profits, the process will continually reduce the absolute differences in the $\epsilon_i$ in each submarket from those existing in the profit-maximization case. It is possible that several, or perhaps all, of the $\epsilon_i$ will be brought to equality, in which case the efficient markup of price over marginal cost will be equal in those submarkets with identical elasticities. Indeed, depending on the extent of the differences in elasticity existing at profit-maximizing prices, it may be possible to have $P_i = MC_i$ in several submarkets, thus reducing the extent of welfare losses that would otherwise occur.

In the previous example, where excess profits are possible through discriminatory pricing, optimality requires that $P_1 = P_2 = P_3 = 10$ and that the elasticities at these prices are $\epsilon_1 = 1/4$, $\epsilon_2 = 1/3$, and $\epsilon_3 = 1/2$, compared with the elasticities at the profit-maximizing prices of $\epsilon_1 = 1.5$, $\epsilon_2 = 1.67$, and $\epsilon_3 = 2$. The absolute difference between $\epsilon_1$ and $\epsilon_3$ is .25 in the optimal case but .5 (or double) in the profit-maximizing case, and similarly for each of the paired comparisons.

This result should not be surprising. Indeed, it is merely a special case of the "rule of proportionality" developed long ago[21] to define

---

20. The costs referred to here are "efficient" costs. Revenues may fail to cover costs because of mismanagement, excessive capacity, and so on. $TR < TC$ should correct the situation if allowed to persist long enough. Indeed, one of the functions of accounting of financial losses is to eliminate excess capacity and inept management.

21. See R. F. Kahn, "Some Notes on Ideal Output," *The Economic Journal,* March 1935; and A. P. Lerner, "The Concept of Monopoly and the Measurement of Monopoly Power," *Review of Economic Studies,* June 1934.

efficiency criteria among industries, all of which are monopolized. Our three submarkets could be construed as three different industries. As $\frac{P_i}{MC_i}$ approached equality in all three "industries" (or submarkets), efficiency in the consumer surplus sense would increase.

However, our optimum price of $10 in each submarket implies that total revenues equal total costs, including normal profit. Assume that, as we have argued is the case for most of the transportation suppliers, the ascertainable $MC$, when multiplied by the quantities sold at $P = MC$, will lead to revenues less than costs including normal profit. Economies of scale, cost indivisibilities, and the like could easily account for such a discrepancy. Assume further that additional revenues are needed to sustain a private operation equal to $M$ per period above those that can be obtained when $P_i = \$10$.

The $M$ can be recouped by permitting the prices in each submarket to rise above $10. In the reverse process, analogous to that for price reductions from the excess-profit situation of a discriminating monopolist, prices would be raised first for the submarkets faced with the most inelastic demands at $P_i = \$10$ (e.g., submarket 1 with $\epsilon_1 = 1/4$). As the price is increased, the elasticity increases for linear demands until it equals or exceeds that of the next most inelastic demand. The process should be continued until the "needed sum of money" over and above the $10 per unit (i.e., $M$) is achieved. In essence, this is the Baumol-Bradford-Walters "theorem" concerning optimal prices subject to a revenue constraint. Whether it is possible to make all $\frac{P_i}{MC_i}$ proportions equal depends on the magnitude of $M$, the extent of the differences between elasticities at identical $P_i = MC_i$, and the extent of differences in the marginal costs of supplying each of the submarkets.[22]

In the numerical example, it can be shown (after tedious manipulation) that $P_1 = \dfrac{60(1 + \lambda)}{1 + 2\lambda}$, $P_2 = \dfrac{50(1 + \lambda)}{1 + 2\lambda}$, and $P_3 = \dfrac{40(1 + \lambda)}{1 + 2\lambda}$. Solving for $\lambda$ (an even more tedious process) yields two solutions to the resulting quadratic equation derived by differentiating the Lagrangian function with respect to $\lambda$. The value of $\lambda$ that satisfies a net revenue constraint of $M = \$100$ is (approximately) $-1.5$. Inserting these values in the above yields "optimal" prices as follows: $P_1 = \$15$, $P_2 = \$12.5$, and $P_3 = \$10$. At these prices total revenues exceed total costs by approximately[23] $100, the extra amount needed to cover the

---

22. Our illustration merely assumes that $MC_1 = MC_2 = MC_3 = \$10$ for simplicity's sake. The same principles apply for varying $MC$s.

23. Considerable rounding was done in the computations: hence the "approximately."

indirect costs. Note that the deviation of $P_i$ from $MC_i$ is bigger the greater the inelasticity of demand, as we would expect.

Obviously, there is some welfare loss, ignoring second-best considerations, because whenever $P_i > MC_i$ there is some diminution in consumers' surplus. Whether deviation from marginal-cost pricing is optimal depends on the magnitude of the welfare loss from the alternatives: direct subsidy and public ownership with indirect subsidy equal to $M. These two options have several problems in common.

First, a subsidy represents an income transfer from taxpayers generally to the users and/or operators of the service being subsidized. Whether such a transfer is desirable is a matter of judgment. Presumably, if it represented a transfer that led to greater equality of income distribution, most people would view it as a move in the right direction. However, in the freight transportation industries, the users and operators are often large industrial enterprises. Since their stockholders are more highly concentrated in the upper levels of income distribution than in income taxation, such a subsidy would doubtless lead to a slight increase in inequality and would be undesirable from this judgmental standpoint.

Second, a subsidy, other things being equal, would require either an increase in tax rates or a bigger deficit at the appropriate level of government. The first would cause distortions in other sectors of the economy, depending on which taxes were increased. Raising income taxes would have some negative effect on work (personal income tax) and the pattern of demands or investment incentives (corporate income tax). Increases in sales taxes would cause other prices in the economy to deviate even further from marginal cost, with consequent welfare losses. Any other tax rate increase to cover the subsidy would occasion similar types of losses elsewhere in the economy.

The other alternative, namely a larger deficit than would otherwise be the case, would contribute to inflationary pressures, assuming that othewise the surplus or deficit planned for stabilization purposes was correct. Such pressures would likewise have income redistribution effects but would also cause a series of repercussions on the price–marginal cost relationship elsewhere in the system that, on balance, would result in welfare losses.

Without a general equilibrium framework of analysis with reasonable parameters, not much can be said other than that a subsidy to one industry imposes costs on other segments of the economy. To determine whether subsidy, direct or indirect, is preferable to value-of-service pricing requires a comparison of the respective welfare losses, which is no easy task![24]

---

24. The issue is really very complex. For example, a subsidy can be administered

Public ownership not only gives rise to the problems noted above but also puts the enterprise even more in the political realm. The political involvement often creates incentives to use the firm to effectuate other social purposes at the expense of internal efficiency. Indeed efficiency criteria are likely to get short shrift in terms of pricing policy (i.e., lower prices or rates to the poor) or investment policy (i.e., location of new investment in depressed areas). There is nothing wrong with such actions as long as no alternative, less costly way or ways of effectuating certain aspects of social policy exist and as long as these actions can produce the desired results. Often this is not the case. Various alternatives normally exist, especially in a modern welfare state. Using direct regulation or ownership of an industry to implement social policy often creates inefficiencies within the industry without compensating net benefits. This appears to be the case with respect to much of contemporary transportation regulation (ICC and CAB) and ownership (Amtrak). We will discuss these issues more fully later.

In short, the much maligned value-of-service pricing turns out to be less undesirable than was frequently alleged in those situations where marginal cost pricing yields operating deficits. At least the alternatives to limited value-of-service pricing *may* occasion costs greater than the welfare loss associated with such pricing. In fact value-of-service pricing may increase output in cases where $MC$ is declining, since rates would be reduced in submarkets where elasticity exceeds unity. That would increase sales by an amount greater than an equivalent price increase in submarkets where elasticity is below unity, thereby leading to a net output increase. This appears to be the situation in many transportation submarkets, especially where intermodal competition or private or unregulated carriage exists. Indeed, the case can be made that for the railroads careful application of value-of-service pricing may be the main route to privately profitable operations.[25]

---

in several different ways: a lump sum agreed upon prior to the year's operations; a guarantee to make up the difference between total revenues and total costs; or a subsidy per unit of sales of some stipulated amount. That these would have different effects on the firm's incentives to be efficient is obvious. The first would provide an incentive to reduce costs, since the lump sum would not change. Subsequent negotiations of the amount of the lump sum in the light of actual experience could provide a continuing incentive to lower production costs. The second alternative provides no incentive to reduce costs—indeed it invites cost "padding." The third provides incentives to expand output, assuming the increased output can be sold at prices $\geq MC$, that might require more sales effort to shift the demand function. Other alternatives such as cost-plus agreements can be envisioned. These additional consequences related to the type of subsidy create further complications, which may or may not make value-of-service pricing the preferred alternative.

25. See Wilson, *Essays*, pp.167ff.

## Peak/Off-Peak Pricing

The marginal-cost and value-of-service pricing principles assumed an even flow of demand per time period—day, week, year, etc. However, in many, if not most, lines of production there are more or less regularly occurring peak demands followed by slack demands within the relevant period. Thus we have the morning and evening rush hours for urban transit, each of which is followed by minuscule demand; seasonal fluctuations in the demand for rail services associated with the agricultural crop season; and heavy demand for air transport at holiday periods. The key problem then is to decide how to price the service during peak periods, when capacity may be fully utilized, and during off-peak periods, when capacity may be substantially underutilized. An associated issue is the determination of the optimal capacity. We will consider the theory of these matters and later apply it to transportation. This application is particularly timely in view of the Railroad Revitalization and Regulatory Reform Act of 1976 (the 4-R Act); one of its purposes is to "promote the establishment of railroad rate structures which are more sensitive to changes in the level of seasonal, regional and shipper demand."[26]

The importance of seasonal freight rates was stressed by Commissioner Daniel O'Neal of the ICC in discussing seasonal or "demand sensitive" rates. After noting that "the number of options available for improving the financial health of the rail industry are limited," he concluded that "the establishment of innovative service, marketing and pricing practices offers a most appealing means to achieving increased efficiency and improved health in the railroad industry."[27] It is therefore important to set forth the efficiency criteria involved in peak/off-peak pricing (or demand-sensitive pricing), apply them to transportation, and note some of the (substantial) problems involved.

### The Classical Theory of Peak/Off-Peak Pricing

There is renewed interest in the theory of peak-load pricing, many years after it had been viewed as settled. As far back as 1949, Marcel Boiteux derived a formal solution to the problem. If we stretch the definition of formality, the solution goes back to H. Hotelling (1938) and before that to J. M. Clark (1911) and J. Dupuit (1844). However, in its more contemporary form, the problem was first solved by

---

26. Public Law 94–210, 94th Cong., S. 2718, Feb. 5, 1976, Sec. 101 (b) (4).
27. Ex Parte No. 324, "Standards and Expeditious Procedures for Establishing Railroad Rates Based on Seasonal, Regional, or Peak-Period Demand for Rail Service," decided Jan. 28, 1977, p.52A.

Boiteux in 1949 and independently by Steiner in 1957. Since Steiner's formulation[28] is the most straightforward and the one most often referred to in subsequent discussions, we will outline his approach here and use it as the point of departure for further analysis.

## THE STEINER SOLUTION

For non-storable commodities (e.g., transportation or electrical service) subject to periodic fluctuations, the problem involves the optimal amount of capacity and the optimal utilization of that capacity. The simplest case, à la Steiner, assumes the following:

1. The cost of providing enough capacity to produce one unit of output is $\beta$ and is constant regardless of the volume of production or the number of units of capacity actually purchased.
2. The marginal operating (non-capital) costs are constant at $b$ dollars per unit per period.
3. Demand fluctuations within the chosen subperiod do not occur or are deemed to be irrelevant.
4. Prices charged within the chosen period are given but may be varied among subperiods.
5. Costs and revenues are determined for equal-length subperiods.
6. Demands in each subperiod are independent of each other and, for simplicity, are assumed to be linear, as are the cost functions according to assumptions (1) and (2) above.

Given these assumptions, Pareto optimality in the sense that the sum of producers' plus consumers' surplus is maximized requires that the total revenue from sales of the product equal total costs. This is the same as stating that resources are optimally allocated when the willingness of consumers to pay for the marginal unit of output equals the cost of producing that unit (given the usual second-order conditions implicit in the above assumptions). We can derive the optimal solution for two cases: the fixed or insignificant peak and the shifting or significant peak.

*Fixed Peak.* For any given plant capacity, including optimal capacity, the demand function at the peak $D_1$ intersects the capacity constraint at a price $P_1 > b > 0$. If there are two subperiods, the off-peak demand function does not intersect at any price $P_2 \geqq b$. This means that sales (= output) in the peak period, $Q_1$, exceed sales in the off-peak period, $Q_2$ (i.e., $Q_1 > Q_2$).

---

28. P. O. Steiner, "Peak Loads and Efficient Pricing," *Quarterly Journal of Economics*, November 1957, pp.585–610.

*Shifting Peak.* For any given plant capacity, including optimal, the demand function for both peak and off-peak periods intersects the capacity constraint at prices $P_1$, $P_2 \geqq b > 0$: hence $Q_1 = Q_2$.

Both of these cases can be visualized by assuming three subperiods. Demand functions vis-à-vis capacity in periods 1 and 2 represent the shifting-peak situation, while the demand function in period 3 represents the fixed-peak case relative to optimal capacity. Figure 3.5 illustrates the solution.

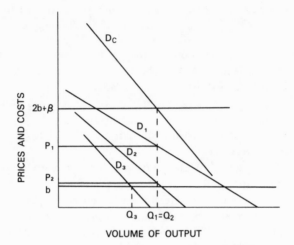

Fig. 3.5

VOLUME OF OUTPUT

The vertical sum of the demands in each subperiod ($D_C$) is the aggregate demand for output, in this case determined by subperiods 1 and 2. Optimal capacity is determined by the intersection of marginal capacity and operating cost ($2b + \beta$) with $D_C$ in the sense that consumers in periods 1 and 2 are willing to pay a "price" equal to $P_1 + P_2$ for the last unit of output costing $2b + \beta$. Consumers in subperiod 3 are unwilling to pay costs of capacity equal to $Q_1$ ($= Q_2$), and hence effective utilization of excess capacity in period 3 requires a price equal to short-run marginal cost, or $b$. Thus "optimal" prices are $P_1 + P_2 = 2b + \beta$ and $P_3 = b$. In essence, consumers in subperiods 1 and 2 share the capacity costs according to the intensity of their demands.

Given the assumptions earlier stated, Pareto optimality (neglecting departures therefrom in the rest of the economy and neglecting problems of income distribution) requires that the firm's total revenues $TR$ equal total costs $TC$, where

$$TR = \sum_{i=1}^{n} P_i Q_i \text{ for the } n\text{-period case, and}$$

$$TC = Q^*\beta + b\sum_{i=1}^{n} Q_i, \text{ in which } Q^* = \text{optimal capacity.}$$

$$\therefore \sum_{i=1}^{n} P_i Q_i = Q^*\beta + b\sum_{i=1}^{n} Q_i.$$

In the three-subperiod case we have $P_1Q_1 + P_2Q_2 + P_3Q_3 = Q_1\beta + b(Q_1 + Q_2 + Q_3)$. But since $Q_1 = Q_2 > Q_3$, it follows that $Q_1(P_1 + P_2) + P_3Q_3 = Q_1\beta + b(2Q_1 + Q_3)$. If we set $P_3 = b$, then $P_1 + P_2 = 2b + \beta$. In the generalized case for $n$ subperiods, the sum of the prices paid by those in the shifting-peak situation equals $nb + \beta$, while the prices paid by off-peak users in the fixed-peak situation equal $b$.

It is simple to show that these prices are optimal under the restrictive assumptions: If capacity were increased by one unit, the cost of producing that unit in each period would be $nb + \beta$, whereas with downward-sloping demand curves the sum of the new prices required to sell the extra unit would be less than $\sum_{i=1}^{n} P_i$. Thus, the marginal consumer's evaluation would be less than the marginal cost. The converse is true for a reduction in capacity of one unit below that we have deemed optimal.

We have described the simplest form of the "classical" solution proposed by Steiner. Figures 3.6 and 3.7 illustrate the Steiner solution graphically.

In the fixed-peak case, we have assumed that the peak demand function $D_1$ is $Q_1 = 100 - P_1$, while the off-peak demand function $D_2$ is $Q_2 = 60 - 2P_2$, $b = 5$, $\beta = 20$. Optimal prices are $P_1 = 25$ and $P_2 = 5$. These prices compare with maximum-profit prices of a single-firm monopoly of $P_1 = 62.5$ ($AA$ in Figure 3.6) and $P_2 = 17.5$ ($BB$ in Figure 3.6). The reader can readily verify that the consumers' plus producer's surplus in the optimal-price situation exceeds that in the profit-maximizing situation.

In the shifting-peak case of Figure 3.7, $D_1$ is as before, the off-peak demand $D_3$ is $Q_3 = 90 - P_3$, and costs are the same as in Figure 3.6. Now the optimal prices are $P_1 = 20$ and $P_2 = 10$. Thus both peak users share the capacity costs in accordance with their intensity of demand at the peak. It can also be shown that the sum of the consumers' plus producers' surplus is greater at these prices than at profit-maximizing prices.

### THE WILLIAMSON "TWIST"

The Steiner formulation is simplicity itself, but the geometry is somewhat unconventional, if one ignores the "pure public goods" analogy. In 1966 Williamson sought, among other things, to render the "awkward and unconventional" geometric techniques more conventional and presumably less awkward.[28] Williamson's "twist" is to take the *"entire demand cycle* as the natural unit against which to express costs. . . . We therefore define short-run marginal costs as the operating costs of supplying the incremental unit of output (at levels of operation less than capacity) over an entire cycle, namely $b$ per unit per

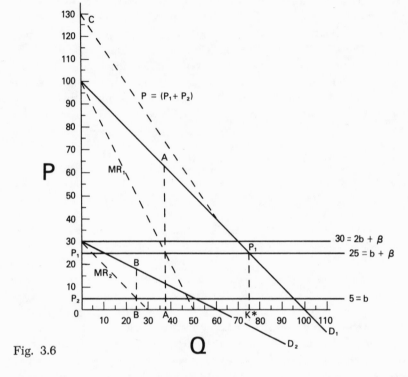

Fig. 3.6

cycle. Since incremental capacity costs continue at the rate of $\beta$ per unit per cycle long run marginal costs are $b + \beta$ per unit per cycle." Similarly, demand must be specified in a consistent way, namely, weighted by "the fraction of the cycle over which it prevails."[29] Thus, in place of the Steiner et al. "additive approach," Williamson adopts a

---

28. O. E. Williamson, "Peak-Load Pricing and Optimal Capacity under Indivisibility Constraints," *American Economic Review*, September 1966, p.810. One of the "other things" Williamson sought to do in this article was to make explicit the social welfare function implicit in the Boiteux, Steiner, and Hirshleifer analyses. This was hardly necessary, as the assumptions take care of that, and, in fact, Steiner was as explicit as Williamson in this connection. See P. O. Steiner, "Peak Load Pricing Revisited," in H. M. Trebing, ed., *Essays on Public Utility Pricing and Regulation* (East Lansing: Institute of Public Administration, Michigan State University, 1971), p.11.

29. Williamson, p.817.

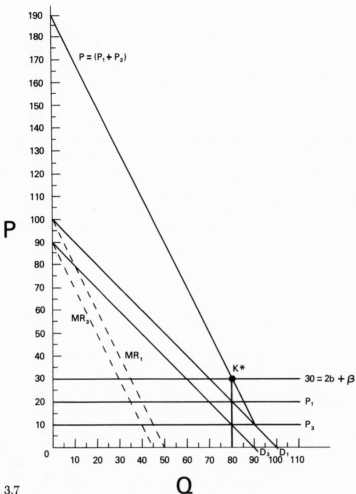

Fig. 3.7

(weighted) "averaging approach" in dealing with subperiods of a given demand cycle.

Take, for example, the data from the two previous exhibits pertaining to the fixed- and shifting-peak cases.

Fixed Peak: $\quad Q_1 = 100 - P_1.$ $\quad (D_1 = \text{peak demand})$

$\qquad\qquad Q_2 = \phantom{0}60 - 2P_2.$ $\quad (D_2 = \text{off-peak demand})$

The Steiner formulation converts these two demands into a single demand by adding vertically to obtain the demand for capacity. Thus

$$P = P_1 + P_2 = \frac{-3}{2}Q + 130 \quad \text{for all} \quad Q \leqq 60. \text{ For } Q > 60, \; P = 100 - Q$$

(i.e., $D_1$, since for $Q > 60$, $P_2 < 0$). Given this demand and linear costs $b = 5$ and $\beta = 20$, optimal capacity is determined by setting $P = 2b + \beta = 30$. Since this capacity determines an output $> 60$, the revelant demand is $P = 100 - Q$. The $MC$ for the single demand, however, is $b + \beta$ (which distinguishes the fixed from the shifting peak); thus optimal capacity occurs when $P_1 = b + \beta = 25$, or at $Q_1 = 75$. Off-peak demanders would consume only 75 units if $P_2 = -7.5$ (i.e., $75 = 60 - 2P_2$). At $P_2 = MC_2 = 5$, consumption is optimal in terms of consumer surplus. (See Figure 3.6.)

In a sense, this reasoning is convoluted, since it requires the determination of optimal prices after determination of optimal output. As Williamson notes, it is "awkward and unconventional." His "twist" is to weight the peak/off-peak demands by the proportion of the demand cycle over which they pertain. The Steiner solution implies (nay, requires) that the periods be equal.

The Williamson "twist" is more compelling in the shifting-peak case.

Shifting Peak:  $D_1$:  $Q_1 = 100 - P_1$.
$\qquad\qquad\quad D_3$:  $Q_3 = \phantom{0}90 - P_3$.

As before in the Steiner approach, $P = P_1 + P_2 = -2Q + 190$ (see Fig. 3.7). At a "price" $= 2b + \beta = 30$, optimal capacity is 80 units (i.e., $30 = 2Q + 190$), and to ration demand to this output, we substitute $Q_1 = Q_2 = 80$ in $D_1$ and $D_3$ to obtain optimal prices $P_1 = 20$ and $P_2 = 10$.

The Williamson approach with $Q_1 = Q_3$ assumes that prices $P_1$ and $P_2$ pertain over the whole demand cycle. Optimality requires that total revenues equal total costs, which in turn requires that the total revenues be weighted by the fraction of the cycle "during which the demand in question prevails" (i.e., $W_1$ and $W_3$ where $W_1 + W_3 = 1$).

In the present example we have total revenues equal to $P_1Q_1W_1 + P_3Q_3W_3$. Since $Q_1 = Q_3$ this expression becomes $P_1Q_1W_1 + P_3Q_1W_3$. Total capacity costs need to be specified somewhat differently since each demand is assumed to pertain over the entire cycle. Thus optimal price for each demand must be $b + \beta$. Since there are two such demands assumed to prevail over the entire cycle, total costs would be $Q_1(b + \beta) + Q_3(b + \beta)$, which must also be weighted by the fractions of the cycle over which they pertain. Thus we have total costs equal to $W_1Q_1(b + \beta) + W_3Q_3(b + \beta)$. Since $Q_1 = Q_3$, total costs become $Q_1[W_1(b + \beta) + W_3(b + \beta)]$. However since $W_1 + W_3 = 1$, this reduces to $Q_1(b + \beta)$. Optimality requires that $P_1Q_1W_1 + P_3Q_3W_3 = Q_1(b + \beta)$. Dividing by $Q_1$, we obtain $P_1W_1 + P_3W_3 = b + \beta$.

In the Steiner approach $\beta = 20$, but in Williamson's approach $\beta = \$10$ for each cycle, since two fictitious cycles were assumed, one for each demand. Thus, the $\beta$ in the Steiner approach needs to be weighted by the proportion of the cycle over which costs are actually incurred. Substituting $P_1 = 100 - Q$ and $P_3 = 90 - Q_3$ in the above equation we have $1/2(100 - Q_1) + 1/2(90 - Q_3) = 5 + 10$. But $Q_1 = Q_3$, $\therefore$ $1/2(100 - Q_1) + 1/2(90 - Q_1) = 15$; and $Q_1 = 80$, $P_1 = 20$, $P_3 = 10$, as in the Steiner solution.

More formally it can be shown in the two-period case that optimal prices are as follows for the two approaches:[30]

$$\text{Steiner:} \quad P_1 + P_2 = 2b + \beta^*$$
$$\text{Williamson:} \quad P_1 W_1 + P_2 W_2 = b + \beta$$

For the $n$-period case we have

$$\text{Steiner:} \quad \sum_{i=1}^{n} P_i = nb + \beta^*$$

$$\text{Williamson:} \quad \sum_{i=1}^{n} P_i W_i = b \sum_{i=1}^{n} W_i + \beta$$

The two approaches are equivalent as long as *either* $\beta = \beta^*$ and $W_i = W_j = 1$, *or* $\beta = \beta^*, \dfrac{1}{n} = W_i = W_j$, and $\sum_{i=1}^{n} W_i = 1$. Alternatively, the two approaches can be rendered equivalent for any given problem as long as the capacity costs and weights are reinterpreted in a manner consistent with either of the conditions noted. The Williamson formulation is somewhat more general in that it can include subperiods of different lengths (i.e., $W_i \neq W_j$), whereas the Steiner solution cannot.

Since the above formulations, considerable extensions of the analysis have been made, mainly by modifying the basic assumptions noted on p.155 by introducing additional considerations such as "uncertainty," the effects of regulation, and heterogeneous productive capacity.[31] In general, these do not profoundly change the basic conclusions of the "classical" approach. Indeed, one is tempted to agree with Steiner that "the purely theoretical debate . . . has gone on too

---

30. George W. Wilson, "The Theory of Peak Load Pricing: A Final Note," *Bell Journal of Economics and Management Science*, Spring 1972, pp.307–10. O. Williamson mildly dissents from this "reconciliation" in "Peak-Load Pricing: Some Further Remarks," *Bell Journal of Economics and Management Science*, Spring 1974, pp.223–28.

31. A bibliography of the more recent literature is contained in the references in the following: E. E. Bailey and E. B. Lindenberg, "Peak Load Pricing Principles: Past and Present," in H. Trebing, ed., *New Dimensions in Public Utility Pricing* (East Lansing: MSU Public Utilities Studies, Michigan State University, 1976), pp.30–31; and "Symposium on Peak Load Pricing," *Bell Journal of Economics*, Spring 1976, pp.206, 230–31, 240–41.

long without a major infusion of new insights."[32] Clearly, however, the simplifying assumptions of the classical approach require further examination, especially as they pertain to transportation. The following section examines each of these assumptions and notes the theoretical implications of altering them. It will be followed by an examination of the problems encountered in applying the relevant principles to the pricing of intercity freight transportation.

## Modification of Assumptions

The first two assumptions concern constant capacity and operating costs per unit of output. The modification to the above analysis by assuming either rising or falling unit capacity and/or operating costs is fairly straightforward and obvious. In the case where both sets of costs are rising after, let us say, a small volume of output, optimal prices in each period ($P_i = MC_i$) will exceed average costs and thus in every period will contribute something to capacity even in the fixed-peak case. The firm will be making excess profits but the sum of producer's plus consumers' surpluses will be maximized. Figure 3.8 illustrates

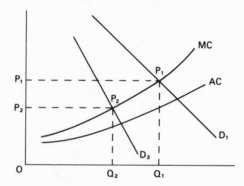

Fig. 3.8

this case with $P_1 = MC_1$ at output $OQ_1$, and $P_2 = MC_2$ at output $OQ_2$. Excess profits $= (P_1 - A)OQ_1 + (P_2 - \beta)OQ_2$ (i.e., price minus average cost times the optimal output). Elimination of excess profits could be achieved by special taxation of the enterprise, which may blunt incentives to be efficient, or by altering prices, which would involve welfare losses. If the firm were nationalized, the excess profits could be returned to the general fund, assuming that the level of efficiency was not adversely affected by public ownership.

---

32. P. O. Steiner, "Peak Load Pricing Revisited," p.20. More pungently and more recently, Steiner has characterized the so-called theoretical debate as a "converging infinite series of contributions whose sum after 20 years is close enough to its limit that there has got to be a better way to spend one's time" (in Trebing, *New Dimensions in Public Utility Pricing*, p.43).

Similarly, if both sets of costs are declining, it is evident that at optimal prices $(P_i = MC_i)$ there would be a revenue deficiency that would require subsidy, ownership, and/or permission to discriminate in pricing. [33] In short, no serious complications ensue from modifying the constant unit-cost assumptions regarding operating and capacity costs.

Modification of the assumption that demand fluctuations within the period do not occur likewise presents no insuperable analytical problem. For if at a given price in some designated time period at certain times there is excess capacity and at others deficiency of capacity, we simply need to redefine the periods and allow the prices to vary between the newly defined periods. There may well be a real cost if "too many" subperiods and "too many" prices are changed, but analytically no problem arises, as Steiner so aptly shows. [34]

These considerations also take care of assumption 4 on p.155, where prices were assumed not to change *within* the chosen subperiod. Clearly, if demand fluctuations are substantial within the period, a single price would lead to welfare losses. With large demand fluctuations, the subperiod needs to be further broken down into shorter periods with correspondingly different prices charged in each.

Assumptions 5 and 6 have been dealt with earlier. Again, their acknowledged unrealism does not deny the basic optimality conclusions, although, in practice, all the modifications toward realism create serious problems of implementation and of finding the correct number of subperiods and correct price within each necessary to approximate optimality.

## Application of Peak/Off-Peak Pricing

The foregoing principles of peak/off-peak pricing are relatively straightforward and plausible. Yet, except for portions of the unregulated sector of freight transportation, there has been remarkably little effort to implement such an apparently rational policy. Indeed, this lack of application elicited a section of the 4-R Act exhorting the Interstate Commerce Commission to encourage such pricing. Thus Section 202(d)(17) of the Act states:

Within one year after the date of enactment of this paragraph, the Commission shall establish by rule, standards and expeditious procedures for the establishment of railroad rates based on seasonal, regional, or peak period demand for rail services.

---

33. Further details can be found in Bailey and Lindenberg, pp.20–24.
34. P. O. Steiner, "Comment" on Bailey and Lindenberg, in Trebing, pp.39–42.

The commission's response was to establish new procedures in the filing and evaluation of seasonal rates[35] with the intent of encouraging greater use of such demand-sensitive rates. However, there are serious difficulties with respect to seasonal freight rates, which largely account for their limited use to date.

In the past, the commission itself has not looked favorably on such pricing practices, largely because of the opportunities for discrimination contained in any such scheme. In fact, in the few instances since World War II when such pricing has been implemented, the ICC, in response to shippers' protests, has kept reduced rates, intended to stimulate demand for a brief slack period, in effect for the entire year.[36] Several experiments with seasonal pricing have been more successful. In 1971, the rail carriers moving grain from North Dakota to Minneapolis and Duluth reduced so-called year-round rates in response to motor carrier competition, but added a special premium of 13% above the rate for the peak months of July, August, and September, when the capacity of both rail and truck systems was being taxed. Though the experiment was partially successful, when world prices changed dramatically after 1972–73, the fixed date for imposing the higher rate became unworkable. In Canada there are seasonal rates for moving potash—a peak rate of $4.50 per ton in March, April, and May and a low rate of $2.00 per ton during the slack season. It is reported that the movement of potash has been leveled substantially as a result. Other experiments have been less successful.

Basic problems beyond ICC reluctance exist. One obvious difficulty is that price is only one of many variables influencing the quantity of shipments by any given mode at any given time. Clearly, even if price were not the overriding factor, a railroad would receive more revenue from rate increases at the peak but would suffer from rate decreases during the off-peak period, if rail demand were inelastic. This raises the question of whether to create a differential between peak and off-peak rates by raising rates proportionally more during the peak, compared with the present year-round rate, or reducing rates proportionally more during the off-peak period. There are an infinite number of combinations of peak rate increases vis-à-vis off-peak rate decreases that in principle could create the "correct" spread.

Since rates are set on particular commodities between specified points, the issue of the capacity constraint is less compelling in transport than in, say, electric power generation. That is, a particular commodity, such as grain, in a given region may have a distinct seasonal pattern of movement. But if the carrier has a widespread geographical

---

35. See Ex Parte 324, February 4, 1977.
36. See Ex Parte 324.

system and/or carries other commodities whose seasonal pattern counterbalances that of the grain, no capacity or box car shortages may be involved. Seasonal pricing in circumstances where the total rail shipments have little seasonality could simply represent a means of increasing carrier revenues if rates were raised during the peak (assuming inelastic rail demand) and maintained during the off-peak season. Rail seasonal grain rates in the Southern territory in September 1977 seem to have been motivated by revenue incentives.

The problem of timing likewise looms large. The higher peak rate could go into effect on a specific date and drop to the off-peak rate at a later specified date. This arrangement has obvious limitations for the most seasonal commodities. With agricultural products, especially grain, the peak period may vary as much as one or two months from year to year because of weather, crop size, or market conditions. Other seasonal commodities, ore, and construction aggregates also exhibit variable seasonality because of weather conditions. To offset the problems of a fixed date and to recognize that for most seasonal commodities demand builds up to a peak and then tapers off, several prices or rates may be offered during the peak season, beginning with small increments and building up to higher ones, then tapering down to the off-peak rate.

If the dates and the different rates are given well in advance, shippers can make plans for storage or diversion to other modes. On the other hand, inflexibility in the face of variable seasonality limits the usefulness of either of these approaches. As a consequence, alternative methods have been considered. As the Kearney report notes, "A more flexible approach is one in which the peak load price is applied and removed [on the basis of] some indicator of demand for rail services."[37] Such indicators as a measure of car shortages, the opening or closing of navigable waterways, the percent of a crop harvested in a given area, or the number of cars ordered by shippers could be used to trigger higher (or lower) rates on a given commodity movement.

Despite these problems, the opportunity both to increase rail carrier revenues and to reduce future car needs is substantial. Over 25 percent of U. S. rail traffic by cars has been identified as "seasonal," where seasonal traffic is defined as a deviation of 20 percent or more above or below the annual average by car type (for 35 commodity classes).[38] The most seasonal commodities are agricultural products (especially wheat, poultry, soybeans, livestock, and "other" field

37. A. T. Kearney, *Seasonal, Peak, and Regional Rates Evaluation,* Task III, Final Task Report, July 15, 1977, p.v-3.

38. ICC, *The Impact of the 4-R Act, Railroad Ratemaking Provisions,* October 5, 1977, p.71.

crops), copper and iron ore, crushed stone, sand and gravel, assembled motor vehicles, and agricultural chemicals.[39] Estimates of the rail transport demand elasticities (in absolute value), using methods noted in chapter 1, exceeded 4 for crushed stone and for sand and gravel; exceeded unity for soybeans, corn, and assembled motor vehicles; and were about 0.8 for wheat and iron ore.[40] Unfortunately, these estimates are annual, national aggregates and do not relate to specific regions and/or times of year. During the peak period, demand elasticities can be expected to become smaller as shippers feel pressure to move their goods. Thus, higher rates during the peak period would be expected to produce more net revenue and, to a lesser extent, help to smooth the peak/off-peak aberration.

Of greater importance than the crude elasticity estimates is the cost of storage to the shipper. For grain it is estimated to range between $0.0338 per bushel per month and $0.0153, with the higher figure applicable to relatively small storage facilities and the lower figure to large installations.[41] Generally speaking, a shipper faced with a higher seasonal rate will incur storage costs up to the point at which such costs equal the savings in transport realized by not shipping at the seasonal rate. An analysis of the impact of seasonal rates designed to limit demand peaks for grain to 20 percent above the quarterly average, in the light of the storage costs, indicates that "a successful peak load pricing strategy could potentially save the railroads as much as $1 billion in capital expenditures between now and 1985."[42] This statement assumes, among other things, that the 20 percent demand peak ceiling can be achieved by sensible peak pricing. Obviously, all the railroads in the region would have to agree on the pricing policy, and independent truckers and barge operators would have to be incapable of moving the traffic during the peak period, because they lack the capacity or for other reasons. Otherwise, the traffic will simply be diverted with little benefit to the railroads and little or no smoothing of the peak.

As noted above, the U.S. experience with seasonal rates in the regulated sector of transportation has been limited. The provision in the 4-R Act designed to encourage peak-load pricing was clearly intended to stimulate experimentation and subsequently monitor the results. The benefits to the carriers, while plausible, are highly problematic. Only three applications for seasonal rates had been received by the ICC by December 1977. Two involved decreases during the off-peak

---

39. Ibid., Table IV-3, p.73.
40. See Table 1.6. These estimates are high.
41. ICC, *The Impact of the 4-R Act*, p.77.
42. Ibid., p.83.

period, and one requested a 20 percent seasonal premium on grain movements to, from, and between points in the Southern territory, Indiana and Illinois, from September 5, 1977 to December 15, 1977. Aside from causing considerable annoyance to shippers and state legislators, the effects of the sudden increase have not yet been evaluated. In any event, the experiment with peak/off-peak pricing has begun, albeit on a limited scale.

This ends our review of efficient pricing criteria. It is difficult to establish clear-cut, unambiguous guidelines that depend on such things as the need or desirability of a revenue constraint or the social costs of subsidy when $P = MC$ and economies of scale exist. The practical problems are even more severe and relate to the inadequate knowledge that exists regarding demand and cost functions. Even such an apparently straightforward problem as seasonal railway freight rates is beset with implementation difficulties and woefully inadequate estimates of results. Will revenues rise or will traffic be diverted? Will significant equipment savings be realized? The questions exist over and above attempts at estimating how much the variables (traffic, revenues, and equipment needs) will change. Yet many transport companies are subject to more or less detailed economic regulation where knowledge of such things is essential for sensible regulatory decisions. We therefore turn now to the economics of regulation.

# The Economics of Regulation

Intercity freight transportation industries have been regulated for many years. The Act to Regulate Commerce was passed in 1887. It had been preceded by a series of regulations in various Western states inspired by the Granger Movement, which was in part a response by agrarian interests to the pattern of rate discrimination employed by the railroads in the previous decade.[1] In this chapter we will examine the economic theory of regulation, conditions required for successful regulation, and the impact of regulation on the economy as well as on the industries regulated.

## The Theory of Economic Regulation

The transportation industries have long been subject to economic as well as safety regulation. During the twentieth century, more and more industries have been brought under various forms of economic regulation, and analysts have sought to explain why certain types of industries at particular times have been subjected to various types of regulation. This is what is meant by a "theory of regulation." There are, of course, many kinds of regulation, and, indeed, all business enterprises are more or less regulated in the sense that they are subject to the rules and constraints applicable to situations ranging from perfect markets through regulated monopolies or oligopolies. All are subject to the general rules established by the plethora of new agencies dealing with the environment (EPA), equality of economic opportunity and nondiscrimination (EEOC), worker health and safety (OSHA), antitrust laws (FTC and Antitrust Division of the Department of Justice), labor laws (NLRB), and many others. However, these types of economic regulation are not industry-specific. Most attempts to develop a theory of regulation have confined themselves to

---

1. The Appendix to this chapter provides a brief historical review of the development of the U.S. transportation regulation.

the regulation of a particular industry by a special agency or commission that is granted broad powers over specific aspects of the industry. The powers granted usually extend to price level and structure, mergers, entry, financial arrangements, and accounting practices and procedures.

Two opposing theories of economic regulation exist in the literature. One holds that "regulation is a device for protecting the public against the adverse effects of monopoly," while the other holds that "regulation is procured by politically effective groups assumed to be composed of the members of the regulated industry itself, for their own protection."[2] But all these theories and their variations do not explain when and why particular industries or groups of firms have been subjected to industry-specific, commission-type regulation.

Consider the following:

1. In the United States, industries varying widely in structure, performance, and other aspects—from trucking to electric power and telephones—have been regulated by commissions. No common economic denominator underlies commission-type regulation, and, ever since the Nebbia case,[3] such commonality is no longer legally relevant.

2. Some commission-regulated industries have sought economic regulation while others have not. There is much ambiguity on this point. Many now believe that because of the periodic breakdown of their privately operated cartels, the railroads actively sought the creation of the Interstate Commerce Commission. The traditional view, on the contrary, holds that regulation was thrust on the railroads as punishment for abuses of economic power. There is indeed a great variation in the extent to which particular industries now regulated by commission actively sought or fought control. A theory of regulation would need to sort out the historical evidence to determine which is the correct interpretation—no easy task in itself. For instance, in the trucking industry we are advised that regulation was favored by the larger trucking enterprises as well as the railroads and the ICC itself, but for the industry as a whole the picture is unclear. In general, there appears to be wide variation among presently regulated industries in terms of the original sources of and incentives toward regulation and the extent to which the now-regulated firms sought to mold the legislation and its subsequent interpretation and enforcement.

3. Commission-regulated industries were subjected to controls at different times, when different overall economic conditions prevailed—

2. R. Posner, "Taxation by Regulation," *Bell Journal of Economics and Management Science,* Autumn 1972, p.22.
3. *Nebbia v. New York,* 291 U.S. 502 (1934).

the railroads in 1887, electricity and gas in 1905, telephone and telegraph in 1910, trucks and airlines in the mid-1930s. Political conditions and varying legal interpretations also had a great deal to do with both the incidence of regulation and its nature, and have to be considered as variables in any theory purporting to explain commission-type regulation. The 1930s, for example, was a period in which society began to question the efficacy of competition as a regulator of business. There was a strong push for "codes of fair competition" under the NRA. In such a milieu, it was easier to justify economic regulation even of competitive industries such as trucking. Similar moods have not prevailed in earlier or later eras throughout the nation as a whole.

4. Some commission-regulated industries were to be restricted in their pricing and other behavior, while others were to be promoted—for example, the air transport industry. Some industries such as shipping were directly subsidized, while others were not.

Given this enormous variety of circumstances, a theory with any predictive or explanatory power is almost an impossibility, and the search for it is probably a meaningless exercise. If we demand of such a theory assertions to the effect that Industry B is likely to be subjected to commission-type economic regulation under a specified set of conditions, whereas Industry A is not, we must specify the particular conditions. If we are unable to specify, measure, "weight," and predict them, we will be unable to predict when or even whether Industry A will in fact be subjected to economic regulation. That is, we need to be able to specify a relationship along the following lines:

Economic Regulation of Industry $A = f$ (structure, practices, and performance of A; the state of the industry and the nation; the political power of industry members vis-à-vis competitors and customers; the relative importance of the industry to the economy and national defense; whether or not Industry B, which provides substitute service, is regulated; and other variables).

Not only is it impossible to quantify many of these variables but also there is no known way for some of them (e.g., political power) to be ranked among industries. Furthermore, most of the variables change over time in ways that cannot readily be envisioned. In addition, the weighting system required for each variable would be inherently subjective, unless, of course, some econometric model could be devised to specify the coefficients in some reasonable form and fashion. Finally, we cannot *a priori* deduce the direction of the relationship for some of the variables. (Does a high degree of political power of the firms in an industry increase the likelihood of regulation or does it increase the likelihood of no regulation at all?) Thus, it seems fair to assert that "continued absence of regulation in some sectors of the economy is the product of historical and political circumstance rather than of any principled policy guiding the activities of American government."[4]

A theory of regulation becomes tautological to the extent that it asserts such things as "regulation occurs when the 'demand for regulation' exceeds the 'supply'" or when "entropy" exceeds the level of "tolerance";[5] tautological because we cannot quantify or even qualitatively rank the variables involved, nor can we test the theories empirically. We take the fact of regulation to mean that the benefits *must* have exceeded the costs or that entropy *must* have exceeded tolerance, which, since we cannot specify the variables or their relative weights and ranking, means that industries are regulated because they are regulated. We cannot therefore predict when particular industries will or even may be subjected to any specific form of regulation—commission or otherwise—even when we confine ourselves to strictly economic variables. However, two aspects of regulation can be fruitfully investigated: the conditions conducive to "successful" economic regulation and the economic consequences of such regulation.

## Conditions for Successful Regulation

The various criteria for "success" depend on the purpose of or reasons for regulation in the first place. A view of regulation designed to benefit the firms so regulated (e.g., more effectively to stabilize a cartel, as is implicit in Kolko's and Hilton's interpretation of the Act to Regulate Commerce[6]) will obviously have different criteria than will a view stressing the necessity to restrain anticompetitive practices in the public interest. Since the stated purpose (whether real or not) of virtually all regulatory agencies is to protect the public or to enhance the public interest in cases where promotion or even protection of the industry is part of the rationale (e.g., the Civil Aviation Act sought, inter alia, to *promote* aviation), we may assume that public interest criteria are most relevant. In chapter 3 we identified such criteria as those that enhance consumer-plus-producer surplus. Thus, successful regulation implies an improvement in economic performance

---

4. A. Altshuler, "The Case for Less Transportation Regulation," paper delivered at the National Transportation Institute, Chicago, March 5, 1975, p.5.

5. G. Stigler, "The Theory of Economic Regulation," *Bell Journal of Economics and Management Science*, Spring 1971.

6. G. Kolko, *Railroads and Regulation, 1877–1916* (Princeton: Princeton University Press, 1965); G. Hilton, *The Transportation Act of 1958: A Decade of Experience* (Bloomington: Indiana University Press, 1969).

(rising output per unit of input) at efficient prices, compared with what would be expected in the absence of such regulation, as long as other important social goals are not adversely affected in the process. Unfortunately, social goals often loom large in regulatory activity at the expense of efficiency. Thus efficient peak/off-peak pricing is frequently eschewed on grounds of equity, as in the case of seasonal freight rates, which are viewed as discriminatory to agricultural interests,[7] or when urban transit fares are held constant during the peak/off-peak periods, allegedly to benefit the working poor. Not only is the peak/off-peak cycle perpetuated, with its resultant excess capacity in the fixed-peak situation, but more importantly there is greater demand for future capacity than would otherwise be the case in response to increased demand. For example, airport congestion, which usually occurs at well defined hours of the day, could be alleviated by efficient peak/off-peak pricing. If such pricing is not implemented, growing demands for air transport over time lead to airport expansion or wholly new airports that would not otherwise be necessary, at least not so soon. Such examples abound in transportation and also include highways and seaports.

There is nothing wrong with considerations of equity or assistance to the poor or to farmers, but when they mean higher prices to all users, higher costs to suppliers, and excess or premature capital expansion, one must question whether direct subsidy or tax relief would be less costly ways to redress real or imagined inequities.

All regulatory commissions have multiple objectives. The ICC, for example, has argued that, in any important case involving rate changes, mergers, or abandonments, it must "consider the economic effects on all shippers, on towns, cities, ports and regions, on the carriers themselves, and, of course, on the consumers."[8] In addition, the Act to Regulate Commerce requires "consideration" of the needs of commerce, national defense, and the postal service. More recently, environmental considerations have come to be weighed in every decision, especially in terms of the differential air pollution and energy consumption proclivities among the modes. However, the commission has, understandably, never defined its preference function or specified the relative importance of each of these often conflicting interests.[9]

As a consequence, the commission is able to "justify" every decision regardless of its impact on the efficient provision of transport services. Indeed, it is often alleged, with some justification, that the commission seldom concerns itself with the productivity or efficiency of the car-

---

7. See chapter 3, pp.163–67.
8. ICC, *The Regulatory Issues of Today* (Washington, D.C.: 1975), p.2.
9. I have referred to ICC regulation in this connection as a "Grand Benthamite Design." See Appendix to this chapter for further elucidation.

riers involved in any case brought before it. Equity, discrimination, and fairness loom large in commission decisions. Without knowing the relative weights accorded to the many economic and noneconomic criteria, we cannot judge the commission's performance objectively in terms of its own goals or those of the Act.

However, limiting ourselves to efficiency criteria, which assume either that the noneconomic goals are best satisfied by policies external to the industry or that pursuit of efficiency will not jeopardize other goals, we can specify four conditions in the industry being considered for regulation that yield a high probability of "successful" regulation:

1. External benefits and costs are large. If there is a wide gap between privately perceived benefits and costs relative to social benefits and costs, and if these cannot, for a variety of economic and noneconomic reasons, be brought closer to equality through efficient public pricing (e.g., emission charges) or taxation (e.g., fuel tax for use of publicly provided right-of-way), then private, unregulated decision making will lead to pricing, output, and investment decisions that are inefficient in the sense of maximizing net social benefits. The wider the gap between social and private costs and benefits, the greater the possibility of successful regulation.

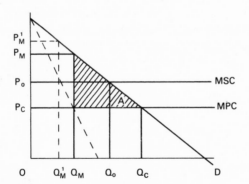

Fig. 4.1

The theory here is quite straightforward. In Figure 4.1 the difference between marginal private costs $MPC$ and marginal social costs $MSC$ is assumed for illustrative purposes to be linear. If the social or external costs cannot be internalized, a competitive industry would produce too much (i.e., $Q_C$ at a price of $P_C$) will cause a welfare loss equal to the area labeled $A$; a monopoly would produce too little (i.e., $Q_M$ at a price of $P_M$) and a welfare loss equal to the total shaded area. The optimum is, of course, $P_0$, $Q_0$. If the external costs (equal to $P_0 - P_C$ in Figure 4.1) cannot be internalized, in the competitive situation, regulation *could* specify a price of $P_0$. In the monopoly case, even if the external costs could be internalized, an even larger loss of net consumer surplus would result. Here again, a regulatory authority *could* establish a price of $P_0$, given the requisite information. The greater the divergence of $MSC$ from $MPC$, the greater the possibility of significant improvement through rate or price regulation. In the monopoly case, this possibility exists even if the externalities can be internalized.[10] The same is not true in the competitive situation.[11]

2. Costs not assignable to specific sales units are large. If there are high fixed or joint costs, or costs that are not assignable on a cost-occasioned basis to particular sales units because of a difference between the size of a unit of sales and the minimum feasible unit of output, it is not possible to recover total costs by pricing the sales units on the basis of the costs occasioned by virtue of producing any particular unit. This means that price discrimination of some sort, including an arbitrary allocation of indivisible costs to units of sales and subsidy are the only two ways for a private enterprise to break even. A private firm seeking maximum or even satisfactory profits is likely to discriminate in a fashion inconsistent with other public policy goals. Under these circumstances a regulated pricing structure *can* render price discrimination that is more consistent with other objectives in a fashion that would not necessarily be more inconsistent with efficiency than a privately established price structure. The greater the magnitude of nonassignable costs, therefore, the greater the possibility of establishing a pricing structure in the public interest with a less adverse potential impact on efficiency.[12]

3. The industry is inherently "monopolistic" because of economies of scale, limited markets, or high initial investment. These traditional justifications for imposing price regulation to protect the public from higher prices and restricted output ensue from attempts to maximize pecuniary profits under monopoly as compared to competitive conditions.[13]

---

10. For example, if the firm's costs are increased to $MSC$, profit-maximizing behavior will equate $MR$ to $MSC$, which implies a price $P_M^1$ and output $Q_M^1$ and a movement even further away from the optimum.

11. The analysis can be extended to situations where the marginal social benefits exceed the prices pertaining to the demand schedule—i.e., external benefits of production. I have discussed these in D. McConaughy and C. J. Clawson, *Business Logistics—Policies and Decisions* (Los Angeles: University of Southern California, 1968), chap. 4.

12. Recall that efficient pricing in a multiproduct enterprise subject to a constraint that revenues equal costs or exceed costs by a "fair" or "normal" amount *requires* that individual prices systematically deviate from marginal cost on the basis of the reciprocal of the elasticity of demand (see chap. 3).

13. See J. C. Bonbright, *Principles of Public Utility Rates* (New York: Columbia University Press, 1961); E. Clemens, *Economics and Public Utilities* (New York: Appleton-Century-Crofts, 1950).

4. The costs of regulation, including the impact of regulation on efficiency and technological change within the firm or firms regulated, are not excessive, or perhaps are favorable to efficiency and technological change. Such costs depend in part on the number of firms in the industry. Other things being equal, the larger the number of firms and the greater their diversity, the more cumbersome and costly the regulation. The overriding problem in motor carrier regulation may be the existence of thousands of carriers, offering widely diversified services, most of which are not subject to any economic regulation at all.[14]

Opposite conclusions with respect to the probability of successful regulation hold to the extent that these four conditions do not prevail. In general, economic regulation is capable of improving economic performance and/or reducing undesirable side effects from the public viewpoint where the above conditions exist. If only some of these conditions exist, as is likely in most cases, the assessment of the probability of "successful" economic regulation becomes more complex, as difficult trade-offs emerge. Very careful advance appraisal of the industry is needed before imposing regulatory restraints.[15]

It should also be noted that several of these conditions are interrelated. For example, the ease and hence the cost of regulation are vastly simplified if only a single firm is involved—though there are troubles aplenty with the Bell telephone system. In addition, some portion of the nonassignable costs and externalities are directly related to factors rendering the market inherently or "naturally" monopolistic. However, these conditions are not necessarily interrelated. Regulatory costs are partly dependent on the type of regulation imposed. Cost indivisibilities of various kinds exist in nonmonopolistic markets as well. Externalities, as already noted, depend in part on the attempts of public authorities to price publicly provided facilities economically and to recapture or to internalize external costs. The magnitude of the gap between private and social costs is not something dictated by the inherent nature of the commodity or the productive process.

Finally, in this connection, one must admit that measuring these conditions, or even specifying orders of magnitude, involves considerable guesswork and, in the final analysis, especially as regards the fourth condition, must be judgmental. Nevertheless, the possibility of successful economic regulation by an independent, objective, and

---

14. The impact of regulation on technological change is discussed later in this chapter.

15. An obvious condition for successful regulation is the appointment of capable regulators and staff. For some comments on this non-trivial matter, see the Appendix to this chapter. More details on the performance of ICC regulators and staff are contained in A. Hoogenboom and O. Hoogenboom, *A History of the ICC: From Panacea to Palliative* (New York: Norton, 1976).

competent regulatory commission is heavily dependent on these conditions even if the measurement of many of the variables is largely
judgmental.

## Application to Transportation

At the outset we must face up to the question of what constitutes
an industry. The usual definition runs in terms of cross-elasticities of
demand. An industry is deemed to consist of a group of firms producing a product whose cross-elasticity vis-à-vis the products of the
other firms in the group is high, or in the case of perfect competition, infinite. On the other hand, where the cross-elasticity among the
products of two or more firms or groups of firms is low, the firms be-
long to different industries.[16]

In the transportation field the ease with which the various modes
can substitute for one another depends on the nature of the commodity to be shipped (its density, value, and elasticity of supply and
demand), particular shipper circumstances, the value to the shipper
of the qualitative elements of the several transport alternatives, and
other special services. Between any pair of cities or combination of
production and sales centers there may be many or few different
transport "industries" with a corresponding variation in degree of
competitiveness, independent of extra market arrangements or agreements among the firms involved. Furthermore, the identification of
a transport "industry" in terms of a particular technology is fallacious.
Substitute conditions cut across the various media on the basis of
the criteria mentioned above, which themselves are subject to change
over time and do not neatly confine themselves to technical characteristics.[17]

Yet in transportation we persist in analyzing the modes separately
as if they each constituted a distinct industry. More and more we

---

16. There is not much recent literature on the issues of elasticity and cross-
elasticity. Many of the problems using these concepts were extensively explored
some years back. See R. L. Bishop, "Elasticities, Cross-Elasticities, and Market
Relationships," *American Economic Review*, December 1952, pp.779–804; R.
Heiser, "Comment," ibid., June 1955, pp.373–82; and R. L. Bishop, "Reply," ibid.,
pp.382–86. These discussions were more concerned with identifying the nature
of market competition in terms of varying levels of elasticity. Ross M. Robertson
has extended the analysis and sought to define the relevant market in terms of
categories of uses for the output of what often appear to be different industries. See
his paper "On the Changing Apparatus of Competition," *American Economic Review*, May 1954. I have applied some of Robertson's analysis specifically to the field
of transportation. See George W. Wilson, *Essays on Some Unsettled Questions in
the Economics of Transportation* (Bloomington: Indiana University, 1962), especially pp.24–30.

17. For a detailed discussion of this point, see George W. Wilson, "On the Output Unit in Transportation," *Land Economics*, August 1959.

acknowledge the existence of intermodal relationships, but we still discuss them using conclusions derived from the modal approach. As long as each mode remains under separate ownership and control, the modal approach is not especially misleading. But as transport coordination proceeds despite legal, institutional, and psychological roadblocks, this approach will no longer do. Furthermore, the failure to specify the industry more precisely or even to acknowledge the complexities involved leads unconsciously to the homogeneity assumption regarding the alleged product of transport enterprises, tonmiles. To add up rail, truck, ship, air, and pipeline ton-miles and presume that a meaningful aggregate is obtained is to misinterpret the diversity within transport. Our knowledge of the nature of the industries with which we are dealing is seriously impaired by the failure to construe them in other than modal terms.

Thus, from the outset we are beset with conceptual ambiguity and confusion that have become institutionalized. In reality, any given transport market is supplied by firms having a wide variety of technical and economic characteristics. To talk about the "representative firm" and deduce cost and demand functions on the basis of such an abstraction, even in the fuzzy state in which Alfred Marshall left it, is scarcely conducive to an understanding of reality. In short, it is at best difficult to determine whether the transport industries possess the characteristics that render them eligible for regulation on strict economic grounds. One is forced, therefore, to defer to the conventional wisdom and adopt the modal approach once more. In what follows, we will concentrate on rail, truck, barge, and oil pipeline transport and examine the extent to which each possesses the features conducive to improvement by economic regulation.

*Externalities.* Despite these ambiguities, it is possible to discuss the first two conditions in at least a general sense with respect to intercity freight transportation. There is no question that externalities constitute a significant aspect of the provision of transport both in a positive sense (social cohesion, defense, effective administration of a large nation-state, opening up new regions) and a negative sense (air pollution, especially from trucks; noise pollution; water pollution from oil and barge spills).[18] As an input into the production and distribution of all commodities, changes in the costs and prices of providing transport services create external economies or diseconomies for virtually every industry and locality. Although, as emphasized in chapter 1, the freight rate ratio is generally quite low, it nevertheless represents a rather ubiquitous input. Hence, as is so often stressed, the efficient

---

18. See chap. 2, pp.60–61.

provision of transport is a necessary, though not sufficient, condition for the maintenance and development of any economy. In this sense, it is an important industry and an especially important part of what is usually and loosely deemed "social overhead" or "social infrastructure."

By themselves these considerations scarcely justify commission-type economic regulation. After all the "food-producing" industries[19] are also quite important, and society has not yet seen fit to establish an overall regulatory agency to pass judgment on prices, entry, exit, and merger. Yet public regulation of transportation is partly linked to the early and heavy public involvement in the creation of the rights-of-way as manifested by land grants to the railways and the construction of roadways. For better or worse, all governments become deeply involved in the initial and often continuing provision of such infrastructure. It is thus easy to move from such involvement into even deeper and more detailed concern with rates and prices.

None of this "justifies" the present panoply of economic regulation. Nor does it deny that efficient utilization of both rights-of-way and rolling stock or vehicles would be possible under a more laissez-faire approach. It merely suggests that the industry is important, gives rise to relatively large externalities, and has always been deeply involved with government. Thus, the *possibility* of efficient pricing exists either to close the gap between $MSC$ and $MPC$ where negative externalities exist and/or to ensure a closer coincidence between marginal costs and rates or at least to ensure more efficient price discrimination of the sort noted in chapter 3. To the extent that these things would occur without commission-type regulation, the justification of the latter diminishes and vice versa.

*Cost Indivisibilities.* We have repeatedly stressed in chapter 2 that for rail, truck (including highways), and barges the magnitude of joint, indivisible, and other costs not assignable to the basic units to be priced is extremely large. Hence this condition for successful regulation is fulfilled in intercity freight transportation.

*Economies of Scale.* As stressed in chapter 2, the various empirical studies regarding rail and truck transport yield conflicting conclusions. Barge and pipeline transport, however, do appear to be subject to economies of scale, although this conclusion may be due to the dearth of studies of this issue for these modes.

Market limitations between any city-pair or production and consumption points will obviously depend on the relative size of the points to be served. The number of transportation enterprises "needed" will obviously be greater between, say, New York and Chicago than

---

19. Note the ambiguity of what constitutes an industry, as noted earlier.

between two rural communities. The number of firms will also depend on the modal composition. From this point of view most city-pairs or production-consumption points within the United States or any other nation have market limitations because either monopoly or oligopoly in the transport sector prevails. However, these limitations need not justify economic regulation if there are enough shipper options and freedom of entry to preclude monopoly-like pricing with large divergences between $P_i$ and $MC_i$. In the United States, for example, virtually all city-pairs have highway as well as rail access and to a much lesser extent barge and pipeline access. Thus, if a single railway serves any two points, the threat of monopoly-like performance is considerably reduced if there is free entry in, say, the trucking industry. Even if no trucking firm existed that served the two points, the threat of entry would severely restrain the railroad in its pricing, output, and quality decisions by a process long ago examined by Bain, referred to as "limit price" analysis,[20] and, even earlier, by Schumpeter and his notion of the process of "creative destruction" or the existence of "potential" competition.[21]

Thus many railroads claim that particular rates are often based on their estimates of the costs of an efficient trucking concern (especially those of independent operators) even where trucking service is not presently available. The fact that movements of many commodities between particular points are predominantly or completely confined to a single mode does not necessarily mean that the rates on such movements deviate significantly from $MC$. Indeed, given the likely behavior of costs in, say, rail-truck or rail-truck-barge competition for particular commodities, an all-or-nothing outcome is not only to be expected but likely to be the most efficient. For example, assume that the aggregate elasticity of demand for transport is zero at $OM$ ton-miles (see Figure 4.2). Without regulation, rates would gravitate toward the average avoidable costs for the total traffic of each carrier type. If both carriers know the total potential traffic, the carrier rate that is lowest depends on the relationship between the cost functions and the amount of potential traffic. There are several possibilities. If the cost functions intersect as in Figure 4.2, the low-cost carrier depends on the traffic potential.

---

20. Joe S. Bain, "Pricing in Monopoly and Oligopoly," *American Economic Review*, March 1949, pp.448–64.

21. Potential competition "disciplines before it attacks. The businessman feels himself to be in a competitive position even if he is alone in his field . . . ," J. A. Schumpeter, *Capitalism, Socialism and Democracy*, 3d ed. (New York: Harper, 1962; 1st ed., 1942), p.85. Chap. 7 of this work discusses "The Process of Creative Destruction."

Assume the truck long-run average avoidable cost is constant at $OC$ while the rail cost declines with volume along $C_1C_1$, with the intersection at $C$, $M$. If the traffic potential lies to the left of $M$, say at $M_1M_1$, and truck rates are set slightly in excess of $OC$, all the business will move via truck. In this instance total economic costs involved in the movement by truck would only be $OC(OM_1)$, which is less

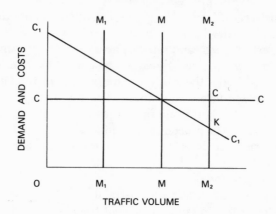

Fig. 4.2                    TRAFFIC VOLUME

than if the rails participated. Indeed, no rail participation is economic, for up to the total potential of $OM_1$ (indeed, up to $OM$), avoidable economic rail costs are in excess of truck costs. Hence any rail movement represents some economic waste. Given the general superiority of truck service, there is no doubt that at a truck rate of $OC$ both shippers and society are benefited.

Assume, on the other hand, a volume potential of $MM$. If both carriers set rates based on average avoidable costs of $OM$ (that is, $OC$), it is possible that some rail shipments will be made since there may be certain shippers whose circumstances create no preference for truck service over rail service. But it is unlikely that all shippers would be so situated. As a consequence, some sharing of the $OM$ potential would take place. Unlike the previous situation, however, with a rail rate of $OC$, any traffic moving by rail in volume less than $OM$ will result in out-of-pocket losses because the rail cost function declines. The rail rate of $OC$ is only justified (compensatory) if the *total* traffic potential in fact moves by rail. With rate parity between rail and truck, this is extremely unlikely. Thus, society suffers some unnecessary economic waste through sharing the traffic. Such waste can only be eliminated by giving all the business to rail or to truck. The social waste would be even greater through traffic sharing if the truck long-run cost function also declined. This, of course, points up the fact that in setting a rate based on such avoidable costs, the traffic potential must be accurately assessed; otherwise, the rate set, though profitable at the projected volume, will prove to be noncompensatory. Eastman recognized this possibility when he argued that "if the reduced rates actually succeed in materially increasing the volume of traffic carried, the added expenses may take on a character very different from what it would take if the increase were inconsequential. This is particularly true if the volume is materially increased in the direction of predominant loaded movement."[22] Though Eastman envisaged a situation of rising long-run cost, whereas we have assumed decreasing per-unit avoidable cost, the general truth of the proposition is evident. This implies that so-called incentive rates depend on very accurate traffic forecasts if they are to prove compensatory.

In the example of a traffic potential of $OM$, the sharing of the traffic would not persist in the long run because the rails would recognize the avoidable losses. Hence, in this situation trucks would obtain all the business at a rate of $OC$, and the net economic costs to society would be $OC(OM)$ less nontransport cost savings accruing from any superiority of truck service.

A more complicated situation emerges if the traffic potential is larger than $OM$, say, $OM_2$. Here a rail rate of $M_2K$ would secure all the business and minimize the economic costs but only if the value of the superior truck service was less than $KC$ for all shippers. If not, then trucks would obtain some business at the rate of $OC$, which would be remunerative. However, any sharing of the traffic due to such circumstances would push the rail volume to the left of $OM_2$ and raise the rail average avoidable costs above the quoted rates. Hence an increase in the rail rate would be needed, which would cause more diversion to trucks and a further gap between the rail rate and costs. The rail rate would have to keep rising until it reached a level along $CC_1$ between $M$ and $M_2$ such that no more shippers valued truck service by an amount equal to $OC$ minus the rail rate.

From the short-run point of view, it is evident that the competitive outcome, which forces rates down to average avoidable costs, minimizes economic costs. In all situations, with the possible exception of the third example, this results in an all-or-nothing outcome; that is, either the rails or the trucks capture the total business, but it is generally uneconomic for any sharing to take place under the conditions postulated.

*Regulatory Costs.* The final condition for "successful" regulation, namely, reasonable costs of regulation, is the most difficult of all to

---

22. Joseph B. Eastman, *Pick-up and Delivery in Official Territory* (1936), 218 ICC 441, 490–93.

anticipate prior to the imposition of economic regulation. Indeed, it is extremely difficult to assess the costs of regulation even after the fact, as we discuss in the latter part of this chapter. Much, of course, depends on the type of regulation and its extent. While there is some analysis of particular kinds of regulation (e.g., rate-of-return regulation, discussed below), the quantification of costs is exceedingly complex. Obvious areas where regulation does or may raise costs are the budget of the regulating commission, the costs of hearings, proceedings and court cases, the impact of regulation on technological change, and managerial efficiency. Except for the first two, the quantitative assessment of the costs may be very subjective. Similarly, any analysis of benefits tends to be complex. Thus attempts to assess costs vis-à-vis benefits normally do not take place prior to the establishment of regulatory machinery.

We may conclude that at least two of the conditions required for successful economic regulation exist in transportation but there is much ambiguity with respect to the others. The case for regulatory change or regulatory reform, especially as advanced since President Kennedy's message on transportation to the Congress in 1962, rests heavily on three main beliefs. (1) Since the 1930s the number of shipper transport alternatives between most city-pairs has increased to the point where at worst the situation is oligopolistic and at best is "workably" competitive. Since most markets in other sectors of the economy appear to be no better, yet remain unregulated, continued detailed economic regulation of transportation is an anachronism. (2) The ability to regulate an industry, or set of industries, comprising 20,000 or more firms surrounded by an unregulated competitive component comprising about 80,000 more is not feasible. Add to this the necessity to make fine and usually arbitrary distinctions among common, private, exempt, and contract carriage and to attempt to monitor millions of freight rates, thousands of which change daily, to determine whether they are "just and reasonable," to say nothing of the other variables subject to ICC jurisdiction—an impossible task even if there existed better demand and supply evidence than we have examined in chapters 1 and 2. (3) The economic "costs" of regulation to society for transcend any "benefits" that can be discerned or measured.

These three beliefs are partly interrelated. To the extent that competition, though far from perfect, is at least "workable," any given level of regulatory costs would lead to progressively reduced *net* benefits as the workability of competition increased. Since "workability" of competition is associated with either an increase in the number of firms serving any market or a decrease in the size dispersal among firms that increases competitive equality, the task of economic regulation, beyond the antitrust laws, grows and with it the costs. In short, the belief is that changes in the transportation industries, especially those associated with technological changes in the automotive industry and the accompanying massive public investments in highways, have created conditions that make unsuitable the type of economic regulation imposed in 1887 and designed, ostensibly at least, to stop abuses of economic power by a dominating monopoly.[23] Such changes have raised the economic costs of regulation at the same time as they have reduced the potential economic benefits.

## The Economic Consequences of Regulation

The economic consequences of regulation depend on the type of regulation imposed as well as its effective enforcement. The general economic literature has been most concerned with two types: price regulation and rate-of-return regulation under conditions of complete monopoly.

### Direct Price Regulation

The monopoly is assumed to face the following demand and production conditions, which are assumed to remain static over the period of the analysis:

The inverse demand is $P = p(q)$, where $P$ represents the single price (no discrimination) for the single, homogeneous commodity $q$; the production function $q = f(L,K)$ where $L$ is the amount of "labor" utilized and $K$ is the amount of capital ($L$ is deemed to include other inputs such as raw materials). The "wage" rate is given and assumed to be invariant with respect to this firm's purchases of it at $w$ per unit of $L$; likewise, the cost-of-capital is given as $r$ per unit of $K$ in percentage terms, while a unit of $K$ is valued at $1.[24] The firm is assumed to seek maximum profits ($\pi$).

From these assumptions we can specify the profit function as follows:

$$\pi = pq - rK - wL = pf(L,K) - rK - wL.$$

To maximize profit take the partial derivatives of this function with respect to $K$ and $L$, respectively, and solve by setting each equal to zero (the functions are assumed to satisfy the normal second-order conditions).

The results will show that the maximum-profit employment of $K$ and $L$ occurs when $MRP_K = r$ and $MRP_L = w$, where $MRP_{K,L}$ is the

---

23. See the Appendix to this chapter.
24. This value is for convenience only. Different values of $K$ can be assumed, but the results will be unchanged.

marginal revenue product of $K$ or $L$. With these quantities of $K$ and $L$ employed, the maximum-profit quantity of output $q$ is determined from $q = f(K,L)$, which, given the inverse demand, yields the maximum-profit price.

To anticipate the later discussion of rate-of-return regulation, the above equalities of marginal products of $K$ and $L$, with their respective prices, satisfy the efficiency criterion in the sense that every output level, including the optimum, is produced at least cost.[25] That is, the least cost of producing any given output occurs whenever the $MPP_{K,L}$ (the marginal physical product) are equal to $r$ and $w$, respectively, or,

$$\frac{MPP_K}{MPP_L} = \frac{r}{w} = \frac{\frac{\partial f}{\partial K}}{\frac{\partial f}{\partial L}}.$$

These conditions ensure that the maximum profit output (where $MC = MR$) is produced at lowest cost, thus maximizing profits, $\pi$.

A bit of geometry may help at this point. Assume a single isoquant $I$, as shown in Figure 4.3. It shows the alternative combinations of $K$

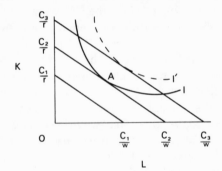

Fig. 4.3

and $L$ required to produce a fixed quantity of output $\bar{q}$. For any total level of expenditures, say, $C_i$, the firm can hire $\dfrac{C_i}{w}$ units of $L$ and $\dfrac{C_i}{r}$ units of $K$. Assume an expenditure of $C_1$. The firm can hire any com-

---

25. For example, we seek to minimize total costs $(rK + wL)$ subject to producing a given output $q = f(K,L)$. Construct the Lagrangian function

$$\mathfrak{L} = rK + wL - \lambda[f(K,L) - \bar{q}].$$

Take the first partial derivatives with respect to $K$ and $L$ and set them equal to zero to obtain:

$$r - \lambda \frac{\partial f}{\partial K} = 0, \text{ and } w - \lambda \frac{\partial f}{\partial L} = 0; \text{ or } \frac{\frac{\partial f}{\partial K}}{\frac{\partial f}{\partial L}} = \frac{r}{w}.$$

bination of $K$ and $L$ along $C_1$, given $r$ and $w$. However, an expenditure of $C_1$ does not permit a level of output along $I$ (i.e., does not permit employing enough $K$ and $L$ to produce $\bar{q}$). Consider an expenditure of $C_3$—now the firm can hire enough $K$ and $L$ to produce *more* than $\bar{q}$ (i.e., with an outlay of $C_3$ the firm can produce $\bar{q}$ but it can also produce more for the same cost along a higher isoquant $I^1$). This is clearly not the least-cost outlay to produce $\bar{q}$. However, for an outlay of $C_2$ the firm can just spend enough and hence hire enough $K$ and $L$ to produce $\bar{q}$ at point $A$—the point on the isoquant that is just tangent to $C_2$. The slope of $C_2$ (and of $C_1$ and $C_3$) equals $\dfrac{C_2}{r} \div \dfrac{C_2}{w} = \dfrac{w}{r}$. The slope of the isoquant at this point (called the marginal rate of technical substitution of $K$ for $L$) equals $\dfrac{MPP_L}{MPP_K} = \dfrac{\frac{\partial f}{\partial L}}{\frac{\partial f}{\partial K}}$ .

Thus, $\dfrac{w}{r} = \dfrac{\frac{\partial f}{\partial L}}{\frac{\partial f}{\partial K}}$, or $\dfrac{r}{w} = \dfrac{\frac{\partial f}{\partial K}}{\frac{\partial f}{\partial L}}$ , as shown before.

The maximum profit output is determined as noted before and illustrated in Figure 4.4 for (assumed) linear demand, where $MC$

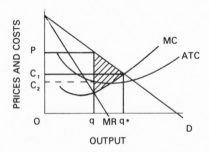

Fig. 4.4

$= MR$. To maximize profits, this output must be produced at least cost. For any output the above relationship between factor prices and marginal products will obtain.

The unregulated monopoly leads to excess profits at $(P - C_2)q$. Profits are "excessive" since normal profits are assumed to be included in the average total cost $(ATC)$ curve. There is also a welfare loss equal to the shaded area, analogous to the discussion in chapter 3. Since optimal output occurs where $MC$ intersects the demand curve, the regulatory agency could establish a price at this point ($C_1$ in Figure 4.4) *and* require the firm to satisfy all demand at this price

$(q^*)$.[26] We are making the rather large assumption that the ICC knows the level and shape of the demand and cost functions! However, most analyses of the economics of regulation make this assumption either implicitly or explicitly.

In the case depicted in Figure 4.4, $MC$ is rising. At the point where $MC$ intersects the demand curve, price will exceed $ATC$ and some excess profits will result. They may be taxed away via a lump sum tax or required to be spent in certain ways, say on R and D. Were $MC$ constant no such "problems" would emerge. When $MC$ is declining at a slower rate than demand, setting a price at the intersection of $MC$ and demand would yield net losses. Society may provide subsidy, permit some form of price discrimination, or set the price at the point where *average* cost intersects the demand curve and permit some welfare loss (see chapter 3).[27]

In contrast to rate-of-return regulation, price regulation does *not* involve misallocation or inefficient factor combinations. For example, suppose the price is fixed by the regulatory authority at $P^*(=MC = AR)$. Profits are now $\pi = P^*f(K,L) - rK - wL$. Taking partials with respect to $K$ and $L$ and setting them equal to zero yields the efficiency conditions, namely, equality of marginal products with factor prices. This does *not* occur under rate-of-return regulation.

### Rate-of-Return Regulation

Some regulatory commissions specify a rate-of-return constraint to guide decisions concerning raising or lowering prices. That is, after specifying the so-called rate base to include the value of the assets needed to produce the service, an allowable rate of return on that base is determined at some percentage figure. In transportation the fair-return-on-a-fair-value concept was enunciated and enshrined long ago in *Smyth* v. *Ames*. The Supreme Court stated, inter alia, that "what the company is entitled to ask is a fair return upon the value of that which it employs for the public convenience."[28] At various times the ICC has specified a rate of return for the railroads between 5.5 and 6.0 percent, but it has become a moot point since the 1920s. More recently the DOT has specified that the railroads "need" a rate of return in the range of 10.86 to 12.5 percent. The commission does not specify a

---

26. That is, in the case of transportation, make the firm a common carrier holding itself out to serve all customers at the known price.

27. Joan Robinson has discussed these alternatives in *The Economics of Imperfect Competition* (London: Macmillan, 1946), chap. 13. Her somewhat different results arise in part because she permits the monopolist to adjust output at the fixed price to the point where $MC = MR$. We have imposed the requirement that, at the set price, the firm is obligated to satisfy all the demand.

28. 169, U.S. 466 (1898), p.547.

rate of return for motor carriers. Rather, it uses the operating ratio (i.e., operating costs divided by operating revenues) on the grounds that since the capital investment in the industry is so small relative to total operating costs, the "margin of revenues over expenses required to pay a normal rate of return . . . would be so small that a slight miscalculation of probable revenues or expenses could leave the carrier with revenues insufficient to pay operating expenses."[29] However, since the commission has indicated from time to time that a 93 percent operating ratio is "normal" or fair for motor carriers, one can infer that a fair return on investment is between 20 and 40 percent![30] The Civil Aeronautics Board has specified a fair rate of return of some 12 percent for scheduled air carriers.

Fortunately, we need not concern ourselves with the accounting intricacies of what to include in the rate base, how to value the assets (reproduction or original cost and all that), or what to include in costs and revenues. These pragmatic issues are well covered in most public utility and transportation texts. Rather, we will examine the economic consequences of any form of rate-of-return constraint.

*The A-J-W Effect.* Assume that the same nondiscriminating monopolist produces a single homogeneous product or service, and that the firm seeks to maximize the absolute value of profits in each period. Impose a rate-of-return constraint[31] $s$ that lies between the opportunity cost of capital $r$ and the rate of return $r^*$ the firm could make by charging the maximum-profit price $OP$ (in Figure 4.4) and producing

---

29. D. Philip Locklin, *Economics of Transportation*, 6th ed. (Homewood, Ill.: Richard D. Irwin, 1966), p.702.

30. For example, let the normal operating ratio for motor carriers be $\alpha_1 = \dfrac{C_1}{R_1}$, where $C_1$ is operating costs and $R_1$ is operating revenues. Let the fair return for rails be $B_2 = \dfrac{R_2 - C_2}{K_2}$, where $K_2$ is the fair value of the capital invested (the rate base). The fair return for motor carriers will be $B_1 = \dfrac{R_1 - C_1}{K_1}$.

But $C_1 = \alpha_1 R_1$.

$\therefore B_1 = \dfrac{R_1 - \alpha_1 R_1}{K_1} = \dfrac{R_1}{K_1}(1 - \alpha_1)$.

Define the capital turnover ratio as $T_1 = \dfrac{R_1}{K_1}$. $\therefore B_1 = T_1(1 - \alpha_1)$.

For motor carriers $T_1$ varies between 3 and 6. The commission's definition of $\alpha_1$ as .93 implies a fair return of between 21 and 42 percent. (See George W. Wilson, "The I.C.C. Profit Criteria—Rail vs. Truck," *Transportation Journal*, Fall 1966, pp.17–20, for further elaboration.)

31. There has been substantial literature on this since the seminal articles by H. Averch and L. Johnson, "The Firm under Regulatory Constraint," *American Economic Review*, December 1962; and S. Wellisz, "Regulation of Natural Gas Pipeline Companies: An Economic Analysis," *Journal of Political Economy*, February 1963—hence the designation as the A-J-W effect.

the maximum-profit output $Oq$. The firm thus seeks to maximize profits subject to a rate of return $\le s$. Formally we have the following:

$$\text{Max. } \pi = pf(K,L) - rK - wL, \text{ subject to } \frac{pf(K,L) - wL}{K} = s.$$

Note that $s$, $r$, and $r^*$ are percentages, and $r < s < r^*$. This means that the regulatory agency will not set a rate of return equal to or below the opportunity cost of capital. If it did the firm would have zero or negative profits and, in the latter case, would cease production. If $s$ were set equal to or greater than $r^*$, there would be no regulatory restraint. Indeed $s$ *could* not be greater than $r^*$ since $r^*$ is the maximum possible profit. Thus, the assumption of the allowable rate of return lying between the two extremes of $r$ and $r^*$ implies effective regulation and allowing the firm some profit, depending on the level of $s$ vis-à-vis $r$. It is also assumed that the firm is capable of earning at least $s$, unlike the railroad situation, where a fair return is, say, 12 percent, but the ICC can in no way ensure that a 12 percent return is achievable. In the above situation the firm is clearly capable of receiving net revenues that yield a return at least equal to $s$, whatever it might be, because $s < r^*$. This means that the constraint can be written as an equality since the profit-maximizing firm would never accept a rate of return less than the maximum allowable. Since none of the values of the variables are negative, the problem simplifies to one of maximization of the type noted in chapter 3.

Thus we form the Lagrangian

$$\mathcal{L} = pf(K,L) - rK - wL - \lambda[pf(K,L) - wL - sK].$$

Taking partials with respect to $K$ and $L$ setting them equal to zero yields

$$\frac{\partial f}{\partial K}\left(p + \frac{dp}{df}\right) = \frac{r - \lambda s}{(1 - \lambda)} \text{ and } \frac{\partial f}{\partial L}\left(p + \frac{dp}{df}\right) = w.$$

The ratio of the marginal products of $K$ and $L$ is therefore $\dfrac{MPP_K}{MPP_L} = \dfrac{1}{w}\left(\dfrac{r - \lambda s}{1 - \lambda}\right)$.

To determine whether the expression on the right-hand side differs from $\dfrac{r}{w}$ (the efficiency condition) requires an evaluation of $\dfrac{r - \lambda s}{1 - \lambda}$. Rewrite this as $r - \dfrac{\lambda(s - r)}{(1 - \lambda)}$ and determine whether $\dfrac{\lambda(s - r)}{(1 - \lambda)}$ is positive or negative. The expression will be positive if $\lambda$ lies between zero and one, since $s - r > 1$ by our previous discussion. It can be shown that indeed $0 < \lambda < 1$.[32] As a consequence, the unconstrained equilibrium has $\dfrac{MPR_K}{MPP_L} = \dfrac{r}{w}$, while the constrained equilibrium has $\dfrac{MPR_K}{MPP_L}$ $= \dfrac{r-a}{w}$, where $a = \dfrac{\lambda(s-r)}{(1-\lambda)} > 0$. In short, the firm under regulatory constraint has relatively more capital vis-à-vis labor than is required to produce any given output. Thus, any output is produced at higher cost than efficiency requires or, as Averch and Johnson put it, such a firm "operates inefficiently in the sense that [social] cost is not minimized at the output it selects."[33]

But additional implications emerge from this approach. Without providing the proofs here (indeed the mathematics have taken some years to verify), it can be shown that:

1. As regulation becomes tighter in the sense that the allowable rate of return is pushed closer to the opportunity cost of capital, the optimal-profit capital stock of the firm increases.
2. The firm will increase output and reduce price while the level of capital outlays will continue to deviate from least cost of production on the introduction of a rate-of-return constraint.

The intuitive rationale for these statements is that if a firm is assured a rate of return on its capital base higher than the cost of capital, it has an incentive to produce more than the unconstrained monopolist using more capital, even though it must suffer price reductions. The increase in the capital base will continue until the profit reductions due to price reductions occasioned by higher output are no longer offset by the higher returns to capital $(s - r)$ guaranteed by regulation. The maximum profit output that results will be less than the Pareto optimal output but greater than that of the unconstrained monopolist. Figure 4.5 illustrates this for rising $MC$. As $s$ decreases toward $r$, output will expand from the unconstrained level $(Oq_1)$. However, since the additional output is produced at higher marginal cost $\left(\dfrac{dc}{dq}\right)$ than would be the case with an unconstrained monopolist $(MC)$, output will only expand to $Oq_2$, which is less than Pareto optimality $(Oq_3)$.[34]

There have been many extensions of this situation, including attempts at quantifying the relative importance of such overcapitalization. For example, Wellisz also notes that if capital is expanded in the peak/off-peak situation, under rate-of-return constraint, peak prices

32. See W. Baumol and A. Klevorick, "Input Choices and Rate of Return Regulation," *Bell Journal of Economics and Management Science*, Autumn 1970.
33. Averch and Johnson, 33. p.1052.
34. E. Sheshinski, "Welfare Aspects of a Regulatory Constraint: Note," *American Economic Review*, March 1971, pp.175–78.

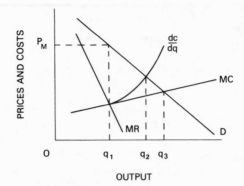

Fig. 4.5                          OUTPUT

will be lowered and off-peak prices raised, not only aggravating the cycle but further reducing producer-plus-consumer surplus (refer to Figure 3.6). If a rate-of-return constraint is imposed and optimum capacity expanded at the peak, the economic losses therefrom must be recouped from the off-peak customers by raising prices or rates, thereby narrowing the spread between *efficient* peak and off-peak prices. While it may be questioned why, if the firm is already at the optimum, including zero profits, anyone would *want* to impose a rate-of-return constraint, this is always possible in the real world.

Westfield has further concluded that under plausible conditions there will be an added inducement for suppliers of the monopolist to "conspire" and charge higher prices, because there is less incentive for the buyer (the rate-of-return regulated monopolist) to resist the higher prices since he obtains a "profit" on each increment of capital, whether due to price or quantity, equal to $s - r$.[35]

In addition, the A-J-W assumptions have been modified to introduce such things as the cost of capital not equal to \$1;[36] regulatory lag;[37] uncertainty;[38] and alternative firm objectives, such as maximization of sales, output, or return on investment[39] rather than absolute profit-maximization and alternative regulatory constraints such as fixed markup over cost and fixed total profit.[40]

The analytical approach is relatively straightforward, and for the latter two extensions of the original Averch and Johnson discussion it

35. F. M. Westfield, "Regulation and Conspiracy," *American Economic Review*, June 1965.
36. Ibid.
37. Baumol and Klevorick, "Input Choices."
38. E. Zajac, "A Geometric Treatment of Averch-Johnson's Behavior of the Firm Model," *American Economic Review*, March 1970.
39. E. Bailey and V. Malone, "Resource Allocation and the Regulated Firm," *Bell Journal of Economics and Management Science*, Spring 1970; M. Kafoglis, "Output of the Constrained Firm," *American Economic Review*, September 1969.
40. Bailey and Malone, "Resource Allocation."

merely involves taking alternative firm objectives (sales, profit, output, or return on investment) and maximizing subject to alternative regulatory constraints (rate of return, markup over cost, fixed profit per unit of output, or fixed total profit). The various combinations are then worked out by familiar Lagrangian techniques, and, not surprisingly, rather different consequences emerge than under the A-J-W assumptions. Such consequences for the most part conclude either that there is no tendency to raise the capital-labor ratio beyond the efficient level or that there may actually be undercapitalization. The varying conclusions are fully specified elsewhere[41] and need not be repeated here. The upshot of these modifications is, as Bailey and Malone state, that "the status of resource allocation in a regulated firm is extremely difficult to assess."[42]

## Quality Variation and Price Regulation

Price and rate-of-return regulation influence the quality of output as well as the costs. For example, under price regulation the firm may engage in a level of sales effort or quality variation (intended to shift the demand function so that higher profits would be reaped) greater than would be the case in the absence of price regulation.

An early analysis of the equilibrium (i.e., maximum-profit) position of the firm with and without a fixed price deduced the following equilibrium conditions for a demand function of the form $q = f(p, x)$ and an average cost of production function of the form $C = c(q, x)$, where $x$ represents the level of quality that both shifts the demand curve to the right and raises the curve of average cost. The condition for joint optimization of price and quality without the price constraint is

$$\frac{P}{C} = \frac{\epsilon_d}{\epsilon_q}, \tag{1}$$

where $\epsilon_d$ is the ordinary elasticity of demand and $\epsilon_q$ is the elasticity of demand with respect to quality variation defined as $\epsilon_q = \dfrac{c\,\dfrac{\partial f}{\partial x}}{q\,\dfrac{\partial c}{\partial x}}$

(i.e., "the ratio of the percentage change in demand to the percentage

---

41. Ibid. It is worth noting that *effective* operating-ratio regulation would create inefficiencies the opposite of those indicated in the A-J analysis of rate-of-return regulation. That is, a firm subject to an operating-ratio constraint has an incentive to use less capital and more labor than required for efficiency. For the analysis, see R. Cherry, "The Operating Ratio Effect and Regulated Motor Carriers," in *Motor Carrier Economic Regulation,* Proceedings of a Workshop, April 7–8, 1977 (Washington, D.C.: National Academy of Sciences, 1978), pp.269–89. Of course, the ICC's implicit operating restraint of 92.5–93.0% is not "effective," and the trucking industry is far from being a single-firm monopolist.

42. Ibid., p.141.

change in average cost, both induced by a small change in quality"[43]).

Equation (1) indicates that profits are maximized when the price markup over average cost equals the ratio of the two elasticities. In the fixed-price case, say, a price below the one that is implicit in the unconstrained case above, the equilibrium condition is

$$\frac{P^*}{C^*} = \frac{1}{\epsilon_q} \frac{P^*}{(P^* - MC)}, ^{[44]} \qquad (2)$$

where $P^*$ is fixed by a regulatory authority. Equation (2) is derived from the consideration that "for profits to be maximized the marginal cost of production plus the total increase in quality cost necessary to sell one more unit at the given price must be equal to the given price ($P^*$)" and that "the average increase in quality cost necessary to sell one more unit at the going price is the increase in quality cost per unit increase in the quality index, divided by the increase in sales at the going price per unit increase in the quality index."[45]

We may now compare quality level and the markup of price over average cost with and without price regulation. That is, is the level of quality expenditure and/or the price markup greater under price regulation than otherwise? Note that using the relationship $MR = P\left(1 - \frac{1}{\epsilon}\right)$, where $\epsilon = \frac{P}{P - MR}$, equation (1) can be written as $\frac{P}{C} = \frac{1}{\epsilon_q}\left(\frac{P}{P - MR}\right)$.

The difference between $\frac{P}{C}$ and $\frac{P^*}{C^*}$ then depends on the differences among $P^*$, $P$, $C$, $C^*$, and $MR$ and $MC$. Under effective price regulation $P^* < P$ and output will expand if the firm is also required to satisfy all the demand at the lower price. An $MC$ that is constant or rising will necessarily result in narrowing the gap between $P^*$ and $C^*$.

---

43. R. Dorfman and P. Steiner, "Optimal Advertising and Optimal Quality," *American Economic Review*, December 1954, p.834. The derivation of equation (1) is spelled out in the article and further elaborated in F. Bass et al., *Mathematical Models and Methods in Marketing* (Homewood, Ill.: Richard D. Irwin, 1961), pp.214–19.

44. See Dorfman and Steiner for derivation.

45. Dorfman and Steiner, p.844. Perhaps, more intuitively, using discrete changes we may note that when "quality is changed by $\Delta x$, this raises the costs of all previous units sold by an amount $\Delta c$. If we improve quality just enough to increase sales by one unit, then total costs become $q\Delta c + MC$, whereas total revenues become $p(q + \Delta q)$; hence the new level of profit is $p(q + \Delta q) - q(c + \Delta c) = MC$ and the *change* ($\Delta R$) from the previous level of profit is" $\Delta R = q\Delta c - p\Delta q + MC$. However, by definition of $\epsilon_q$, $q\Delta c = c\frac{\Delta q}{\epsilon_q}$. $\therefore \Delta R = c\frac{\Delta q}{\epsilon_q} - p\Delta q + MC$. In equilibrium $\Delta R = 0$, $\therefore c\frac{\Delta q}{\epsilon_q} = p\Delta q - MC$. In this case $\Delta q = 1$. Substituting in the above, inverting both sides, and multiplying by $p$, we obtain equation (2) in the text (Bass et al., p.201).

If there is any net profit to be gained by improving quality, it will increase output even further and narrow the gap even more. Thus, we may conclude that a price-regulated firm will spend more on quality, expand output, and realize a closer coincidence between price and average cost (as well as $MC$, where $MC$ is constant or rising).

However, it is not completely clear that the restrained monopolist will, in fact, spend more on improving quality. Suppose the market contains persons or groups with identical demand functions but with varying responses to quality changes. If we permit price differences, it will pay the firm to sell different qualities at different prices. In this case we cannot tell whether total quality expenditures will exceed those of a firm charging a regulated price $P^*$. If, however, "as frequently happens, those members of a market who have relatively high sensitivity to price changes have low sensitivity to quality and vice versa, then a spectrum of qualities will be offered."[46] This indeterminacy in the monopoly case has recently been noted using a somewhat different form of analysis.[47]

No normative judgment can be made concerning the social preference for a price-restrained monopolist selling a higher quality of output (than would be the case in unconstrained, *single*-price monopoly) and the situation where the constrained monopolist is permitted to charge different prices for different qualities. Indeed, this is the welfare conundrum posed by Chamberlin long ago, when he noted that "the explicit recognition that product is differentiated brings into the open the problem of variety and makes it clear that *pure competition may no longer be regarded* as in any sense an 'ideal' for purposes of welfare economics."[48] A similar analysis can be made for advertising expenditures, in which case the desirability of increased sales effort, especially the "persuasive" variety, becomes more suspect; hence price regulation may not achieve much in the way of net benefits to society as a whole.

### Quality Variation and Rate-of-Return Regulation

If the price for a homogeneous product produced by a monopoly is not regulated, but the overall rate of return is, the firm has two variables to manipulate—price and quality—subject to the constraint.

---

46. Ibid., p.833.
47. L. White, "Quality Variation when Prices Are Regulated," *Bell Journal of Economics and Management Science*," Autumn 1972, pp.429–30.
48. E. Chamberlin, *The Theory of Monopolistic Competition*, 6th ed. (Cambridge: Harvard University Press, 1948), p.214. A more recent attempt to come to grips with the problem is A. Dixit and J. Stiglitz, "Monopolistic Competition and Optimum Product Diversity," *American Economic Review*, June 1977, pp.297ff.

In the unconstrained case, every increase in expenditures of the firm to improve quality will shift both the cost and the demand curve. For every alternative level of quality expenditures, there will be a different demand and a different cost: hence a different maximum-profit price.

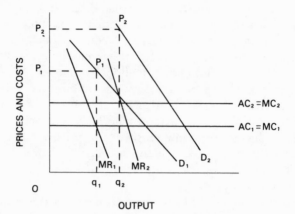

Fig. 4.6                                     OUTPUT

Consider Figure 4.6. Assume $D_1$, $MR_1$, and $AC_1$ are the demand, marginal revenue, and cost functions associated with a given quality of output. The maximum-profit position of the unrestrained monopolist is, of course, $P_1$ with an output of $q_1$. Assume that a quality improvement raises average costs to $AC_2$ and shifts the demand to $D_2$. A new maximum-profit position results at $P_2$, $q_2$. Assuming an infinite number of such maximum-profit prices corresponding to alternative demand and cost functions, the latter varying with quality changes, which also affect demand, we may construct a curve $LAR$, representing the locus of maximum-profit prices (or average revenues), and a curve $LAC$, representing the locus of the corresponding average costs, as shown in Figure 4.7

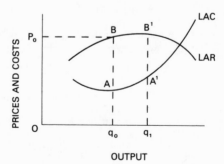

Fig. 4.7                                     OUTPUT

The curves are assumed to have these shapes because, after a point, further increments in quality improvements become progressively more costly. In transportation, for example, guaranteed faster delivery time requires higher fuel consumption for motor carriers and improved monitoring of vehicles. As the guaranteed delivery time diminishes, costs rise progressively faster. Similarly, the value of quality improvements to any buyer is subject to diminishing returns in terms of his willingness to pay ever higher amounts for improved quality. Given these shapes of *LAR* and *LAC*, the maximum maximorum profit occurs at the output where their slopes are equal $(Oq_0)$ with a price $P_0$.[49] This says that joint optimization of price and quality occurs when "the effect on profit of arbitrarily small changes in price and quality . . . have precisely offsetting effects on sales."[50] More formally this can be shown as follows: $q$ = sales per period, $c$ = average cost, $p$ = price, $\pi$ = net profit, and $x$ = a quality variable that affects sales and costs. Therefore, $q = f(p, x)$ and $c = c(q, x)$. Therefore $\pi = pf(p, x) - f(p, x) c[f(p, r), x]$. Taking partials of $\pi$ with respect to $p$ and $x$ and setting them equal to zero yields

$$-\frac{\partial f}{\partial p} = \frac{\dfrac{\partial f}{\partial x}}{\dfrac{\partial c}{\partial x}}.\text{[51]}$$

The left-hand side of the equation is the slope of the demand curve, and the right-hand side is the ratio of the increase in sales due to increases in average cost that arise from improvements in quality.[52]

We have been discussing the unconstrained case. If we now impose a rate-of-return constraint less than that implicit in the above, how will equilibrium price and quality change? The firm is guaranteed a rate of return, $s > r$, as noted above. It will therefore want to expand its capital base. This means that output will increase.[53] The firm may also expand its quality outlays. In short, the firm will expand output using more capital (along with some other complementary factors, previously

---

49. See Wilson, *Essays*, pp.102–107.
50. Dorfman and Steiner, "Optimal Advertising."
51. See Bass et al., pp.215–16, for details of derivation.
52. By simple substitution the above equation can be transformed into a form similar to that of the fixed-price case of the preceding section, $\dfrac{p}{c} - \dfrac{\epsilon}{\epsilon_q}$. See ibid.
53. This is not merely an assumption. A firm would not "pad the rate base" by adding useless capital when it can obtain some additional return by adding useful capital. Thus an increase in the capital base will expand output because the added capital is used for productive purposes: i.e., $Q = f(K, L)$. See Zajac, pp.124–25, for a formal proof.

designated $L$) and, in essence, will move along the $LAR$ and $LAC$ curves of Figure 4.7 until the total profits—say, at $q_1$ (which equal $(B^1 - A^1)q_1$)—are reduced relative to the maximum maximorum such that the ratio of the profits at $q_1$ to the original capital stock required to produce $q_0$ efficiently, say $K_0$, plus the incremental capital required to produce $q_1$, equals $s$; or $\dfrac{(B^1 - A^1)q_1}{K_0 + \Delta K} = s$. Depending on the shapes of $LAC$ and $LAR$, there will be a combination of increased quality outlays and price reduction to achieve the allowable rate of return. In general, however, it is apparent that quality will be higher and price lower than in the unconstrained case,[54] and, of course, quantity of output will be greater, assuming efficient production.

There may, however, be four sources of inefficiency that negate these more positive results: expense padding, inefficient production due to the A-J-W effect, entrance to new markets at a loss, and "encouraging" higher prices from equipment suppliers.

*Expense Padding.* A firm faced with an effective rate-of-return constraint may meet the constraint not only by expanding its capital base but also by incurring higher expenditures to produce any given level of output. Since the firm is assured a rate of return equal to $s$, there will be a tendency to be lax regarding costs not only in the A-J-W sense but also with regard to operating costs. More personnel may be hired than necessary, factor payments or fringe benefits may be higher than elsewhere, or amenities may be more substantial than in the case of firms subject to price regulation. An assured rate of return on an expanded base and the absence of competitive pressures can readily lead to behavior that does not minimize costs. Since the firm can adjust prices within the constraint, it can recoup whatever extra costs are occasioned by such laxity and, depending on demand and cost elasticities, can maintain the same aggregate level of profit.[55] At the very least, such a firm has little incentive to search actively for means to reduce unit costs. The "quiet life" in relatively sumptuous surroundings will certainly dull the incentives to lower unit costs and ferret out unnecessary expenditures.

*The A-J-W Effect in the Context of Quality Variation.* If the firm produces whatever output level it chooses inefficiently, then the $LAC$

---

54. If both the $LAR$ and $LAC$ functions have equal slopes at a point below the maximum of $LAR$, it is possible for the price to be higher under rate-of-return regulation. Quality and quantity will likewise be higher.

55. A regulatory constraint relating profit to total costs will obviously encourage cost padding. See Bailey and Malone, pp.139–40, for an analytical interpretation. The public utility literature abounds with concern for expense padding and what expenditures, both capital and operating, are "allowable" in calculating the rate base and the level of profits. See, for example, H. Trebing, "Toward an Incentive System of Regulation," *Public Utilities Fortnightly*, July 18, 1963.

function will rise above the level portrayed in Figure 4.7 beyond point $A$, analogous to the function $\dfrac{dc}{dq}$ in Figure 4.5. The new equilibrium output will be less than $Oq_1$ in Figure 4.7, the quality improvement less than in the unconstrained case, while the price may or may not be higher, depending on the shape of $LAR$. These results will be reinforced to the extent that cost padding is practiced.

*Entrance to New Markets at a Loss.* One of the implications of the A-J-W effect is that the firm has an incentive to expand into other regulated markets even if it has to take a loss or lower return, as long as the allowable profits on the additional capital employed in the other markets exceed the loss. Thus the firm could either drive out other firms in such secondary markets or discourage entry even though actual or potential suppliers in these markets were more efficient, as long as the firm is allowed to include the extra capital in its rate base.[56] This, of course, increases the resources needed to serve the other markets and stifles at least potential competition in them.

*Encouraging Higher Supply Prices.* Since the rate of return is calculated on the basis of the value of the capital base, the regulated monopoly may be relatively indifferent to the prices it pays for equipment. Indeed, under plausible conditions the firm "may not only fail to suffer a decline but actually experience an increase in profit if suppliers of capital goods collude to raise their prices."[57] Whether profits rise or remain the same depends on the slope of the total net revenue product of capital function (equals Max. $[pf - wL]$) function at the intersection of the ray through the origin equal to $sK$, when $r < s < r^*$. For reasonable shapes of the first function, the above conclusion holds whether the rate base is calculated on original or reproduction cost.[58]

These analytical developments have remarkably little relevance to contemporary transportation regulation. Nor has the analysis of the effects of regulation on transportation been developed to a comparable degree. Beyond the conclusion that rate-of-return regulation in natural gas and electric utilities may encourage firms to expand into submarkets at zero profit or even at an operating loss (because the enlargement of the rate base permits an increase in profits that more than offsets the loss[59]), there is little applicability to present-day regu-

---

56. Averch and Johnson, pp.1057–59. For an illustration and brief discussion, see H. Wein, "Fair Rate of Return and Incentives—Some General Considerations," in H. Trebling, ed., *Performance Under Regulation* (East Lansing: Michigan State University, 1968), pp.42ff.
57. Westfield, "Regulation and Conspiracy."
58. The interested reader should consult Westfield for details.
59. Wellisz, p.37; Averch and Johnson, pp.1057–58.

lation of transportation.[60] All the analyses assume total and effective regulation of one or a few variables and the existence of static monopoly power, but ignore the possibilities in what Leibenstein refers to as "X-efficiency."[61]

Hardly any of these assumptions are fulfilled in contemporary U.S. transportation regulation. In fact, such regulation extends well beyond price, rate of return, markup over cost, or other variables discussed in the literature noted above. It includes entry control, authority over mergers, abandonment, security issues, and operating rights and practices. ICC regulation is, in addition, partial, involving dynamic, not static adjustments. Indeed, as Kahn has argued, the static misallocation inherent in "too much capital" may provide a vehicle for technological advance if the additional capital is of a more efficient type and in the longer run may offset the static misallocation.[62] ICC regulation has also become more and more oriented toward the preservation of existing common carrier enterprises than the prevention of abuses of monopoly power. Furthermore, the specific regulatory criteria within transportation are often deliberately noneconomic and occasionally inconsistent. For example, there is a stress on average cost rather than on marginal cost; the approach toward "discrimination" is deliberately noneconomic and occasionally inconsistent; and in the case of the motor carrier industry, emphasis is placed on the operating ratio rather than on the rate of return. This means, of course, that any assessment of the actual impact of the existing regulation of transportation in the United States requires an analysis going beyond anything yet attempted—useful and challenging as these analyses are.

If rail, truck, and barge transportation become more concentrated (e.g., CONRAIL) and potentially capable of obtaining excess profits, the various considerations noted under the A-J-W effect will become more relevant. However, if we acknowledge that most transport markets have at least several suppliers of the same or different modes (i.e., that even under regulation with entry control, they are effectively oligopolistic or monopolistic), some insight into the consequences of transport regulation may be gained by examining the effect of price and rate-of-return regulation on non-monopoly structures.

---

60. Even in this case, operation in unprofitable submarkets in transportation is largely due to legal compulsion (i.e., refusal to permit abandonment) or ignorance of costs. It is not induced by rate-of-return regulation.

61. Harvey Leibenstein, "Allocative Efficiency vs. X-Efficiency," *American Economic Review*, June 1966.

62. A. E. Kahn, "The Graduated Fair Return: Comment," *American Economic Review*, vol.58, 1968.

## Regulated Oligopoly

The key feature of markets served by a "limited"[63] number of producers is a recognized mutuality of interest among the firms. Each firm is aware that its rivals will react in some way to its independent price, output, and quality charges, and thus each firm considers the most likely reaction of its rivals before making changes in any of these variables. Since rivals' reactions are likely to vary, depending on the economic circumstances facing each firm (e.g., the extent of excess capacity), determinate solutions are difficult to come by. To simplify the problem, we will assume here that each firm has excess capacity, the usual assumption leading to the "kinked" oligopoly solution.[64] A firm that has excess capacity will be anxious to increase its sales, but since each firm is aware that all the others are in the same boat, no firm will alter its price once a price for all firms has been established. Thus, each firm believes that if it raised its price, the others would *not* match the increase. Since the products are highly substitutable, the firm initiating the price increase would suffer a sales loss proportionately greater than the price increase—its demand for price increases is believed to be highly elastic. On the other hand, a firm that reduces its price to capture more business largely at the expense of its rivals can expect to have price reductions matched more or less promptly—its demand for price decreases is believed to be substantially less elastic or even inelastic at the prevailing price.[65]

In essence, the firm faces two extreme demand curves—the more inelastic demand $d_1d_1$ (in Figure 4.8) assumes all price changes are matched, and the more elastic demand $d_2d_2$ assumes no price changes

63. "Limited" number may refer to three to a dozen or more firms and/or situations in which the four or eight largest firms account for, say, 50 percent or more of the industry's output, regardless of the number of suppliers. Obviously, the economic outcome will vary as the number of firms increases substantially above three, and/or the share of the largest firms decreases. It is partly for this reason that clear-cut analytical answers in the oligopoly situation are difficult to derive without additional assumptions regarding the firms' behavior.

64. For details of the oligopoly problem, see any intermediate microtheory text, such as F. Scherer, *Industrial Market Structure and Economic Performance* (Chicago: Rand McNally, 1970), chaps. 5–8.

65. Of course, since everyone knows this, it may well be that price increases are matched and decreases are not matched. The firm raising its price may do so as an "invitation" to the others to follow, knowing that otherwise the price will not be sustained. Conversely, firms may be loath to match price reductions, at least promptly, since they would all be matching revenue losses and in essence invite the "chiseler" to raise its price to the previous level before too much business is stolen from them. In fact, if the firms do not have excess capacity, and a seller's market exists, an opposite kink to that shown in the text may exist. (See C. W. Efroymson, "A Note on Kinked Demand Curves," *American Economic Review*, March 1943.)

are matched. The prevailing price is assumed to exist at the point of intersection of $d_1d_1$ and $d_2d_2$, or $A$. The "kinked" demand—the one the firm believes to exist—consists of $d_2d_2$ above and to the left of $A$ and $d_1d_1$ below and to the right of $A$. The associated marginal revenue function $MR$ thus has a discontinuity at $A$, the dotted line $BC$. If the marginal cost curve intersects the $MR$ curve in the area of discontinuity, the maximum profit price and output are $A$ and $Oq_0$, respectively. In addition, for any change in $MC$ between $B$ and $C$, this will remain the equilibrium price and output combination: hence the traditional price stability or rigidity under oligopoly. Whatever competition exists takes place on the basis of sales effort and/or quality variations. What will happen to the equilibrium price, quantity, and quality when regulation is imposed?

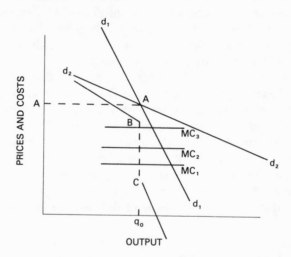

Fig. 4.8

*Price Regulation under Oligopoly.* The economic consequences of price regulation depend on the level of the price to be established. If the price set is below the kink but above $MC$, output of each firm will expand slightly along $d_1d_1$, since that is the demand assuming complete retaliation. Given price regulation, all firms are subject to the price set. Even if the price is set at the level of the kink, the previous price, there will be some repercussions. Price setting by a regulatory agency at any level reduces one aspect of uncertainty. Before regulation or any formal arrangements designed to eliminate price competition, there was always the possibility of occasional price changes initiated by a firm with perhaps a somewhat different perception of the state of the market, costs, or degree of excess capacity. Once a regulated price has been set, this possibility is removed. Competition or rivalry will thus be focused even more than before on quality variation and/or more advertising. If competition is sufficiently strong, the incentive to incur expenditures to "improve" service quality will tend to push marginal cost toward the regulated price. As Kahn notes, "If price is prevented from falling to marginal cost (due to regulation) then, to the extent that competition prevails, it will tend to raise *cost* to the level of *price*. Only when . . . marginal cost is once again equated with price will the tendency to service inflation be halted."[66] The air passenger industry provides abundant evidence of the consequences of non-price competition and the incentives to alter quality by such things as free, lavish meals and overscheduling arrivals in important travel markets at the best times (which contributes to airport congestion). Likewise, when airline profits turned to losses in 1969–70, schedules were cut back, charges were made for in-flight movies, and meals became less lavish and, in some cases, turned into sandwiches.[67]

Not surprisingly, the airline industry provides the setting for the more formal analysis of quality variation under price regulation. Assume an oligopolistic industry that produces two outputs, say, transportation and "meals," which is a quality aspect of the primary output, transportation service.[68] Each firm can vary the number (and quality) of meals it offers per passenger per trip. In terms of freight transport, each firm can vary the quality of service per shipment. In this case the quality variable is tied to the primary output. The demand for transport and "meals" can be specified as $Q_T = f(P_T, P_M)$ and $Q_M = g$ $(P_T, P_M)$, where $P_T$, $P_M$ are the prices of transport and meals, respectively, and $Q_T$, $Q_M$ the quantities demanded.

Profits for a "representative" firm are $\pi = P_T q_T + P_M q_M q_T - C_T q_T - C_M q_M q_T$, where $q_T$, $q_M$ are the outputs of the firm and $C_T$ and $C_M$ the costs of producing transport and meals, which are assumed to be constant for all output levels.

If the industry comes under price regulation and cannot charge separately for "meals," then each firm can charge only $P_T^*$ for transport but is free to vary the quality. Its profits are now $\pi = P_T^* q_T - C_T q_T - C_M q_M q_T$. The only variable subject to the firm's discretion is $q_M$. To maximize $\pi$, we take the first derivative of the profits function

---

66. A. E. Kahn, *The Economics of Regulation* (New York: John Wiley and Son, 1971), p.209. See also T. Keeler, "Airline Regulation," *Bell Journal of Economics and Management Science*, Autumn 1972, pp.421–23.

67. Kahn, pp.209–10, n106.

68. L. White, "Quality Variation When Prices Are Regulated," *Bell Journal of Economics and Management Science*, Autumn 1972, p.426. The following discussion is based on this work.

with respect to $q_M$, set it equal to zero, and with some rearranging obtain

$$q_M = \frac{P_T^* - C_T}{C_M} - \frac{q_T}{\dfrac{\partial q_T}{\partial q_M}} . \qquad (1)$$

Note that the greater $\dfrac{\partial q_T}{\partial q_M}$ the greater $q_M$ and vice versa. If the industry were monopolized, the firm would view $\dfrac{\partial q_T}{\partial q_M}$ as being smaller than in the case of oligopoly. For a monopolist, variation in $q_M$ can only induce an increase in demand along the *industry* demand curve. Under oligopoly, a single firm would expect to obtain not only new customers for the industry as a whole but also customers lured away from its rivals. The firm's demand in the oligopoly situation is perceived as being more elastic with respect to quality variation than the monopolist's. Similarly, the greater the number of firms in the industry the higher $\dfrac{\partial q_T}{\partial q_M}$ is believed to be: hence the higher the level of quality outlays. In the extreme case of perfect competition, $\dfrac{\partial q_T}{\partial q_M}$ is infinite. Thus the last term in equation (1) disappears, and we are left with $q_M = \dfrac{P_T^* - C_T}{C_M}$, which means that each firm expands $q_M$ "until the cost of quality (per unit of sales which equals $q_M C_M$) . . . just equals the potential net revenue $(P_T^* - C_T)$ from basic transportation."[69]

Thus a price-regulated oligopoly will offer more quality than either an unregulated oligopoly or a price-regulated monopoly. In addition, the larger the number of firms the greater the quality outlays. This also implies that if the regulatory agency seeks to reward an oligopoly with higher profits by establishing a higher price, the higher profits will not materialize because they will be competed away through higher quality costs per unit of sales. Unless the regulatory agency also imposes controls on quality outlays and prevents entry, simple price regulation alone will lead to the above consequences.

*Rate-of-Return Regulation under Oligopoly.* The analysis is much more complicated and tenuous in this case. Assume a rate of return set at $s$ as before. It must refer to the *industry* capital stock $K$ so that the firms as a whole are constrained to aggregate net profits equal to $sK$. No individual firm, however, is guaranteed a rate of return of $s$. Indeed, depending on relative firm efficiency, market circumstances, and other characteristics, some firms could reap returns greater than $s$

69. Ibid., p.428.

and others less than $s$, as long as the sum of the profits of each firm, relative to total industry capital, equals $s$. Thus, if the profits of the $i^{th}$ firm during any period are $\pi_i$ and the capital stock of the $i^{th}$ firm is $K_i$, we require only that $\dfrac{\sum\limits_{i=1}^{n} \pi_i}{\sum\limits_{i=1}^{n} K_i} = s$, even though no particular $\dfrac{\pi_i}{K_i}$ would equal $s$. Thus, even in the days when there were lingering hopes that railways as a whole might earn a fair return on a fair value,[70] in 1940 when the overall return was barely 3 percent, 60 of 131 Class I railroads had returns below 3 percent (16 of them ran deficits) and 29 carriers had stated returns over 6 percent, or double the average.[71] Similarly, the airline industry exhibits substantial differences between the earnings of individual lines and those allowable for the industry as a whole.

The problem then is that the imposition of an allowable rate of return for the industry will find some firms with actual rates of return above, at, and below that rate. If $s$ is below the previous industry level, it is not clear how firms in each of these three categories will react in terms of output, price, and/or quality changes. Those firms making more than $s$ will not necessarily be induced to reduce their profitability by expanding their rate base and lowering their price from the unconstrained case because their rate-base expansion will lead to a rise in allowable total profits for the *whole* industry. The amount of benefits accruing to this group of firms from such an action is unknown. A sensible strategy for such firms would be to continue to maximize and hope that the profits vis-à-vis the capital base of the other firms will be such as to change nothing for them (i.e., to ensure that total industry earnings relative to total industry capital equals $s$, while continuing to maximize profits in the same fashion as before the imposition of the constraint).

In a similar fashion, those firms earning $s$ will have no obvious incentive to change, while those earning less than $s$ will have an incentive to apply to the regulatory commission to "do something" to permit a rise in their earnings to the allowable level. However, if the commission has only the regulatory tool of an overall rate-of-return constraint, there is nothing it can do.

In the railroad industry this was known as the weak and strong line problem. If the ICC set a general rate level adequate to yield the weak lines a "fair" return, the returns to the strong lines would be

---

70. Even though the revised rule of rate making in 1933 eliminated all reference to fair return on fair value.

71. See Locklin, Table 18, p.330; and Table 20, p.346.

exorbitant; while if the rate level were set so that the strong lines obtained a "fair" return, the weak ones might soon be bankrupt. Attempts to merge the weak with the strong lines so that, inter alia, less disparity in individual lines' rate of return would result, came to naught during the 1920s.

In short, under rate-of-return regulation with sharp variation in individual firms' rates of return, the actions of particular firms to imposition of an industry rate of return lower than they previously earned depend on their views of the prospects of the other firms in the industry. If the number of rivals is fairly large and no great size dispersion exists, the reactions of each to a rate-of-return constraint is likely to be negligible. If it leads to an excessive rate of return for the industry (i.e., $> s$), the regulatory agency needs to have the authority to force a series of rate changes or a rate decrease over all, which should lower profits in an oligopoly. The results will be precisely the same as those noted under price regulation with increased emphasis on quality competition, sales effort, and control of entry and exit.

If the number of rivals is small, say five or six, or if a small subset of a large number of firms dominates the industry in terms of $\pi_i$ and $K_i$, the binding constraint will induce a pattern of behavior analogous to that of the A-J-W effect, modified only to the extent of uncertainty of the economic success and capital expansion activities of the rivals. If the firms are equal in size and making similar rates of return ($r^* > s$), the probability of A-J-W-type responses is greatly enhanced, especially if each firm believes the others will play the game of roughly equivalent capital expansion in response to the regulatory constraint.

## Regulated Competition

In freely competitive markets the automatic, impersonal outcome leads to a long-run optimal price and quantity, if externalities are ignored. Figure 4.9(a) shows the "typical" firm's cost functions, where its output is so small relative to total industry output that it believes it can sell all it is capable of producing without influencing price. It is a price taker and thus has only one decision to make, namely, how much to produce to maximize profits. Figure 4.9(b) shows the basic market demand and supply for the homogeneous commodity. Its scale is far larger than that of the firm in panel (a), and the abscissa is labeled $Q$, as distinguished from $q$ for the firm ($\Sigma q = Q$). Since each firm is a price taker, the price in the market is equivalent to marginal revenue. Thus, profit-maximization implies $P = MR = MC$. Each firm will produce an output at the point where $P = MC$, and the industry supply will be the sum of their output at $P = MC$—hence the industry supply curve reflects the firms' $MC$. In Figure 4.9 the

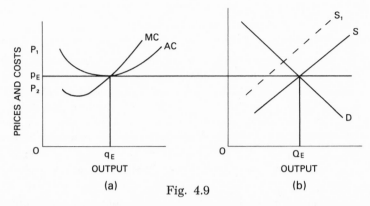

Fig. 4.9

(a)                                                    (b)

equilibrium price $P_E$ equals $MC$ and also equals $AC$, implicit in which are normal profits yielding a normal rate of return on the capital invested. This price will automatically tend to be established in the long run. If actual price exceeded $P_E$, each firm would produce a larger output, at which the higher price, $P_1 = MC > AC$, implying excess profits. This would induce new entrants, shift the industry supply curve from $S_1$ to $S$, and eliminate excess profits and hence stop new entry. If the price $P_2 < P_E$ existed, precisely opposite effects would take place. Thus, as Bain put it so well many years ago:

> Although each seller regards price as outside his control and simply adjusts his output to whatever the going price may be, it is thus clear that the combined actions of many such sellers unequivocally determine a definite market price at which the individual profit-seeking adjustments of all sellers can be maintained consistently with the aggregate desires of buyers. We see, first in the instance of short-run adjustments, that a market in pure competition is "automatically regulated" or "self-regulating" to a certain end. "An invisible hand," as Adam Smith described it, harnesses the essentially selfish adjustments of each of many sellers to produce a price result that none of them has planned.[72]

Since all this automatically leads to such economically desirable results, why would the government seek to regulate such an industry? The usual explanation points out that agriculture, an industry often assumed to possess most of the characteristics of a competitive industry, experiences frequent shifts in demand and supply because of crop failures or surpluses that are related to the weather in the United States and abroad. The degree of price and income instability (since both supply and demand are believed to be highly price-inelastic) has

72. J. S. Bain, *Pricing Distribution and Employment* (New York: Henry Holt, 1953), p.139.

been deemed "excessive." A similar rationale was used to justify motor carrier regulation in the 1930s although, as we have seen, the industry does not have all the features required for a perfectly competitive industry. Nevertheless, price instability, whatever its cause, often elicits private attempts to forestall it (e.g., the railroad pools and rate bureaus of the late nineteenth century) and/or public regulation.

Under competitive conditions, rate-of-return regulation is unnecessary since only normal returns can persist in the long run without regulation. We need examine only price regulation and its effects. If price is set above $P_E$, say, at $P_1$, the firms will be making excess profits. Indeed, this may be one of the purposes of such regulation, especially if those being regulated are politically powerful. However, to retain the price $P_1$ and the resultant excess profits, entry into the industry must be controlled. Furthermore, at $P_1$ there is excess supply in the market, which requires stockpiling of the excess, if it is a storable commodity, or maintenance of excess capacity for each producer (e.g., crop acreage restrictions in agriculture, narrowly construed operating authority in trucking).

If the price is set below $P_E$, say, at $P_2$, exit from the industry must be prevented. What is needed is a subsidy equal to $P_E - P_2$ for every unit sold to maintain each firm's financial viability combined with a rationing of the excess demand at $P_2$, or a greater subsidy than $P_E - P_2$ per unit to induce output to the new quantity demanded at the lower price.

## Conclusion to the Theory of Regulation

Economic regulation of any group of firms is beset with difficulties as far as efficiency criteria are concerned. Even regulating a single-product, nondiscriminating monopoly by means of a rate-of-return constraint may induce A-J-W inefficiencies as well as cost padding. Price regulation in such circumstances may induce excessive expenditures on quality or advertising or may lead to a spectrum of qualities and a whole price structure that in turn needs to be subject to the purview of the regulatory agency. When we move from single-firm monopoly to oligopoly and competitive industries, the workload of the agency mounts rapidly.[73] Indeed, the agency must control entry and exit, perhaps administer a subsidy, take jurisdiction over a complex structure of rates, attempt to ascertain marginal costs in specific situations, control quality variation and the rates related thereto. It must perform all these functions in addition to determining fairness ("fair return on a fair value"), controlling mergers, establishing uniform accounting rules,

---

73. See Appendix to this chapter for an example of the ICC's workload following passage of the Motor Carrier Act in 1935.

deciding what are "allowable" expenses and "allowable" inclusions in the rate base.

Regulating additional industries or extending the scope of transport regulation in the United States may pose formidable problems and may be more costly to society than any potential benefits. It is easy to understand the cries for regulatory reform or even for total deregulation of some of the areas now subject to ICC jurisdiction. Largely because of these problems, which have always existed but seemingly have worsened in transportation, attempts have been made to assess the consequences of regulation by the ICC and by other agencies.

## Economic Consequences of the ICC

In transportation there are an enormous number of markets for intercity freight transport (movement of particular commodities or classes of commodities between various origins and destinations). The market "structure" therefore is highly variable among them. Unless one selected a few major markets and attempted to deduce the number, size, and type of transport firms serving each one, the market-structure approach is not generally applicable to examining specific economic consequences. Furthermore, the ICC has limited jurisdiction over some modes (especially truck and barge). Thus, a somewhat different approach needs to be adopted in trying to sort out the effects of ICC regulation. In what follows we will briefly outline the main ingredients of such regulation and examine the most likely consequences of each, some of which are predicted from the above analysis of market structure.

### Rate Policy

In 1887 the aims of the Act to Regulate Commerce were to enhance rate stability by reducing "excessive" rate competition ("rate wars") and eliminate or moderate other forms of rate or price discrimination. Given the myriad of transport submarkets, it was natural for the ICC to treat each market (and each case) as sui generis. Each market would tend to have different numbers and types of competitors by mode; each commodity would have its own transport demand elasticity and level. It might even have unique transport costs, which, in turn, would differ by mode and perhaps among different carriers of the same mode. Thus, very few firm or specific rules are laid down with respect to what level of rate or rate change will be authorized in particular cases. The following represent the ICC's criteria with respect to rates:

1. No rates are to fall below out-of-pocket costs, based on the carriers'

or the ICC's cost evidence, reference being made to long-run marginal cost (*LRMC*).

2. Each rate is to contribute a "fair" share above *LRMC*, the amount depending on implicit elasticity estimates or judgments.

3. Existing certificated carriers serving particular submarkets are to "share the traffic" and not eliminate one another through rate competition.

Other aspects of policy relating to mergers, entry, operating rights, and modal separation are largely designed to sustain this type of rate structure, based less on cost than on demand or value-of-service factors, except where unregulated carriage poses a threat to those with common or contract status. Under these circumstances, allowing regulated rates closer to *LRMC* will ensure some of the traffic potential at "compensatory" rates. Where nonregulated traffic poses less of a threat, the commission is likely to moderate rate competition among the regulated carriers and permit them jointly to exploit the overall inelasticity of demand for transport for particular commodities.

Combining these criteria with regulatory stress on "noneconomic" factors[74] and considerable averaging of costs among carriers in the ICC computations of *LRMC* lead to the conclusion that economic regulation of rates causes a higher level of rates than would otherwise occur, assuming that most major transport markets would be at least workably competitive in the absence of such regulation. Under workably competitive conditions, a far closer relationship between rates and short-run marginal costs of efficient carriers (certainly below *LRMC* as now calculated) would result.

This conclusion is further supported as far as regulated carriers are concerned by the imposition of common carrier obligations. Among other things, "holding out to serve generally" requires a greater degree of excess capacity than would be needed if the carriers could be more selective. Furthermore, the difficulty of abandoning even obviously unprofitable lines leads to a higher degree of excess capacity, especially in rail transport, and hence higher overall costs than would exist without regulation.[75]

---

74. See pp.172–76 above.

75. For example, 25% of the mileage in the Midwest and Northeast Region accounts for only 4% of the carloads originated or terminated (*Rail Service in the Midwest and Northeast Region,* A Report by the Secretary of Transportation [Washington, D. C.: U. S. Department of Transportation, February 1, 1974], Part I, p.3). Studies of particular railroads indicate similar evidence of excess capacity. For example, almost 30% of the Pittsburgh and Lake Erie's lines carried only 2% of the traffic in 1953 (J. Conant, *Railroad Mergers and Abandonments* [Berkeley: University of California Press, 1964], p.7); 6% of the Chicago and Northwestern's mileage accounted for 50% of its revenue ton-miles, according to a 1966 study

The tendency toward excess capacity is further aggravated by the ICC's refusal to sanction many peak/off-peak rates, a policy that leads to more capacity than would otherwise be needed despite the difficulties of implementing such a pricing policy.[76] Of course, not all the current excess capacity, especially in rail but also to a lesser extent in trucking, can be attributed to ICC regulatory policy. Indeed, probably the major source of excess capacity is to be found in the declining rail share of intercity ton-miles, due largely to the development of alternative modes assisted by other aspects of public policy, mainly the creation of an extensive highway network. In fact, railway mileage has steadily decreased from some 253,000 miles in 1920 to less than 200,000 miles by 1975.[77] Much excess capacity still exists, of course, but there has been about a 20 percent reduction. The remainder is not due solely to regulation, although regulation has retarded the process.

Costs of providing common carrier service have also increased compared with, say, private or unregulated carriage by the filing of tariffs and schedules; regular reports to the ICC, often in forms calculated more to serve the needs of the regulators than to provide information necessary for improved managerial performance; costs of proceedings, including extensive and costly justification for or opposition to rate changes, abandonments, and the like; and higher insurance requirements and higher tax liabilities for similar assets.[78]

Most but not all of these added costs are attributable to economic regulation (e.g., differential state and local taxation). Nor are all

---

(ICC Finance Dockets Nos. 24182, 24183, and 24184); a 1973 study of the Lehigh Valley Railroad found that 90% of its traffic moved on 17% of its mileage (Testimony of the Federal Railroad Administrator in Hearings Before the Senate Surface Transportation Subcommittee on S.1031, 93rd Cong., 1st sess. [Washington, D. C.: U. S. Government Printing Office, 1973], Part 2, p.273, May 30, 1973).

Harbeson concludes from such evidence that "a systematic program of line abandonment much more extensive than hitherto contemplated or permitted" is necessary for rail financial viability (R. Harbeson, "Some Policy Implications of Northeast Railroad Problems," *Transportation Journal*, Fall 1974, p.8). See also Conant, chap. 1, for a discussion of rail excess capacity and overinvestment.

76. See chap. 3, pp.163–67.

77. Exclusive of yard tracks, sidings, and parallel tracks (AAR, *Yearbook of Railroad Facts*, various years).

78. As has been noted, private carriage "escapes certain costs . . . including the costs of tariff publication, solicitation and certain supervision aggregating eight percent or more of total costs" (E. W. Williams, Jr., *The Regulation of Rail-Motor Rate Competition* [New York: Harper, 1958], p.10). There are also differential tax burdens among private, contract, and common carriers by truck (see Wilson, *Essays*, pp.177ff.). The differential taxation of railway property at the state and local levels is notorious and has prompted several legislative efforts to remove such discrimination on the grounds that it constitutes an unlawful burden on interstate commerce (see J. Spychalski, "The Taxation of Railroad Property in Indiana," dissertation, Indiana University, 1962).

of them undesirable (e.g., higher insurance costs). However, whatever their source or justification, their effect is to raise computed costs, which in turn raise general rate levels. At the same time attempts to maintain a value-of-service rate structure result in higher levels of rates above the higher costs.

Not only are costs and rates higher under regulation but also there is less correspondence of particular rates to their costs. This is not only related to the value-of-service rate structure but also caused by the attempt to maintain rate stability in the face of often highly variable specific costs and by the lengthy proceedings that prevent rates from adjusting to cost variation. It should be noted, however, that only a tiny fraction of the rates and tariffs filed each year are subject to formal proceedings.[79] This does not mean that rate regulation is ineffective; the formal proceedings have widespread effects and influence rate proposals that are not subject to such proceedings or may not need to be since they are consistent with prior rulings.

In the past the commission has been reluctant to grant even cost-justified quantity discounts (or volume rates) much beyond the traditional CL-LCL (and TL-LTL) rate differentials. This policy was originally designed to protect small shippers who normally could not ship in multi-carload lots. Such a policy clearly establishes a narrower range of rate differentials than could be cost-justified. During the 1940s the policy was changed, as the commission removed many of the regulatory constraints concerning multi-car and unit train rates. However, it was not until the 1960s that the railroads themselves sought increasing numbers of volume rate reductions, most of which were approved by the commission.[80] Thus, as a source of inefficient pricing the question of quantity discounts is no longer significant.

In general, regulation rather systematically violates efficiency criteria $(P_i \neq MC_i)$ in many submarkets and leads to higher costs of providing a given amount of transportation service. It is worth noting that not all rates are systematically higher than $MC$. Indeed, various estimates exist that suggest that as many as 30 percent of rail rates may be below ICC-computed $LRMC$.[81] This situation leads to similar kinds of inefficiencies, as $P_i > MC_i$, but it does tend to reduce the average rate level. Similarly, regulation perpetuates a certain amount of excess capacity. Later we will examine several attempts to quantify the amount of economic waste involved in maintaining a non-cost-oriented rate structure and excess capacity.

79. Possibly as few as one in 300. See L. S. Goodman, "Recent Trends in Transport Rate Regulation," *Michigan Law Review*, June 1972, pp.1225–26.

80. For details see Goodman, pp.1240–45.

81. ICC, *The Impact of the 4-R Act, Railroad Ratemaking Provision*, October 5, 1977, Table 1-1, p.9.

## Effects of Entry Control

One of the instrumentalities needed to maintain this pattern of rate regulation is the ability to restrict supply. The effects of entry control and operating rights are therefore in the same direction as the other aspects of regulatory policy discussed above. However, several aspects of the supply control problem are worth noting.

First, to the firms so protected, the effectiveness of supply control is of considerable importance. For many firms it represents a kind of quid pro quo for acceptance of the common carrier obligations and their associated higher costs. It is particularly important to the regulated firms, since they can expand capacity without much fear of new (regulated) entrants.

Second, attempts to restrict supply provide an additional source of inefficiency, especially in the motor carrier industry, where route, back-haul, and commodity restrictions reinforce the already strong tendency toward excess capacity and/or underutilization of equipment. In addition, however, the commission, in its role of protector of regulated transportation, has imposed costs on private carriage as well—especially in denying operating rights on back-haul traffic for private or exempt carriers. A recent study shows that "private tractor-trailer combinations return empty 62.4 percent of the time versus 38 percent for ICC regulated vehicles" and that this is due in part at least to regulation.[82] A later survey of empty mileage was conducted by the ICC during 1976. It found that "the percentage of empty truck miles for ICC authorized, exempt . . . and private trucks were 16.2, 21.2, and 27.3 percent, respectively."[83]

Third, in only one major area (rail transport) is entry severely circumscribed by virtue of high capital requirements. Thus entry controls require detailed administrative hearings. The problems of supply control, especially when entry is technically easy, are increased substantially when a large segment of an industry escapes from regulation, as in the trucking industry. The regulated sector of the industry is at a considerable competitive disadvantage because it lacks the flexibility to respond quickly to changed circumstances and thus incurs higher costs. The regulatory agency is then forced to exploit more rigorously whatever degree of monopoly power may exist in other submarkets where exempt or unregulated carriage poses little threat. Of course, the incentive to enter is partly a function of the price level relative to costs. The commission has to play a rather delicate game,

---

82. E. Miller, "Effects of Regulation on Truck Utilization," *Transportation Journal,* Fall 1973, p.11.

83. ICC, *Empty/Loaded Truck Miles on Interstate Highways During 1976,* April 1977, p.3.

for which it is singularly ill equipped, in establishing such rates at a level analogous to Bain's "limit price," above which so many new entrants appear that a lower price turns out to be more profitable.[84] More recently it has been concluded that "higher barriers to entry result in an increased expected utility, and if the hazard rate is reduced, the optimal limit price is increased."[85] Entry control in transportation constitutes a "higher barrier" and undoubtedly leads to higher prices despite the uncertainties involved.

Indeed, there is a fairly impressive, though not unambiguous, body of empirical findings indicating that the level of *regulated* trucking rates is higher than would otherwise be the case.[86] Maister has carefully reviewed these findings and several more-recent empirical studies and concludes that

(1) little confidence can be held in the results of previous attempts to apply regression techniques to detect the effect of regulation in Canada; (2) applying these techniques to more recent (and reliable) data suggests that there is no strong relationship between *rate* regulation and the level of trucking rates in Canada, although because of multi-collinearity and omitted variables this cannot be considered a definitive conclusion; (3) there is weak, but suggestive, evidence that there is no significant effect of *entry* regulation on rates; and, finally, that the problems associated with the application of regression techniques to this problem are numerous and complex, and that all such applications should be examined and interpreted with the utmost care and attention.[87]

In addition, rates on exempt commodities tend to be considerably lower than rates on non-exempt commodities.[88] Furthermore, when certain agricultural commodities were deregulated some years back, their rates promptly fell substantially with no apparent service de-

---

84. J. S. Bain, "A Note on Pricing in Monopoly and Oligopoly," *American Economic Review*, March 1949.

85. D. P. Baron, "Limit Pricing, Potential Entry and Barriers to Entry," *American Economic Review*, September 1973, p.673.

86. J. Sloss, "Regulation of Motor Freight Transportation: A Quantitative Evaluation of Policy," *Bell Journal of Economics and Management Science*, Autumn 1970; D. McLachlan, "Canadian Trucking Regulations," *Logistics and Transportation Review*, no.1, 1972; J. Palmer, "A Further Analysis of Provincial Trucking Regulation," *Bell Journal of Economics and Management Science*, Autumn 1973.

87. D. Maister, "Regulation and the Level of Trucking Rates in Canada," in *Motor Carrier Economic Regulation*, Proceedings of a Workshop, April 7–8, 1977 (Washington, D.C.: National Academy of Sciences, 1978), pp.226–27.

88. R. Farmer, "The Case for Unregulated Truck Transportation," *Journal of Farm Economics*, May 1964; C. Linnenberg, Jr., "Agricultural Exemption in Interstate Trucking—Mend or End Them," *Law and Contemporary Problems*, Winter 1960; J. Ulrey, "Problems and Issues in Transportation Policy and Implications for Agriculture," *Journal of Farm Economics*, December 1964.

terioration.[89] As further evidence of the extent to which regulated trucking rates exceed costs, the value of operating rights has been increasing rapidly. Some estimates indicate that the value of such rights rose by 16 percent per year between 1962 and 1972.[90] The Council on Wage and Price Stability estimated the total value of all operating authorities in 1974 at between $3 billion and $4 billion.[91] Such values represent rates of return greater than those required to attract capital and, in essence, are a form of capitalized monopoly return. Even totally bankrupt firms can often sell their operating rights for large amounts.[92] The ICC recently reported on 43 transactions in operating rights covering the period 1967–1971. On the average, the value of these rights had increased at a compound rate of 17 percent per year, or 13 percent adjusted for inflation.[93] The American Trucking Associations likewise argues that "operating rights, the value of which tend to increase rather than decrease with time, are the single most important asset of the motor carrier."[94] The reason such rights are important and increase in value over time is related to the higher rates and greater potential profits resulting from regulatory restraints on competition. The rights have value because they are scarce relative to the profit prospects. As Kafoglis concludes, "the 'paradox' of valuable operating rights in a 'competitive' industry can be explained by the existence of regulation that permits little real competition."[95] The bulk of the evidence thus supports the view that rates in general are higher than they would be in the absence of economic regulation.

This relatively high rate level, compared to cost, is supported not only by entry restrictions but also by rate bureaus, which provide a

---

89. USDA, Marketing Reports 224 (1958), 316 (1959), and Supplement (1961). When movement of poultry and fruits and vegetables was deregulated in the mid-1950s, rates dropped by 33 percent and 19 percent, respectively.

90. Testimony of J. Shenenfield, Assistant Attorney General, Antitrust Division, before the Subcommittee on Antitrust and Monopoly of the Committee on the Judiciary, U. S. Senate, Concerning Economic Regulation of the Motor Carrier Industry, October 27, 1977, p.11.

91. Ibid., p.12.

92. S. M. Aug, "Truckers Pay $20 Million for Licenses of Associated," *Washington Star*, July 12, 1976.

93. For details, see M. Kafoglis, "Valuable Operating Rights in a 'Competitive' Industry: A Paradox of Regulated Trucking," *Regulation*, September/October 1977, pp.27–32. For a critique of Kafloglis's position, see D. Kamerschen and C. Paul, "The Value of Operating Rights in Regulated Trucking: Paradigm Lost," *Transportation Research Forum, Proceedings—Nineteenth Annual Meeting, 1978* (Oxford, Ind.: Richard B. Cross, 1978), pp.374–81.

94. T. Flanagan, "Are Motor Carriers' Operating Rights Really Intangible?" *Motor Freight Controller*, September 1978, p.6.

95. Kafoglis, p.32.

forum for motor carriers in a particular territory, collectively to establish rates. Such price fixing would be *per se* illegal under the antitrust laws. As a consequence, in 1948 Congress passed the Reed-Bulwinkle amendment, Sect. 5A of the Interstate Commerce Act (over the veto of then-President Truman), which provided rate bureaus in transportaion with antitrust immunity subject to ICC approval and other conditions. A body of contentious literature has arisen concerning the pros and cons of rate bureaus, especially the extent to which they inhibit rate reductions, limit the "right of independent action," foster stability, assist in "coordinating" shipper and carrier needs, and facilitate interlining.[96] Rate bureaus, along with entry control in trucking and ICC rate policy, are part of a system that tends to support higher rate levels and more rate stability than would otherwise exist.

## Regulation and Technological Change

The rate of technological change for a nation or an industry depends on the rate of invention and the rate of diffusion of an invention. The major determinants of either rate are not well known, nor are the circumstances under which the rates may be varied. Inventive activity, including a firm's expenditures on research and development (R and D) may require a certain degree of monopoly power. On the other hand, too much power may inhibit change and experimentation. Furthermore, a good many inventions are still made by individuals not attached to large corporate research laboratories[97] and whose motivations and psychology may loom large in determining the propensity to invent. Similar complexities arise in determining the speed with which particular firms in specific industries adopt an existing invention. Are large, highly profitable, rapidly growing firms (or industries) likely to be innovative (i.e., adopt an invention) more rapidly than smaller, less-profitable firms? The former have the ability to do so but may lack the will, while the latter may have the will but lack the (financial) ability.

Since one of the major evils charged to regulatory agencies, especially the ICC, is that they inhibit technological change, let us inquire

---

96. Some of these issues are discussed in the testimony of Shenenfield, cited above. For a favorable view of rate bureaus in a study commissioned by various traffic associations, see J. Friedman, *Collective Ratemaking in Trucking: The Public-Interest Rationale*, Washington, D. C., October, 1977. A short but more balanced discussion is contained in C. Barrett, *The Theory and Practice of Carrier Rate-Making*, reprinted from *Transportation and Distribution Management*, Washington, D. C. (no date). See also G. Davis and C. Sherwood, *Rate Bureaus and Antitrust Conflicts in Transportation* (New York: Praeger, 1975).

97. V. Jewkes, D. Sawers and R. Stillerman, *The Sources of Invention* (London: Macmillan, 1960), chap. 5.

in what ways regulation may influence both the rate of invention and the rate of diffusion.

TECHNOLOGICAL CHANGE IN THE TRANSPORTATION INDUSTRIES

We should first note the apparent rate of technological change in the transport industries. Since technological change leads to pro-ductivity increases (i.e., increases in output per unit of input) one indicator of technological change would be data pertaining to pro-ductivity. Unfortunately, in transportation such data suffer from enormous deficiencies and may yield misleading results. For example, using as a measure of productivity "net ton-miles and passenger-miles per man-hour" (a frequently used and misused indicator), the Bureau of Labor Statistics shows that in the rail industry productivity grew at a rate of 5.2 percent per year between 1947 and 1970 and at 6 percent per year between 1957 and 1970.[98] These rates far exceed not only those of the private economy as a whole and major sectors thereof but also those of intercity motor trucking (3.1 percent per year) and inland water transport (0.7 percent per year).[99] Others have noted a similar apparent relative technological dynamism not only for railroads but for transportation as a whole.[100]

It is difficult to reconcile such findings with the financial distress of much of the transport system, especially the railroads. Such rapid rates of productivity growth "should have enabled the rail industry to grant competitive wage increases, to increase its profit rate, and at the same time to keep its relative prices down so as to fend off com-petition from other modes of transport and transport alternatives."[101] Economic regulation may account for part of this paradox. However, even if the ICC prevented downward rail rate adjustments consistent with the apparent rate of productivity growth, rail profits on the existing traffic volumes should have risen. Furthermore, as noted above, the measured productivity growth of trucks and barges was substantially below that of rail, suggesting a relative increase in

---

98. See *Indexes of Output Per Man-Hour, Selected Industries, 1939 and 1947–1970*, Bureau of Labor Statistics Bulletin no.1692, 1972, p.107. Other studies by the BLS also indicate rail productivity growth between 5 percent and 6 percent per year using such measures as car-miles per man-hour. (See *Improving Railroad Productivity*, Final Report of the Task Force on Railroad Productivity, Washing-ton, D.C., November, 1973, p.53 n1.)

99. J. W. Kendrick, *Postwar Productivity Trends in the United States, 1948–1969* (New York: National Bureau of Economic Research, 1971), pp.5–11.

100. See R. J. Barber, "Technological Change in American Transportation: The Role of Government Action," *Virginia Law Review*, June 1964; and E. Mansfield, "Technical Change in the Railroad Industry," in *Transportation Economics* (New York: National Bureau of Economic Research, 1965).

101. *Improving Railroad Productivity*, pp.53–54.

rail's competitive position since rates in the unregulated segments of the truck and barge industries (the major portion of these industries, by far) more closely reflect costs. In addition, there is no evidence that wages paid to railway labor are out of line either with those of industry in general or in terms of the value of the product of railway labor.[102]

The key to this apparent paradox must lie in the measurement of productivity. Since productivity is a ratio of some measure of output to some measure of input, the problem resides in either or both indicators. Studies showing a rapid rise in rail productivity invariably use ton-miles (net or gross) as the output indicator. We have already stressed the problems of such an output measure in cost estimation in chapter 2. The same difficulties emerge here. The composition of rail aggregate ton-miles has shifted dramatically over the period covered by these productivity measures. Passenger traffic has sharply declined relative to freight traffic. The average length of haul has risen. Carload and bulk movements of relatively low-valued, high-density commodities (coal, grain, iron ore, lumber) have virtually displaced LCL movements of higher-valued commodities. The quality of railroad service has also deteriorated as rails have deferred much maintenance. Since all of these changes in the composition and quality of output imply a substitution away from high labor-intensive to low labor-intensive output, it is apparent that any measure of ton-miles per unit of labor input will overstate real efficiency gains in the sense that a given output is produced with fewer labor inputs.[103] Similarly, on the input side, there has been a rapid rise in the capital-to-labor ratio and also in the proportion of raw materials to labor. In other words, each unit of labor has increasing amounts of other inputs with which to work.

The changing composition of both output and input systematically leads to an overstatement of the ratio between the two. There are various types of adjustment that can be made to render such changes, which do not reflect real efficiency growth, more meaningful in the context of productivity.[104] However, when a series of (not unreason-

---

102. G. Wilson, "Wages and Productivity of Railway Labor," *Quarterly Review of Economics and Business,* Spring 1963. Updating the data through 1972 yields similar conclusions, namely, that increases in railway labor costs have roughly coincided with the rise in value productivity of labor.

103. A good discussion of these points is contained in *Improving Railroad Productivity,* pp.54ff.; and Paul Banner, "Capital and Output in the Railroad Industry," *Papers—Ninth Annual Meeting of the Transportation Research Forum, 1968* (Oxford, Ind.: Richard B. Cross, 1968), pp.129–47.

104. See ibid. for a good summary of the necessary adjustments. A discussion of the whole issue of transport productivity measurement is contained in R. Scheppach, Jr., and L. Woehlcke, *Transportation Productivity* (Lexington, Mass.: D. C. Heath, 1975).

able) adjustments are made, labor productivity appears to have risen by 2.7 percent to 3.7 percent per year between 1947 and 1970.[105]

A better measure of productivity change involves relating a (deflated) output measure to total factor inputs, not merely one, and weighting the inputs by their relative proportion of costs. When this is done, rail total factor productivity appears to have grown by 0.8 percent to 1.8 percent per year from 1947 to 1970, depending on whether 1970 or 1947 factor weights are used,[106] a figure well below the 2.5 percent growth of total factor productivity for the entire private domestic economy. This estimate seems to be more reasonable in that it is consistent with the rail financial malaise.

However, some of the data adjustments needed to obtain these estimates are questionable, and the data leave a good deal to be desired. It is clear, therefore, that productivity measures are extremely tenuous at best and, in the present state of the art, with existing data sources, need to be taken with a large grain of salt. The situation is even worse with respect to the other freight transportation modes, especially those where man-power requirements are relatively fixed over a wide range of output variation (e.g., rail, barge, and pipelines).[107]

It is for these reasons that we do not hazard here any tenuous or even judgmental empirical estimates of the rate of productivity or technological growth for the several modes of intercity freight transportation. This clearly inhibits any assessment of the impact of regulatory policy on (some unknown) degree of technological change. To analyze this issue we are forced to revert to nonempirical techniques. In the next sections we therefore examine what little is known about the determinants of invention and innovation and the most likely direction (not the magnitude) of the impact of regulation on each.

## DETERMINANTS OF INVENTIVE ACTIVITY[108]

The most comprehensive attempt to analyze the economics of invention is the work of Jacob Schmookler, who views invention as an economic activity. After rather carefully discussing the (now) well-known defects in patent statistics, he concludes that such statistics are reasonable indexes of the number of economically significant inventions.[109] He derives a simple model that assumes that in-

105. *Improving Railroad Productivity*, p.74.
106. Ibid., p.78.
107. G. Wilson, "An Influence of Demand upon Productivity," *Canadian Journal of Economics and Political Science*, August 1956.
108. Material through p.223 appeared in slightly different form in G. Wilson, ed., *Technological Development and Economic Growth* (Bloomington: Division of Research, Indiana University, 1972), chap. 7.
109. Jacob Schmookler, *Invention and Economic Growth* (Cambridge: Harvard University Press, 1966), p.23.

ventive activity is closely related to expected gains. He defines expected gain as

$$\pi_i = s_i S \frac{[P_i - C_i]}{P_i} - E_i,$$

where $E_i$ = expected cost of inventing machine $i$ at any given time
$s$ = percent of the market $S$ captured by $i$ for machines of
that general class, where $s_i = \dfrac{P_i X_i}{S}$
$X_i$ = number of machines of type $i$ expected to be sold at $P$
$C_i$ = expected cost of producing each machine $i$

Then, since $\dfrac{P_i - C_i}{P_i}$ is simply the percentage markup, if we assume rough "competitive equality among industries," it is evident that "the number of machines it will pay to invent will vary directly with S, the expected size of the market."[110] After examining the data Schmookler concludes that "the amount of invention is governed by the extent of the market,"[111] and later notes that "Man's efforts to satisfy his wants better . . . [are] intimately related to the ways in which he satisfies his wants now. Since invention is usually costly—in time if not in money—its volume is bound to be somewhat sensitive to the return expected from it."[112] Thus, invention is neither exogenous nor autonomous.

Furthermore, patented inventions are distributed among firms or industries in a fashion consistent with maximizing behavior. That is, cross-section studies (from 1900 to 1950) show that patented inventions that lead to improvement of capital goods tend to be distributed among U. S. industries in proportion to the industries' value added, with inventions lagging behind investment or value added in the particular industry. In short, a high volume of capital goods sales in a field is presumptive evidence that invention in it will be profitable.

Others have generally corroborated Schmookler's findings. For example, F. M. Scherer relates the number of patents to sales for a large number of firms (448) and concludes that "the greater the sales of a firm in any given market, the more incentive and resources the firm has to generate patentable inventions related to that market."[113] There are, however, large differences among the 14 industries in

110. Ibid., p.115.
111. Ibid., p.163.
112. Ibid., p.207.
113. F. M. Scherer, "Firm Size and Patented Inventions," *American Economic Review*, December 1965, p.1100. See also J. Schmookler and O. Brownlee, "Determinants of Inventive Activity," *American Economic Review*, May 1962; and Schmookler, *Invention and Economic Growth*.

which the firms are involved. In general, Scherer finds that the higher an industry's average patent output per dollar of sales, the less variable patenting tends to be relative to size. This is interpreted to mean that in technically progressive fields such as electrical equipment and general chemicals, technological competition forces firms to match each other's inventive efforts.[114] In essence, a vigorous scientific climate in any industry may exert something of a push, and size of market, however measured, cannot be regarded as the sole determinant. Even though the scientific climate is important, most observers tend to believe that the pull of demand is the predominant influence on inventive activity—a conclusion that certainly is consistent with Adam Smith's dictum that "the division of labor is limited by the extent of the market," or the even more ancient saw that "necessity is the mother of invention." However, the rate at which any industry adopts an existing invention (the rate of diffusion) is critical in determining observed rates of technological change.[115]

---

114. Scherer, p.1100, n6.
115. More sophisticated attempts to explain inventive activities in economic terms have recently been made. Although such studies have not yet gotten much beyond Schmookler, they have opened up some promising areas of research. However, most of these recent analyses generally assume that once inventive activities have been carried to the point where they are ready to be implemented or embodied in a new process or product, the productive capacity of the system is immediately raised to the extent implicit in the process or product. Such a view emerges from the public-goods aspect of inventions that is continually stressed (see, for example, W. D. Nordhaus, "An Economic Theory of Technological Change," *The American Economic Review*, May 1969, p.19) or from the general view that "the cost of dissemination of technical knowledge is typically very low in comparison to its production cost" (Karl Shell, "Inventive Activity, Industrial Organization and Economic Growth," Discussion Paper no.163 [Philadelphia: University of Pennsylvania, 1970], p.4). Thus, once the inventing is done the implication is that widespread application or diffusion of it will follow in short order—or even immediately in the absence of patents or inventor secrecy. For example, Nordhaus relates the lag that occurs before an invention is generally adopted exclusively to "the life of the patent, the average lead time or the length for which secrets can be held" (Nordhaus, p.19) and thus makes the rate of technological change (the rate of change in the capacity of the system, assuming no change in quality or quantity of labor and capital) a simple function of the number of inventions produced at a given time (p.21). (Nordhaus modifies the function by assuming diminishing returns to additions to the stock of knowledge, but this modification is not relevant to the present discussion.) Few seriously believe that diffusion or innovation is held back solely by patents and secrecy. Even if all new knowledge or inventions were pure public goods or could be used universally at zero marginal cost, there would not be immediate universal adoption. There is always a lag between the best practice technique and what may be termed the average level of technology, an average composed of operations embodying both best-practice and less-than-best-practice techniques. Indeed, this is doubtless what Nordhaus means by "average lead time." It takes time for people to perceive and react to new knowledge or, as Arrow puts it, "the transmission of the observation or of the revised probability judgments must take place over channels which have a limited capacity and are

## The Economics of Diffusion

The rate of capacity growth of an economy or an industry, aside from quantitative and qualitative changes in labor and capital, depends on the rate of introduction of new technology and its rate of diffusion. To take the simplest case, assume an invention that can lower production costs by $\rho$ percent. If we assume a constant rate of diffusion of this invention or new technique among firms in an industry or in the whole economy of $k$ percent (in the sense that after the first introduction of the new technique, $k$ percent of the firms who have not adopted it in period $t$ will in fact adopt it in period $t+1$) and that the same reduction in production costs will occur for all firms, the increase in capacity for the industry or economy over time is:

$$kN(1+\rho) + \sum_{t=1}^{n} (1-k)^{(t-1)}(1+\rho).$$

In this equation all firms are considered to contribute the same proportion of value added, and $N$ is the number of firms in existence.

Over time, the increase in capacity in response to this given innovation approaches zero as all firms in the industry or the economy adopt it. Obviously, the ultimate change in capacity is precisely equal to the original gain in efficiency, namely $\rho$ percent.[116] The diffusion process simply spells out the rate at which the original gain spreads as more and more firms adopt the innovation.

Graphically, for any $\rho$ there is a set of growth paths approaching a capacity level of $Q(1+p)$, depending on $k$. Figure 4.10 shows two such paths labeled $Q^*A$ and $Q^*B$.

Under this simple construction, an industry or the economy as a whole approaches the capacity limit (as defined by the level of technology and ignoring changes in labor and capital) at the decreasing rate $(1-k)^t$. That is, while at time zero, potential capacity is $Q^*(1+\rho)$, it is not realized unless $k=1$. For if $k<1$, which is to be

therefore costly" (Kenneth J. Arrow, "Classification Notes on the Production and Transmission of Technological Knowledge," *The American Economic Review*, May 1969, p.32). He further notes that "the diffusion of an innovation becomes a process formally akin to the spread of an infectious disease" (Arrow, p.33). Irving Siegel notes that "the main role of research is to multiply technical and economic opportunities, but the quality of entrepreneurship, market conditions and other factors determine whether or not such opportunities will be realized" (see Irving Siegel, "The Role of Scientific Research in Stimulating Economic Progress," *The American Economic Review*, May 1960, p.340).

116. That is, the growth in capacity is a series of percentage changes in $Q$ beginning with $kN(1 + \rho)$ in period 1, when $k$ percent of the firms innovate, and continuing at the rate $(1 - k)^{(t-1)}$. The sum of such a series is

$$kN(1+\rho) \left[ \frac{1}{1 - (1\text{-}k)} \right] = (1+\rho)N.$$

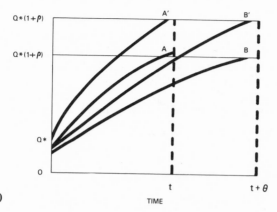

SET OF GROWTH PATHS APPROACHING CAPACITY LEVEL OF Q* (1+ρ)

Fig. 4.10                                    TIME

expected, the gap between actual and theoretical capacity (or between best and average practice techniques) progressively narrows for any $k > 0$ and $k < 1$. Ultimately, in the extreme, when all firms have adopted the invention, the industry moves along the capacity ceiling $Q^*(1 + \rho)$ until another invention appears. Note that in this formulation $k$ and $\rho$ are assumed to be independent, although this assumption is questioned later. This means that regardless of the size of $\rho$, the industry or economy will reach $Q^*(1 + \rho)$ or $Q^*(1 + \rho')$ over the same time interval as indicated by $Q^*A$ and $Q^*A'$ or by the slower rate of diffusion shown by $Q^*B$ and $Q^*B'$, depending on the size of $k$. Clearly, for any given invention the actual rate of growth of capacity depends solely on the rate of diffusion.

However, it is evident that technological innovation is not a once-and-for-all proposition. A more realistic model, therefore, should incorporate continuous technological change that also raises potential capacity. The simplest formulation is to assume a constant rate of such progress; thus, we may write the growth in capacity as $\Delta Q_t = kN$ $(1 - k)^{(t-1)}(1 + \rho)^{(t-1)}$, $t = 1, \ldots, n$.

Assuming discrete time intervals, the capacity line on a graph will shift upward each period by an amount $\Delta Q_t$ (see Figure 4.11). The actual growth path *ABCD* is a combination of sequential technical progress with a given rate of diffusion; *AA'*, *BB'*, and so on are the paths associated with a given change in $\rho$ and are thereafter totally dominated by the rate of diffusion. Thus, as firms diffuse the innovations occurring during period 1 over several time periods (such as *AA'*), depending on the size of $k$, new innovations occur during every period. In turn, they are diffused and thus "pile up," as it were, on previous actual growth rates.

ILLUSTRATION OF GROWTH IN CAPACITY

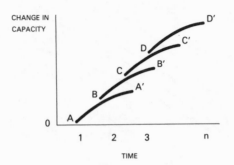

Fig. 4.11

THE VARIABILITY OF DIFFUSION RATES

The rate of diffusion $k$ for the economy as a whole is a weighted average of diffusion rates among industries. That is:

$$k = \sum_{i=1}^{n} \frac{Q_i}{Q} k_i,$$

where $Q$ refers to GNP, $Q_i$ is the value added of industry $i$, and $k_i$ represents the rate of diffusion of the $i^{th}$ industry. For $k$ to vary over time implies that $k_i$ varies among industries and over time, and, in addition, that the share of the $i^{th}$ industry in GNP changes over time.

What do we know about the variability of $k$ among industries? Mansfield has conducted the only consistent set of studies that attempts to compare rates of diffusion among industries, although Griliches has examined different diffusion rates within agriculture. The conclusion regarding the determinants of the rate of diffusion among industries based on Mansfield's work is that the rate is a linear function of the profitability $P$ of the innovation and the size of the investment $S$ required to install it. This is true in the sense that an equation based on his proxy measures of $P$ and $S$[117] seems to account for the observed variation in "how rapidly the use of twelve innovations spreads from enterprise to enterprise in four industries."[118]

However, while $P$ and $S$ may "explain" the observations, for identical values of $P$ and $S$ there are significant variations in the rate of diffusion among the four industries. Of interest for this study, one of the four industries was rail transportation. Its rate of diffusion was the slowest of the four examined, the others being coal, steel, and brewing, in

---

117. See his caveats in Edwin Mansfield, *Industrial Research and Technological Innovation* (New York: W. W. Norton & Company, Inc., 1968), pp.143–44 and p.143 nn20, 21. Note also the similarity to Schmookler's determinants of inventive activity.

118. Mansfield, p.133.

descending order of slowness (i.e., larger $k$ for brewing and steel than for coal or railroads). In different terms, the average period that elapsed between the time when 10 percent of the firms and when 90 percent of the firms in the industry had adopted the invention is 22–23 years in rail transportation, about 20 years in coal, 16 years in steel, and 8–9 years in brewing.[119]

This may somewhat overstate the slowness of the rail rate of diffusion (i.e, understate $k$). For example, the diesel was one of the most significant railroad innovations. In 1946, some 10 percent of all the locomotives in the industry were diesel; by 1957, the industry was 90 percent dieselized, over a period of only 11 years, about half the time estimated by Mansfield.[120]

This is not, of course, a fair comparison, since Mansfield's data for railroads included not only diesel locomotives but also CTC and car retarders in deducing the average elapsed time. In addition, his data referred to percentage of firms while the AAR estimate referred to the industry as a whole, thereby implying that the larger firms adopted new ideas faster.[121] Finally, the expected profitability $P$ and relative size of investment $S$ for railroads were doubtless different from the values used in his interindustry comparison.

Mansfield's data limitations (the use of proxy measures of important variables, such as *ex post* profitability rather than *ex ante*, and other difficulties) make the results only of limited or questionable validity. However, two other implications from the model are of some interest: the rate of diffusion tends to be positively related to the growth rate of the industry's output; and the interindustry rate of diffusion tends to be inversely related to the degree of industrial concentration or positively related to the degree of "competitiveness," factors we need to examine in assessing the regulatory impact on the rate of diffusion.

It is noteworthy that the rate of technological change seems to be related to somewhat similar characteristics among industries, although there is much uncertainty about the relationship between firm size

119. Edwin Mansfield, "Innovation and Technical Change in the Railroad Industry," in National Bureau of Economic Research, *Transportation Economics* (New York: Columbia University Press, 1965), p.187.

120. Data on number of diesel and total units from AAR, *Railroad Transportation: A Statistical Record, 1921–1955* (Washington, D. C., December, 1956), p.11; and AAR, *Statistics of Railroads of Class I in the United States, Years 1957–1967*, August 1968, p.11.

121. This is partially borne out in an earlier study by Mansfield seeking to determine the proportion of all innovations in any industry carried out by the four largest firms. Using parameters derived from the steel and petroleum industries and applied to the railroads, he notes that the top four railroads would be expected to introduce 54 percent of the innovations (based on the model), whereas they actually introduced 65 percent. (See Mansfield, "Innovation and Technical Change in the Railroad Industry.")

and market structure, on the one hand, and technological change, on the other.

### VARIATION OF THE RATE OF DIFFUSION OVER TIME

Thus far $k_i$ has been treated as a constant, although there is no warrant for such an assumption. In fact, a more likely behavior pattern of $k_i$ over time is a slow initial rate of diffusion as a few firms in the industry adopt the invention. As the invention more or less proves itself, a bandwagon effect (Schumpeter's "herd of imitators") may occur, and the rate of diffusion will accelerate. Finally, after a majority of firms have adopted the innovation and only the last holdouts remain, the rate of diffusion will slow down again. If this behavior pattern is plausible, the most appropriate assumption is that $k_i$ follows a kind of logistic function pattern over time.

The data of Mansfield and Griliches tend to support this general behavior of $k_i$.[122] However, they also indicate sharp variation among industries (or regions) in the nature of the S-shaped diffusion pattern. Mansfield notes a variation from less than one year to about 15 years before one-half of the firms in various industries introduce a particular invention. Similarly, Griliches estimates that the time interval between a 20 percent and an 80 percent adoption level for hybrid corn varied between three and eight years, depending on the particular state or region of the firms (farms). Other studies generally support these findings.[123]

In short, variation in $k_i$ over time appears to depend on factors other than variation among industries, although it is difficult to distinguish the factors. This finding suggests that the focus of the analysis of diffusion ought to be the individual firm rather than the industry. What characteristics of firms may account for differential rates of diffusion or imitation? On *a priori* grounds, one would consider the following factors important: the cost of introducing the technique and the profit expected from it; the size and growth rate of the firm; the firm's level and growth of profit and liquidity; the age, amount, and durability of the firm's capital assets; the age, educational level, values, attitudes, and contacts of the managers; and the strength of competitive or social pressures to be innovative or imitate. It would be expected that such factors vary substantially among firms as well as among industries. The direction of influence of each is obvious, but

---

122. Mansfield, *Industrial Research and Technological Innovation*, chap. 7; and Z. Griliches, "Hybrid Corn: An Exploration in the Economics of Technological Change," *Econometrica*, October 1957.

123. See E. Rogers, *Diffusion of Innovations* (New York: The Free Press of Glencoe, Inc., 1962).

for some firms these factors may work at cross-purposes, and to assess the net direction of change requires some estimation of the relative importance of each in the diffusion process.

Unfortunately, few studies have attempted to analyze more than a few factors at a time. Even in these studies, many of the factors were found not to be statistically significant.[124] It is difficult to obtain suitable proxy data for some of the variables and to specify the inter-relationships and the nature of the underlying functions to be fitted to the data. Although one may succeed in explaining some observed diffusion and imitation patterns using a limited number of variables, as the intriguing work of Mansfield has shown, the data in general are so sparse and tenuous that not much confidence can be placed in the results. Even as we know little about the causes of technological change and invention, we know little about the diffusion process and its varying rates. The problem is compounded when we consider the inter-relatedness of new techniques and their diffusion. That is, $k_i$ may in part depend on $P_i$, and vice versa. Indeed, the cost and expected gains from a new technique have generally been viewed as important influences on $k_i$. The separate treatment given these variables here should not be taken to mean that they are independent.[125]

## REGULATORY IMPACT ON INVENTION AND THE RATE OF DIFFUSION IN THE TRANSPORTATION INDUSTRIES

*Impact on Invention.* The previous analysis indicates a close relationship between inventive activity and industry sales (and hence expected profitability of any invention for that industry). Railway freight operating revenues for 1977 totalled $18.9 billion. Gross intercity freight revenues of all ICC-regulated motor carriers were about $26 billion in 1976 and non-ICC-regulated over $30 billion. These are large industries by any relevant comparison.[126] Furthermore, many individual railroads and some motor carriers are large. For example,

124. See Edwin Mansfield, *Industrial Research and Technological Innovation*, chaps. 7 and 8; and Mansfield, *The Economics of Technological Change* (New York: W. W. Norton and Company, Inc., 1968), chap. 4 and the references cited therein.

125. An illustration of the kind of interrelationship of these variables is given in R. R. Nelson and E. S. Phelps, "Investment in Humans, Technological Diffusion and Economic Growth," *American Economic Review*, May 1966, pp. 69–75.

126. Direct comparisons with other 3-digit industries, according to the 1972 Census of Manufacturers, indicate that with rail freight operating revenues in that year of $12.6 billion, ICC-regulated intercity truck revenues of $18.7 billion, and non-ICC-regulated of $21.3 billion, the intercity freight market far exceeds the value of shipments of such 3-digit industry groups as meat products ($26.1 billion), beverages ($13.8), industrial chemicals ($17.3), petroleum refining ($25.6), blast furnaces and basic steel products ($14.1). Some of these industries invest heavily in R and D. On the basis of sales volumes, one would therefore expect that the intercity freight market would be one of the leaders in terms of inventive activity.

the nine largest railways (by sales) would rank among the top 200 industrial corporations, and the four largest trucking firms would rank among the second 200 largest corporations. Thus there is support for the view that the intercity freight transport industries ought to be typified by substantial inventive activity, and to some extent it is true. Inventive activity, as measured by the number of patents or expenditures for R and D, is relatively high in the transportation equipment industry, even excluding aircraft.[127] But by far the greatest proportion of inventions for this market have been made by outsiders, namely, equipment suppliers. The firms themselves do little inventing and, indeed, allocate few resources to R and D.

For example, total R and D spending by both the AAR and the Federal Railroad Administration amounted to only 0.3 percent of gross industry operating revenues in 1977.[128] On the other hand, manufacturers of motor vehicles and other transportation equipment (excluding aircraft) had average R and D expenditures over many years (1961–1974) of about 3.3 percent of sales, over ten times that of the railroads.[129] In addition, over 80 percent of such railroad expenditures on R and D is accounted for by the FRA. A recent AAR document notes that this "dominance" of the industry's own research efforts "has reduced the industry's ability to attack those major problems it considers most important."[130] The evidence with respect to the motor carrier industry is not available but doubtless indicates a similar if not more extreme pattern of minimal inventive activity by the industry itself and thus heavy or almost complete technological reliance on equipment suppliers.

There is nothing inherently contradictory between this observation and Schmookler's conclusions regarding the relationship between inventive activity and expected sales and profitability. The intercity freight market, both rail and truck, is, by virtue of its size, attractive to inventive activity, either from within or without. However, Scherer implies that inventive dynamism is located *within* the firms of an industry. In this sense, the firms in the intercity freight market are laggards. Equipment suppliers do most of the inventing in transportation—diesel engines, CTC, computerization, containerization, welded steel rails, car retarders, and specialized box cars and trailers were all products of firms outside rail and truck transport. A similar situation exists with respect to barge lines. Pipelines have a comparable inventive

127. Scherer, p.1101.

128. Office of Technology Assessment, *An Evaluation of Railroad Safety* (Washington, D. C., 1978), p.136.

129. National Science Board, *Science Indicators 1976* (Washington, D. C.: Government Printing Office, 1977), p.106.

130. AAR, "Research and Development," mimeographed (n.d.) p.2.

history, although oil pipelines are best viewed as parts of the oil industry. Product and slurry pipelines, however, are consistent with the above in terms of inventive activity.

This situation is not necessarily undesirable. To be sure, some have argued that outsiders cannot be as acutely aware of the technical problems facing the suppliers of intercity freight service as those suppliers themselves. Hence, whatever they invent, however useful it may be, may not help resolve some of the critical technical problems apparent only to the firms actively engaged in producing for the market. Such inventive activity may suffer from "suppliers' myopia," as has been suggested.

Yet many industries subcontract R and D; hence their small in-house performance or direct R and D may not be so significant. Technical problems may in fact be better resolved by outsiders. Some evidence exists to the effect that contracted R and D is more efficient than the in-house R and D of the large industrial laboratories tied to a specific industry. In any case, such contracting-out to specialized R and D enterprises can readily overcome "suppliers' myopia" (although not completely, as the railroad hot-box problem illustrates).

How does economic regulation influence R and D? If regulation adversely affects profits, it reduces the ability to engage in inventive activity. Likewise, if expected profitability of any invention is reduced because of regulatory constraints or delays, the incentive and the ability to invent will also be reduced. Only incentive is relevant to inventive activities outside of the intercity freight industry itself.

The profitability of the invention to the user (i.e., the railroad or trucking company) depends on the invention's impact on costs, quality, and/or price of the service. The profitability to the outside inventor depends on the sales price of the invention relative to its cost of production and expected sales volume. A regulatory commission cannot directly influence the inventor's profit and only partially influences the user's. Indeed, an effective rate-of-return constraint might stimulate inventive activity since the volume and possibly the price of new machines purchased would be higher (the A-J-W effect), to the extent that effective rate-of-return regulation "invites" conspiracy or lack of competition among equipment suppliers.

Again, if the regulatory agency could effectively control rates and profits of the industry being regulated, as is presumed in the highly stylized single-firm, homogeneous-product monopolist, actions could easily be taken to stimulate inventive activity through extending the regulatory lag, allowing higher rates and profits, and allowing deductions from stated profits for R and D activities.

The problem with ICC regulation of intercity freight transportation is that it is extremely difficult to regulate rate levels effectively because of the large unregulated area in trucking and water transportation. Higher general rate authorizations for the railways are increasingly nullified by flag outs and thus generate smaller and smaller revenue increases per percentage increase in allowable rates. As Commissioner O'Neal of the ICC put it, "Continued reliance upon *general* rate increases seems to be self-defeating."[131]

Even less is the commission able to influence rail or regulated truck profits since it has little effective jurisdiction over service quality or production costs and none over shipper demand elasticities with respect to price and quality variables. Thus the commission has little effect on the extent of the market for a particular invention. While one can argue that the commission's pattern of regulation has discouraged in-house inventive activity, it is difficult to conclude that this is either socially disadvantageous or that the total of inventive activity for the intercity freight market has been adversely affected. Indeed, the ICC's relative ineffectiveness and inability to influence the size of the respective markets and the profitability of particular inventions (to the inventor) may have retarded the rate of invention for this industry. For example, the CAB's far more effective control of air fares may have stimulated an undue or excessive amount of inventive activity for the air passenger transportation market, although even in this case, many other factors were present (e.g., military R and D).

It is probably fair to conclude that the pattern of ICC economic regulation inhibits inventive activity in and for the intercity freight market by limiting profit prospects of specific inventions, by reducing the resources available for either in-house or outside R and D efforts, and by diverting managerial talent away from technical efficiency considerations toward matters pertaining to regulation itself. It is not clear how important this is in terms of inventive activities. However, the major impact of any form of economic regulation is less on inventive activity than on innovation or the rate of diffusion.

*Impact on the Rate of Diffusion.* The rate of diffusion within rail transport has been found to be relatively slower than in any of the other industries examined. Unfortunately, comparable evidence is not available for truck, water, or pipeline transportation. We are therefore forced into a largely *a priori* analysis of the most likely effects of regulation on the main determinants of the rate of diffusion. The two principal determinants, as found to be statistically significant by Mansfield, are expected profitability $P$ and relative size of the investment $S$. How might ICC regulation affect these?

With respect to profitability, a new, cost-reducing innovation should be stimulated by effective rate regulation. Rates set or maintained on

---

131. ICC, Ex Parte 324, January 28, 1977, p.52A.

any traffic at or above the average costs of all carriers in the market should invite such innovations by raising their expected profitability above what would be the case in a more competitive, unregulated environment. The sanctioning of rate bureaus, itself part of the regulatory milieu, reinforces this possibility. In this respect, rate regulation provides a stimulus to innovation which would be expected, *ceteris paribus*, to raise the rate of diffusion.

However, *ceteris* are not always (or even often) *paribus*. Some cost-reducing inventions in transportation (e.g., with respect to rail cars, or truck bodies) require heavier loads or larger minimum size of shipments to achieve lower costs per ton or per ton-mile. Since significantly larger shipment sizes require the shipper to have larger inventories, they impose additional costs (storage, capital costs). Thus, to obtain the heavier loadings requires some rate incentive. It is at this point that "regulatory delay" may reduce the profitability. In important cases where rate reductions are proposed for a new technology, they are likely to be protested by competing carriers not prepared or able to adopt the new, higher capacity units.

The famous, or infamous, "Big John" case dramatically illustrates this point. More than four years passed between the announcement by the Southern Railway of its intention to introduce 100-ton aluminum covered hopper (Big John) cars for moving grain at a 60 percent rate reduction and the final decision that, by and large, authorized the service and the proposed rate reduction.[132] During that period, full exploitation of the profit prospects could not be realized by the Southern Railway (even though limited service of the kind proposed at the lower rates was offered after expiration of the seven-month rate suspension by the ICC) because neither shippers nor receivers would make the investments needed until the extended hearings were concluded. It is estimated that the Southern Railway had invested over $30 million in the Big John cars, which, before and during the period of the hearings, were substantially underutilized. In addition, the time and cost of participating in the lengthy hearings reduced the expected profitability even more,[133] and there was no guarantee that the final outcome would be consistent with the Southern Railway's intentions. Such procedures under regulation therefore add to the already high degree of uncertainty that exists in innovative activities and further inhibit them.

---

132. Details of the case are summarized by A. Gellman in William Capron, ed., *Technological Change in Regulated Industries* (Washington, D.C.: The Brookings Institution, 1971), pp.175–78; and in Ann F. Friedlaender, *The Dilemma of Freight Transport Regulation* (Washington, D.C.: The Brookings Institution, 1969), pp.92–94.

133. For some details, see Gellman and the references cited therein.

Delay in introducing a new invention may arise less through obvious obstruction (in the Big John case) than by differing rate policies of the regulatory agency. One case involved an estimated four- to five-year delay in introducing unit coal train rates to electricity generating stations on the eastern seaboard in the late 1950s and early 1960s.[134] Considerable discrimination (pricing on the basis of shipper demand elasticities) existed on coal rates to major users and were long sanctioned by the ICC. However, any rate reductions occasioned by introduction of a new technology had to be applied to all shippers regardless of their demand elasticities for coal. Since generating stations on the coast could use imported oil instead of coal, their elasticity of demand for coal was high relative to inland stations without alternatives to coal. Unit trains would significantly reduce the costs of transporting coal and would permit rate reductions where necessary—i.e., to the eastern seaboard stations whose elasticity of transport demand was estimated then to have been about $-4.6$, due to the oil alternative, compared with about $-0.39$ for the inland stations lacking an alternative fuel.[135] The requirement to reduce all rates, not only those to the eastern seaboard, pending introduction of unit train service, thus reduced the expected profitability of the innovation.

Another aspect of rate regulation that has received some attention is the "piggyback" decision. It has been alleged that the use of Rail Form A costing formulae misled the railroads into excessive adoption of 80-foot flatcars. Understating actual operating costs had originally led to similar rates for trailer-on-flatcar (TOFC) as for container-on-flatcar (COFC) service, despite the significantly higher costs of the former.[136] After noting that "regulation by formula distorts management's innovative drives as much as it frustrates them," Gellman argues that "if as much energy had been poured into development of the optimum piggyback vehicle . . . as was devoted to finding the vehicle that would yield the lowest Rail Form A costs, it is safe to assume that the cost—and service—aspects of railway piggyback operations . . . would be far more attractive today than they are."[137] In addition, piggyback operations are believed to have expanded more slowly in the United States than in Canada because of "the lack of restrictions in Canada which limited multi-modal ownership, compared with very onerous multi-modal restrictions in the United States."[138]

---

134. P. MacAvoy and J. Sloss, *Regulation of Transport Innovation: The ICC and Unit Coal Trains to the East Coast* (New York: Random House, 1967).

135. Ibid., pp.80–85.

136. Gellman, pp.170–74.

137. Ibid., p.174.

138. W. J. Stenason, "Multi-Modal Ownership in Transportation," *Papers— Eighth Annual Meeting, Transportation Research Forum* (Oxford, Ind.: Richard B. Cross Company, 1967), p.470.

These few, and often-cited, examples illustrate some of the ways that the present pattern of regulation influences both the overall rate of diffusion and the direction of innovation for the railroad industry. Similar, though much less pronounced, effects are believed to occur in the trucking, barge, and pipeline industries. The effects are less pronounced if only because ICC jurisdiction is less complete and the trucks and bargelines use publicly provided rights-of-way. Thus, a major influence on the nature of innovations resides in the size, location, and quality of the right-of-way as well as restrictions on its use (e.g., size, weight, and speed limitations on the highways), few of which relate to ICC regulation.

Even confining ourselves to railways, it is not clear how much the *overall* rate of diffusion is influenced by regulatory policy. Some aspects of regulatory policy positively influence the profitability of specific innovations while others have a negative influence. Only in cases where rate reductions appear necessary to utilize an improvement in equipment capacity is ICC policy directly involved. Where cost savings that do not require rate adjustments can be achieved, commission regulation has little direct influence on expected profitability of any innovation and hence on its rate of diffusion. In fact, labor union resistance to change and its relative strength in rail and truck transport are doubtless far more important in this connection.

The other major determinant of the rate of diffusion, namely, the relative size of the investment needed to adopt the invention, is clearly not linked to regulatory policy in any direct fashion. To be sure, if it could be argued that, because of the A-J-W effect, the present investment in transportation is greater than would otherwise be the case, it should stimulate the rate of adoption of a new invention (i.e., a relatively smaller $S_i$). But the A-J-W effect is not operative in the rail or trucking industries.

Thus, the ICC impact on $P$ and $S$ appears to be rather negligible and confined mostly to cases where rate changes are needed to utilize the equipment more fully. Since $P$ and $S$ were found to be statistically significant determinants of $k_i$, there is little statistically tested (or even testable) evidence that the ICC has had much impact on $k_i$ in any of the modes over which it has some discretionary and legal power. Those who feel that this cannot be the case usually conclude their discussion by noting the fairly rapid productivity growth in transportation and the large number of inventions. However, awareness of the bureaucratic maze of the ICC then leads to a conclusion to the effect that "technological change *might* have been greater,"[139] in the absence of regulation. Statistically, this is impossible to docu-

---

139. Friedlaender, p.98.

ment. Indeed, as we have noted in the case of the airlines, technological change might have been much slower in the absence of regulation. Nor is it clear what normative significance is to be attached to higher or lower rates of diffusion than might otherwise have occurred. Many have argued that technological change is "out of control," that we need a technology "ombudsman" to slow it down and be more selective.[140] To what extent the ICC has "stifled" innovation is most uncertain. More documented cases like the Big John and unit train examples are needed. Yet it remains the case that the commission has not generally paid much attention to efficiency within the transportation industries. Perhaps one can argue that such benign neglect impedes innovation and that regulation slows down the rate of diffusion by its impact on variables other than $P$ and $S$.

Other variables influencing $k_i$ include the rate of growth of the firm's or industry's output, profit, and liquidity; the degree of "competitiveness" of the industry; the willingness of the firms to take risks; and the "technological base" of the industry. Let us examine these briefly on *a priori* grounds to determine at least the *direction* of regulatory influence.

(a) Rate of growth of output. The demand for intercity freight transport is derived from the demand for inputs and outputs, the location of economic activity, and the composition of GNP, none of which are much influenced by regulatory policies. To be sure, there is a long literature on location theory that assigns substantial weight to relative freight rates.[141] To the extent that ICC regulation of relative rates is effective, it can influence industrial location and hence the overall demand for intercity freight movements. For example, value-of-service pricing maintained or stressed by the ICC would support higher rates on finished goods than on material inputs, thereby providing an incentive for firms to locate nearer the markets depending on the extent of weight loss during the production process (Weber's "material index"). The degree of taper in the rate structure is also influenced by regulatory policy, which influences location, *ceteris paribus*. It is, however, impossible to isolate either the direct impact of relative freight rates and rate levels on industrial location or the

---

140. See Alvin Toffler, *Future Shock* (New York: Bantam Books, 1971), chap. 19.

141. See, for example, J. H. von Thunen, *Der Isolierte Staat* (Berlin, 1875); C. Friedrich, ed., *Alfred Weber's Theory of Location of Industry* (Chicago: University of Chicago Press, 1928); A. Losch, *The Economics of Location* (New Haven: Yale University Press, 1959). Many of these are neatly summarized in S. Daggett, *Principles of Inland Transportation*, 3d ed., 1941, chap. XXI. More recent analyses include W. Isard, *Location and Space Economy* (New York: John Wiley & Sons, 1956); L. Moses, "Location and the Theory of Production," *Quarterly Journal of Economics* 72(1958); and M. Greenhut, *A Theory of the Firm in Economic Space* (New York: Appleton-Century-Crofts, 1970).

impact of rate regulation on either of these. More recent analyses argue that once an industrial locational pattern has been established, transport costs become relatively unimportant in either inducing relocation (even if freight rates change) or influencing the location of new investments. This is true because freight charges as a proportion of delivered prices are low, as noted in chapter 1; agglomeration economies are large; locational inertia is strong once a pattern has been established; and non-transport costs in the form of subsidies, tax incentives, and economies of scale tend to swamp the significance of freight charges for new investments.

Economic regulation may, however, lead to higher costs of providing transportation, which may adversely affect profits of the regulated carriers if the costs are not offset by systematically higher rates. Since ICC jurisdiction is not complete, it cannot ensure this—hence, the profitability and liquidity of regulated carriers are adversely affected. The requirement for common carriers to maintain excess capacity, the restrictions on abandonment of unprofitable service, the excess reporting requirements, and regulatory delay also retard innovation.

However, many other factors intrude, so the net effect of ICC policies is impossible to sort out. ICC policy doubtless contributes to the relative decline of common carriage but much less to the overall growth of profits, liquidity, or growth of the total intercity freight market.

(b) Degree of competitiveness of the intercity freight markets. It is virtually impossible to define or distinguish "degrees of competitiveness" among industries. The typical approach is to assess them in terms of industrial structure and industry pricing practices. Clearly, one of the functions of economic regulation is to restrain or prevent price or rate competition. The ICC has likewise been accused of promoting a higher degree of concentration in the regulated segment of transportation than would otherwise exist. Thus, the overall impact of regulation is anticompetitive as far as prices or rates are concerned. But there is no close correlation between this phenomenon and innovation. Indeed, we have already noted Mansfield's findings that the largest firms in the railroad industry do a disproportionate amount of innovating. In truth, the relationship between diffusion rates on the one hand and industrial structure or "degrees" of competitiveness on the other hand is ambiguous.[142] Thus, even if the commission promoted a higher degree of monopoly by its policies with respect to mergers and entry than would be expected, the effect on the rate of diffusion would be uncertain even as to direction, let alone amount.

---

142. See G. Wilson, ed., *Technological Development and Economic Growth*, Appendix to chap. 7, for a summary of the conflicting views concerning firm size, concentration, and innovation.

(c) Willingness of firms to take risks. Since innovation is risky, in that its profitability is at best probabilistic, the greater the willingness to try new things the higher the rate of diffusion. Regulation affects such willingness mostly with respect to those aspects of regulation that influence risk for any given invention. As previously noted, this is mostly confined to cases where rate changes may be required. The direction of impact here is unequivocal—not only is the outcome of the hearings uncertain but the costs are higher and hence for any given "willingness to take risks," the uncertainty is enhanced by regulatory policy and delay. In other cases, regulatory policy is less involved in terms of the impact on managerial risk-taking proclivities. Indirectly, if regulation is responsible for reducing future growth prospects of any industry, that industry may attract fewer managers with high propensities to take risk. Similarly, if regulation promotes stability or requires a large portion of managerial time and efforts to attempt some new technology, the industry so regulated will not be attractive to such persons. So goes the conventional wisdom.

On the other hand, persons with high risk-taking characteristics may find the regulatory milieu especially challenging. Arnold Toynbee's notion of challenge begetting responses is relevant here. The regulatory process, stifling to innovation though it may otherwise be, may in fact attract the kind of management bent on "overcoming" against higher odds. Even the (probably) overregulated railway industry has regularly attracted the Ben Heinemans, John Ingrams, and John Barrigers. The "quiet life," the meek acquiescence to regulatory dicta, are anathema to such people. Within the interstices of the regulatory parameters, "bold, daring entrepreneurs" may be attracted by the prospects of profit and of altering the parameters. The Southern Railway persevered and overcame, albeit at some cost.

Indeed, within the regulatory agencies themselves, entrepreneurship, in the sense of responding to challenges for change, is not lacking. Chairmen O'Neal of the ICC and Kahn of the CAB provide evidence of what can be accomplished even without prospects of personal gain. In a changing regulatory milieu, supply-side enterpreneurship does not appear to be lacking.

To be sure, many decades elapsed before the pressure for regulatory reform grew. President Kennedy's 1963 Message on Transportation triggered renewed emphasis on regulatory reform and stimulated the willingness to take risks and to test long-established rulings and procedures, within both the regulatory agencies themselves and the industries involved.

This movement suggests that past ICC policies and procedures did stifle innovation, as all the critics of regulation argue. Indeed, in the recent past the railroad industry did not attract many "bold, daring" enterpreneurs. The extent to which this lack is or was due to ICC regulation is unknown. Traditional railway practices of promoting from within, over which ICC policy has no influence, may be more important in terms of resistance to change or willingness to take risks. The image of a declining industry, saddled with innumerable regulatory burdens, will naturally discourage all but a few bold spirits. Whether the image is true or not, the effect is predictable. Furthermore, the noninnovators have a convenient scapegoat—regulation itself. In this sense, economic regulation may indeed stifle innovation and account, in part, for the relative slowness in the rate of diffusion detected in rail transport.

(d) "Technological base" of the industry. "Differences in technological opportunity—e.g., differences in technical investment possibilities unrelated to the mere volume of sales and typically opened up by the broad advance of knowledge—are a major factor responsible for interindustry differences in inventive output."[143] If one assumes a direct relationship between inventive output and the rate of diffusion (because those firms actually engaged in R and D would be expected to be more aware of technical possibilities and hence more likely to adopt the promising ones rapidly), then the technological base becomes important as an explanatory variable. Thus, certain fields, such as the electrical and chemical industries and aircraft manufacturing, have what may be called a "vigorous scientific climate."[144] Such a climate exerts a kind of push toward more inventive output and provides a "continuous supply of new technical possibilities,"[145] which *may* induce a higher rate of diffusion.[146]

The issue of regulation and technological change has been belabored here mainly to provide some perspective to the widely held view that the adverse economic consequences of regulation may be most significant. It is easy to chastise the ICC on many counts. It is less easy to pinpoint the ways in which regulatory policy directly or indirectly impedes invention and innovation. Attempts to measure such impacts or even to account for the other variables have been conspicuously unsuccessful,[147] but that does not mean that regulatory policy is neutral with respect to inventive activity and diffusion rates. On

---

143. Scherer, p.1121.
144. Ibid., p.1100.
145. Ibid.
146. Of course, a continuous supply might lead to a wait-and-see attitude with respect to any specific invention.
147. Mansfield attempted to measure the impact on the rate of diffusion of the firm's growth rate, profitability, age of the president (as a proxy for "willingness to take risks"), liquidity, and profit trend. He found that half the estimates had the wrong sign and none was statistically significant. (See his *Industrial Research and Technological Innovation*, p.167.)

balance it doubtless slows both and influences the direction of inventive activity, but the significance of its actions cannot be shown. Many of the determining variables are difficult to measure and "weight," and the influence of regulation on several or most of them is ambiguous or negligible. Nor is it possible to be sure what would have been the situation with respect to technological change in the absence of regulation. Conjectural history of this sort is not highly convincing. Finally, it is difficult to judge whether the actual levels of inventive activity and rates of diffusion in transportation are above, below, or at some putative optimal level. As Friedlaender notes,

the evaluation of the performance of an industry with respect to technical change is difficult because there is no operational standard against which performance can be judged. Since performance can be judged only in terms of opportunities to exploit technical change and innovation, it can be judged only good or bad with regard to the rate at which potentialities are exploited. However, the potential for innovation is by its very nature a nonoperational concept.[148]

The tentative nature of our conclusions in this connection is related to the intangibility surrounding the whole area of technological change and its determinants. Inadequate knowledge precludes definitive judgment with respect to the influence of regulation. The ambiguities of the situation should be viewed as a potential research agenda, especially by those who see the regulatory impact as having seriously retarded and/or distorted technological change in the intercity freight market. With present knowledge, there is no way of calculating the economic costs associated with such adverse impacts, if they exist.

### The Costs of Regulation

There are five main areas where economic regulation may or does cause costs to society. The most obvious is the process of regulating itself: it involves not only the resources of the ICC but also the proceedings, hearings, court cases, and other litigation arising because of the activities of the commission. The second area is the static misallocation as a result of ICC policies that keep freight rates above marginal cost—the "deadweight loss," discussed earlier. Third is the economic waste or loss occasioned by the degree of excess capacity resulting from regulation, such as inhibitions on abandonment of unprofitable service, the common carrier obligation to serve, and the restrictions on rate flexibility, which discourage fuller use of existing capacity. A fourth area is the shift of traffic from low- to high-cost modes because of rate regulation that prevents rates from reflecting

---

148. Friedlaender, p.88. See also Capron, p.221.

relative costs. Finally, as the previous section showed, there is some influence on technological change.

Attempts have been made to estimate the amount of economic "loss" or costs of each of the first four areas. The intent is to estimate how much cost "could" be avoided by elimination of regulation and then to compare this cost with the "benefits" of regulation—to do a sort of benefit-cost analysis of transport regulation by the ICC.[149]

For many years, professional economists tried to convince Congress that detailed economic regulation of transportation was wasteful because most transportation submarkets were in some sense "workably competitive"; the trucking industry, in particular, had most, if not all, the features of a perfectly competitive industry, so that regulation of it was singularly perverse and inappropriate, from an efficiency perspective.[150] Congressional authorities were singularly unimpressed with arguments regarding such an ephemeral concept as "workable competition." The prospect of changing a pattern of regulation dating back to 1887 for railroads, 1906 for pipelines, 1935 for motor carriers, and 1940 for water carriers was not very appealing to a Congress struggling through the 1950s, 60s, and 70s with more important matters. It is easy to understand the reluctance of the average legislator to accept as a mandate for reform the evidence that some portions of the regulated transportation industries seemed to have most or all of the structural features of competitive markets. Thereupon, in the mid-1960s, economists began to estimate the net social costs of contemporary transport regulation, eschewing the generalized and unpersuasive earlier arguments regarding the overall workability of competition in the intercity freight markets. Impressive numbers in the $8 billion to $16 billion range and over (in dollars of 1978) emerged as estimates of the costs of transport regulation. No measured benefits were made. Hence, such figures became estimates of the net social costs.

In terms of political arithmetic, the strategy worked. Congressmen could more readily respond to conclusions that the economic waste of transportation regulation totaled a significant and determinate number of dollars. As with the poverty program, once the numbers and relative significance were shown to be large, political concern grew accordingly and so did support for various reform measures. Let us

---

149. Benefit-cost analysis applied to new transport investments is the subject of Part II of this volume.

150. Indeed, before the Motor Carrier Act of 1935, economists were pointing out the (beneficent) competitive features of the industry. Thus S. Peterson argued as early as 1929 that "the case for regulation—except as it applies to safety and responsibility—is not especially impressive" ("Motor Carrier Regulation and Its Economic Bases," *Quarterly Journal of Economics*, August 1929, p.16).

examine some of the more "well-known" measures and their derivation. We begin by providing a numerical estimate of each category
of the "costs" noted above.

*Costs of the ICC, Proceedings, Hearings, and Other Litigation.* The
ICC budget for fiscal 1978 totaled over $64 million, including $3⅔ million in supplementary funds. Its funding has increased sharply since
1950, when appropriations totaled $11.4 million, although there has
not been a significant increase in staff. The average employment was
2,161 persons in 1950, and the 1978 budget authorized 2,250 positions.
However, the budget represents only the tip of a much larger iceberg.
The commission's activities in attempting to enforce the Act to Regulate Commerce and subsequent amendments impose large expenses
on applicants for and opponents of new operating authorities, abandonment of existing authorities or rights-of-way, and rate and tariff
changes. The lengthy proceedings, hearings and, ultimately, challenges (and defenses) in federal courts use up resources. During fiscal
1977 the ICC's workload included almost 10,000 cases decided. The
duration of each case ranged from an average of 6.8 months for
cases "dismissed or discontinued" to an average of 25.4 months for
cases "decided by final report after service of initial decision." More
than 10,000 new cases were opened during fiscal 1977. In addition,
the commission disposed of over 10,000 informal proceedings and
received almost 327,000 tariffs relating to common carriage alone. In
fiscal 1976 some 2,000 hearing days were held before 60 administrative
law judges, and 267 challenges were brought in federal courts. Each
of these cases, informal proceedings, challenges, etc., involves inputs
over and above the ICC budget from all the parties involved or who
choose to become involved.

Cases must be prepared by applicants and protestants. Many need
to be based on more or less sophisticated prior research and analysis.
The more controversial cases often take years, as we have noted in
connection with a railway innovation requiring rate reductions. A
rail abandonment case, initially filed on March 18, 1975 and decided
by the administrative law judge on November 16, 1978, involved over
150 witnesses (some of whom had prepared elaborate evidence totaling
2,000–3,000 pages) plus 12,000 pages of testimony; many days of oral
hearings in various parts of the country; and considerable legal and
other expert talent.[151]

There is no way to estimate the value of resources outside the
commission that are used up in the process of administering the Act
and providing the opportunity for support, opposition, and cross-

---

151. ICC Docket No. AB-18 (Sub-No. 21).

examination. Five times the present ICC budget seems to be a conservative guess. Even supposing total additional costs of \$300–\$400 million per year in 1978 values, not all of them would be avoidable even if the ICC were totally abolished. Many of the carriers' and shippers' actions would be subject to the antitrust and other laws pertaining to business conduct. Indeed, even with the ICC, the Department of Justice frequently intervenes in transportation matters —often in opposition to commission rulings or in support of one or another of the parties in a particular case. As a rough guess, it may be that present regulation leads to \$100–\$300 million of avoidable cost.

*Costs Due to Static Misallocation.* As noted in chapter 3, the static loss of "surplus" due to prices or rates above marginal cost ($MC$), assuming linear cost and demand functions, is one-half the deviation of price ($\Delta P$) from $MC$ multiplied by the deviation from the quantity demanded ($\Delta Q$) at a price equal to $MC$: the familiar welfare triangle. Thus "deadweight" or static loss may be defined as

$$W = \frac{1}{2} \Delta P \Delta Q. \tag{1}$$

It is very difficult to estimate $\Delta P$ and $\Delta Q$ directly. However, we may recast equation (1) by dividing both sides by total revenues ($PQ$). Thus,

$$\frac{W}{PQ} = \frac{1}{2} \left(\frac{\Delta P}{P}\right)\left(\frac{\Delta Q}{Q}\right), \tag{2}$$

where $\frac{W}{PQ}$ is the *relative* deadweight loss, and $\frac{\Delta P}{P}$ is the ratio of the difference between $P$ and $MC$ to price for the commodity in question $\left(\text{i.e., } \frac{\Delta P}{P} = \frac{P - MC}{P}\right)$. If we recall our definition of $\epsilon_D$, then $\frac{\Delta Q}{Q} = \epsilon_D \frac{\Delta P}{P}$. Substituting this in equation (2), we obtain

$$\frac{W}{PQ} = \frac{1}{2}\left(\frac{\Delta P}{P}\right)^2 \epsilon_D.$$

For rail transportation the ICC regularly publishes estimates of the ratio of rail revenues to out-of-pocket costs for various commodity groups (see Table 1.5), from which estimates of $\frac{\Delta P}{P}$ may be derived.[152] Using the estimate of the aggregate elasticity of rail transport

---

152. For example, for "all commodities" this ratio in Table 1.5 is 1.27, which is interpreted to mean $\frac{P}{MC} = 1.27$. Thus, $\frac{P\text{-}MC}{P} = \frac{\Delta P}{P} \cong .213$.

demand from Table 1.4 of $|.696|$, the *relative* welfare loss because of such price deviation is

$$\frac{W}{PQ} = \frac{1}{2} (.213)^2 (.696) = .016.$$

Railway freight rate revenues in 1977 were $18.9 billion. Thus, deadweight loss may be estimated as approximately $300 million (.016 × $18.9 billion). Using Benishay and Whitaker's higher estimate of $\epsilon_{RT} = .842$ yields a loss of almost $350 million.[153]

A similar exercise can be performed using aggregate truck data and assuming, on the rather flimsy basis of certain past experience,[154] that $\frac{\Delta P}{P} = 16.7\%$, and that $\epsilon_{TT} = |1.912|$.[155] Using these estimates, relative deadweight loss in trucking is .027. Revenues of regulated truckers in 1974 were $26 billion; hence, deadweight loss is approximately $700 million.

The total welfare loss from such value-of-service-type pricing, supported by the ICC, is a little over $1 billion for 1977 for rail and truck regulated intercity freight. If all of this is caused by ICC regulation, as is usually assumed, we must add this figure to the estimates of other costs already, or soon to be, calculated.[156]

Many similar analyses have been made for industries other than transportation.[157] They are all subject to certain well-known defects whose *net* impact on the size of the estimated losses is unknown. As Scherer puts it, we can "give up trying to measure the impact . . . or we can cross our fingers and hope the errors . . . are not too serious."[158]

The above estimate of the static losses due to regulation may be understated since pipelines and water transportation have been excluded, although these omissions are not especially important. How-

---

153. One can make similar estimates for each of the many product classes for which the ICC provides the ratio of revenue to out-of-pocket costs and for which estimates of $\epsilon_{RT}$ exist. Friedlaender, *The Dilemma of Freight Transport Regulation*, has performed such an exercise for the five broad commodity classes noted in Table 1.5. Even finer breakdowns are possible, given some of the elasticity estimates in Table 1.6 and the ICC ratios. However, the method is crude at best, as noted below, and, for broad orders of magnitude, the use of aggregate data will suffice.

154. See p.212, above; and Friedlaender, p.74.

155. See chap. 1, p.18, where the first three estimates (excluding the ICC's) average out to 1.912.

156. Considerations of second-best should reduce these magnitudes somewhat along the lines of Friedlaender, pp.75–77, but we will not attempt this here, in view of the roughness of the data used and the methodology.

157. The first such effort was that of A. Harberger, "Monopoly and Resource Allocation," *American Economic Review*, May 1954. See also D. Schwartzman, "The Burden of Monopoly," *Journal of Political Economy*, December 1960.

158. F. Scherer, *Industrial Market Structure and Economic Performance* (Chicago: Rand McNally, 1970), pp.402–404.

ever, it may be that the "welfare triangle" itself is not the right indicator of the amount of loss but, rather, the whole trapezoid $P_M CAP_0$ in Figure 3.1. The argument is that the existence of obtainable consumer surplus through price discrimination leads incipient monopolists to compete for such gains. Such competition leads to the expenditure of resources on such activities as lobbying and litigation, up to the maximum shown by the trapezoid, which are viewed as socially wasteful—hence the triangular welfare loss significantly understates the total.[159]

We will not debate this viewpoint here. Even if the $1 billion is an underestimate, for the above reason, some of these excess costs may be captured in our previous estimate of the costs of hearings, proceedings, and so on. When we aggregate *all* the cost estimates to be made here, some of the "missed costs" of the above estimate may be captured. In such aggregation, we invoke the law (or hope) of offsetting error. We will not therefore attempt to adjust the $1 billion figure to account for the second-best problem (which overstates the loss) or to include a finer breakdown of commodities for rail (which would doubtless raise the rail estimate). The data base used above, especially the elasticity estimates, ICC costing problems, and the percent price deviation used for trucking preclude much in the way of significant refinement. Furthermore, to attribute all the social waste to the ICC assumes that value-of-service pricing would not exist in rail or truck transportation if there were no economic regulation—a dubious proposition at best, especially for rail. Indeed, as we noted in chapter 3, some degree of value-of-service pricing may be efficient—i.e., efficient pricing in the context of a revenue constraint.

*Excess Capacity Costs.* Friedlaender developed an interesting methodology for assessing these costs for rail transport.[160] She noted that if short-run cost elasticity (or percent variable) is less than long-run cost elasticity, excess capacity must prevail. That is, costs could be reduced if the capital stock were reduced. Cost elasticity refers to the percent change in costs for a given change in output. For

---

159. See G. Tullock, "The Welfare Costs of Tariffs, Monopolies and Theft," *Western Economic Journal*, June 1967; and R. Posner, "The Social Costs of Monopoly and Regulation," *Journal of Political Economy*, August 1975. However, *all* of the trapezoid may not represent social waste, as Posner assumes. Some social benefits may accrue in situations where such costs are incurred to attract more customers from other suppliers. Pustay has argued that in the domestic airline industry in 1969 benefits accounted for between 30 and 50 percent of the costs included in the trapezoid. Thus it is not all social waste (M. W. Pustay, "The Social Costs of Monopoly and Regulation," *Southern Economic Journal*, October 1978).

160. A. Friedlaender, "The Social Costs of Regulating the Railroads," *American Economic Review*, May 1971.

a linear cost function of the form $C = a+bX$, where $C$ refers to total costs and $X$ refers to output, cost elasticity $E = \dfrac{bX}{C}$. Denote the short-run cost function as $C = a+bX$ and the long-run cost function as $C^* = a^* + b^*X$. Thus, $E = \dfrac{bX}{C}$ and $E^* = \dfrac{b^*X}{C^*}$. Therefore $\dfrac{E}{E^*} = \dfrac{bX}{C}$ $\div \dfrac{b^*X}{C^*} = \dfrac{C^*bX}{Cb^*X} = \dfrac{C^*b}{Cb^*}$. If we assume that marginal costs are equal, that is, $b = b^*$, then $\dfrac{E}{E^*} = \dfrac{C^*}{C}$. If we can measure $E$ and $E^*$, we can determine the difference between actual costs and an efficient level of costs. That is, if $\dfrac{E}{E^*} < 1$, excess capacity prevails and efficient costs would be lower than actual costs. However, if $\dfrac{E}{E^*} \geq 1$, no excess capacity exists and actual costs are "efficient." Note that when $\dfrac{E}{E^*} < 1$ (i.e., excess capacity exists), short-run $MC$ will be below long-run $MC$, and that vitiates the assumption that $b = b^*$.

Nonetheless, Friedlaender then computes a long-run cost curve by making a cross-section analysis of 88 Class I railroads using average data for the four years 1961–64. The cost curve was of the form

$$C = a_0 + a_1 F + a_2 P + a_3 F^2 + a_4 P^2 + u,$$

where $F$ = millions of annual freight-car miles
$\quad\;\; P$ = millions of annual passenger-car miles
$\quad\;\; C$ = total cost in millions of 1958 dollars
$\quad\;\; u$ = random disturbance term.

Note that this process assumes that cross-section analysis yields a long-run rather than a short-run cost function because it is believed that the firms in the sample have adjusted capacity to output levels. This is the usual basis for believing that cross-section studies are more reflective of long-run costs, whereas time-series studies are believed to represent short-run costs, as noted in chapter 1.

Thus, to calculate a short-run cost function, Friedlaender selects from the 88-carrier sample those railroads whose capital stock appeared to be constant over the period 1957–64. Using miles of track as a proxy for identifying capital stock constancy, she selected 33 Class I railroads. Quarterly data were used in this regression, which required the inclusion of seasonal dummy variables in the cost equation. No adjustment was made for cost changes related to price changes of the inputs purchased.

However, calculations were then derived for $E$ and $E^*$ for each of the 33 railroads, although no information is provided in the article concerning how the outputs of freight or passenger service were combined to derive a single elasticity coefficient relating to "output." For each railroad, its actual average cost over the period 1961–64 was multiplied by its computed $\frac{E}{E^*}$ when $\frac{E}{E^*} < 1$, to derive an estimate of "efficient" operating cost for each road. If $\frac{E}{E^*} \geq 1$, the actual cost was deemed to be "efficient." The sum of the actual costs for the 33 railroads was then compared with the sum of the "efficient" costs. The ratio of the latter to the former was 0.736 $\left( \text{i.e., } \frac{3288.3}{4466.7} \right)$. "If this ratio can be assumed to hold for all railroads and remain constant over time, the minimum cost of rail operations in 1969 would have been $6,673.9 million, while the actual cost in 1969 was $9066.5 million. Thus the losses from excess capacity in 1969 were $2,392.6 million."[161]

An alternative approach seeks to determine how much output could be increased if existing capacity were fully utilized. The calculations implied that output could have been increased by 33.35 percent, with the efficient size labor force fully utilizing the existing capital stock. Since total operating revenues were $11,450.3 million in 1969, the maximum increase in output would be $3,818.5 million.

The two estimates, $2.4 billion and $3.8 billion, are taken to represent the range of costs to society due to regulation of railways. That is, the ICC is believed to be solely responsible for excess capacity in the rail industry to the tune of $2.4–$3.8 billion. Both estimates are doubtless overstated, even granting the numerous assumptions and the abundant data problems. For example, some excess capacity inevitably exists in the railway industry at all times and would occur whether regulation were imposed or not. How much this "natural" excess would be is unknown but it necessarily exists because it is not possible to have full utilization of the right-of-way, yards, and rolling stock at the same time.

Again, the value of the increased output in the second calculation would be less than $3.8 billion because it is unlikely that a 33 percent increase in sales of rail service could have taken place in 1969 at a constant average revenue per ton-mile. Elasticity of rail transport demand is unlikely to be infinite, as noted in chapter 1. Partly for these reasons, and the erroneous assumption that $b = b^*$, Moore adopts a different approach, admittedly not "very definitive ($n$) or exact."[162]

---

161. Ibid., p.230.
162. T. G. Moore, "The Feasibility of Deregulating Surface Freight Transportation," in *Surface Transportation Legislation*, Hearings before the Subcommittee on Surface Transportation of the Committee on Commerce, U. S. Senate, 92nd Cong., 2d sess. May 12 and 19, 1972, Part 3, p.1087.

Using data from USDA Marketing Reports between 1958 and 1961, when deregulation of certain agricultural commodities promptly led to rate reductions of 12 to 59 percent, without any perceptible change in service quality, Moore assumes that without regulation all truck regulated rates would fall by 20 percent. In short, these agricultural commodities are viewed as a random sample of *all* commodities shipped by truck. In 1968, revenues of Class I and II carriers were $9.6 billion; hence a 20 percent reduction in rates, on the same volume of traffic, would reduce truck revenues by 20 percent, or $1.92 billion. "At this lower level of revenues the industry would presumably *cover its costs* including a normal profit."[163] Thus, excess profits and/or costs would fall. The cost reduction would represent a *real* gain to the economy while a reduction of excess profits is merely an income transfer. Extremely crude estimates of excess profits of between $20 million and $500 million are then subtracted from the $1.92 billion to obtain a range of loss to the trucking industry from economic regulation of $1.4 to $1.9 billion. Thus regulation is viewed as having inflated the costs of regulated truckers by these amounts over and above the static deadweight loss previously estimated or loss from traffic not carried. Note that these are not strictly excess capacity costs although the technique of estimation bears some resemblance to Friedlaender's.

Moore continues with this approach applied to the railroads but with some slight variation. Noting that $\epsilon_{RT} \cong -1$ (by reworking Morton's estimates) and rail cross-elasticity with respect to truck is approximately $+1$ (again by modifying Morton's estimates), he then notes that a 20 percent truck rate reduction will require a 20 percent rail rate reduction if rail volume is to be maintained. With rail revenues of about $10 billion in 1968 and, obviously, no excess profits, costs would have to fall by $2 billion. Adjusting this figure by guessing at overcapitalization, Moore argues that costs would need to fall by only $1.7 billion, which then becomes his lower estimate of the inflation of rail costs, related to excess capacity due to regulation. He accepts Friedlaender's lower estimate of $2.4 billion excess capacity costs as an upper limit to the $1.7 billion. These estimates, crude as they are and based on many assumptions only some of which are reasonable, have been extended to private and unregulated trucking and water carriers. They are even more tentative than those already noted.

*Traffic Misallocation.* Since freight rates do not reflect the relative marginal costs among the modes, shippers are frequently encouraged to use a higher-cost mode. But shippers care only about the freight

---

163. Ibid., p.1084 (emphasis supplied).

rate and quality-of-service differentials when making modal choices, as discussed in chapter 1. Since regulation is believed to support non-cost-oriented rate structures, modal choice is often inefficient from society's point of view. To estimate the costs to society, one needs to identify which modes should, on efficiency grounds, carry various types of traffic and compare the ideal with existing traffic allocations to obtain an estimate of the excess costs due to regulation.

Suppose it is found that for rail-truck competition, all shipments beyond, say, $x$ miles should move by rail because rail costs per ton-mile are, say, 1¢ lower than truck (assume all other things, especially quality of service, are equal). Assume that of the total rail plus truck ton-miles $T$, $y\%$ should, on efficiency grounds, be generated by rail but that actually $z\%$ is so generated (where $z < y$). Total costs due to misallocation would thus be $\$T(.01)(y - z)$.

Clearly, other things are not equal and indeed the least-cost mode depends on the commodity being shipped and the valuation shippers put on the quality-of-service differential, which itself changes over time, as argued in chapter 1. Attempts to calculate the losses of misallocation thus involve a host of assumptions. We will examine one of the more or less heroic attempts to put an aggregate price tag on this form of economic waste, namely, that of Harbeson.[164]

Using data from the Census of Transportation showing the modal tonnage of manufactures by 13 mileage blocks for 1963 (the mileage blocks started with < 50 miles and ended with > 2,000 miles), Harbeson calculated the excess of motor carrier costs per ton over rail costs (inclusive of an estimate of the value of the rail service differential). Multiplying these excess costs by the tonnage moved by for-hire motor carriers for each mileage block yields his estimates of "economic loss." There are many data problems in these computations, as he readily admits. In the first place, the rail and truck cost data are available by regions. To cover all possibilities, two calculations were made: one, using the highest regional rail marginal cost data in comparison with the lowest regional truck marginal cost data, yielded an estimate of $1.129 billion; the other, using the lowest regional rail marginal cost data in comparison with the highest regional truck marginal cost data, yielded an estimate of $2.921 billion.

However, the estimates of the quality of the rail-truck service differential were based solely on the simplistic measures of time-in-transit differences and shipment-size differentials already noted and criticized in chapter 1. In fact, the so-called added cost of using rails vs. trucks from these two sources was relatively small (i.e., under

164. R. W. Harbeson, "Toward Better Resource Allocation in Transportation," *The Journal of Law and Economics*, October 1969, pp.321–38.

10 percent at 150 miles, or 210 miles with adjustment for circuity)
and declined in relative significance with distance (i.e., under 5 percent at 1,350 miles, or 1,890 rail miles adjusted for circuity). As noted
in chapter 1, such estimates of the value of the quality differentials
are seriously understated. Recognizing this, Harbeson adjusted these
estimates upward by 50 percent. Using the higher rail service disadvantage estimates and repeating the two calculations noted above,
he obtains an economic loss between $1.042 and $2.834 billion. The
50 percent increase is, of course, arbitrary, but doubtless in the right
direction. More important is the assumption that each shipment was
average in the sense that the cost estimates assumed 33.7 tons per carload and 16.6 tons per truckload. The difficulties of cost finding, further averaging, adding to truck costs an estimate of the underpayment
large trucks made for use of the publicly provided right-of-way (based
on the incremental method of highway cost allocation), and the usual
data problems raise serious doubts about the results despite the many
ingenious attempts to account for data inaccuracies. Despite these
problems, Moore believes these are "the most careful estimates of the
costs of shipping by rail and truck."[165] Despite the caveats, Harbeson
concludes that "the development of intercity for-hire motor transportation has very considerably overstepped the boundaries marked out
by relative economy and fitness."[166] No attempt was made to calculate
the economic loss for water carriers vs. rail, rail vs. pipelines, etc., because the cost and other data are simply inadequate.

*Total Costs Attributed to Regulation.* In the various attempts to measure the different kinds of "costs" imposed on society by virtue of economic regulation the authors freely admit the frailty of their estimates
in light of the assumptions made and the data and methods used. It is
therefore hazardous to add up all the categories of costs, even in terms
of a low and a high range of estimates, since the resulting hodgepodge
would be difficult to interpret. Furthermore, the assumption that these
costs are caused solely by economic regulation and could to some degree be removed by deregulation is based on faith, not solid evidence.
Yet such totals are impressive despite their ambiguity. Accordingly,
they are presented in Table 4.1. Economic losses in the range of $8 to
$16 billion in current prices may represent part of the costs of regu-
lation as far as railroad and for-hire trucking are concerned. The range
may even be understated since costs imposed on other carriers[167] and
the impact of regulation on technological change are ignored.

---

165. Moore, p.1090.
166. Harbeson, p.334.
167. Some estimates have been made on even shakier grounds than those noted
above. For water carriers, see Moore, p.1089. Other estimates for motor carriers
are summarized by D. Maister, "Regulation and the Level of Trucking Rates in

TABLE 4.1

Estimates of Economic Loss
in Rail and For-Hire Trucking from Regulation
( $billions, 1977–78 )

| Type of Loss | Low | High |
|---|---|---|
| Direct regulatory costs | 0.1 | 0.3 |
| Static welfare loss | 1.0 | 1.1 |
| Excess capacity costs* | 5.3 | 9.7 |
| Traffic misallocation costs** | 1.9 | 5.6 |
| Totals | 8.3 | 16.7 |

*Adjusted upward from the 1968 estimates by the GNP deflator.
**Adjusted upward from the 1964 cost estimates of Harbeson by the GNP deflator.

An alternative calculation uses an aggregative production function of standard Cobb-Douglas form. Since the capital and labor resources devoted to commercial intercity freight transportation are approximately 10 percent and 5 percent, respectively, of total U.S. capital and labor, then if, because of regulation, 10 percent of these are excessive and could be shifted to other industries, real output could increase by 0.65 percent, assuming the share of capital and labor in national income are 0.3 and 0.7, respectively.[168] Since GNP in 1977 was $1,872 billion, in current dollars, the estimated economic loss due to regulation or potential gain from deregulation (assuming that 10 percent of the $K$ and $L$ in freight transportation is excessive and due to regulation) amounts to slightly more than $12 billion, or approximately the midpoint of the above aggregate estimates for rail and truck. Again, we must stress the crudeness of this and all the other estimates of economic loss and the heavy reliance on often dubious assumptions and even more doubtful statistics, to say nothing of the alternative method-

---

Canada," in *Motor Carrier Economic Regulation* (Washington, D. C.: National Academy of Sciences, 1978); and L. Darby, "An Evaluation of Federal Regulation of Common Motor Carriage," Ph.D. diss., Indiana University, 1969. The higher empty mileage for private, exempt, and other non-ICC-authorized carriers is another source of waste related to regulation. For some data, see William Tye, P. Roberts, and J. Altonji, "Load Factors of Motor Carriers on the Interstate Highway System," in *Motor Carrier Economic Regulation* (Washington, D.C.: National Academy of Sciences, 1978), pp.528–59. On the basis of earlier estimates of percent empty by varying types of vehicles, Moore calculated the loss to private trucks between $170 million and $1,700 million (in values of 1977–78)—a rather large range indicating the crudeness of the estimation procedures.

168. That is, if $Y = A + CL + (1 - C)K$, where the bar $(-)$ indicates rates of change, $C = 0.7$, and $A$, $L$, and $K$ are, respectively, an index of technological change (or the residual), labor utilized, capital utilized. A 10 percent shift out of commercial freight transportation can be viewed as a 1 percent increase in $K$ and ½ percent increase in $L$. Thus, $Y = A + .7(.005) + .3(.01) = .0065$. (See G. Wilson, "Transportation and Price Stability," *American Economic Review*, May 1969.)

ologies. Yet regulation surely costs something, and these attempts yield an order of magnitude, at least.

As might be expected, the ICC belatedly responded to such attempts by performing its own calculation of costs vs. benefits of regulation of surface freight transportation. In a rather unfortunate report,[169] the commission concluded that the benefits vastly exceeded its scaled-down estimates of the above-mentioned costs of regulation. The costs were scaled down largely by reestimation of both the direct price and the cross-elasticities (rail vs. truck) derived by Morton and by counting as benefits the assumed amounts (on the basis of a U.K. study) by which rates are lower than they would have been in the absence of economic regulation. Crude as the earlier cost estimates were, this performance by the commission is far more suspect in both data and methodology. There is much room for improvement in estimating the costs of regulation, but the commission's report is too blatantly self-serving to be convincing or worthy of further notice here. However, the commission's report does highlight the issue of benefits. It is one thing to argue that the costs of regulation may be of the order of $12 billion ± 30 percent; it is another to argue that they are "too high" relative to the benefits conferred.

## The Benefits of Economic Regulation

It is necessary to distinguish between net benefits to society as a whole and transferred benefits from one group to another. Net benefits refer to the increase in the quantity and/or quality of output from a given level of resource inputs due to regulation, while transferred benefits merely shift incomes without a concomitant increase in income or output due to regulation.

The net benefits of contemporary regulation refer to such effects as greater rate stability, preservation of common carrier service with its greater assurance of service regularity, uniform bills of lading, minimum liability, and absence of "discrimination." Several of these are "goods" in and of themselves (e.g., reduced discrimination), while others may contribute to greater output. For example, to the extent that rates are more stable and service is more reliable under regulation than without it, firms can plan future production and distribution with greater certainty. Productivity for the goods-producing industries is raised because fewer resources are needed to hedge against uncertainty. This is likely to be of special importance to small, sporadic, or non-regular shippers.

---

169. ICC, *A Cost and Benefit Evaluation of Surface Transport Regulation*, Statement No. 76-1 (Washington, D. C., 1976).

However, the increased rate stability under regulation may also increase static inefficiency because rates are adjusted more slowly to cost and demand changes than would otherwise be the case. Nor is it clear how much more stable particular rates are under regulation. It is not therefore possible to assess the quantitative importance of an unknown degree of enhanced rate stability to increased efficiency of production planning. Our previous finding that freight rates are a relatively small component of production costs suggests that freight rate stability is not very important. One cannot assess the benefits of improved service reliability and availability not only because the extent of such improvements under regulation is conjectural but also because their relative importance is unknown.

Thus, it is not surprising that no estimates of net benefits to contrast with the "economic losses" estimated above have been made. To be sure, there may be some net satisfaction to certain shippers to know or believe that there is a presumably objective commission oriented toward their interests and to which they may appeal in the event of a dispute with a common carrier. But, again, even without such a commission, there exist other governmental agencies designed to prevent monopoly abuses and discrimination and to protect shipper interests. The net advantage of the ICC in this regard is even more conjectural.

As far as transferred benefits are concerned, their magnitude is doubtless greater than net benefits but their evaluation is even more hazardous, especially as it involves matters of income redistribution—a subject notorious for its subjectivity. For example, the ICC study makes much of the "fact" that freight rates have increased less under regulation than they would if there had been none. Even if that were true, it would represent a shift of income from carriers to shippers, assuming that rates should have gone up faster because of cost increases. Whether this is a net social good or not depends largely on one's value judgment. Certainly, not many rail carriers can be accused of reaping excess profits, and the fact that perhaps a third of rail rates are below out-of-pocket costs (by Rail Form A calculations) suggests that such transfers may have negative economic repercussions. Again, excess profits in the motor carrier industry may not exist, even if one knew how to define "excess," because there is some evidence that the regulatory milieu may have encouraged unions to bargain for higher wages to capture whatever excess profits might exist because of regulatory constraints on competition.[170] In addition, it is alleged that small

---

170. See, for example, J. Annable, "The ICC, the IBT and the Cartelization of the American Trucking Industry," *Quarterly Review of Economics and Business*, Summer 1973; and T. G. Moore, *The Beneficiaries of Trucking Regulation* (Wash-

shippers and small communities benefit by virtue of the common carrier obligations to serve, because the excess profits on high-density routes, protected by regulation, are then used to "subsidize" operations to and from small communities, which would otherwise have lower quality (or no) service and/or higher rates. Thus shippers on higher-density routes are indirectly subsidizing other shippers.

These and other examples of transferred benefits[171] cannot readily be quantified and even less readily justified. Nor is it evident in each case whether such transfers really exist or would cease to exist in the absence of economic regulation. However, the vehemence with which the supposed transfer beneficiaries protest any significant move toward reduction of the scope of economic regulation indicates that such benefits transcend by far any net social benefits of regulation. Indeed, the transferred benefits have become the focal point of those opposing "regulatory reform."

## Consequences of Deregulation

Predicting the consequences of any major changes in the rules and regulations applicable to an industry over long periods of time cannot be done with much accuracy. Indeed, opponents of change often use this fact as a tactic to discourage any change at all. For example, it has been stated that regulation "is attacked *solely* by *theorists* who *think* that a different system might work as well or better but who do not know with *certainty* what the outcome will be."[172] The failure of theorists and other proponents of reform in transportation to be certain and specific is merely a reflection of honesty. But, to insist that no changes be made without certain and specific predictions is an invitation to inertia. What we can legitimately insist on is a careful examination of the most probable consequences of regulatory reform based on the best evidence and reasoning available. Such a careful examination has been made many times by many people without a vested interest in the outcome. The results of these investigations all

---

ington, D. C.: American Enterprise Institute, 1976); and Statement of the Council on Wage and Price Stability before the ICC, Washington, D. C., in Investigation and Suspension Docket No. M-29772, "Southern Motor Carrier Rate Conference, Inc.," July 5, 1978, where it is shown that wages in regulated industries, including rail and truck, have increased more rapidly than in other sectors of the economy.

171. For example, the incomes of many lawyers, economists, statisticians, and accountants would be sharply reduced if the activities of the ICC were curtailed or eliminated. The lengthy proceedings of innumerable cases provide healthy sources of income to many of these professionals.

172. Statement of Gene T. West, Senior Vice President, Consolidated Freightways, Before the National Commission for the Review of Antitrust Laws and Procedures, July 26–27, 1978, p.17 (emphasis supplied). This statement also refers to "the scrapping of a good thing in favor of a *totally unknown* quantity."

support the view that the nature of sensible changes lies in the direction of greater reliance on competitive forces, especially if combined with appropriate user charges for publicly provided facilities, a careful monitoring of anticompetitive mergers, freedom of the nonregulated carriers to eliminate unprofitable services with dispatch, and more cost-effective public transportation investments.

The underlying belief for these views is that in virtually all the intercity freight markets there exists an actual or potential number of shipper options so that at least workable competition would prevail, with the efficient results that typify many other segments of the U. S. economy not subject to direct economic regulation. The vast extension and improvement in right-of-way and increase in vehicles have left few shippers or communities captive to a single carrier. At best, therefore, continued detailed economic regulation, first conceived under rail monopoly abuses of power in 1887 and extended in 1935 to motor carriers under conditions and philosophies determined by the Great Depression, is unnecessary; at worst, it is incredibly wasteful for the few (mostly transfer) benefits it confers.

Under present and probable future circumstances, the existing patterns of economic regulation are and will become increasingly burdensome and complex. Indeed, effective regulation is now administratively infeasible. It is (comparatively) easy to regulate a single-firm monopoly, although even here serious problems emerge. But when the number of independent entities to be regulated increases into the thousands, administrative and enforcement difficulties mount exponentially. When the firms being regulated differ enormously by size, offer a wide variety of services, have substantial cost and quality differences, and serve thousands of different markets, regulatory problems mount. Combine these features with the legal necessity to exempt totally a large proportion of firms in the same general industry and partially exempt others, all under the mandate of an act which itself contains serious inconsistencies and ambiguities, and we have pretty much described the dilemma of U. S. transport policy. To suggest perpetuation or even extension of such a regulatory milieu, in the hope of making it more effective, independent of its alleged consequences, is surely unrealistic.

Thus, the alternatives to at least *some* relaxation of present regulation are singularly inappropriate. It is important to outline the most probable consequences of regulatory reform, if only to respond to the predictions made by opponents of such changes. The analysis, however, need not only be in *a priori* or conjectural terms. Deregulation of parts of the transportation industries has already occurred both within the United States and in other market-oriented countries. Canada,

Australia, the United Kingdom, France, Germany, Japan, and the Netherlands, among others, have all had experience with direct economic regulation, especially of rail and truck transport, that contains many (but not all) of the features of contemporary U. S. regulation. All these countries have already moved toward regulatory reform or complete elimination of certain forms of regulation, especially those pertaining to rates and entry restrictions.

The consequences of such deregulation have, in every case, been judged to have been favorable.[173] There has been no "chaos" in any of these countries. Both rail and truck pricing have become more rational, and more concern with specific costs has been evident everywhere. In no country is the railroad free from subsidy but there has been increased incentive to link the subsidy more closely to unprofitable services that the government requires be offered. In short, the results of relaxation of regulatory controls over rail and truck rates and entry into trucking have conformed rather closely to what one would expect from policy changes emphasizing competitive forces rather than attempting to restrict one or another of the competing modes. To be sure, not all transport problems have been solved. The issues of public investment in transport infrastructure, appropriate user charges, and labor relations in transportation remain, but they exist independently of the regulatory milieu.

Within the United States when certain agricultural commodities, hitherto regulated, were declared to be exempt, the rates on their shipment promptly fell about 20 percent with no sign of service quality deterioration.[174] In certain states, intrastate trucking not subject to ICC-type regulations has established rates on comparable shipments that are well below the rates of interstate truckers. In New Jersey, rate differentials between 9 percent and 15 percent have been recorded.[175] More recently, the air cargo and air passenger industries were exempted from economic regulation. While it is too early to make any definitive judgments, the results to date appear to be distinctly beneficial to both carriers and customers. Some rates and fares have increased (partly because of deregulation but largely because of general inflationary pressures), others have decreased. Over all, there has been a sharp increase in rate (fare) quality options, including seasonal rates.

---

173. For details see J. R. Nelson and H. O. Whitten and Associates, *Foreign Regulatory Experiments: Implications for U. S.*, November, 1977, prepared for U. S. DOT; and T. D. Heaver and J. C. Nelson, *Railway Pricing under Commercial Freedom: The Canadian Experience* (Vancouver: Centre for Transportation Studies, University of British Columbia, 1977).

174. See above, p.212.

175. C. G. Burck, "Truckers Roll Toward Deregulation," *Fortune*, December 18, 1978, p.78.

Air passenger and cargo traffic has increased sharply, and, thus far at least, the carriers' profits have risen or been maintained. While these illustrations do not prove that similar results would occur if rail, truck, barge, and pipelines were to be deregulated, they do support the view that most of the allegedly undesirable consequences will not occur. Let us examine the undesirable results that opponents of regulatory reform believe would happen.

*"Chaos" Would Result.* The term "chaos" is never very clearly defined. However, the frequent references to the experience, especially of the trucking industry, during the Great Depression provide a clue. In fact, the "chaos" argument is used almost solely with reference to the trucking industry apparently on the assumption that the rail, barge, and oil pipeline industries are structurally oligopolistic and would not be subject to "cutthroat" competition.

Conditions in the trucking industry in the 1930s may be viewed as chaotic. During the Depression, rates were often barely enough to cover fuel costs. Owner-operators, desperate for business, often failed to cover their imputed wage costs. As a result, revenues adequate for maintenance, depreciation, insurance, and liability coverage were not forthcoming for the marginal operations. Operations were unsafe and shippers were uninsured. The trucking industry indeed became a "haven for the unemployed"; it created enormous excess capacity and volatile, uneconomic, unsafe, and uncertain service, especially on the part of the innumerable marginal operators.[176]

In the more than 40 years since the Depression, the infant trucking industry has by and large matured. Many trucking enterprises are large and increasingly employ sophisticated managerial techniques and computer skills. Replication of the results of the 1930s cannot be expected, even if another slump of comparable proportions were to occur. Not only has the industry matured but also society now has a fairly comprehensive system of unemployment compensation. Thus the unusual entry into a single industry of large numbers of marginal, inexperienced carriers, as occurred in the past, would not happen. Stripped of its rhetoric, "chaos" seems to mean nothing more than rate-service competition, something the antitrust laws are pledged to enhance. In the absence of economic regulation, without even the Reed-Bulwinkle Amendment (since the trucking industry has most of the structural features of a workably competitive industry), one would expect workably competitive results, namely, a closer coincidence of

---

176. Some details of the situation in the 1930s and indeed the evolution of the trucking industry itself from World War I through the mid-1950s are contained in M. J. Roberts, "The Motor Transportation Revolution," *Business History Review*, March 1956.

rates and costs, a sharp reduction in monopoly rents in terms of the value of operating rights, and a larger range of rate-quality alternatives.

*Impact on Small Communities.* First, there is no evidence whatever that rates to and from small communities are subsidized in the sense that rates are below out-of-pocket or marginal costs. Indeed, a recent study found such service to be profitable,[177] and an even more recent study found that as far as the motor carriers themselves were concerned, traffic to and from small communities was regarded as desirable.[178] If it is both profitable and desirable, there can be little presumption that operating losses are incurred under present regulatory schemes. Even under present regulation, if the service is unprofitable at established rates, the normal procedure is to cut back on service, make it so sporadic and irregular that the "demand" for such service does not materialize, or raise the rates. In fact, there are many present operating authorities not in use. A "use-it-or-lose-it" policy has never been seriously implemented by the ICC.

Second, no carrier would willingly quote rates below out-of-pocket costs. This presumes a higher degree of cost knowledge than exists in most areas of transportation, but if the carrier did believe that its existing rate was less than the costs of service, it would simply discontinue providing such service or request a rate increase. In fact, rates below out-of-pocket costs are illegal under present regulations. Thus, no regulated carrier has either an incentive or legal mandate to quote rates that may be considered subsidized: it has precisely the opposite incentives and mandate.

Third, small communities utilize the whole gamut of available transport facilities, as far as trucking is concerned, running from common to contract to private and exempt. A survey of shippers from small communities (under 25,000 population) indicates a relatively high degree of satisfaction with the panoply of services presently available, not all of which are common carriage. Nor is all the existing common carriage forced on the common carriers. One conclusion of the 1978 study is, "A large percentage of shippers in small communities regard private carriage as a workable alternative in the event of deteriorated common carriage service. This is especially true of the smallest communities (1,000–2,500 population)."[179]

---

177. R. L. Banks & Associates, "Economic Analysis and Regulatory Implications of Motor Common Carrier Service to Predominantly Small Communities" (Washington, D. C., June 1976).

178. *The Impact on Small Communities of Motor Carrier Regulation Revision* (Washington, D. C.: Government Printing Office, 1978).

179. Ibid., p.101.

Thus, if presently regulated carriers are not losing money serving small communities, are not forced to do it in any event, and are not providing exceptional service now compared to non-common carriage, there can be absolutely no justification for trying (by entry control and rate regulation) to ensure excess profits on major intercity routes to compensate for nonexistent losses on frequently not-offered service in small communities. Nor is there any Congressional mandate requiring use of the trucking industry to subsidize small communities. The following seems to be a reasonable conclusion to this issue:

> The predicted impact of *total* deregulation of motor carriage on small communities is surprisingly undramatic. Effects are not so specific to small communities but are largely those which would be felt throughout the economy. On balance, they are positive effects—including a decline in general rate levels and an increase in the variety of price-service options available to shippers. Adverse effects would not be expected for small communities as such but would be felt by some individual shippers, within large and small communities alike, who currently benefit from particular irrationalities in the current pricing structure.[180]

But suppose, all of the evidence to the contrary notwithstanding, that common carriers are providing superior service to small communities at rates below out-of-pocket costs. Protection of rates above marginal cost on traffic to and from large communities is thereby necessary to sustain such service to small communities. Does it follow that substantial deregulation, and especially greater freedom of entry, would jeopardize the interests of small communities?

With more competition spread unevenly among the innumerable submarkets, some rates would fall and others would rise, as determined by the improved functioning of the markets. Where rates declined, there would be pressure on the carriers to improve their efficiency and, in particular, to increase their utilization of equipment and facilities. Since no carrier would willingly quote rates below cost, and given the illegality of such rates in any event, there would be a greater coincidence of rates with more efficient levels of costs. Furthermore, it would occasion a higher sense of cost-consciousness on the part of the carriers themselves and improve the rate structure. It is not at all evident that this would adversely affect small shippers or small communities. Deprived of the excess receipts in some of the high-volume markets, regulated carriers would have an incentive to cultivate other markets more effectively. At the present time, as the "small shipments" problem suggests, the incentive to provide inadequate service to the lower-volume markets is substantial.

---

180. Ibid., p.132 (emphasis supplied).

Now the regulated motor carriers say they cannot stand such pressures, that rates well above costs on some traffic need to be maintained so that they can internally subsidize traffic needed to support small shippers and small communities. The logical response to this, even though the opposite consequences are equally probable, as just argued, is that if small shippers and communities need special protection, it is inefficient to require a private industry to provide it. If rates for such purposes are now uneconomically low, they should promptly be raised to cover costs. If society decides that special protection is desirable, it can and should be provided directly, not indirectly through the privately owned segment of the transportation industry.

*Safety and Deregulation.* We need to distinguish very carefully between safety regulation and economic regulation. Economic regulation pertains to the establishment and enforcement of rates, operating authority, mergers, and the like. It is concerned with the overall viability and profitability of the currently regulated carriers, as well as issues of discrimination and national defense. Safety regulation, on the other hand, concerns accident prevention and reduction. It is more the purview of state authorities and different federal agencies. It involves the establishment and enforcement of highway weight, speed, and size limitations; equipment regulations; restrictions on reckless driving; driver training. Safety standards and enforcement are the parameters within which trucking operations and economic regulation take place. Indeed, the only connection between safety and economic regulation is in the overall economic health of the carrier. A carrier in poor financial shape may try to skimp on certain safety measures, such as driver training and supervision and equipment maintenance in the short run. Economic regulation has no authority over specific categories of expenditure for the carriers, safety or otherwise. Nor does economic regulation influence the driver hiring practices or even internal discipline. To be sure, flagrant safety violations may lead to suspension or denial of operating authority by the ICC, but in such instances the unsafe drivers and/or vehicles should long since have been forced off the road or the carrier forced out of business by safety enforcement agencies. The establishment and enforcement of economic regulatory criteria are independent of the safety parameters, even though changes in the latter influence total carrier costs.

The lack of relationship between economic and safety regulation has recently been manifest in the transference of safety authority from the economic regulatory agencies themselves to the National Transportation Safety Board and the Federal Highway Administration of the Department of Transportation. Like the FAA, itself long since separated from the CAB, these agencies establish certain qualifications for drivers and equipment and record, report, and investigate accidents. Since the safety function is completely separate from the economic function, one can quite readily argue for stringent enforcement of new or existing safety regulations and, at the same time, argue for a substantial reduction in economic regulation.

The apparently better safety record of ICC-regulated carriers[181] can be explained by the fact that such carriers tend to be bigger and have more extensive operations. Larger carriers, in general, have more sophisticated and extensive safety and training programs than do small owner-operators. The latter occasionally drive too long, undermaintain their equipment, and otherwise present something of a hazard. Yet even this is not certain. An owner-operator has a vested interest in properly maintaining *his* own vehicle. A driver for a large carrier may not accurately or adequately report the conditions of a rig he may not use again. Nor is it always true that larger firms do a better maintenance job than smaller ones. Thus, subjecting the latter to economic regulation would not change the frequency of safety violations. Indeed, a comprehensive study of the whole highway safety issue concluded that traffic accidents are most meaningfully viewed as failures of the "system" rather than as a failure of any single component, such as the driver, the vehicle, or the environment.[182] The same study went on to note that "there is no single factor identified in the literature which can be labeled a principle 'cause' or highway hazard and which could be easily remedied to reduce traffic accident losses markedly."[183] If this is true, then the fact that a particular truck may be carrying regulated commodities at legal rates should have no influence one way or the other on the accident rate. And, certainly, it should make no difference whether the truck is operating under an ICC authority or some state authority or is moving under exempt conditions. This means that changing the parameters of economic regulation should not adversely affect safety, unless, at the same time, it reduces the financial health and viability of carriers with better than average safety records and induces them to cut back on safety-related activities. It is difficult to believe that this would be one of the consequences of significant relaxation of regulatory restrictions.

Although it is impossible to make a certain prediction, on *a priori* grounds, it is likely that the existing large firms in the trucking industry would become even larger in the absence of detailed economic

181. See testimony of D. Wyckoff before the National Commission for the Review of Antitrust Laws and Procedures, October 18, 1978.
182. Arthur D. Little, Inc., *The State of the Art of Traffic Safety* (Boston, June 1966), p.31.
183. Ibid.

regulation, especially for LTL service, where there may exist mild economies of scale and where service quality, including safety, is generally better.[184] In other areas of trucking, the size distribution of firms is unlikely to change—or at least unlikely to change in any predictable direction. Thus, even if size, stability, and financial viability correlate with safety, a tenuous correlation at best, regulatory reform is unlikely to change much in this connection. Even if the financial health of the larger firms were to be adversely affected, an even more dubious possibility, it is questionable that safety-related expenditures would be much affected. It should also be recalled that most deregulation proposals require that applicants be "fit, willing and able."

## Conclusion

The case for regulatory reform with reference to the intercity freight market is rather compelling and indeed at present writing (December 1978) appears to be imminent with respect to rail and truck transport. New, but, one hopes, more simplified, rules of the game will be introduced, along with a considerably enhanced degree of individual carrier discretion with respect to rates, abandonments, and entry. Collective rate making will be sharply reduced. However, the end result is likely to be singularly undramatic. In a workably competitive environment, rid of much of the patent wastes of innumerable regulatory minutiae, net economic benefits from deregulation, depending on its extent, should rise slowly but cumulatively over time. Since most major markets are effectively oligopolistic, rate wars will not suddenly break out. Some rates may change sharply, up or down; some carriers and shippers will fare better financially than others; but the industry as a whole as well as the national economy should benefit by the changes being proposed.

Four major factors lead to the belief that regulatory reform is an idea whose time has come: experience elsewhere, economic theory, changed conditions in transport markets, and various empirical studies as enumerated in this chapter.

When or if substantial deregulation occurs, it should be viewed as an experiment designed to improve a set of regulatory arrangements whose net benefits have become increasingly dubious at the least and may even represent net social losses. At a time when the business

---

184. They should not, however, get large solely because of merger but because of entry into new areas. Whether or not they would get larger than would be the case under continued ICC regulation is impossible to predict. Indeed, the commission has in general favored a policy of merger among existing carriers, which would tend to suggest that it has fostered a certain amount of oligopoly in markets that might have been somewhat less oligopolistic in the absence of regulation.

community is becoming increasingly restive because of the spread of non-industry-specific rules and regulations in connection with environmental issues, concerns over sex and racial discrimination in income and employment, worker health and safety, and product safety, it may indeed be fitting that the trend is in the opposite direction in the industry that was the first to be subjected to extensive regulatory controls.

# Appendix

## Regulation through the Years

The purpose of this Appendix is to present a broad overview of the development of economic regulation of transportation in the United States and to explore its impact on the industries so regulated. In general, it is doubtful that economic regulation has had much of an impact on the underlying strength or weakness of the transport industries. If that statement is true, it implies that substantial *de*regulation would be unlikely to improve significantly the performance of the surface transportation industries. This does not mean that economic regulation has no effect, nor that the attempt to reform regulation is misguided, for there is indeed much that is wrong. Mainly, this Appendix seeks to develop the theme that the causes of the present and past conditions in surface transportation involve much more than economic regulation. In fact, economic regulation, when one considers the totality of factors impinging on transportation, may be of only marginal significance. The "other things" that affect the transportation industries are outlined below, not in any particular order of priority. Indeed, one would be hard pressed to say which are the more significant.

*Technological change* has obviously been a major factor, since different modes suffer or benefit from technological change at different times and at different rates. The whole question is even more complex when one considers that most of the technological change has taken place in the equipment supplying areas, beyond the purview of the transportation firms themselves, since they do very little in the way of R and D. Thus, it may be, as some have argued, that technological change in the transport industries suffers from "suppliers' myopia."

*Differential state and local regulations* refer primarily to size and weight limitations for trucking but also affect certain railway activities (state rail full crew laws, differential taxation of railroad property, etc.).

*Different labor conditions and labor relationships* among the modes of transportation affect the cost structure and, to some extent, the cost levels among the different modes.

The pattern of *public investments in transportation and the level of user charges* are perhaps of greater importance. Since public investments in right-of-way are not rationalized in any economic sense, they clearly distort the relative advantages and cost structures of the various modes in ways that would not necessarily have occurred had economic criteria prevailed. Accompanying the issue of public investment in transportation is, of course, the level of user charges and the question of whether the various users of the publicly provided facilities pay their "fair" share. There are significant differences among the modes with respect to this category, as noted in chapter 2.

*Public subsidies to transportation* have taken place in differential amounts and at different times. They have tended to warp the economic outcome over and above the issue of whether specific commercial users do or do not pay their fair share for the inland waterways and/or the publicly provided highways.

*Public taxation of transportation* is another cost-warping factor. Such levies as the gas tax or differential state tax on railroad properties are not neutral among the modes or in the aggregate.

The *legal milieu,* that is, the varying interpretations of the Act to Regulate Commerce and subsequent legislation may be almost as important as the details of the acts themselves. Certainly, this was true in the early years.

Other forms of *federal, state, and local legislation* affect the transportation modes differentially. I refer here, of course, to environmental protection, OSHA rules, the antitrust laws, energy conditions, and the energy proposals of the Carter administration.

*Changes in the economic structure of the economy* in terms of location and composition of GNP require different relative emphasis on quality of service vis-à-vis cost of service, mostly to the disadvantage of rail and barge service.

All these factors have differential impacts on the different modes, which, in turn, affect their cost structure, cost level, and, to some extent, cost behavior and service qualities. The totality of these nonregulatory forces suggests that economic regulation by the Interstate Commerce Commission may have had a relatively minor influence on the economic performance of the surface transportation industries. Given that the impact of these other factors varies over time, and, in addition, that the impact of economic regulation varies over time, it follows that the *relative* economic impact of regulation will differ from time to time.

## Historical Development of Regulation

There appear to be seven fairly distinct phases in the development of transportation regulation: (1) the period before passage of the Act to Regulate Commerce, in 1887, which witnessed growing concern over railroad practices; (2) the period extending roughly to 1904–1906, when the authority the ICC thought it had was stripped away bit by bit; (3) from 1904–1906 through World War I to 1920, when the commission reacquired the authority it thought it had earlier and proceeded to restrain general rate increases, leaving the railroads in relatively poor shape by the war's end; (4) the beginning of promotive regulation and an abortive attempt at systemwide planning, to which we have now returned; (5) from the Great Depression to World War II, during which the commission could do little to help or hinder in the face of overwhelming economic forces, even though its authority was expanded to cover trucking, waterways, and bankruptcy issues; (6) from World War II to the late 1950s, when there was a temporary resurgence of the railroads during the war and a subsequent reversion to steady relative decline, with the commission vacillating inconsistently and increasingly being attacked for ineptitude; and (7) from the late 1950s to the present, a period that saw a sharp break from past reactions to problems of regulation and difficulties within transportation; namely, instead of expansion of the authority of the regulating agency, there have been mounting pressures to reduce or even eliminate economic regulation altogether. In a sense, we have come full circle; in the twenty years after the Act was passed, court interpretation stripped away all ICC power; in the last twenty years, after restoring the powers and enlarging them substantially, we are now in the process of taking them away once again.

### First Period

Discrimination, rebates, instability, and the creation and breakdown of railroad pools led to considerable agitation by farmers, merchants, and independent oilmen for state regulation of railroads. So-called Granger Laws were duly passed in several Midwest states, the most important of which was in Illinois. The laws generally provided that rates be established by a regulatory commission or by a legislature, prohibited long-/short-haul discrimination, and sought to limit rail consolidation and to prohibit free passes to public officials. Though most of these laws were later repealed, their constitutionality was upheld on the grounds that rail transport was "affected with the public interest" and that railways were "common carriers."

In the meantime, there was agitation for some kind of federal action. In 1874, for example, the Windom committee found many abuses but recommended national or state ownership of one or more railroads to "serve as regulators of other lines," in a rationale analogous to that for the TVA. The issue of regulation was constantly emerging in Congress, and one house or the other passed legislation of various kinds. Indeed, over 150 bills for federal regulation were introduced in Congress in the twenty years preceding the ultimate enactment in 1887. In 1884 the House passed a measure, and the following year the Senate passed a different measure, both based on the Cullom report, which stressed that the primary evil was discrimination among places and shippers. Federal regulation became urgent after the 1886 Supreme Court decision on the Wabash case, which held that a state could not control rates on interstate traffic. Finally, in 1887 the Act to Regulate Commerce was passed, the first major incursion into the hitherto sacrosanct realm of private enterprise. Why did it happen to the railroads?

There are two diametrically opposed views. The conventional wisdom has it that the railroads so abused their monopoly power that society retaliated by regulation designed to eliminate their abuses and to punish them. The alternative view is that because the railroads were unable to police themselves, as evidenced by the breakdown of the pools in the early 1880s and the outbreak of cutthroat competition, they supported some form of regulation, in principle at least, to restore stability to the industry. In other words, they sought regulation as a device to establish a more permanent and efficient cartel.

The truth of the matter appears to be that after the constitutionality of the state laws was upheld and certainly after the Wabash case,[1] some form of federal regulation appeared to be inevitable. As the president of the Chicago, Burlington, and Quincy put it in 1878, "The public *will* regulate us to some extent and we must make up our minds to it."[2] Railroads thus sought to shape the federal regulation and clearly preferred it to the tougher state regulations that were then in existence. Thus on February 4, 1887, President Cleveland signed the Act to Regulate Commerce, which created a five-man commission; outlawed pools and rate discrimination; required that rates be just, reasonable, and published; authorized the commission to investigate any interstate railway and empowered it to compel witnesses to testify and to secure relevant documents; and required railroads to submit regular reports and to adopt a uniform accounting system. At the end

---

1. *Wabash Railway Co.* v. *Illinois,* 118 U.S. 557 (1886).
2. Cited in A. Hoogenboom and O. Hoogenboom, *A History of the ICC from Panacea to Palliative* (New York: W. W. Norton, 1976), p.12.

of March 1887, with five commissioners and eleven staff members, the ICC set out to eliminate abuses of economic power of the largest industry in the country. At that time railroads employed almost 800,000 workers and had over 100,000 miles of track.

## Second Period

After several early decisions, mostly with respect to long- and short-haul discrimination, the *Chicago Tribune* proclaimed that "The Interstate Commerce Act is working wonders and the rail magnates are trembling."[3] This was not the case, however. In the course of the next fifteen years, virtually all the commission's powers were emasculated by Supreme Court rulings. By 1903 the commission itself lamented that all it could do was "investigate and report and such orders as it can make have no binding effect."[4] Specifically, the kinds of Court rulings the commission faced were as follows: the commission was required to obtain a court order to uphold its rulings if they were not obeyed voluntarily (and they were not). On top of this was the issue of judicial review, in which the Court even entertained additional evidence and often, as has been said, "the same case" was not heard by the courts. Hence commission decisions were often overruled. Add to this the length of court cases, which considerably diminished the effectiveness of commission rulings. The Court also held that the commission could not in fact compel witnesses to testify. The power to prescribe maximum rates was destroyed in the Maximum Freight Rate case in 1897; Section 4 was emasculated in the Alabama Midland Case in 1896; and the courts even ruled that the commission had no power even to suspend a rate that the railroads proposed. The ineptitude of the commission in the early years cannot be attributed to its efforts but, rather, to the efforts of the courts to strip away whatever powers the commission thought it had.

## Third Period

By 1910 the Congress had given back all the powers originally believed to have existed in a long series of acts (the Expediting Act of 1903, the Elkins Act of 1903, the Hepburn Act of 1906, the Mann-Elkins Act of 1910), and the courts finally and "voluntarily" limited the scope of judicial review in 1910, arguing that they would not substitute their judgment for that of the commission as long as the commission's judgment was based on its authority as interpreted by the courts and adequate evidence. The commission thus had a second chance, and its ac-

---

3. Ibid., p.23.
4. ICC, *17th Annual Report, 1903*, p.17.

tivities increased dramatically. By 1909, only 3 years after the Hepburn Act, formal complaints to the ICC numbered 2½ times the total number of formal complaints during its first 19 years.[5] With its new-found powers, the commission denied a series of requests for general rate increases or sanctioned lower increases than in retrospect were needed— thereby impairing railroad earnings and jeopardizing new investments. However, the commission did not tamper with the rate structure, nor did it seek to "rationalize" or coordinate the entire rail system. Since wartime needs required both higher rates and "rationalization," President Wilson bypassed the ICC and set up the Railroad Administration in 1917; by general order no. 1, the director general of railroads required the pooling of all equipment and facilities, ordered new routings, denied shippers the right to route, and sought to operate all railroads as a national system. Subsequently, rates were raised and the service was much better coordinated.

## Fourth Period

After World War I there were increasing demands, mostly from shippers, for restoration of private control and a return to ICC regulation. Other proposals (e.g., the Plumb Plan) bear a striking resemblance to ConRail. The Transportation Act of 1920 broadened the commission's authority; legalized railroad combinations, subject to an overall "plan" that the commission was to devise; enshrined the rule of rate making into law (fair return on fair value); and gave the commission control over security issues and service. In general, the idea was to "rationalize" the system and abandon the emphasis on competition, with considerable "leadership" assumed to emanate from the commission, which itself was to begin to fashion a national, coordinated railroad system.

However, the commission was reluctant to exercise leadership—it even refused to formulate a final plan and begged to be relieved of such responsibility. As Sharfman noted, the ICC did not "free the railroad industry . . . of the accumulated burden of past ills," nor did it "establish principles and practices for this regulated industry beyond and above those recognized in the general competitive field."[6] In addition, the commission had not pressed the railroads to reduce their bonded indebtedness or to consolidate into a few economically viable systems. This meant that when the Great Depression arrived, the railroads suffered far more than would otherwise have been the case, and the commission, regardless of its legal authority or regardless of any

---

5. I. Sharfman, *The Interstate Commerce Commission* (New York: The Commonwealth Fund, 1931), vol.I, p.41n40.
6. Ibid., p.617.

sudden infusion of leadership zeal, not hitherto apparent, was power-less in the face of such overwhelming economic forces.

## Fifth Period

In face of the economic disaster, new regulatory authority was en-acted—a kind of knee-jerk, "pass-a-law" syndrome so common in the face of emergencies. The Emergency Transportation Act of 1933 sought to encourage cost reductions by eliminating unnecessary dupli-cation and facilitating pooling and joint use of tracks, but it accom-plished little and died an ignominious death in 1936. It did create a Federal Coordinator of Transportation (one of whose major reports led to the regulation of motor carriers) and repeal the recapture clause and the rule of rate making of the 1920 Act. Section 77 of the Bankruptcy Act made it easier to reorganize the debt level and struc-ture of a railroad to make it consistent with "future earning power." Neither of these did much good at the time and in fact did some harm (e.g., the latter led to wiping out many stockholders because the ICC underestimated post-Depression earnings of some bankrupt roads).

The Depression also spawned the Motor Carrier Act of 1935, which extended the ICC's authority to regulate the trucking industry. Sud-denly the workload of the commission burgeoned enormously—by November 1, 1936, there were about 86,000 applications for certificates and permits, half of which were protested; over 53,000 tariff publica-tions; almost 17,000 schedules; and 2,000 contracts filed with the ICC.[7] In addition, it had to make fine distinctions among common, contract, exempt, and private carriage as well as determine what is an agricul-tural product. More important, it later had to determine what "pres-ervation of inherent advantages"—especially between rail and truck—meant in practice.

As if this were not enough, an already swamped and confused com-mission was soon given jurisdiction over coastwise, intercoastal, in-land, and Great Lakes common and contract water carriers in inter-state and foreign commerce by the Transportation Act of 1940. The Act also enunciated a national transportation policy that is wonderful in its ambiguity and inconsistency:

It is hereby declared to be the national transportation policy of the Congress to provide for fair and impartial regulation of all modes of trans-portation . . . to promote safe, adequate, economical, and efficient service and foster sound economic conditions in transportation and among the several carriers; to encourage the establishment and maintenance of reason-able charges . . . without unjust discriminations, undue preferences or ad-

---

7. Hoogenboom and Hoogenboom, p.132.

vantages or unfair or destructive practices . . . all to the end of developing, coordinating and preserving a national transportation system by water, highway and rail, as well as other means, adequate to meet the needs of the commerce of the United States, of the Postal Service and of the national defense.[8]

## Sixth Period

However, World War II had already begun in Europe and the railroads, on the verge of total financial collapse in 1938, picked up sharply and achieved record tonnages, passenger movements, and overall revenues during the war years. But the ICC was not asked to coordinate transportation during the war; rather, President Roosevelt established the Office for Defense Transportation but did appoint J. B. Eastman as director. The ICC emerged from the war with expanded authority but with little sense of direction. With the death of Eastman, perhaps the ablest commissioner ever, the ICC lacked leadership as well.

Rail prosperity was short-lived. With the resurgence of truck and car transportation, water, and oil pipelines, rail traffic shares dropped from 62 percent of freight in 1939 to barely 50 percent in 1957, passenger traffic declined sharply, and large accounting losses were recorded. By the mid-1950s the railroads were again in serious financial difficulty partly due to ICC regulation (i.e., restrictions on even compensatory rail rate reductions, slowness in permitting abandonment of unprofitable service, restraints on innovations that might injure other common carriers). Indeed, the scope of ICC regulation decreased with the rise of exempt and private carriage itself in part because of rigidities and delays imposed by the regulatory process, in which everybody has a right to his day in court.

In addition, the ICC's case-by-case approach fostered confusion, especially with regard to relative rate relations between competing modes. Indeed, ICC rate regulation has been characterized as a "Grand Benthamite Design."

The argument went as follows:

Rate regulation as practiced by the ICC, if completely effective, would maintain higher rates on specific traffic than would otherwise occur, involve greater rigidity, tend to preserve a demand-oriented rate structure, reinforce misapplication of value-of-service pricing but emphasize commodity discrimination as the most effective way of covering the nonassignable costs, frequently allow more than one mode to participate in a given piece of business regardless of relative costs, consider a wide variety of noneconomic objectives and externalities, treat each case as *sui generis,* more effectively prevent rates from falling below marginal cost, and force a kind of public

8. Public Law No.785, 75th Cong., 3d sess., 1940, pp.2–3.

accountability and greater cost consciousness on the common carriers. Insofar as one can impute rationality to contemporary regulation, the overall impression is that the commission seeks a rate structure such that all non-traceable costs, including those additional costs arising from pursuit of noneconomic objectives and the added duties of common carriage, are recouped from shippers on the basis of willingness and ability to pay; that is to say, the markup over computed out-of-pocket costs would be determined by the relative level and elasticity of the demand for transport of particular commodities. Individual rates would be adjusted from the maximum profit level by consideration of external economies and diseconomies as far as regulated carriers are concerned and overall profit limitation is implied. Rate regulation, if completely effective, thus attempts, albeit in a crude and implicit way, to assess the benefits to the regulated carriers as a group and weigh these against whatever externalities appear to emerge in particular instances. It is true, of course, that, unlike Bentham, the ICC does not explicitly add up the net benefits to each shipper, carrier and community involved or affected and then strike the balance, approving those rate changes for which the sum of the net benefits exceeds zero and disapproving all others. But the frequent references to injury or noninjury to some shippers, regions, defense interests, or other carriers due to proposed rate changes, suggests that an interpretation of rate policy in terms of Bentham's felicific calculus may not be so far-fetched as it seems on the surface.[9]

But, of course, because of incomplete jurisdiction (barely one-third of motor carrier ton-miles and between 10 and 15 percent of inland water ton-miles), this Grand Design cannot be fulfilled. More fundamentally, of course, it fails because of the reasons for the failure of Bentham's felicific calculus, namely, the inability to measure or even provide appropriate weights for the conflicting or complementary benefits and costs. But, finally, almost all the noneconomic objectives can now be fulfilled by more direct techniques than by using a particular industry as an instrument. Regional growth and adjustment to change, overall stabilization policy, antitrust considerations, and national defense, which have so often provided the rationale in the past for uneconomic decision making by the ICC, can now be attacked in a more forthright fashion than was the case thirty to fifty years ago. Society's concern at the industry level should now be with efficiency and technological progress, neither of which a regulatory agency in a semicompetitive market is in a position to promote. If we grant these largely insuperable problems of the Grand Design and acknowledge the enormous costs of regulation, it is difficult to disagree with the policy recommendations of the last five administrations, whose general thrust

9. G. Wilson, "The Effect of Rate Regulation on Resource Allocation in Transportation," *American Economic Review*, May 1964, pp.167–68.

was and is toward "greater reliance upon competitive forces in transportation."

In any event, by the middle to late '50s, the ICC was being increasingly criticized, sometimes unfairly but often with justice. Naturally, there was another law, but the Transportation Act of 1958 solved nothing. As one judge put it, "The legislators had tackled a tough problem, had looked long and hard at it, and, then, caught between conflicting pressures, had come up with a whimper."[10]

### Seventh Period

The attack on economic regulation was then taken up by professional economists, and when President Kennedy took office, he supported some of their views, namely, that "a chaotic patchwork of inconsistent and often obsolete legislation and regulation has evolved from a history of specific actions addressed to specific problems of specific industries at specific times. This patchwork does not fully reflect either the dramatic changes in technology . . . or the parallel changes in the structure of competition."[11] The Doyle report concluded that "regulatory policy has produced a general program of preserving the status quo which is in direct opposition to the over-all objective of a dynamic transportation system. . . ."[12]

The attack on the regulatory agencies, especially the ICC, had begun in earnest. More and more professional economists turned their attention to the transportation industries and in the Kennedy, Johnson, Nixon, Ford and Carter administrations, their views became those of the administration as far as economic regulation was concerned. Each annual report of the Council of Economic Advisors contained increasingly bitter indictments of economic regulation, which, at least in transportation, was believed to have shifted from regulation of monopoly to regulation of competition. The pleas for "regulatory reform" are essentially based on the belief that in the 1960s and beyond all major and most minor transport markets (i.e., city-pairs) have enough shipper transport options that they would be workably competitive in the absence of economic regulation; and that entry controls, rate regulation, requirements to maintain unprofitable service, internal subsidization, and legalization of rate bureaus are anachronistic hangovers of an earlier era when most transport markets had less shipper choice and were therefore subject to abuses of monopoly power. It was and is also widely believed that these aspects of regulation have resulted

---

10. Cited in Hoogenboom and Hoogenboom, pp.155–56.
11. John F. Kennedy, "The Transportation System of Our Nation," message to Congress, April 5, 1962.
12. *National Transportation Policy*, 87th Cong., 1st sess., 1961, p.405.

in static misallocation (i.e., $P_i > MC_i$), excess capacity, and retarded innovation, and that the "costs" of these to society may exceed $10 billion per year as of 1977, not counting the costs of regulation itself. Since no comparable net benefits could be found, it was believed that regulation was causing perhaps as much as $10 billion in net avoidable economic waste.

Legislation following President Kennedy's message on transportation (the first ever—and this only because the President adlibbed in a speech that he was going to deliver such a message), which urged "less Federal regulation and subsidization," got nowhere. Following Kennedy's death, President Johnson declared that transportation reform was high on the agenda of national priorities. However, before he could submit proposals along the lines of President Kennedy, the United States became preoccupied with the civil rights movement and the Indochina wars. Transport regulatory reform got short shrift.

However, President Johnson did succeed in creating the Department of Transportation (DOT) to coordinate the executive functions of the transportation agencies. It began operation on April 1, 1967. Though not in direct conflict with the ICC, the DOT has generally supported "regulatory reform," and for many years, especially since the early 1970s, it has made legislative proposals along these lines that have been more or less supported by the White House. Most of them got nowhere, as powerful lobbies, especially the American Trucking Associations and the Teamsters Union, succeeded in blocking any major relaxation of regulatory constraints, even though every President from Kennedy through Carter has endorsed regulatory reform. It has become rather like "motherhood." The wave of railroad bankruptcies in the Northeast triggered the Regional Rail Reorganization Act of 1973 and an emphasis on planning and coordination, but regulatory reform lay in the future.

Under the Ford Administration a new argument was added to the basic critique of regulation, namely, that as currently practiced, transportation regulation contributed to "stagflation"—that the regulated industries reinforced the downward inflexibility of the U. S. price level in addition to causing inefficiency. More and more, the urgency of regulatory reform was stressed. Cries of "abolish the ICC" were heard, even from a few leading Congressmen. Bills designed at least partially to deregulate railroads, trucks, and airlines were regularly submitted but seldom got out of committee. Finally, on February 5, 1976, the 4-R Act was passed, less, one suspects, because of its stress on regulatory reform than for its promise to provide more than $6 billion in subsidy or loan guarantees to upgrade rail right-of-way as a kind of last-ditch effort to prevent more ConRail-types of nationalization and preserve private railroad operation.

Although the Act sought more rate freedom, seasonal rates, more flexible rate bureaus, and an improvement in the rails' competitive position, the provisions were surrounded with exceptions. For example, if a railroad is found to have "market dominance," it is not free to raise its rate by 7 percent. The ICC was to define what market dominance means, but under its definitions, preliminary studies indicate that at a maximum only 20 percent of rail traffic is not market-dominant. In virtually every section of the Act, there is room for interpretation. It is clear that the commission will interpret it in such a way as to narrow the extent of change from pre-existing practice. Recently an ICC commissioner stated that since any relaxation of trucking regulations will threaten the new public policy under the 4-R Act designed to make railroads financially viable and will put in jeopardy the large public investments in railroads, we may need re-regulation (not deregulation) of the trucking industry! Other features of the Act are mandated requirements for speedier hearings and easier abandonment of unprofitable service, the ultimate effects of which are uncertain.

The new thrust toward coordinated system planning has taken place outside the regulatory milieu. The two are not unrelated, of course, but it is noteworthy that once again the ICC has been bypassed in actual or incipient emergencies.

### Lessons from History

1. The ICC has never concerned itself with performance or efficiency criteria with respect to transportation. As the Magnuson Committee Staff Analysis put it, "Since the regulatory process does not . . . relate particular actions to performance objectives . . . there has been no incentive for the railroads to change operating practices to bring greater service effectiveness or more refined investment choices."[13] This arises in part because the ICC has interpreted its mandate as having broad, multiple, and conflicting objectives, as noted in chapter 4.

A more single-minded emphasis on efficiency, performance, and technological dynamism within the regulated industry is obviously called for. Other interests affected can or should be dealt with directly via federal tax and subsidy policy whenever detrimental effects outside transportation are deemed worthy of offset.

2. It is relatively easy to regulate a growing, prosperous industry and even to make such regulation appear successful by effectively limiting earnings and prices to "reasonable" levels. On the other hand,

---

13. *The American Railroads: Posture, Problems, and Prospects,* staff analysis for the Senate Committee on Commerce, 92d Cong., 2d sess. (Washington, D.C.: Government Printing Office, 1972), p.7.

when a regulated industry gets into serious financial and/or economic trouble, there is little a regulatory agency can do. It is far easier to restrain burgeoning prices and profits than to stimulate them in the face of sharply decreasing demand. As has been said in another context, "It is easier to pull on a string than to push." Furthermore, the adversary process becomes self-reinforcing; the industry spends a disproportionate amount of resources blaming regulation for its malaise, thereby diverting talent away from resolving the real problems. In response, since the regulatory agency has so many other interests to consider, it is likely to pay little attention even to legitimate complaints, which in turn provoke more complaints and recriminations.

3. There is nothing in the Act to Regulate Commerce as it now exists to prevent the ICC from doing any or all of the things that the proponents of regulatory reform recommend. The reason we have been forced to legislation is that the commission will not do them, although things seem to be changing under Commissioner Daniel O'Neal (1977). With new commissioners and upper-level staff, there could be far more flexibility and much less need for legislation. Flexibility is clearly preferable to new legislation, which is inevitably ambiguous and subject to interpretation. Indeed, there is a potential lawsuit in every section and for every interpretation of the 4-R Act. History suggests that, with their heavy caseload, the commissioners rely to a great extent on the staff. As a recent study notes, "In proportion to its weakness and inexperience, the ICC depended increasingly throughout the twentieth century on its long-time staff members, who had reason to protect a comfortable status quo. . . . The ICC has become a powerful commission composed of weak commissioners, superimposed upon an entrenched staff."[14] This has now been changed.

Whether these faults are inherent in any long-term regulatory agency is difficult to say. But clearly the inability to improve the transportation situation during the 1930s, for reasons largely beyond the reach of the commission, and the failure to help sustain the railroads' financial viability after World War II, for reasons only partly beyond its reach, testify to its malaise, ineptitude, and status-quo mentality.

In retrospect, therefore, it is clear that the quality of the commissioners and the senior staff is the crucial variable, far more so than enabling legislation as long as such legislation is deliciously vague and subject to interpretation.

---

14. Hoogenboom and Hoogenboom, p.189.

# PART II

# *Efficient Expansion of Transport Capacity*

## Introduction

To this point we have emphasized certain pricing principles and regulatory changes that should improve existing transportation facilities. However, as transport structures deteriorate with use, as industries shift location and patterns of output, and as overall economic growth continues, replacement decisions and additional transportation capacity decisions have to be made. They can obviously be made using various criteria—political, military, social, economic. Indeed, especially for public sector transport investments, noneconomic criteria have tended to predominate in the past in most countries. Transportation investments have often been justified on the basis of social cohesion, defense, political unification, regional balance, and even national prestige (e.g., the SST). Even when such noneconomic criteria are not invoked, emphasis is often placed on the assumed stimulus to economic growth and development that are uniquely attributable to new transportation investment.

Over the past decade or so, there has been increased awareness that most economies are devoting too many resources to the transport sector, and that transport investment, by itself, is not the strategic key to regional and national growth that many believe it to be. These two findings or concerns are obviously interrelated. The belief that transport investments have some special properties related to economic growth obviously encourages more investment in transport, especially by public authorities. This belief may be referred to as the "Grand Transportation Mystique" (GTM). Thus Hawkins asserts that "the one sure generalization that can be made about the underdeveloped countries is that investment in transport and communications is a vital factor."[1] Rostow claims that the railroad was "historically the most powerful single initiator of take-offs. . . . [and that] the preparation of a viable base for a modern industrial structure requires that quite revolutionary changes be brought about in two nonindustrial sectors: agriculture and social overhead capital, most notably in transport."[2] The motto of an Indian automotive club even proclaims that "Transportation Is Civilization"!

There are some valid reasons for the existence of this belief. Historically, rapid periods of economic growth in Western Europe and North America have been associated with (but not necessarily caused by) sharp increases in expenditures, first on canals and then, in the mid-

---

1. E. K. Hawkins, *Roads and Road Transport in an Underdeveloped Country* (London: London Colonial Office, 1962), p.26.

2. W. W. Rostow, *The Stages of Economic Growth* (Cambridge: Cambridge University Press, 1960), pp.25, 26, 55.

to late-nineteenth century, on railroads. Secondly, a major transport investment (bridge, railroad, road, port, or airport) often represents a major architectural or engineering feat; it is durable and tangible and has obvious properties that appeal to political authorities; it is akin to statues and monuments, but with more apparent utility. Furthermore, it is difficult to demonstrate in advance that a particular transport investment may significantly violate efficiency criteria, for such an investment is often viewed as "necessary" for military, social, or prestige reasons. Finally, it is true that any economy seeking to promote economic growth must "specialize," and that requires the ability to move people and goods from one place to another. It is for this reason that transport investment, especially in infrastructure, has been viewed as an indispensable prerequisite to economic growth.

These are all plausible reasons for the GTM. Yet there are serious reservations concerning each. The past historical associations between transport investments and growth do not imply causation or any close causal connection. Indeed, the overbuilding of the U. S. railroad system well in advance of demand has been viewed by many as slowing down the overall rate of growth—that investments elsewhere would have increased the growth rate beyond that actually recorded.

Likewise, the apparent attribute of being an indispensable prerequisite, a necessary condition, does not also imply that it is *a* or *the* dominant cause. Note also that while a spatially specialized economy must be able to have access to both production and consumption points, the kind of access is not specified—in some cases a single-lane road might be adequate, rather than a four-lane highway or a railway or something more grandiose and more capital-intensive. It is at this point that the "monument" attribute frequently determines the type of transport investment. In developed countries, transport investment constitutes some 10 to 14 percent of annual gross domestic investment, while in poor countries the share is often double these percentages.[3]

Yet in most countries, the share of value added or GDP (gross domestic product) originating in the transport sector relative to total GDP is considerably smaller. Similarly, the percentage of the total economically active (employed) who are employed in transport is low —barely 4 to 5 percent in the U. S. and Canada, for example. Furthermore, for most commodities the proportion of the delivered or f.o.b. prices attributable to freight charges is extremely low—normally well below 5 percent in developed countries or 10 percent in developing

---

3. G. W. Wilson, B. Bergmann, L. Hirsch, and M. Klein, *The Impact of Highway Investment on Development* (Washington, D. C.: The Brookings Institution, 1966), p.2.

countries, except for extremely low-valued, bulky commodities, as noted in chapter 1.

This relative unimportance of the transport sector and freight rates suggests that much of the emphasis on transport may be misplaced or that the GTM is still operative. At this point defenders of the GTM will stress the strategic nature of transportation. A major strike of transport workers can have serious effects on many industries and people, but the same is true of producers of other intermediate inputs widely used in many industries. Somehow it is believed that transportation inputs are more significant than other inputs—a belief that is difficult to substantiate.

Yet it is true that an improved transportation system can lead to lower freight rates or passenger fares, which, in turn, can lead to a wider market or greater net satisfactions (especially to the poor, in the case of lower fares), which, in turn, can lead to greater specialization and overall efficiency. As Adam Smith long ago remarked, "the division of labor is limited by the extent of the market." But note that at each step in the chain there is only the possibility that these results will happen. For example, many obstacles prevent lower freight costs from leading to lower freight rates; lower freight rates need not result in lower prices of goods to customers, hence no widening of the market; and, even if there is a widening of the market, efficiency over all will improve only if there are economies of scale or new technologies to take advantage of the wider market. In short, institutional, technological, and even psychological factors well beyond the bounds of transport may break the chain of causation at each point. Numerous examples exist.

Again, it is often argued, that to "open up" new regions, transport investment, certainly for access purposes, is essential. This is the basic rationale for feeder roads. Yet if there is little in the region to be developed, the provision of access will accomplish little or nothing, and the investment in access facilities will be wasted. Even if there are resources to be developed in the hitherto isolated region, little growth will occur unless the persons aware of the improved access respond to the new economic opportunity and additional investments beyond those in transportation are made. In this case, the investment in transport is merely part of the complementary set of investments, each of which is worthless without the others, and certainly none is more strategic than any other. Many feeder roads have failed precisely because these factors were missing. A study of such roads indicated that two main preconditions were necessary if a region were to benefit significantly from improved access: the region was already growing and beginning to exceed the capacity of existing transport facilities; and the region had an abundance of easily exploitable natural resources along the right-of-way.[4] A transport improvement by itself cannot be expected to generate benefits proportionate to the costs.

*Efficiency within Transport vs. Other Social Goals*

Transport policy and transport investment in virtually all countries have frequently been used to promote other (desirable) goals than simply moving more people and goods. Highway expansion has often been used to promote employment or reduce regional disparities. Contraction of the railway system reduces railway employment and is resisted even if traffic is declining and deficits are rising; and urban transit fares are often kept low to assist the urban poor. There is nothing wrong with these and other objectives, but using the transport system as a means of achieving them raises a serious question. Is freight rate policy or transport investment policy the most feasible way (i.e., least-cost, most effective way) to accomplish the noneconomic objectives, especially since such policies create inefficiencies within the transport sector? Note that uneconomic expansion of highways to create employment opportunities or reduce regional disparities represents misallocation of capital in the efficiency sense; hence it "costs" the economy in terms of overall growth with no guarantee that the highway expansion will reduce regional disparities or create permanent employment opportunities after the work is done. Other, less costly approaches need to be considered.

The failure to contract railway operations that are definitely financially nonviable can result only in growing deficits for the railways, which must or will be made up by the government. This increases the overall public deficit and contributes to inflation (where the incidence is often greater for the poor or those without the resourcefulness to combat it) or higher tax rates, both of which jeopardize overall growth. A similar problem, or set of problems, exists with respect to urban transit rates that are kept too low, in addition to the fact that if the rates are too low, a private operation will either go out of business or defer maintenance, drive excessive hours, and contribute to the accident rate. In short, using transport to effectuate various nontransportation goals needs to be carefully scrutinized to see if the costs are excessive and the results are as anticipated.

The general goals of most economies can be specified roughly as follows:

1. Overall growth of GDP within a 4 to 8 percent range per year and rising income per head, depending on the country and particular circumstances

---

4. Wilson et al., chap. 8.

2. Reduction of population growth to between zero to 2 percent per year over the next 5 to 10 years—again depending on the country and particular circumstances

3. Reduction of inequality by raising living standards of the poor generally

4. Reduction of regional disparities in income per head

5. Reduction of movement from rural to urban areas

6. Modernization of agriculture, especially for Third World economies, and expansion of rural amenities

7. Other social, political, military, and religious objectives.

All these goals are interrelated—clearly income per head will rise more rapidly if population growth slows; improvement of regional disparities and the rural sector will contribute to raising living standards of the poor, and vice versa; modernization of agriculture will raise rural incomes, stimulate net proceeds from exports, and raise or maintain the overall growth rate.

What is the role of transport in all of this? Let us take each goal separately, even though they are closely interrelated, and examine what role "improved transportation" may have to play.

1. Overall growth of 4 to 8 percent per year: If overall growth continues, sooner or later additional capacity will be needed for specific transport links. If alternatives are fully considered, there will be many cases where transport investment will be economically justified. If, in the meantime, institutional restraints have been removed where such exist, the overall efficiency of the capital market will be improved, and ongoing economic growth will be facilitated. This is probably the major contribution that improved efficiency in transportation can make toward the goal of high, sustained, overall growth.

2. Reduced rate of population growth: Transport policy or investment has obviously no direct link here. Even overall growth has only an indirect link through its effect on birth and death rates.

3 and 4. Reduced inequality among persons and regions: The overall distribution of personal income will not be significantly altered by policies in the transport sector except indirectly through considerations of the role of transport in overall economic growth (see 1. above). Even rapid overall growth will not lead to more equality of income distribution unless explicit public policies are invoked, such as progressive taxation and expenditures for health, education, and unemployment compensation that are designed to channel the economic growth in the direction of more equality. The modern welfare state of the Western developed economies required massive public involvement

along the above lines to attain the present income distribution. Transport has little to do with any of these things on a large scale.

However, regional disparities can be somewhat more effectively influenced by rate and investment policies in transportation. One of the problems is that improved or cheaper access to a relatively poor region has two conflicting tendencies: Easier access to the relatively poor region tends to increase the penetration of the region from the outside, often to the detriment of local businesses hitherto "protected" by the high transport cost barrier. On the other hand, improved access may stimulate the local economy if it makes it easier to develop hitherto underdeveloped natural resources. The net effect depends on local conditions but, in general, a "transport-mainly" policy will not have much effect unless the previously untapped resources were, in fact, untapped solely because of transport cost barriers. Clearly, if there were no or few resources, there can be no certainty that regional disparities would narrow, and, in this case, the investments would be inefficient to boot—a cost to the economy with the equal probability of results opposite to those desired. If, however, the improved access or less costly transport were accompanied by policies designed to encourage new industries in the region, to locate additional government facilities there, and to create more public facilities such as schools and hospitals, the prospect for effective utilization of the added transportation facilities and for a reduction of regional inequality would be considerably brighter.

5 and 6. Reduced migration from rural to urban areas, modernization of agriculture, and improvement of urban amenities: Modernization of agriculture usually implies sharp increases in output per hectare and output per man by use of machinery, and a substitution of capital for labor. Since the share of agriculture in GDP progressively decreases with economic growth, further modernization will reduce manpower requirements unless vast new tracts of land are brought under cultivation or other investments are made to utilize the excess manpower. Transport can assist in the latter but only as a component of an overall rural strategy involving other investments, possibly agricultural price support programs, extension of rural credit and marketing facilities, rural electrification schemes, a "county" agent system. Once again, the problem is not uniquely related to transportation. Thus there is no reason to misdirect investment in rural transport facilities in the vain hope that this will have the desired effect. There may indeed be a major inconsistency in a rapid modernization of agriculture and a reduction of the rate of rural migration.

7. Other objectives: Aside from the role of a relatively ubiquitous transport system in facilitating administration, defense, and security,

there is little direct connection with transport infrastructure. To be sure, many highways around the world have been built primarily for defense purposes but, again, at an efficiency cost in terms of misallocation of scarce capital.

Concern is often expressed about transport vehicles and their role in noise and air pollution. Antipollution legislation will become a growing necessity as vehicles per capita increase, as they will with further economic growth. Restrictions on automotive emissions as well as on imports will be desirable and can, in fact, be justified in terms of benefits (cleaner air, improved balance of payments) vis-à-vis costs. Similar views pertain to vehicle accidents; sensible and improved safety regulation is clearly justifiable.

## Conclusion

Efficiency within transportation, both in terms of use of existing infrastructure, vehicles, and rolling stock, which was the subject of Part I, and in terms of investment criteria should be the overriding goal of national transportation policy, deviations from which require special justification on a benefit-cost basis. Part II outlines efficient investment criteria along benefit-cost lines.

*Efficient Expansion of Capacity.* There are often trade-offs between policy changes and investment needs. Assume a policy, practice, or regulation exists that impedes the use of a given transport facility. For example, assume that an airport is closed down at night because of noise pollution, as is increasingly the case in North America and Western Europe. Obviously, the capacity of the airport will be reduced, but at the same time air cargo carriers will increase their use of the airport at other times of the day. As traffic at the airport expands, additional runways or an entirely new airport will be needed earlier than would otherwise be necessary. If the policy of nighttime closing were changed, new capacity might not be needed at all, or at least not so soon. Similarly with pricing policy—if airports were to charge significantly higher prices per landing at peak hours than at off-peak times, the arrivals could be evened out during the day and the amount of congestion at peak times could be reduced. Thus the time at which additional capacity would be needed would be delayed, assuming steady overall traffic growth per year.

Some countries have restrictions on what commodities a given licensed trucker can carry on the back haul. This means a greater number of empty or partially filled truck miles, and requires more truck miles to move a given volume of freight than would be the case without the restriction. The back-haul restriction also places a higher load on the highway and effectively reduces its capacity. Removing the restriction would enhance the road's capacity without adding new lanes.

Thus we see that certain rules and policies with respect to pricing, use of vehicles, or hours of operation often have the effect of reducing the capacity of an existing transport facility. Such rules and regulations abound in transportation in virtually all countries, largely because the provision of the right-of-way usually involved public funds. There was a natural disposition on the part of the public authorities to set certain terms and conditions of use. Nonetheless, such rules are frequently unduly restrictive or have become outmoded. In other ways they may reduce effective capacity, leading to demands for new investment to offset these effects, as the discussion of the ICC in chapter 4 indicated.

Looked at the other way around, any new investment will create less capacity than otherwise if there are constraints on its use. For any given or projected traffic volume, therefore, the amount of investment needed will be greater the more severe the policies.

Investments in infrastructure, which tend to be very large and which once made are committed in a locational sense, should therefore be made only after the possibilities of institutional, policy, or regulatory changes have been fully investigated. In addition, infrastructure investments should be considered after or concurrent with an analysis of equipment needs. It is often possible to increase the utilization of existing right-of-way for all modes by additional or improved equipment. The latter is generally low cost on a per unit basis, and the units are not irrevocably committed to a particular facility. If an error is made, such units can be used at other facilities or, in many cases, can be sold, since there often exists a ready second-hand market.

After the capacity-enhancing prospects of changes in policy and additions or improvements to equipment have been made or considered, new or upgraded rights-of-way may still be required, but the extent of such additions or upgrading may be less if full advantage is taken of the first two possibilities. These points are stressed here because they are often neglected in favor of more grandiose, visible, and politically appealing construction projects. The first problem is to identify areas where and when new capacity or specific transport projects may be needed. In the following chapters we will examine techniques of efficient project identification in transportation and discuss project appraisal, the more familiar benefit-cost analysis.

# Transportation Project Identification

## Introduction

Projects may be identified in a variety of ways. A regional or local political authority may decide that a new highway, railway line, waterway, port, or airport is desirable for its constituency because other constituencies have one or more of them. The increased employment associated with such relatively large-scale undertakings may appear very attractive, especially if the region has unduly high unemployment levels. Sometimes projects are identified on the basis of certain apparent "gaps" in the transportation network; the interests of symmetry may suggest particular transport projects; or sparsely settled regions may invite consideration of more transport infrastructure.

In the real world such political identification appears to be the primary source of projects. Indeed, grandiose projects, such as the one-time Canadian "roads to resources" program, are often concocted without much thought for the future traffic potential. Military or prestige considerations are often important, as in the U. S. National System of Interstate and Defense Highways or the SST project. Reinforced by the GTM, such projects are frequently implemented despite limited traffic prospects. National transportation investment "policy" becomes a hodgepodge, or shopping list, of a large number of politically inspired projects with little overall concern for their relationship to other investments in transportation elsewhere or among themselves. Less-costly alternatives are often not explored, with the result that excessive resources are devoted to transportation.

A better method of project identification is desirable. In this section an approach highlighting the derived-demand nature of transportation services will be outlined along with illustrations of its use in several developing countries. A simplified, broad outline of the approaches used in several comprehensive transportation studies will be made, but details of the computations and the large number of models and submodels will be omitted. The intent is mainly to provide the reader with a sense of the overall steps, data, and methods needed to perform such a systems analysis. The interested reader will find intriguing details and sophisticated analyses by examining the studies themselves.[1]

## A Comprehensive Approach to Transport Planning

At the outset, it will be useful to specify the end result to be obtained from a comprehensive planning approach. The aim is to deduce future traffic volumes between as many points within a nation as is feasible to distinguish. The whole economy is divided into zones, or nodes (or centroids), which are geographic regions containing at least one urban center. Traffic volumes are then projected in terms of tons of commodities and numbers of passengers, usually expressed as two-way flows for each internodal pair. Table 5.1 is an example of an internodal or nodal trade flow matrix (*NTFM*). Each $X_{ij}$ is the

TABLE 5.1

*Internodal Trade Flow Matrix 19xx*

| FROM ＼ TO | Zone 1 | Zone 2 | Zone 3 | . . . | Zone n |
|---|---|---|---|---|---|
| Zone 1 | $X_{11}$ | $X_{12}$ | $X_{13}$ | . . . | $X_{1n}$ |
| Zone 2 | $X_{21}$ | $X_{22}$ | $X_{23}$ | . . . | $X_{2n}$ |
| Zone 3 | $X_{31}$ | $X_{32}$ | $X_{33}$ | . . . | $X_{3n}$ |
| . | . | . | . | . | . |
| . | . | . | . | . | . |
| . | . | . | . | . | . |
| Zone n | $X_{n1}$ | $X_{n2}$ | $X_{n3}$ | . . . | $X_{nn}$ |

number of tons or passengers for a base year or for selected future years. Separate matrices are needed for goods and for passenger movements and for each of the years to be forecast, along with the base year. For example, $X_{32}$ might be the estimated annual tonnage moving from zone 3 to zone 2 in 1990, and $X_{23}$ the tonnage moving

---

1. Harvard University Transport Research Program, *An Analysis of Investment Alternatives in the Colombian Transport System* (Cambridge, 1968); D. Kresge and P. Roberts, *Techniques of Transport Planning*, vol. 2 (Washington, D. C.: The Brookings Institution, 1971); Arthur D. Little & Associated Consultants, *Southeast Asian Regional Transport Survey* (Manila: Asian Development Bank, 1972), referred to as RTS; G. Wilson, L. Orr, et al., *Regional Transport Survey for the Khmer Republic, Kingdom of Laos, and Republic of Vietnam* (Kuala Lumpur: Southeast Asian Agency for Transport and Communications (SEATAC), 1975), referred to as the Mini-RTS; The ADAR Corporation, *The Sudan Transport Study* (August 1975); *Estudio Centroamericano de Transporte, 1974–1976* (San Salvador, April 1977); Louis Berger, Inc., *Final Report of the Transportation Advance Planning Study* (October, 1972).

from zone 2 to zone 3. The sum of the two would be the total commodities load that the transport links between the two zones are expected to carry in 1990. Compare this load to the estimated capacity of the existing system between zones 2 and 3. A load-to-capacity ratio $\frac{L}{C}$ greater than one indicates that additional transport capacity of some kind may be desirable and may generate a "project" or set of alternative projects in the area to which further analysis may be directed for determination of feasibility and optimal choice. When each link is so examined for each year, it is possible to develop an efficient transportation investment program time-phased over the length of the planning period. Such a plan, of course, is not written in stone and needs to be constantly updated as various projections turn out differently or contingencies arise. Nevertheless, such an approach is a valuable and rational means to identify projects in the transportation sector. The crucial problem is how to obtain reasonable estimates of the $X_{ij}$. The issue of capacity estimation will be discussed more fully in chapter 6.[2]

The amount of traffic in the aggregate and between major nodes depends on the overall population and production of the whole economy as well as its regional (nodal) demographic, production, and distribution patterns. Thus to estimate $X_{ij}$ requires an overall appraisal and projection of the economy, sectoral output, regional production and consumption patterns, and exports and imports.

Since "consumption is the sole end and purpose of all production," as Adam Smith long ago noted,[3] the starting point must be an assessment of the number of people that an economy needs to provide for 10 to 20 years in the future. Population estimates are also needed to compute the probable future labor force, a necessary input for calculating future real output (GNP). In most countries such projections already exist under various assumptions regarding birth, death, fertility rates, and net migration. Where such projections do not exist, analysts must do the best they can with whatever information is available, especially in poor countries, where the current population figure is itself a rough estimate, depending on when the last census was taken and how thorough it was. Crude growth rates (e.g., 2 to 3 percent per year) can be used to determine future population totals, from which labor force estimates can be made on the basis of other information concerning the age and sex composition of the population

---

2. See chap. 2 for some conceptual and empirical problems in railroad and highway estimates of capacity.

3. Adam Smith, *An Inquiry Into the Nature and Causes of the Wealth of Nations*, Modern Library ed. (New York: Random House, 1937), p.625.

and labor force participation rates. Many alternative demographic models exist, the sophistication of which depends on the extent and reliability of past and present data. By whatever means they are gathered, estimates of total population and the labor force are a necessary beginning for a comprehensive transport study since they will influence the volume of production and consumption and hence the amount of goods and people that will need to be moved over the future transportation system. In addition, population, labor force, and production estimates need to be made for each region of the country that the analysis decides on. We will examine the problems involved in identifying economic regions later. The next step at the macro-economic or national level is to deduce future GNP and its major components.

## Developing a Macroeconomic Model

Since we are seeking to identify a set of national transport projects phased over time (i.e., a national transport investment program), we must provide estimates of the future growth of the overall economy by major aggregate components. As the Colombian (or Harvard) model put it, the macroeconomic model "must provide the transport model with estimates of the demands which will be placed upon the transport system and of the general economic conditions within which the system will operate."[4] More specifically, a macro model is needed to deduce the value of imports and exports (and their tonnage when divided by unit prices) in order to provide likely overall magnitudes and growth rates of specific sectors and thus a consistency check on growth rates of specific commodities. It is therefore necessary and customary to develop a macroeconomic model to make projections for the next 10 to 20 years. The standard simplified model is based on the major GNP components where $GNP = C + I + G + (X - M)$. Consumption $C$ is usually linearly related to GNP with a time lag. Depending on the availability and quality of the data, a relationship of the form $C_t = a + b(GNP)_{t-1}$ is often adequate, especially for relatively poor and simple economies. Investment $I$ may be estimated by some form of accelerator relationship plus some estimate of autonomous investment. Thus, $I_t = d(GNP_t - GNP_{t-1}) + I_a$. Where capital markets are reasonably well developed, an interest rate and other variables may also be included. Where the private sector is not the major source of national investment, government plans or the amount of investment "needed" to sustain a predetermined growth of GNP (along the lines

---

4. Harvard University Transport Research Program, p.42.

of the often misused incremental capital-output ratio) may be calculated.

Government noninvestment spending $G$ can be ascertained by examining past trends relative to GNP and future goals. Exports $X$ may be estimated by forecasting the growth of world demand for the major categories of exports from the country, while imports $M$ can be deduced from estimates of import propensities or "needs." A separate trade forecasting model is often used, which specifies the likely origin of particular import needs and destinations of major exports, as in the RTS and Harvard analyses.

Alternatively, a feasible or target overall growth rate of GNP can be determined (e.g., 5 to 6 percent per year), and the other components can be estimated on the basis of past ratios and trends therein. Again, since one has at this stage an estimate of the labor force for future years (or a set of high, low, and medium estimates), future GNP can be calculated by estimating present and future labor productivity and assuming some full employment–unemployment rate. Aggregate GNP can then be decomposed into its components on the basis of equations of the type noted above or other parameters.

However the estimates are done (and there is a wide variety of forecasting techniques), forecasts of production by major economic sectors are required. Where input-output tables exist, they are preferred. Where they do not (most poor countries do not have them and, even if they did, the coefficients would probably be unreliable guides to the future since the essence of economic development is to *change* those relationships, including input-output coefficients), alternative approaches have to be considered.

The RTS and the Mini-RTS examined the various productive sectors or "industrial origin of GNP" (or GDP) in value terms, in a series of special sector studies of particular concern to the countries of Southeast Asia. The overall results of these separate studies were then reconciled with the macro model forecasts to ensure consistency.

At this point, the research has estimates of value added by major commodity-producing sectors for a series of future years, usually at five-year intervals from some base year where the values are known, until the end of the projection time horizon, often 20 years beyond the base year. These value projections need to be converted into tonnage. One approach is to divide each of the industrial values by some "price" per ton where such information is available. Where the industrial or commodity producing sectors are finely divided, this approach can yield not unreasonable results.

Alternatively, or as a double check, projections of physical output can be made for the major commodities in each sector. For example, in agriculture estimates of tonnage can be made for the main crops by considering acreage planted and yields per acre. For poor countries, extensive data usually exist for major crops such as rice, cotton, bananas, and coffee, most of which are produced for export. The estimated growth of output in physical terms needs to be compared with the overall growth of value added and adjusted to ensure consistency. Indeed, one of the purposes of the macro projections in constant value terms is to provide a consistency check for the physical output projections of the major sectors.

We thus have national aggregate production estimates for major commodities and sectors in tonnage terms for the forecast years. To these must be added imports by commodity class in tonnage terms, these data made consistent with the import values deduced in the macro model.

It is now necessary to determine national consumption of each commodity produced and imported. If per capita consumption of commodity $k$ was $x$ metric tons in the base year, one could assume on the basis of past trends or future "needs" that it will rise or fall at a given rate per year and stabilize after a certain period of time. The per capita figures are then multiplied by the population estimates to obtain total consumption of the commodity.[5]

Alternatively, consumption can be estimated using income elasticities of demand. The overall growth rate in GNP can provide part of the needed data. Thus consumption of commodity $k$ in period $t$, or $C_{kt}$ is: $C_{kt} = C_{k0}[ 1 + \epsilon_y( \%\Delta Y)]$, where $C_{k0}$ is consumption of $k$ in the base period and $\epsilon_y$ is the income elasticity of $k = \dfrac{\%\Delta C_k}{\%\Delta Y}$. Similar estimates are made for each commodity and/or sector.

## Determination of Regions or Nodes

For transport purposes, national aggregates are not very helpful. What is needed is an estimate of internal commodity flows. Thus the country must be divided into distinct regions or nodes. Ideally, one would like to define economic regions, i.e., regions having distinct economic characteristics vis-à-vis other regions but with similar internal characteristics. While all nation-states have subdivisions (states, departments, provinces, etc.), they do not usually conform to any economic criteria. Indeed, few political boundaries either

---

5. For example, the RTS estimated that rice consumption in the (then) Republic of Viet Nam was .195 metric tons per capita in the base year. It was assumed that consumption would grow at 0.4 percent per year for five years and stabilize thereafter at .199 metric tons per capita. Total consumption for each forecast year was then estimated by multiplying the per capita consumption by the population estimates in each forecast year.

within or between nations make any economic sense. It is therefore necessary to compromise in determining nodes both in terms of the number of nodes to consider and in the boundaries of each node, especially since existing data on population, production, or consumption are based on provincial or political boundaries. The number of nodes to consider depends in part on the country, its size, and its regionally distinct features, as well as on the time and resources available for the analysis. The greater the number of nodes, the much greater the number of two-way internodal traffic flows to consider. The number of internodal pairs or links that need to be considered is $\frac{n!}{2(n-2)!}$, where $n$ is the number of nodes (four nodes give rise to six internodal links; 10 nodes generate 45 links; 20 nodes, 190 links). Intranodal homogeneity, internodal distinctiveness in economic terms, data availability, and budget must all be considered in determining the appropriate number of regional or nodal divisions. However, it needs to be emphasized that the smaller the number of nodes identified (or the larger the geographical area of each node), the greater will be the amount of intranodal traffic relative to total and vice versa. The diagonals of the *NTFM* will contain relatively large numbers and thus a large amount of traffic will escape the analysis. The opposite is true for a large number of nodes. The decision on the number of nodes to consider is thus largely judgmental and involves various trade-offs. The studies noted in footnote 1 used from 3 to over 100 separate nodes for particular countries. In any event, a node will usually consist of an aggregate of adjacent provinces or a single province, largely because of data availability on a provincial basis.

Each node must be described as fully as possible in terms of population, area, topography, major production of specific commodities, and, of course, the existing transportation network within the node and between it and each adjacent node. Our purpose is either to allocate the previously forecast total population and national production and consumption for each commodity to each node, or to build up the national totals (subject to the macro model consistency check) from specific forecasts of each node's population, production, and consumption of each commodity.

The nodal population projections start from each node's population in the base year. Then on the basis of assumed birth and death rates and future internal migratory patterns or goals, the population of each node is estimated. Neither this projection nor any other is free from judgment or easy. Specific checks for plausibility and feasibility of each projection, be it of population, specific commodity production, or consumption levels, are constantly required, and alternative assumptions for each need to be examined. Nodal production and consumption estimates by commodity can be made in a similar fashion as those at the national level.

## The Construction of Nodal Trade Flow Matrices

With estimates of production and consumption of each commodity in each node, there will be surpluses or deficits within each node for each commodity. The surpluses need to be routed. One study routed the surpluses in any commodity from the surplus node in that commodity to the nearest deficit node in the same commodity and continued to other deficit nodes until all deficits were met or the surplus was exhausted. A national surplus would be routed to the nearest port for export, and a national deficit would be remedied by imports through the port nearest the last remaining deficit node for the specific commodity. Other, more sophisticated ways of routing the surpluses are linear programming techniques designed to minimize transportation costs and gravity models. What technique is used depends on data availability, computer capability, time, and resources.

Briefly stated, the linear programming approach to least-cost routing of the surpluses to the deficit nodes for each commodity is to find that set of nonnegative flows ($T_{ij}$ = flows between nodes $i$ and $j$) between origins ($O_i$ = surplus sectors in a given commodity) and destinations ($D_j$ = deficit section in the particular commodity) that minimizes transport costs and at the same time fulfils the "requirements" at $D_j$. The model takes the form

$$\text{Min. } C = \sum_i \sum_j T_{ij} C_{ij},$$

where $C$ = total transport costs and $C_{ij}$ = the marginal cost to transport a given commodity between nodes $i$ and $j$; and subject to the following constraints

$$\sum_i^m T_{ij} = D_j, \text{ where } j = 1, 2, \ldots, n$$

$$\sum_j^n T_{ij} = O_i, \text{ where } i = 1, 2, \ldots, m$$

$$\sum_i O_i = \sum_j D_j, \text{ for all } i \text{ and } j$$

$$T_{ij} \geq 0, \text{ for all } i \text{ and } j$$

In routing the surpluses and deficits in a minimum marginal cost pattern, the foregoing represents the optimal flows for homogeneous commodities under perfect competition.[6]

---

6. A. Scott, "An Introduction to Spatial Allocation Analysis," *Association of American Geographers, Resource Paper* no. 9, 1971, p.2.

A gravity model has also been used frequently in determining interregional commodity flows. This model takes as given the surpluses and deficits by node and seeks to replicate past internodal flows. It is then used to predict future flows with empirically derived constants on the basis of changes in the independent variables (i.e., surplus and deficit). The model often takes the general form

$$T_{ij} = K \frac{Y_i^\alpha Y_j^\beta}{C_{ij}^\gamma},$$

where $Y_{i,j}$ represent "attraction factors" such as nodal income or population; $C_{ij}$ is, as before, the cost or impedance factor; and $K$, $\alpha$, $\beta$, and $\gamma$ are empirically derived from past data.[7]

This model does not guarantee that the generated flows actually add up to the total requirements of the deficit sectors, as does the linear programming approach. Some recent investigations indicate that this version of the gravity model is a relatively poor predictor of internodal traffic flows compared to cost-minimization models.[8] In general, though, it appears that "a pattern of commodity flows that is well explained by one model is also well explained by the other . . . when the number of supply and demand regions is limited."[9] For different kinds of commodities, the results of the two models appear to differ somewhat—at least in one experiment designed to evaluate them.[10] However, as Gordon notes, the gravity model suitably constrained can "generate a trading pattern which approximates closely to the linear programming solution."[11] Thus the choice in practice would seem to rest on the kind and quality of data available and the extent to which it is desirable to maintain past interregional trade patterns or to modify them in conformity with least-cost criteria.

In any event, the surpluses and deficits for each commodity give rise to a series of commodity flows between nodes. To take a simple example, assume four nodes or regions and the production and consumption of a particular commodity in a particular forecast year as shown

---

7. Other versions of the model are possible. The selection depends on availability of data and goodness of fit.

8. J. Hartwick, "The Gravity Hypothesis and Transportation Cost Minimization," *Regional and Urban Economics*, vol.2, no.3, 1972. See also I. Gordon, "The Gravity Hypothesis and Transportation Cost Minimization," *Regional and Urban Economics*, vol. 4, 1974, for an attempt to improve the gravity model in this connection.

9. K. Mera, Appendix A, "An Evaluation of Gravity and Linear Programming Models for Predicting Interregional Commodity Flows," in J. Meyer and M. Straszheim, *Techniques of Transport Planning*, vol. I: *Pricing and Project Evaluation* (Washington, D. C.: The Brookings Institution, 1971), p.302.

10. Ibid., pp.304ff.

11. Gordon, p.8.

TABLE 5.2

| Node | Production | Consumption | Deficit or Surplus |
|------|-----------|-------------|--------------------|
|      | *(thousands of metric tons)* | | |
| 1 | 200 | 600 | −400 |
| 2 | 400 | 250 | +150 |
| 3 | 300 | 500 | −200 |
| 4 | 800 | 300 | +500 |

in Table 5.2. Node 1 "needs" 400,000 MT. If it is cheaper to ship from node 2, then 150,000 MT will move from node 2 to node 1, exhausting the surplus at node 2. The remaining 250,000 MT will move from node 4 to node 1. Node 4 will also ship 200,000 MT to node 3 to cover its deficit, leaving node 4 with a surplus of 50,000 MT, which will be exported. The resultant traffic movement in this commodity will be:

node 2 → node 1 = 150,000 MT

node 4 → node 1 = 250,000 MT

node 4 → node 3 = 200,000 MT

If node 2 lies between nodes 1 and 4, the shipment from node 4 to node 1 will also give rise to a movement through node 2 and hence between node 2 and node 1 of 250,000 MT, which need to be added to the movement node 2 → node 1. If the 50,000 MT surplus in node 4 needs to be shipped through a port that exists in node 3, it must be added to the internodal movement between node 4 and node 3. Thus total internodal movements of this commodity are:

node 2 → node 1 = 400,000 MT

node 4 → node 1 = 250,000 MT

node 4 → node 3 = 250,000 MT

The internodal flows will differ if the port is located in another node and if node 3, not node 2, lies between nodes 1 and 4. Obviously, if there are many nodes, the routing pattern can take various forms and thus impose different loads on particular internodal links. For each commodity, similar procedures are followed. The movements are then aggregated to obtain the internodal trade flow matrices for each of the forecast years and will take the form shown on p.283 above.

Two-way flows between each nodal pair may then be derived by adding $X_{ij}$, $X_{ji}$, and the through traffic. We thus have a set of internodal trade flows for the base year and each forecast year in terms of tonnage. Such tonnages then need to be allocated over the various existing internodal links. That is, between any pair of nodes there will frequently exist one or more highways, a railway, and/or a waterway or air connection. It is essential to determine the anticipated load on each of the links in order to develop load-to-capacity ratios or to deduce the changing costs over each connection in response to rising traffic.

There are various techniques for link loading. Let us examine the situation where one highway and one railway connect two nodes. Suppose we have estimated that a total of $X$ MT will move between the nodes. How much would be expected to move by rail and how much by highway? One approach to link loading or modal split analysis is to extrapolate past trends, if they have been fairly definite or stable and where data exist to establish such trends. Thus, if the rail share is decreasing relative to truck at a specified rate, we may simply assume the trend will continue unless there are reasons to believe it would not. For relatively short periods, say, five years, this projection might be reasonable, but for longer periods it might be questionable. One might specify that after, say, five years, the modal split would stabilize, but this is highly conjectural without specific reasons to expect it.

An alternative is to determine the costs of transportation for each commodity by road and by rail. This determination requires some information about their respective cost functions—or at least unit costs—as well as some estimates of the service qualities. Since these data will vary with the quality of the road and rail links, vehicle type, etc., a detailed description of each is required (e.g., four-lane, paved highway through mountainous or flat terrain, etc.; two- or ten-ton truck, etc.). Some studies seek to "rate" particular links in terms of waiting time, link travel time, travel time variability, probability of shipment loss or damage, freight cost or charge per ton. The costs of each can be estimated, and the links can be ranked accordingly.[12] These costs will, of course, vary with the commodity. We can see from our analysis of costs and cost functions in chapter 2 that none of these calculations are easy nor can they be done with a high degree of confidence regardless of the quantity and quality of the data. Nor is the calculation of the value-of-service quality differences between rail and truck any easier. Indeed, as noted in the last part of chapter 1, such quantification is highly subjective and variable—indeed, shipper-specific. Thus, this approach, which is obviously better than mere extrapolation, requires a range of data and judgments that may preclude its application except on a partial and subjective basis. However, it is in this area that elaborate engineering—economic simulation models of rail, truck, port, pipeline, internodal transfer—has been developed.[13]

---

12. See Kresge and Roberts, pp.48–55.

13. For some details, see Kresge and Roberts, Appendixes A, B, and C; and the various Working Papers from the Economics Department of the International Bank for Reconstruction and Development (IBRD), Washington, D. C.

Their data requirements are extensive, and many of the relationships are questionable, but they hold out substantial promise when used with care. In any event, data permitting, least-cost routing assignments can be made for each commodity and the respective total loads on each link can be determined.

We have now estimated or simulated total goods flows between and through each nodal pair for the entire nation for the base year and each of the forecast years and over each existing link.

### Estimating Internodal Passenger Traffic

Estimating internodal freight represents a prodigious amount of time and effort and frequently accounts for the overwhelming proportion of the total study budget. Yet, in terms of traffic (e.g., vehicle movements), internodal freight does not account for the major part of highway traffic, which is heavily concentrated in passenger car and bus traffic. In many countries, rail passenger traffic still constitutes a large portion of total rail business. This is less true of water movement, but obviously true for air transport. In short, all the previous efforts at analytical rigor, logical consistency, simulation, and data development provide little insight into what is often the major traffic movement.

Internodal movements of passengers are less directly linked to production and consumption patterns than are commodity movements. Indeed, the complex motivations in intercity passenger travel defy simplistic attempts at relating such travel to strictly economic variables. Most attempts at estimation use some form of gravity model where the number of passengers moving between nodes $i$ and $j$ is positively dependent on some "attraction" variables (e.g., population or income in the respective nodes) and inversely related to some "impedance" factor (e.g., distance, cost of travel, travel time).[14] For most developing countries (and many developed nations), data adequate to calibrate any of the several forms such a model may take are nonexistent. Indeed, it is often difficult to obtain estimates of base year internodal passenger movements. Where there is a rail link, rail passenger traffic between particular nodes can, often with some effort, be estimated. Highway passenger traffic presents serious estimation problems. Occasionally, traffic counts are available from specific points along the right-of-way. If broken down by vehicle type (truck, bus, car), it is possible—but hazardous—to build these counts up to

---

14. For a brief outline, see J. Meyer and M. Straszheim, *Techniques of Transport Planning*, vol. I: *Pricing and Project Evaluation* (Washington, D.C.: The Brookings Institution, 1971), chap. 9.

annual passenger movements by certain assumptions regarding the average number of occupants per vehicle. Account needs to be taken of seasonality when annual totals are being estimated. Commercial bus companies can provide useful information as well. But for most developing countries, passenger travel estimation does not have a very solid or reliable data base.

Because of the lack of much past data to calibrate a gravity model, recourse must be had to traffic counts or surveys for highway travel. Data on air travel are easier to come by as domestic airlines usually keep information on number of passengers enplaning and deplaning at each point. Rail passenger information can be recast into internodal flows as noted above. Thus, the annual total estimates are generally very tenuous even for the base year, largely because of the frailty of highway passenger data. However, from this point, one can derive at least an estimate for the base year.

Projections from the base year are closely bound up with internodal population and/or income projections by node. Since passenger traffic usually rises faster than either population or income, its growth from the base year annual total estimate may be expected to be one or two percent higher than the projected population or income growth. The exact amount is difficult to estimate unless some prior trends have been determined, and a range of growth rates may be desirable, say, between 4 and 8 percent per year. This range is not very satisfactory and suggests the need for ongoing traffic counts to obtain more accuracy. Indeed, one of the positive benefits of attempting an overall systems analysis, including both freight and passenger traffic, is to pinpoint the kinds of data gaps that are important to fill, which should then lead to a future research program of specific data collection needs and analysis.

However the estimates are made, at this point the analysis has aggregate annual internodal passenger movements. These need to be assigned to each of the specific internodal links in a fashion similar to that used with the internodal commodity movements (i.e., on the basis of costs and performance characteristics of the various modes and/or projections of past modal shares). With this set of information on hand, we need to compare the passenger-plus-freight loadings with the capacity of each internodal link to derive load-to-capacity ratios.

## The Calculation of Capacity

Tenuous as much of the data and the interrelationships of nodal traffic are, the most problematical set of estimates concerns the measurement of rail, highway, and port capacity. In chapter 2 we noted the set of variables that can influence what may be termed "practical" capacity and the problems involved in attempting to express capacity in economic as well as quantitative terms. These caveats need to be kept in mind. In what follows, we will summarize some approaches or rules-of-thumb that have been adopted to obtain some quantitative expression for the "capacity" of particular modal infrastructures.

Let it be recalled, however, that in economic terms capacity refers to that degree of utilization of an asset (rail line, highway segment) beyond which unit costs begin to rise more or less rapidly (i.e., the segment becomes "congested," and that reduces average speed with consequent higher unit costs per ton, ton-mile, or vehicle-mile). A capacity constraint specified as, say, one million tons per mile of track or route per year does not mean that no more than one million tons can physically be moved across that link. Rather, it means that more than that quantity can be moved only at higher unit cost for each traffic unit per period. If this point can be ascertained, then an increase in the capacity may be called for if the reduction in operating costs so occasioned exceeds the cost of the incremental capacity. This latter set of calculations constitutes benefit-cost analysis, which will be discussed in chapter 6.

## Rail Capacity

The usual estimates of rail capacity refer to line-haul capacity and assume that motive power (engines) and rolling stock are available. Problems of yard capacity are generally ignored. The capacity estimates thus assume a certain number of trains per day, average number of cars per train, and average load per car. Thus the RTS, using a prior ECAFE study relevant to single-line, meter gauge rail, assumed a theoretical capacity of such a line of 60 trains per day and 20 cars per train, with an average load of 10 tons per car.[15] Assuming such theoretical operations each day of the year yields an annual capacity of 4.38 million MT per year.

If there are no breakdowns and bad weather, if traffic is available and maintenance is adequate, this figure is a sort of upper bound to what might conceivably be carried under the best of circumstances. Only the Thai railroads came close to this level of tonnage over the internodal rail links examined.[16] The average capacity experienced was well below 50 percent. Other illustrations of rail capacity estimates are given in chapter 2 (pp.86–90), along with a discussion of measurement problems and the meaning of such measures. Despite all

15. Economic Commission for Asia and the Far East (ECAFE), *Introduction to Transport Planning* (New York: United Nations, 1967).
16. RTS, Book Two, Part One, p.167.

these difficulties, it is important to obtain some sense of the capacity of each particular rail internodal link in terms of tonnage, from which load-to-capacity ratios for the several forecast years may be derived. A ratio approaching or exceeding unity indicates a "project" in the sense that, for the particular internodal link, more rail or other capacity may be justifiable, or some industrial relocation may be necessary. This is the problem posed for benefit-cost analysis.

## Highway Capacity

The calculation of highway capacity encounters problems similar to those of rail capacity estimation. In addition to all of these difficulties, highway capacity is further affected by the traffic mix, average speed of the total vehicle flow, variation in total traffic per hour, day, etc., and different service levels, as noted in chapter 2 (pp.98–99). However, some empirically derived estimates of highway capacity were developed by the Highway Research Board in the early to mid-1960s.[17] For highways of different type and design (e.g., two, three, four, or more lanes; asphalt surface; etc.), measures of capacity were developed for various service levels (e.g., average speed) and lane widths, along with considerations of "obstructions" at different distances from the lane edge. Adjustment factors for terrain and different traffic compositions (e.g., share of trucks and buses of total traffic) were also derived.

The following will illustrate the use of the *Manual* and provide more insight into the notion of highway capacity. Assume a particular service level. For example, level E for a two-lane, paved highway is described in the *Manual* as a level of service where "operating speeds will usually be in the neighborhood of 30 m.p.h. but may vary considerably."[18] Under these conditions, the basic capacity is $C = 2,000 \ W_c T_c B_c$, where $C =$ capacity defined as mixed vehicles per hour, total in both directions; $W_c =$ an adjustment factor ($0 < W_c \leq 1$) for lane width and lateral clearance; $T_c, B_c =$ adjustment factors for the proportion of trucks and buses, respectively, in the traffic consist *and* in terms of passenger car equivalents (*pce*). More specifically, $T_c = \dfrac{100}{100 - P_T + P_T \ (pce_T)}$ and $B_c = \dfrac{100}{100 - P_B + P_B \ (pce_B)}$, where $P_T =$ percent of traffic that is truck, and $P_B =$ percent of traffic that is bus.

Essentially, $W_c$, $T_c$, and $B_c$ scale down the maximum uninterrupted flow of 2,000 passenger car units per hour because of width and clearance restrictions and the presence of trucks and buses in varying

17. Highway Research Board, *Highway Capacity Manual*, Special Report 87 (Washington, D. C., 1965).
18. Ibid., p.300.

proportions. Note that the higher $P_T$ or $P_B$ and *pces* are, the smaller is $T_c$ or $B_c$, and vice versa. The *pces* also vary with the nature of the terrain. For example, the *Manual* estimates that for service level E the truck *pce* on level terrain is 3, on rolling terrain 5, and on mountainous terrain 12.[19]

The above capacity equation refers to number of vehicles per hour. To convert to average daily traffic *ADT*, one does not multiply by 24. In fact, from U.S. experience:

When highway capacity is expressed in number of vehicles per hour, this should not be interpreted as meaning that the annual average daily traffic would be 24 times the design value for hourly traffic. Traffic volumes are much heavier during certain hours of the day and during certain periods of the year. . . . It has been found that approximately 15% of the annual average daily traffic would equal the volume observed during the 30th highest hour for rural locations.[20]

The volume of *ADT* observed during the thirtieth-highest hour is viewed as the design hourly volume and is lower than the maximum capacity noted in the above formula for *C*. To convert it into "practical" *ADT*, the calculated *C* is multiplied by 6.67 $\left(\text{or } \dfrac{1}{.15}\right)$, in accordance with U. S. experience.

To illustrate the use of this method, the mini-RTS identified a particular internodal highway link in one of the Southeast Asian nations as a two-lane, relatively smooth asphalt highway with nine-foot lanes, having numerous obstructions on both sides. From the relevant table in the *Manual* for service level E, $W_c$ is estimated at .58. Traffic surveys over the links indicated that 24 percent of the vehicles were trucks and 30 percent were buses, and that these proportions were expected to persist. The terrain was level—hence $pce_T$ was estimated as 3 and $pce_B$ as 2. Capacity (per hour) was thus

$$C = 2000(.58) \left[\frac{100}{100 - 24 + 3\,(24)}\right] \left[\frac{100}{100 - 30 + 2\,(30)}\right] = 603.$$

To convert to *ADT*, multiply by 6.67; the estimate of capacity of this particular link is 4,022 *ADT*. For each highway internodal link, similar calculations need to be made.

### Load-to-Capacity Ratios

Since we previously assigned passenger and freight traffic to each railway and highway link, as well as to water and air where such

---

19. Ibid., Table 10, 9a, p.304.
20. L. J. Ritter, Jr., and R. J. Paquette, *Highway Engineering*, 3d ed. (New York: Ronald Press, 1967), pp.126–27.

links exist, it is now a simple matter to calculate load-to-capacity ratios. Suppose for railways the practical capacity of a particular link was estimated as 1 million tons. Actual traffic in the base year was estimated as 1 million persons and 500,000 tons of freight. Assume that passenger and freight traffic are each expected to grow by 5 percent per year. If one passenger is assumed to be "equivalent" to .25 tons (in terms of cost occasioned), base year traffic is therefore equivalent to 750,000 tons. At 5 percent growth, the load-to-capacity ratio will equal or exceed unity between the fifth and sixth year from the base year.[21] If we accept the many assumptions underlying such calculations and assume a two-year construction lead time, a feasibility study of an expansion of rail capacity might be scheduled some four years after the base year, allowing one year for the study.

Similar types of calculations can be applied to highways. One needs to convert number of passengers and tons into *ADT* by observing the average number of passengers per car and bus and the average tonnage per truck. Where the vehicle fleet is heterogeneous, we need to calculate average loads for a large number of different vehicles as well as the proportion of each type of vehicle expected to use the particular link. In this manner the projected *ADT* may be compared with the capacity estimates. A similar approach may be applied to seaports, inland waterways, and airports.[22]

When this procedure is done for each link, we have a set of "projects" in the sense that capacity will become a constraining force on further traffic growth for particular links at various dates within the planning time horizon. This then establishes specific geographic regions or points that may need more capacity, rerouting of some traffic to less congested links (via pricing or tariff changes, for example), or some relocation of industry. The various alternatives at each location may then be subjected to benefit-cost analysis to determine the preferred option. In this way, an efficient program of transportation investments can be scheduled year by year.

## Conclusion

There are, of course, many difficulties and problems involved in the preceding approach. Indeed, there are many alternative approaches, such as that of the Harvard model, which involves feedbacks *from* the transport system *to* the whole economy rather than the other way around. Improved cost models for particular modes may be able to

---

21. That is, $750,000 \ (1.05)^5 \cong 960,000$, and $750,000(1.05)^6 \cong 1,005,000$.
22. For some details, see RTS.

determine the point beyond which increased volume of traffic over an existing facility will begin to raise unit production costs. This would preclude use of the rather crude approaches to capacity estimation noted above. In addition, the above approach routinely transports nodal surpluses of specific commodities to deficit nodes or exports. No price effect was considered. Yet in nodes containing surpluses, one might expect prices of such commodities to fall, causing adjustments in output such that most of the surplus will be eliminated. This is especially important in the agricultural sector for items such as fresh fruits and vegetables.[23]

In all the many different approaches, the key estimates involve the nodal or internodal trade flow matrices, the link loading procedures, and the apparent shipper costs. The approach that is finally adopted must be tailored to the existing data base and whatever new data can be easily obtained (e.g., from sample surveys, traffic counts). None of it is easy. Judgment is required at every step. Yet imperfect as this procedure is, it is more logical than the political approach so much in evidence in all countries when it comes to large-scale transportation investment. It is potentially capable of effecting substantial savings in investment in the transport sector by attempting to tailor capacity expansion to evolving traffic needs. Furthermore, as the data base is expanded and improved in quality, there will be better knowledge of the interrelationships between transportation and the rest of the economy. The sensitivity of the results to specific assumptions and relationships can be tested to determine which ones require more information and analysis. Viewed as an ongoing process, the approach has great promise, especially for the poorer countries.

Let us assume that a set of "projects" has been ascertained by the above approach or some other. Each project then needs to be analyzed to determine its feasibility in economic terms. The next chapter examines the usual method of such evaluation, namely, benefit-cost analysis.

---

23. The mini-RTS in fact did not route such commodities.

# Benefit-Cost Analysis

## Introduction

All investments in relatively durable assets yield, or are expected to yield, a stream of net benefits or net profits, over a period of future time. Indeed, in the private sector, the expected net profitability of an investment in new plant or equipment is what causes it to occur. In the private sector, such investments are usually made to produce commodities or services that have a market price. The benefits, as perceived by the "investor," are merely the expected net revenues per period arising from the new asset. In the case of public investments, the goods or services generated by the asset are normally not sold in markets for a market-determined price even though user charges in one form or another may be collected.

Nevertheless, the general form of the private investment criteria is readily applied to public investment even though the ingredients may differ. Thus in the private sector, an investment in new plant or equipment may be said to be economically feasible whenever the present value of its net expected future receipts exceeds the present value of its costs. A similar criterion may be applied to public investments, except that "net expected future receipts" is replaced by "net expected future social benefits" in cases where the output is not marketed or does not have a market-determined price.

Thus social benefit-cost analysis involves a quantitative estimate of future benefits $b_t$ (regional, national, or local, depending on the scale of the project), from which are to be deducted any future incremental costs $c_t$ associated with obtaining such benefits. The present value of such net future expected benefits, $b_t - c_t$, is determined by discounting with an appropriate interest rate $r$, sometimes referred to as the social rate of discount. The figure so derived is then compared with the cost of the investment being evaluated $k_t$, where the time required to construct or improve the asset is normally much shorter than the time-span over which net benefits are expected to be reaped (e.g., often 2 to 4 years for the former, compared with 20 or more years for the latter for many forms of public transportation investment).

The usual format for such comparisons is

$$\sum_{t=1}^{n_1} \frac{b_t - c_t}{(1+r)^t} - \sum_{t=1}^{n_2} \frac{k_t}{(1+r)^t} \gtrless 0,$$

where $n_1 > n_2$, the first summation is the present value of the net future benefits, and the second summation is the present value of the net future capital costs. If the difference between the two is positive, the project is said to be economically feasible—the benefits exceed the costs in the present-value sense. Conversely, if the difference is zero or negative, the project is said to be marginal or not economically feasible.

## Evaluation of a "Single" Project

Suppose that the results of the link loading exercise outlined in chapter 5 lead to an expected $L/C$ ratio greater than one in some immediate future year over a particular highway, thereby implying that an expansion of highway capacity between the two nodes may be "feasible" in the above sense. Assume also that all other alternatives (such as more rail capacity) and policies designed to reroute traffic have been ruled out. The expansion of highway capacity then takes on the attributes of a "single" project to be evaluated. In reality there are many alternatives even in this simple case involving questions such as how to expand the highway capacity: reduce the curvature or gradients, expand the number of lanes or shoulder width, eliminate obstructions along the roadside, improve the surface, or any combination of the above? Suppose we select one of the numerous alternatives and wish to examine its economic feasibility. The important ingredients in public investment criteria are the variables $b_t$, $c_t$, $r$, and $k_t$.

### Benefits ($b_t$)

The usual benefits considered in a transportation project involving improvements in the right-of-way or other basic facilities, vehicles, or rolling stock and/or equipment are reduced operating costs, time savings, and reduced accidents and damage. Increased comfort and convenience for passengers are also considered from time to time. It is not easy to evaluate time savings, accident reduction, or passenger comfort in pecuniary terms, although it is possible to do so using careful judgment.[1] For many transportation projects, savings in vehicle operating cost will be more important for justifying new invest-

---

1. For a useful, nontechnical discussion, see H. A. Adler, *Economic Appraisal of Transportation Projects* (Bloomington: Indiana University Press, 1971), pp.22ff.

ments along the existing transport network since such savings represent the release of resources that can be used to produce more capital equipment elsewhere in the economy, assuming that they are or will be productively invested.

The estimation of such savings normally involves a comparison of operating costs with and without the project. Frequently, such cost savings are deduced on a ton-mile, passenger-mile basis, or vehicle-mile basis. There are no incremental costs $c_t$ to deduct from such savings except in cases where the increased use occasioned by the user savings may augment pollution or involve certain external costs. Thus $b_t$ represents net benefits in most cases when improvements to existing highways, railways, waterways, and canals are being considered. The technique in these instances is relatively straightforward, namely, deduce the operating cost per service unit that can be expected to prevail now and in the future *without* the project and from this, for each year, deduct the operating costs expected to prevail *with* the project. If traffic is expected to increase, as is normally the case, present operating costs will tend to increase *without* the project, so that the unit cost savings $b_t$ will rise over time.

When such unit cost savings are multiplied by the expected future traffic, in terms of the relevant service units, total savings per year are readily deduced over the expected economic life of the project. When suitably discounted by the social rate of discount, the present value of the stream of benefits is determined and needs to be compared with the costs $k_t$ of constructing the project.

Where competitive links exist (e.g., highway, railway, waterway, coastal), the decision on which—if any—to expand requires not only computations analogous to those just mentioned but a careful appraisal of likely traffic shifts from one mode to another and rate and service responses of the users of the link not experiencing improvement. In some cases, it may prove economically desirable to expand the capacity of more than one of the links as long as the benefits vis-à-vis costs exceed those of alternative uses of public funds.

The vehicle operating cost savings approach is shown graphically in Figure 6.1. Along the existing right-of-way, unit costs $OC_1$ are constant up to a traffic volume equal to $OT_2$, beyond which they increase along $AC_1$. Marginal costs increase along $MC_1$ (i.e., "congestion" occurs beyond $OT_2$). Assume demand in the base period is $D_1$ and $OC_1$ includes an efficient user charge. Thus traffic in the base period will equal $OT_1$, and the net social benefits will equal the triangular area designated $B$ (the net consumers' surplus). Suppose we then consider a "project" designed to improve the internodal link. Such an improvement is estimated to reduce unit operating costs to $OC_2$. What are its benefits? Assuming demand per period to remain $D_1$, the increase in net consumers' surplus will be the rectangle $C_2C_1C_1G$ (the vehicle operating cost savings multiplied by the existing traffic or $(OC_1 - OC_2)T_1$) plus $GC_1F$ (the net increase in consumers' surplus

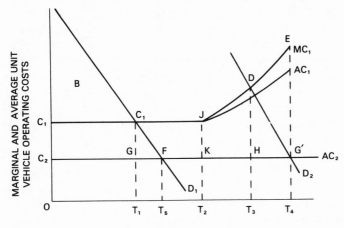

Fig. 6-1                    TRAFFIC VOLUME

due to generated traffic, which equals $\frac{1}{2}(OC_1 - OC_2)(T_5 - T_1)$ for the linear demand $D_1$). Define this total area as $b_t$. If $D_1$ remains constant, the present value of the net social benefits is equal to $\sum\limits_{t=1}^{n}$ $\frac{b_t}{(1+r)^t}$, where $b_t$ is the same in each future period.[2]

However, $D_1$ is unlikely to remain constant, given the assumptions of rising real GNP and population made in chapter 5. Suppose, then, in period 2, demand shifted to $D_2$. "Benefits" in period 2 would then equal $(OC_1 - OC_2)T_3 + JKG'E$, which clearly exceeds $b_1$, and similarly for successive outward shifts of $D_i$ associated with the growth of

---

2. If $b_t$ is assumed to be constant, this summation becomes a form of an annuity whose present value is $(1+r)^n - 1 \div r(1+r)^n$. If $r = 10$ percent and $n = 10$ periods, the present value of a constant $b = \$1$ million per period is $\$6.145$ million. (A particularly useful set of tables for compounding and discounting has been produced by the World Bank. See J. P. Gittinger, ed., *Compounding and Discounting Tables for Project Evaluation*, EDI Teaching Materials Series no. 1 [Washington, D. C.: Economic Development Institute, International Bank for Reconstruction and Development, 1973].) If the present value of the construction costs is less than $\$6.145$ million, the project would be deemed "economically feasible." This does not mean it is optimal, because for a similar investment cost in another project, net benefits may exceed $\$6.145$ million, in which case the other project is to be preferred. All we can say in the present case is that this single project is feasible.

population and output forecast in the process of project identification. For each year, then, $b_{t+1} > b_t$ and its present value must be deduced and summed. It should be stressed that the with-and-without approach will substantially underestimate benefits if it is assumed that unit costs without the project remain constant at $OC_1$. It is critical, then, to develop cost models that show the traffic volumes beyond which unit costs begin to rise, the vexing problem of capacity once again.

In addition to vehicle operating cost savings as a measure of benefit, certain other benefits such as reductions in accidents or damage or the value of the time savings for passengers may be included. Although their pecuniary values are far more difficult to compute than vehicle operating cost savings, estimates are frequently made, and they raise the benefits by varying amounts. In principle, they are simply added to vehicle operating cost savings to obtain total benefits per period of $b_t$.

An alternative way of making the determination of economic feasibility is to deduce what is referred to as "the internal rate of return" (*IRR*), which is defined as the rate of discount $d$ that makes the present value of the expected net benefits equal to the cost of the asset. Assume the present value of the cost of the asset equals $C$. The *IRR* involves calculating $d$ such that $\sum_{t=1}^{n} \frac{b_t - c_t}{(1+d)^t} = C$. If $d > r$ (the social rate of discount), the project is said to be feasible; if $d < r$ it is not. Note that this statement is formally identical with the net present value (*NPV*) criterion, since $NPV > C$ implies $d > r$, and vice versa. For example, for $NPV > C$ we have

$$\sum_{t=1}^{n} \frac{b_t - c_t}{(1+r)^t} > \sum_{t=1}^{n} \frac{b_t - c_t}{(1+d)^t},$$

where the first summation is *NPV* and the second equals $C$ from the previous equation. Since the only differing terms are $r$ and $d$, *NPV* can exceed $C$ only if $d > r$. Similarly, $NPV < C$ requires that $d < r$.[3]

Some analysts prefer the use of the *IRR* because it seems easier to grasp a concept of "rate of return" than a dollar aggregate referred to as net present value. It also reduces the extent of reliance on a precise estimate of the social rate of discount $r$. As we discuss below, the calculation of $r$ is beset with many conceptual and empirical problems, some of which are avoided in the *IRR* calculation. However, some notion of the relative magnitude of $r$ is essential to contrast with $d$,

---

3. Some difficulties or discrepancies between the *NPV* and *IRR* approaches emerge in ranking projects or alternatives. These are discussed below. For a single project, the two approaches yield the same results regarding feasibility.

the *IRR*. The same projections of traffic and operating savings are required for each method, and for a single project each yields the same result in terms of feasibility. Note also that the benefits measure is really a measure of the change in consumers' surplus whatever the specific ingredients used in the calculation.

## THE NATIONAL INCOME OR REGIONAL VALUE-ADDED APPROACH

When a project involves a totally new transport facility in a region hitherto largely inaccessible (e.g., feeder or penetration roads), the operating cost savings approach is inapplicable because there were no previous operating costs or traffic. Thus, it is not possible to compute the change in consumers' surplus. The cost savings approach applies only to an existing transportation link. Many transportation invest-ments—especially in poor countries—involve opening up remote re-gions. Thus "benefits" must be calculated differently. Indeed, the lack of generality of the cost savings approach suggests that some alterna-tive calculation is more relevant not only to a wholly new link but also with regard to existing links. One such approach has been termed the "national income" method, or the expected increase in national or regional output arising from the new investment.

Assume an improvement in any productive process (e.g., a better highway or rail connection, or some innovation) that will permit the same amount of resources to produce a greater output per time period. If the increased output $\Delta Q$ is valued at prices prevailing before the improvement, the increased value of output is $P_1 \Delta Q$. It may be used as the measure of benefits for this and subsequent periods, to which may be applied the *NPV* or *IRR* approaches discussed above.

If the demand per period is $Q_D = 100 - P$ and the initial price = unit costs of production = \$40, then 60 units of the commodity per period will be produced and sold. Assume that an improvement in efficiency leads to a \$20 decrease in the unit cost of production and a corresponding price reduction. The output and sales will then rise to 80 units, an increase of 20 units. At the earlier price, the increase in value of output will be \$800, assuming the same amounts of resources are used. If more resources are used, the net increase in value added will be lower because these resources would be shifted from other employment and production there would decrease.

We can compare the \$800 increase in national or regional income with the calculation of the change in consumers' surplus using the same data. The consumers' surplus increase will be the original quan-tity bought (60 units) multiplied by the unit cost savings (\$20) plus one-half the benefits of the "generated" demand or traffic (to use transport terminology), or $\frac{1}{2}(20 \times \$20)$. The total change in consumers' surplus is then $1,400—quite a different figure from the national income approach. Part of the difference is explained by the elasticity of demand[4] and part by valuing the increased output at the price before the improvement. In reality, since the two approaches measure different things, there is "no reason to suppose that any alteration in an economy that leads to a change in national income will lead to a change of equal magnitude in consumers' surplus."[5]

For relatively small investments in transportation or elsewhere, the consumers' surplus approach may yield results akin to the national income approach, although only under some fairly restrictive assumptions.[6] For large investments, however, the changes in production or national income may fail to be captured accurately by estimates of transportation cost savings. Productive relations, relative prices, and increases in resources hitherto idle or unemployed may all emerge from a relatively large transport investment. Indeed, as we later suggest, such large transport investments may affect attitudes or may stimulate more market-oriented activities that influence the production of a large range of goods and services, not merely those expected to use the transport facility.[7] This is especially true in the case of feeder or penetration roads.[8] The logic of the national income approach is preferred to that of consumers' surplus because it treats changes in real income or output associated with transport investments, which are the primary aim of such investments, especially in poorer countries or regions. However, the data requirements of this approach are more substantial. In addition, since regional or national output growth requires more than transport investment (e.g., clearing the land or the application of other capital inputs, such as irrigation, in the case of agricultural development), it is erroneous to attribute the increase in output solely to transport. What we have is a package of investments of which transport is only a part. There is no logical way to

---

4. As a simple test, the reader should verify that if $Q_D = 100 - 2P$, with initial price = $40, the national income approach for a production cost decrease of $20 per unit will yield a value of $1,600 (using initial price to value the increase in output), while the consumers' surplus approach yields only an $800 increase.

5. H. Mohring, *Transportation Economics* (Cambridge, Mass.: Ballinger, 1976), p.111.

6. For a detailed discussion, see R. Brown and C. Harral, "Estimating Highway Benefits in Underdeveloped Countries," in Highway Research Record No. 115, *Transportation and Economic Development, 6 Reports* (Washington, D. C.: Highway Research Board of the National Academy of Sciences—National Research Council, 1966), pp.29–44.

7. Ibid., p.42.

8. Some examples of the effects are given in G. Wilson, B. Bergmann, L. Hirsch, and M. Klein, *The Impact of Highway Investment on Development* (Washington, D. C.: The Brookings Institution, 1966), chaps. 2, 3, 4.

separate any component of the package as being causally related to the incremental output. Care must also be taken to net out the transfers of labor and capital from other sectors or regions, since they will have been contributing some output in their previous employments. The national income approach is therefore more difficult to employ. As a consequence, most transportation benefit-cost analyses use a variant of the consumers' surplus approach.[9]

Whichever approach to net benefit calculation is employed, the present value must be determined using $r$, or the internal rate of return must be calculated and compared with the social rate of discount $r$.

### The Social Rate of Discount ($r$)

The future streams of benefits $b_t$, costs $c_t$, and capital outlays $k_t$ must be rendered commensurate and must take into account the fact that benefits occurring in the future are less valuable than those occurring today. The usual way to acknowledge this is to discount the future streams by a suitable rate. How shall we determine such a rate? Clearly, the present value calculations and comparisons are highly sensitive to the rate chosen as well as to the time shape of the net benefit and capital outlay streams. Projects feasible at a discount rate of 5 percent may be infeasible at 8 or 10 percent. It is important therefore to be as precise as possible in specifying an appropriate magnitude or at least an appropriate range for $r$.

Unfortunately, the notion of the social rate of discount is controversial not only conceptually but empirically as well. The literature abounds with arguments, pro and con, using the subjective rate of time preference or the opportunity cost of capital or both as the appropriate criterion. Should the social rate of discount vary depending on the sources from which the capital resources are drawn or the means by which they are acquired for public investments (e.g., taxes or borrowing)? Should the rate, however chosen, also vary over future periods so that estimates of $r_t$ need to be made for each period? How does one treat the problem of differential risk or capital market imperfections?[10]

No consensus exists on the conceptual adequacy of any of these issues. Even less agreement exists when it comes to measuring the social rate of discount. Yet clearly if we are to urge more rational public investment decisions in general and within the transport sector in particular, it is necessary to specify some general criteria that,

---

9. For some examples of the national income approach, see ibid., chaps. 2, **4**.
10. Some of these issues have recently been reexamined in R. F. Mikesell, *The Rate of Discount for Evaluating Public Projects* (Washington, D. C.: American Enterprise Institute for Public Policy Research, 1977).

while conceptually subject to controversy, are at least defensible and potentially empirical.

In market-oriented economies, with a relatively large private sector and at least workably competitive capital markets, the resources for any new public transportation (or other) investment will be derived largely from the private sector through taxation or borrowing. If tax monies are used private consumption and investment expenditures would be reduced, and the resources so released would then be shifted to the public sector to construct the project; while for borrowed funds, the public sector would be bidding for the resources to construct the project. In either case, a new public project involves a shift of resources to the public from the private sector, where they were or could have been used to produce private output. In short, there is an opportunity cost in the form of private output foregone whenever resources are so shifted. Thus, suppose the government is considering a new transportation project (such as the Interstate Highway System, the Tennessee-Tombigbee Waterway, a third New York City airport, the St. Lawrence Seaway) that will require an estimated $W$ man-hours of labor, $X$ tons of materials, $Y$ units of transport service, $Z$ kilowatts of electricity, etc. If such resources were left in the private sector, they could produce an output with an expected rate of return of, say, $k$ percent. If the rate of return expected from their use in the public sector exceeds $k$ percent, other things being equal, efficiency would suggest that they should be shifted, and, conversely, if the expected rate of return in the public sector were less than $k$ percent, they should not. Thus, the appropriate rate of discount for public projects should in principle equal the rate of return expected from a similar batch of employed resources in the private sector. If the resources were or were expected to be unemployed, in whole or in part, the opportunity cost would, of course, be zero or some fraction of $k$ percent. This latter situation has often been used to justify certain transport investments when national or regional unemployment rates have been judged to be "too high." Yet such justifications are spurious unless the specific public transport investment contemplated was shown to yield greater net benefits than any other, and unless there was no more effective means of restoring "full employment" by monetary or fiscal policies. In what follows we will assume that full employment can be attained by more sensible general monetary and fiscal policies than have been used in the past and hence that real opportunity costs exist whenever a public transportation project is being considered. This is something of an heroic assumption but seems reasonable, in view of the pervasiveness of the Grand Transportation Mystique, as a legitimate offset.

Thus, the appropriate social rate of discount for public projects is based on the opportunity cost of the resources required to produce them in terms of their expected yield in the private sector for market-oriented economies. There are, as will be appreciated, several problems even with this apparently simple commonsense statement, problems not unlike those associated with determining the marginal social cost of transportation for purposes of efficient pricing.

In the first place, the data needed to calculate the opportunity cost are ex post, accounting data, whereas the logic applies to ex ante, economic data. Different accounting procedures among corporations may yield different stated rates of return unrelated to the underlying economic situation. In the final analysis, profits (and hence actual rates of return) are whatever the accountants, in conjunction with the Internal Revenue Service, say they are. While in principle rates of return among different industries should tend to equalize in the long run as capital and other resources flow from industries with low to those with high rates of return, in actuality large differentials exist and tend to persist over time.

For example, after-tax rates of return on stockholders' equity varied among industries in 1960 from a low of 3.6 percent for lumber and wood products to 16.8 percent for drugs. Twelve years later, the range was from 5.9 percent in primary nonferrous metals to 18.6 percent in drugs. Furthermore, the industries with high (and low) rates of return in 1960 were similarly situated in 1972.[11] Any convergence toward equalization of interindustry rates of return is conspicuous by its absence. In addition, large variances in rates of return exist among firms in different industries and within the same industry. Net income as a percent of stockholders' equity ranged from highs exceeding 30 percent (e.g., Mattel, Columbia Pictures Industries, Memorex) in 1976 to −10 percent and worse (e.g., Lockheed, White Motor, Genesco, Litton Industries), among *Fortune's* 500 largest U. S. industrial corporations.[12] Even within industries similar variance among firms exists and in many industries persists over time. Other measures of rates of return, such as pre-tax net income related to value of assets, indicate similar disparities. Thus "data on real capital markets indicate little, if any, tendency . . . to approach equilibrium. . . . Investment resources simply do not flow across firms and industries so as to equalize real rates of return."[13] Thus attempts to estimate *the* or a *single* opportunity cost of capital from rates of return of industrial or nonindustrial corporations can yield a large range of estimates. Average

11. Federal Trade Commission, *Quarterly Financial Reports for Manufacture Corporations* (Washington, D. C.: Government Printing Office, first quarter 1961 and first quarter 1973).
12. *The Fortune Double 500 Directory,* 1977.
13. L. Thurow, *Generating Inequality* (New York: Basic Books, Inc., 1975), p.146.

or median rates can, of course, be used, but the variance about them needs to be kept in mind.

Recourse can be had to financial markets, but a variety of rates is also in evidence there not only because of risk factors but also depending on which rates one looks at. For example, in 1978 yields on ten-year U. S. Treasury securities were 8.41%; on high-grade municipal bonds, 5.90%; corporate Aaa bonds, 8.73%; prime commercial paper, 7.99%; the prime rate, 9.06%.[14] The variance here, however, is much less than indicated for so-called real rates of return, largely because financial resources are more easily shifted than real resources.

The differences among these various rates or yields relate to taxes, risk, and externalities. In principle, the treatment of taxes is easy. If corporate or business profits taxes equal 50% and the riskless rate of return is 6%, then the opportunity cost of resources removed from the private sector is 6% (the after-tax rate) divided by 50%, or 12%. The resources would have returned 12% if left in the private sector, half of which would have been transferred to the public sector because of the tax structure. In general, then, if the riskless rate of return in the private sector is $i$ (in percent), the social rate of discount will be $i$ divided by the fraction of the returns that remains to the private sector after taxes. In the above example, half the returns remain in the private sector; thus the appropriate social rate of discount is $2i$. If the tax rate were one-third, then two-thirds would remain in the private sector, and the appropriate social rate of discount would be $\frac{3}{2} i$.

However, in most economies, tax rates on profits differ, depending on the form of organization (i.e., corporation, partnership, single proprietor), and the effective tax rates differ among industries, depending on such things as special allowances and differing treatments of depreciation. Again, in principle, this can easily be handled as long as we know the relative quantities of resources withdrawn from the several sectors or firms and the effective profits tax rate of each. For example, if 30% of the resources were withdrawn from a sector whose effective tax rate were one-quarter and 70% from a sector with an effective tax rate of one-half, and the riskless rate of return were 6%, the social rate of discount would be $.30 \times \frac{4}{3} \times 6\% + .7 \times 2 \times 6\% =$ 8.4%. In general, the appropriate social rate of discount is a weighted average of the fraction of the returns that remains to different sectors or firms after taxes, multiplied by the riskless rate of return. The riskless rate of return may be calculated as the long-term government

14. *Economic Indicators, January, 1979* (Washington, D. C.: Government Printing Office, 1979), p.30.

bond rate. This implies that the appropriate rate of discount may vary among public projects, depending on the sources in the private sector from which the resources are drawn. "If [the government] derives [its] resources from different sectors or [varies] in the proportions in which [it] draws upon the different sectors, then . . . opportunity costs may vary."[15] Thus, the use of a single rate based on some formula may be misleading.[16]

The calculation of the appropriate social rate of discount is closely linked to the "riskless" rate of return. The degree of risk varies among industries and among firms. A low-risk industry or firm can be expected to attract resources at lower anticipated rates of return than can a high-risk industry or firm. Thus actual rates of return and their stability or instability over time, which in large part determine the expected risk of new investments in particular enterprises, will already contain a risk premium. The belief that government investments are less risky does not alter the fact that when resources are transferred from the private sectors, the opportunity cost will still involve the total return expected in the private sector that will be sufficiently high to include both the risk and profits tax. As Baumol puts it, "the very absence of real risk [from public investments] means that the private risk discount should also enter the social discount rate. Here private risk plays precisely the same role as the corporation tax. It induces firms to invest in such a way that the marginal investment yield is higher than it would otherwise be. And the transfer of resources from the private sector imposes a correspondingly high opportunity cost."[17] Thus no further adjustment needs to be made to account for risk when the opportunity cost is calculated from evidence for the private sector. If, then, the riskless return is taken as the rate on long-term government securities, it only needs to be adjusted for the profits tax as noted above.

---

15. William Baumol, "On the Discount Rate for Public Projects," in *The Analysis and Evaluation of Public Expenditures: The PPB System*, A Compendium of Papers Submitted to the Subcommittee on Economy in Government of the Joint Economic Committee, Congress of the United States, vol. 1 (Washington, D. C.: Government Printing Office, 1969), p.496. Baumol's presentation of many of the above points is particularly lucid.

16. For example, a formula for evaluating water resource projects established in 1974 specified that the appropriate discount rate should be based on "the average yield during the preceding Fiscal Year on interest-bearing marketable securities of the United States which, at the time the computation is made, have terms of 15 years or more remaining to maturity . . ." (Section 80 of the Water Resources Development Act of 1974, Public Law 93-251). For the period October 1, 1976 to September 1, 1977, the rate was set at 6-3/8% (AWO, *Weekly Letter*, November 25, 1976, p.7).

17. William Baumol, "On the Social Rate of Discount," *American Economic Review*, September 1968, pp.795–96.

Much has been written about the issue of externalities, which are often alleged to favor a lower rate of discount for public investments, in order to encourage them, than private markets would determine. That is, the opportunity cost of resources taken from the private sector is too high because the private sector ignores external benefits, especially to future generations. The final analytical verdict on this issue is not yet in. However, identifying and measuring the externalities is an extremely uncertain business. As the reader will already have noted, the estimates to be used in benefit-cost analysis already have a large subjective or judgmental component. Adding externalities would render the exercise even more subjective. But more compelling is the following statement:

There is no defensible basis for the argument that a lower rate of discount should be employed for evaluating public projects as a means of transferring resources from the present to future generations. First, future generations are not served by increasing public investment at the expense of private investment, but by increases in the general level of investment, which is a function of the market rate of interest and a number of other factors that influence both saving and investment. Second, there is no defensible welfare argument for transferring income and consumption from the present to future generations, especially since future generations are . . . likely to have higher per capita incomes than the present.[18]

There is much more to the story, and, indeed, an enormous literature exists, part of which differs substantially from Mikesell's view.[19] Construing the social rate of discount in terms of opportunity cost, rather than as collective subjective time preference, appears eminently reasonable and lends itself to quantification to a far higher degree than does any alternative. It requires a large, relatively competitive private sector in both product and capital markets. In addition, for measurement purposes, rates of return in the various segments of the private sector must be known, along with the effective rate of profits tax. Each of these raises problems in calculating the social rate of discount. Finally, it is extremely difficult to ascertain from which area of the private sector and in what proportion resources will in fact be shifted to fund a public project.

When a particular project is being evaluated, it is necessary to test the degree of sensitivity of the results to the rate of discount actually used. For example, if the project is feasible at 10%, we may check to determine whether it is also feasible at 15%. If so, then even a 50%

---

18. Mikesell, p.39. See also Baumol, "On the Social Rate of Discount," for similar views.

19. For details see the bibliography in Mikesell; and the papers in *The Analysis and Evaluation of Public Expenditures*.

underestimate of the discount rate does not affect feasibility. If we use the internal rate of return and the discount rate turns out to exceed 15%, even though the estimated social rate of discount is 10%, our confidence in the desirability of the project will be enhanced. Indeed, it should be stressed that all the variables used need to be tested by postulating reasonable upper and lower bounds and examining how the results regarding feasibility are affected. Since all the $b_t$, $c_t$, $k_t$ are estimates to be held with varying degrees of certainty, the calculations should be checked for ranges of variation in the estimates. An alternative would be to assign probabilities to the various estimates and then indicate the probability of achieving specific *NPVs* or rates of return. The decision maker's willingness to take risks (his subjective probability) would then determine whether the project should go forward.[20]

In the absence of a large private sector with at least workably competitive markets, calculation of the social discount rate is more difficult. Recourse is often made to national income accounts, even acknowledging the wide margins of error in their estimation, especially for poor countries. Nevertheless, where national accounts exist, it is possible to derive an estimate of the average rate of return to capital that can serve as a not unreasonable proxy for the social rate of discount. The figure required is the ratio of the income accruing to capital during a year to the national stock of capital at the beginning of the year. Unfortunately, neither estimate is easy, and the latter is especially troublesome, indeed, normally nonexistent. Ingenious ways have to be found to develop the estimates, themselves depending on the data available. A simple way is to calculate the income accruing to capital, by deducting wage and salary payments, i.e., labor income $L$ from national income $Y$. Problems arise in treating the income of individual and unincorporated enterprises because such income is often treated as profits when in reality much of it represents compensation for labor. Assuming adjustments can be made in this regard, the income accruing to capital may be estimated as $Y - L$ for a particular year or years. Capital stock may be estimated indirectly from data more likely to be available. For example, $I = (g + d)k$, where $I =$ gross investment, $g =$ the rate of growth of the capital stock, $d =$ the rate of depreciation of the capital stock, and $k =$ capital stock; or $k =$

---

20. For some theory and details of this approach, see D. Luce and H. Raiffa, *Games and Decisions* (New York: Wiley, 1957); H. Raiffa, *Decision Analysis* (Reading, Mass.: Addison-Wesley, 1968). A transportation application involving part of the above has been reported in R. L. Keeney, "A Decision Analysis with Multiple Objectives: The Mexico City Airport," *Bell Journal of Economics and Management Science*, Spring 1973.

$\dfrac{I}{(g+d)}$ . If the estimates of $I$, $g$, and $d$ are believable, it is a simple matter to calculate $k$. The average rate of return to all capital is then $\dfrac{(Y-L)(g+d)}{I}$ . For example, U. S. national accounts data for 1978 in current values imply an average rate of return of slightly over 15 percent, using estimates of these variables.[21] Crude as this method is, for many countries it may be the only alternative.[22] However it is estimated, the social rate of discount is an important element in benefit-cost analysis and needs to be derived as carefully as data and judgment permit.

### The Capital Cost of the Investment ( $k_t$ )

The third crucial element in assessing the economic feasibility of a project is an estimate of the costs of creating the asset and an estimate of the time-frame of disbursements. Except for relatively small projects, the costs and time required for completion will usually extend over several years, and, invariably, both estimates will differ from actuality. The literature abounds with statements about "cost-overruns" and "unavoidable delays." Part of the cost-overrun is attributable to inflation, which is normally ignored in evaluating benefits and costs, including capital costs. The usual grounds for ignoring any given and even anticipated inflation rate is that if we inflate $b_t$, $c_t$, $r_t$, and $k_t$ by the same rate, everything cancels out, making the inflation adjustment unnecessary. This is true if we refer to the benefit-cost ratio rather than to the difference between the present value of the net benefits less the present value of the capital costs. However, if we refer to the former and adjust the numerator by an estimated rate of inflation $i$, so that we have $(b_t - c_t)^t(1+i)^t$ and adjust the denominator by $[1+r(1+i)]^t$ or by $(1+r+i)^t$, identical results do not emerge, as in the unadjusted case. The difference is likely to be insignificant if more than half of net benefits is reaped in the early years and if $i$ is relatively small. However, if this is not the case and if the rate of inflation is expected to rise over time, an inflation adjustment factor may change the results regarding feasibility. Furthermore, it is unlikely that inflation would have the same impact on each of the variables, in which case even more dramatic changes from the unadjusted calculations may be expected.

---

21. Data from *Economic Indicators*, January 1979, yield the following: $Y - L$ = 403 billion, $g = 4\%$, $d = 9\%$, and $I = 345$ billion; $g$ is approximate and assumes a normal growth of $K$ equal to that of $Y$.

22. For an example of a similar, though more detailed, calculation, see A. Harberger, *Project Evaluation* (London: Macmillan, 1972), chap. 6, "On Estimating the Rate of Return to Capital in Colombia," and the estimate for India, pp.185–92.

It is, however, extremely difficult to estimate either the overall rate of inflation or its varying rate or impact on the respective elements of the benefit-cost analysis. Indeed, such an adjustment or set of adjustments would add another element of subjectivity to an already overburdened set of (often) subjective elements. Hence the usual practice is to employ prices existing in the year when construction is expected to begin.

The other reason for the typical underestimate of costs and the time required for construction frequently is the bias of the investigator in favor of the project. While it is not always conscious or deliberate, it frequently exists whenever cost (as well as benefit) estimates are particularly uncertain. The traditional ways to offset such bias involve such things as "assuming the useful life of the project . . . to be less than its most likely physical or economic life . . . , adding a risk premium to the interest rate used for discounting . . . [and/or] reducing final net benefits by some rule-of-thumb proportion . . . ."[23] It goes without saying that such adjustments are "unscientific" and often capricious. Nonetheless, this is an understandable response to the great uncertainties that exist in all the estimates, especially when they are made by persons with vested interests. A completely unbiased and disinterested consumer of an analysis of a particular project may adjust by some rule of thumb in the face of such uncertainties.[24]

However the estimates of $k_t$ are done, they are ultimately based on the design parameters of the project and costed at current prices. As such, they properly reside in the domain of the engineer. Most economists will take such estimates as data and conduct the subsequent analysis along the lines indicated above.

### Other Problems of Public Transportation Investments

Keynes long ago remarked that most of the world's major investments were not made on the basis of rational calculation along the lines of benefit-cost analysis.

Most, probably, of our decisions to do something positive [e.g., construct a new highway, railway or port], the full consequences of which will be drawn out over many days [or years] to come, can only be taken as a result of animal spirits—of a spontaneous urge to action rather than inaction, and

---

23. J. Meyer and M. Straszheim, *Techniques of Transport Planning*, vol. I: *Pricing and Project Evaluation* (Washington, D.C.: The Brookings Institution, 1971), p.217.
24. O. Eckstein, "A Survey of the Theory of Public Expenditure Criteria," in *Public Finances: Needs, Sources, and Utilization* (Princeton: Princeton University Press for the National Bureau of Economic Research, 1961), p.469.

not as the outcome of a weighted average of quantitative benefits multiplied by quantitative probabilities.[25]

In our attempt to make public expenditures more rational, account needs to be taken of this phenomenon. As previously noted, considerations of efficiency often take second place to political expediency, national prestige, defense, the desire of elected officials to "do" something—the "monument mentality" noted in the introduction to Part II. Though the investment criteria applicable to the private sector are formally identical with those applicable to public investments, there are some special features—especially with regard to transport investments—that compound these difficulties.

In the first place, the role of noneconomic factors looms much larger in public investments than in private. The government is not in business to make profits—nor should it be. Thus the efficiency criteria are likely to get short shrift in comparison with other, more compelling and vivid criteria. Proposals to build the Kra Canal in Thailand; the East West Highway in Malaysia; the Port of Taichung in Taiwan; and in the United States, the Arkansas River, Tennessee-Tombigbee, and Wabash canal projects and the Appalachia roads program are clearly more oriented to defense and/or regional development purposes than to their putative impact on national income growth or overall efficiency. External effects are likely to be overemphasized as well as more realistically present than in the case of private investments.

Secondly, the public officials (elected or not) who make the investment commitments do not generally suffer the consequences of error that a market test would provide. Indeed, if a mistake is made, there are few or no self-correcting mechanisms. On the contrary, there is a very high incentive to rescue an obvious mistake by allocating even more resources. The "AMTRAK decision" may be a conspicuous recent exception to this generalization. Frequently the public investment will constitute a monopoly (e.g., the highway system) and thus will not be a price taker in the "market." Thus, a separate decision on nonmarket grounds needs to be made with respect to efficient pricing.

All these, and other practical difficulties, are compounded with reference to the poor countries. Markets there tend to be far more imperfect than in developed, market economies. Thus existing prices may not adequately represent real opportunity costs. Wage rates may not be indicative of the social opportunity cost of labor. Import and export prices may diverge widely from efficiency criteria because of artificial exchange rates. As a result, the ability to measure the social benefits

---

25. J. M. Keynes, *The General Theory of Employment, Interest and Money* (London: Macmillan, London, 1951; 1st ed., 1936), p.161.

and costs accurately is sharply reduced and so-called shadow prices are used, which in turn add another element of subjectivity to benefit-cost calculations. External effects, which are difficult to measure and include in the analysis under the best of circumstances, are likely to be more substantial in poor countries than elsewhere. For example, the proposal to construct a second tunnel between Hong Kong island and Kowloon was believed to have required so much labor that severe upward pressure on the national wage rate would ensue.

Investment commitments in poor countries tend to be more subject to corruption and lack of administrative capability. This situation is compounded by the dearth of usable data, the enormous instability caused by chronic warfare, new-nation status, or rural insurrection, all of which make future projections of traffic especially problematical and uncertain.[26] All past relationships among economic variables are therefore seriously distorted. Indeed, even without chronic warfare, the essence of development requires a break from past relationships often in an ambiguous and uncertain way.

These and other difficulties raise (or lower) the analysis of benefits and costs for public transportation investments to the status of an uncertain art, especially in poor countries. Some have referred to it as an "ideology" or even a "bastard science."[27] Nevertheless, believing that careful analysis, using the best data, methods, and judgment available, can improve the efficiency of public transport investment planning and execution, we turn to the other specific issues, namely, the distribution of the benefits and costs, shadow pricing, and "other" concepts of benefits.

## Distribution of the Costs and Benefits

The costs and benefits of any project will be paid by or accrue to different industries, social groups, and/or regions. If it is part of social policy to favor some industries, groups, or regions, account may need to be taken of such relative impacts or redistributions. For example, in the improvement of a port facility in a poor country, substantial savings in ship turnaround time will be a major measure of benefits. However, the value of such time savings accrues to the shipowners.

---

26. The present author once undertook an analysis of the Indochina states and sought to project GNP, traffic, and the like (à la chapter 5), assuming "peace" would arrive in 1975. All past data reflected some 20 to 30 years of chronic warfare and hence was unusable as a basis for projection in peacetime.

27. L. Tribe, "Policy Science: Analysis or Ideology," and A. Wilhains, "Cost-Benefit Analysis: Bastard Science? and/or Insidious Poison in the Body Politick," in *Benefit-Cost and Policy Analysis, 1972* (Chicago: Aldine, 1973), chaps. 1 and 2.

If they are mostly foreigners from the developed countries, a large portion of the benefits will be lost to the poor countries; hence income will be redistributed in favor of the rich, something that may not be deemed desirable. To be sure, the poor country may capture some of these benefits by effective port pricing, but that is another matter. A straightforward benefit-cost analysis along lines thus far developed will not consider this issue, but assumes that a benefit (cost) is a benefit (cost) regardless of who receives (or suffers) it.

Similar kinds of redistributions occur within a country. Different regions, groups, and/or industries will therefore be differently affected. Large differential impacts need to be accounted for, but how? The usual procedure is to weight the benefits (costs) in terms of their most likely impact. If the benefits of a project will accrue to a low-income group A and a high-income group B, and if social policy favors A over B, one might weight the benefits to A higher than those to B in evaluating total social benefits. For example, out of total benefits of $100, group A may be expected to receive $75 and B $25. If the groups are weighted equally (i.e., one to one), then we have the same total benefits. If, however, it is decided that an increase in benefits to A is twice as important as an increase in benefits to B, then we need to "weight" or multiply A's benefits by $\frac{4}{3}$ and B's by $\frac{2}{3}$ to obtain socially weighted total benefits of 116.67, i.e., $\frac{4}{3}$ (75) $+ \frac{2}{3}$ (25).[28] Alternative distributions of the benefits will lead to different socially weighted benefits. In this way, it is possible to consider distributional criteria as conceived by the decision maker.

All alternative ways[29] of taking account of such matters involve formidable data problems in identifying the recipients of benefits or the incidence of costs as well as in specifying the weights. The last is inevitably judgmental or solely reflective of the subjective value judgment of the decision maker. Often such considerations are tacked on to the formal analysis as unquantified "additional benefits" to the income distribution, regional balance, or similar additional costs to the extent they can be identified. In fact, distribution weights are not needed if the government or decision maker values the costs and benefits equally among their recipients or if income can be redistrib-

---

28. In general, if we have $n$ groups identified as receiving portions of the total (efficiency) benefits, we may calculate efficiency and redistributive benefits by weighting the benefits of each of the $n$ recipients by $\alpha_1 + \alpha_2 + \ldots + \alpha_n = n$, where the $\alpha_i$ are the weights. If each $\alpha_i = 1$, in essence, no weighting takes place —a benefit to A is equivalent to the same benefit to B, C, D, etc.

29. For an example, see L. Squire and H. G. van der Tak, *Economic Analysis of Projects* (Baltimore and London: published for the World Bank by the Johns Hopkins University Press, 1975), pp.51–56, and chap. 7.

uted relatively costlessly through fiscal policies. Neither course generally obtains and especially not for poor countries. However, except for large public investments, formal inclusion of the redistribution impact is probably not warranted, although where such redistributions are likely to be large, they need to be examined as far as the data, analysis, and judgment permit. Where two alternative projects, one of which influences the income distribution positively and the other negatively or not at all, yield the same *NPV*, the former should be selected. In practice the *NPV* are unlikely to be equal, and the choice then reflects the value of the decision maker places on redistribution whenever the *NPV* of the former is less than that of the latter.

Although it is extremely difficult to identify formally the distribution of the benefits and costs and assign reasonable weights, the issues posed are exceedingly important, especially as society becomes more and more concerned with equity in addition to efficiency. In the United States and elsewhere, past decisions regarding public investment and other programs have ignored such impacts, often to the detriment of the whole program. As has been argued, "the cost of our past ignorance of distributional impacts is clearly high. There is no need to persist in such error. But we must now collect the data and do the analysis of the distributional impacts that are needed for today's decisions."[30] Thus, as the ICC once put it, referring to marginal cost, "Cost has never been out of mind though it has not always been in sight," so we might paraphrase, "Equity has not always been out of mind but frequently out of sight!"

The issue of who receives the benefits, however, extends beyond that of "simple" income redistribution and equity considerations. Regardless of relative incomes, if the benefits are reaped by an especially enterprising socioeconomic group, it is likely to use such benefits to enhance production and efficiency even further. On the other hand, if they are reaped by a less enterprising group, the response may be much less or even none at all. Hence the output expansion contingent on the particular project may differ sharply, depending solely on which groups receive the benefits and how they respond to them. This issue is discussed further below under the heading of "Other Benefit Criteria."

### Shadow Prices

If markets for the inputs and outputs of a particular project are not at least "workably" competitive, the prices used to evaluate inputs

---

30. J. T. Bonnen, "The Absence of Knowledge of Distributional Impact: An Obstacle to Effective Public Program Analysis and Decisions," in *The Analysis and Evaluation of Public Expenditures*, p.447.

and outputs may not reflect the marginal, social opportunity costs. As a consequence, it is often recommended that whatever prices exist need to be "adjusted" to take account of this fact. While the need for such adjustments is most apparent in the developing countries, where market imperfections of various types abound, they are not confined to such nations. In the United States, for example, the minimum wage law is deemed partially responsible for the relatively high rate of unemployment among teenagers because the minimum wage exceeds the value of the marginal product of much teenage labor. Use of the minimum wage to price some of the inputs needed for a new transport investment would thus "overstate" the real (i.e., opportunity) cost of the project. Unemployment among certain classes of labor means that if some of the project inputs utilize labor that would otherwise have been unemployed, the "real" labor cost is effectively zero even if a money wage has to be paid. This issue has been extensively discussed in the context of "labor surplus" with special reference to agriculture in developing countries.[31] The principle of "surplus" labor is frequently important with respect to both developed and developing or poor countries, namely, how to adjust existing prices (wages, foreign exchange rates, other inputs) where they fail to reflect opportunity costs.

The problem may be illustrated as follows: Assume that to construct a particular transportation facility, it is estimated that 100,000 homogeneous man days of labor will be required along with specified quantities of other inputs (capital, raw material). Assuming we need adjust only the labor input because actual money wage rates are "artificially" raised by minimum or legal rates or union pressures, we need to value the 100,000 man days by some estimate of the marginal opportunity cost of labor ($MOC$). If the actual money wage is $\$X$ per man day and the estimated $MOC$ is $\$Y$ (where $X > Y$), the real labor cost component of the project will be less than the actual money cost by 100,000 $(X - Y)$. How shall we calculate the $MOC$ of labor or any other input produced in circumstances of seriously imperfect or even nonexistent markets?

Since we are dealing with an individual project, we must put emphasis on the prices existing within a particular locale. Thus shadow prices derived from the dual of a linear-programming solution to a resource allocation problem pertinent to the nation as a whole would resources and activity *aggregates*,"[32] they are not applicable to specific Since shadow prices, interpreted as a dual, are "scarcity measures of

---

31. The literature here is virtually endless, but the original impetus came from W. A. Lewis, "Economic Development with Unlimited Supplies of Labour," *The Manchester School*, May 1954; and J. Fei and G. Ranis, "A Theory of Economic Development," *American Economic Review*, September 1961.

resource and activity *aggregates*,"[32] they are not applicable to specific projects.

Alternatively, if data permitted, one might specify a production function for one or more of the major productive sectors in the appropriate region and deduce from it the marginal product for those inputs suspected of being over- (or under-) priced in the market. However, not only are suitable data usually unavailable but also the most appropriate form of the production function is difficult to determine.

Because of these and other problems associated with estimating *MOC*, several authors have concluded that existing prices, with all their imperfections, may be preferable to any attempt to adjust them by the general techniques available. For example, Weckstein argues that "although it is plausible to seek substitute prices to improve on actual imperfect market prices, on examination of many cases, market prices turn out to be the best prices to use, and there is no known source of shadow prices that generally gives better guidance to investment choices."[33] But many would disagree with him.[34]

The situation for the practicing project analyst would appear to be that if there is reason to believe that the prices of the inputs to be used in constructing a particular project are seriously defective as approximations of *MOC*, and if there exists a reasonable means to estimate *MOC* more accurately, the attempt should be made. However, since much of the actual adjustment is judgmental, the sensitivity of the results to it, in terms of *NPV* or *IRR*, needs to be checked. If the project can only be justified on the basis of an estimate of *MOC* below prevailing prices, it is probably at best marginal. In addition, since actual prices have to be paid, regardless of the estimated shadow prices, the project may require a higher public subsidy if adopted. All the additional distortions previously indicated with respect to subsidy would then pertain here as well. The analyst needs to be aware of such distortions and not accept the engineering estimates of the

---

32. R. S. Weckstein, "Shadow Prices and Project Evaluation in Less-Developed Countries," *Economic Development and Cultural Change*, April 1972, p.477; Weckstein outlines many other problems associated with such a measure of shadow prices.

33. Ibid., p.474. See also Harberger, p.180.

34. See D. Lal, *Methods of Project Analysis: A Review*, World Bank Staff Occasional Papers no.16 (Baltimore: The Johns Hopkins University Press, 1974), chap. II. R. Haveman has made some estimates of the ratio of social labor cost to market cost by regions in the United States, depending on the extent of unemployment ("Evaluating Public Expenditures Under Conditions of Unemployment," in *The Analysis and Evaluation of Public Expenditures*, pp.547ff.). H. Chenery, "Comparative Advantage and Development Policy," *American Economic Review*, March 1961, and references cited therein.

cost of the project without examining the prices actually used. But considerable restraint is needed in making large-scale adjustments in the prices of individual inputs, especially labor.

One other shadow price, especially relevant to poor countries, is often used in project appraisal. Where the project requires substantial imports of capital equipment and materials, evaluating them at official exchange rates may be extremely misleading. Official exchange rates typically overvalue a nation's currency, and so undervalue imports. A key test of whether and to what extent the currency is over- or undervalued at the official rate is the existence of a chronic trade deficit and a large disparity between official and black market rates. If they are large, some downward adjustment of the official rate (i.e., from, say, 6 rupees per dollar at the official rate to, say, 12 rupees at the opportunity cost rate)[35] may be sensible. As in the case of shadow pricing for local inputs, many of these adjustments are necessarily judgmental. If adjustment of actual prices and exchange rates is done extensively for any project, the degree of subjectivity of the estimates mounts rapidly and provides even more scope for biased results.

*The Exclusion of Indirect Taxes.* The market prices of many inputs and outputs often include sales or excise taxes, and imported goods may be subject to a special duty that raises their price. Such taxes or duties do not reflect a use of more economic resources, as far as the nation as a whole is concerned. Thus, prices containing such taxes overstate the resources used up or benefits received, and the taxes need to be deducted. Usually, this is much simpler than shadow pricing. The tax on gasoline, for example, is usually well specified and can readily be deducted from the price actually charged to ascertain a portion of "vehicle operating costs." Similarly, license fees or other imposts on equipment need to be deducted. In general, such charges are transfers from purchasers of the taxed items to the government and do not represent value added by use of additional resources.

## Choosing among Projects

We have examined some of the principles and problems involved in appraising a given transportation investment project. In reality, there are always alternative projects that need to be compared. These alternatives are of two main types. (1) Projects that are independent of one another (i.e., mutually exclusive) in the sense that the benefits and costs accruing to one project would not be expected to change if any or all of the other alternatives were undertaken. Transport in-

---

35. Adler, p.9, adjusts the official rate by 1.75.

vestments between different nodal pairs may not affect each other except in a remote systemic sense. In general, the construction or improvement of a road between A and B would not influence the benefits and costs of port expansion at C or a new rail investment between M and N. Likewise, a transport investment in one region may be totally unaffected by investments in health, education, or some industry in another region. (2) Projects that are interdependent in the sense of being complementary or competitive so that the benefits or costs of one will be influenced by the construction of another. A road or rail improvement to a port will influence the benefits and costs of a port expansion project. Investments to improve agricultural output in any node will influence the benefits and costs of transportation investments linking that node to some other. A pipeline to a new oil well will obviously enhance the benefits and reduce the costs of improved extractive facilities.

Indeed, this raises the question of project complementarity and project definition. If the transport investment is an indispensable part of the overall investment (as in the case of an oil well), it cannot be treated separately. The "project" thus becomes the whole set of complementary investments and their expected total benefits, and it is not always easy to decide which investments are complementary (i.e., have at least *some* impact on others) and which are independent (i.e., have little or no impact on others). Improvement of a highway or railway to a port may not be considered by the port authority when deciding on a port expansion. Yet if the port capacity expansion leads to large tonnage gains, most of which move over the existing highway, considerable increase in wear and tear on the highway may result and should be added to the costs of the port project. The definition of the scope of a project in terms of what outside benefits and costs it may occasion thus creates another area of difficulty, especially in a highly interdependent economy that may be politically fractionated along geographical lines and/or along lines of agency jurisdiction. The highway department will not generally consider projects proposed by the railway administration or the port authority, for example. Yet their activities may often be highly complementary.

In order to distinguish, in practice, the boundaries of any "project," it is necessary "to pinpoint the exact locus of decision-making power. . . . the distinction has to be made on the basis of what falls outside and inside the terms of reference and area of concern of the decision-maker or analyst."[36] If the locus is narrowly defined, many external

---

36. T. Kuhn, *Public Enterprise Economics and Transport Problems* (Berkeley: University of California Press, 1962), p.8.

effects or interdependencies may be ignored; if broadly defined, such effects will not be ignored but many of them may be highly problematical and difficult to determine with accuracy. The broader issue in project identification or demarcation is thus closely linked to the issue of centralization or decentralization of public decision making, a subject likely to evoke much emotion and irrationality (e.g., states' rights).

Let us abstract from this tempting problem[37] and assume we have identified a set of mutually exclusive projects. How do we choose among them? The answer is simple. If there is no budget constraint, to maximize the net present value for any selection of projects, simply undertake all those for which $B_i - C_i > 0$. If there is a budget constraint in the public sector that precludes undertaking all having positive net benefits $\left( \text{i.e.,} \sum_{t=1}^{n} C_i > \text{Budget Constraint} \right)$, rank all the projects by their $\frac{B_i}{C_i}$ ratio and undertake those projects in order, starting with the highest value and continuing down the ranking until the budget constraint is reached $\left( \text{i.e., when} \sum_{t=1}^{n^*} C_i = \text{the constraint} \right)$.

More problems emerge whenever there is project interdependence. At one extreme is a set of completely competitive projects, in the sense that only *one* will be selected. Such an either-or choice may occur when it is decided to increase transport capacity between a particular nodal pair—the decision may be road vs. rail or one particular road improvement vs. another.[38]

The first problem is that the internal rate of return (*IRR*) approach will not always give the same answer as the net present value (*NPV*) approach. Thus, if our decision criterion is to maximize *NPV*, the *IRR* will not always provide the optimal choice. Consider the following net benefit streams associated with an identical investment of $1 (thousand, million, etc.) in period 0.

|  | Period 1 | Period 2 |
|---|---|---|
| Alternative (1) | 0 | 4 |
| Alternative (2) | 2 | 1 |

At any (external) rate of social discount less than 50%, the net present value of alternative (1) exceeds that of alternative (2) $\left( \text{i.e., the } NPV \right.$ of $\frac{0}{1+r} + \frac{4}{(1+r)^2} - 1$ exceeds $\frac{2}{1+r} + \frac{1}{(1+r)^2} - 1 \left. \right)$. For example, if $r =$

---

37. Kuhn, chap. 2, has a good discussion.
38. See Appendix to this chapter for a simple illustration.

0, the $PC - C$ of alternative $(1) = 3$ and of $(2) = 2$. If $r = 10\%$, $NPV$ of $(1) = 2.306$ and of $(2) = 1.645$. Beyond $50\%$, the opposite is true.

However, the $IRR$ of $(1) = 100\%$ $\left( \text{i.e., } 1 = \dfrac{0}{2.00} + \dfrac{4}{(2.00)^2} \right)$, while that of $(2) = 141.4\%$ $\left( \text{i.e., } 1 = \dfrac{2}{2.414} + \dfrac{1}{(2.414)^2} \right)$. Thus at "low" rates of interest, $(1)$ is preferred to $(2)$, while at high rates of interest, $(2)$ is preferred to $(1)$ on the $NPV$ criterion. On the other hand, using $IRR$, one would always select alternative $(2)$. Thus, when it comes to ranking projects, the $IRR$ is not always correct if the criterion is to maximize $NPV$.[39]

A second problem involves the extent of project interdependence among a set of projects both positive or negative. Formally, the problem is not especially difficult if it is possible to estimate the value of the interdependencies. Assume four projects—A, B, C, and D—A and B are competitive, while C and A and C and D are complementary. If both A and B are built, the impact of B on A will reduce or eliminate a large portion of A's benefits, and vice versa. If both A and C are built, their concurrent or subsequent impacts will enhance each other's benefits; similarly with C and D. If we can assign values to these interrelationships as well as to the benefits of each project stand-

---

39. Another problem with $IRR$ is that it does not always yield unique solutions in a multiperiod net benefit stream if "several" of the net benefits in particular years are negative. Descartes' rule of signs asserts that the number of solutions is at most equal to the number of reversals of sign in terms of the net benefits sequence. Thus, a three-period net benefit sequence has, at most, two $IRR$, a four-period sequence at most three $IRR$. For example, if the net benefits stream for a $1 (thousand, million, etc.) investment is 6, −11, 6, three values of $IRR$ are possible, namely, 0, 100%, and 200%. Note that this is really a four-period sequence, with net benefits equal to −1 in period zero. Thus, three $IRR$ are possible, given three reversals of sign, à la Descartes (e.g., −1, +6, −11, +6).

In most transport projects, however, negative benefits after the investment are not generally encountered since major rehabilitation, say, after five or ten years, is not normally envisioned. Rather, annual maintenance expenditures adequate to maintain the highway, railway, port, or airport are included in the calculation and these, with an upgraded facility, are often less than with an unimproved facility; hence, the net benefit stream after the capital construction is invariably positive in every year because both operating costs and maintenance costs are believed to be lower with the improvement than without. In addition, if we add to net benefits estimates of time savings, accident reduction, and the like, the unit net benefits per ton, ton-mile, vehicle-mile, passenger-mile, are invariably positive. Furthermore, the number of service units is growing; thus the net benefits are not only positive but increasingly so. Thus, the second criticism of the $IRR$ is in practice not overly significant as far as transport projects are concerned. The first problem, however, combined with the latter, suggests that, however difficult it is to calculate the social rate of discount or the marginal productivity of capital in any economy (especially in a poor country), there is really no way out. The $IRR$ needs to be compared with $r$ whenever there are budgetary limitations when project selection is involved.

| Effect of | Effect on | | | |
|---|---|---|---|---|
| | A | B | C | D |
| A | 500 | −600 | 120 | 0 |
| B | −500 | 600 | 0 | −30 |
| C | 90 | 0 | 20 | 50 |
| D | 0 | −30 | 40 | 100 |

ing alone, we can derive a matrix showing the effects of each project on itself and the others. The diagonal indicates the effects of A on A, B on B, etc., which are the present values of the expected benefits of each project by itself. Since A and B are completely competitive, the effect of B on A is to wipe out all of A's benefits (−500), and, similarly, with the effect of A on B (−600). The effect of C on A is to enhance A's benefits by 90, and the effect of A on C is to enhance C's benefits by 120. Thus, if both A and C are constructed, total benefits will be the sum of the single-project benefits of each (i.e., 500 + 20) and the indirect benefits (i.e., 90 + 120), or 730. The present value of each combination of the interdependent projects can similarly be calculated. The number of different combinations of $n$ projects is $2^n − 1$. Thus with four projects there are 15 combinations that need to be examined (A, B, C, D, AB, AC, AD, CD, BD, BC, ABC, ABD, BCD, ACD, and ABCD). With estimates of the costs of each project, it is a simple matter to select that combination yielding the largest net present value.[40]

The difficulty lies in the determination of the indirect or system effects. Indeed, since A and C are such close complements, it might be advisable to treat them as one project. Similarly, since C and D are complements, they might reasonably be packaged with A so that the project choice boils down to A (including C and D) and B, which is formally identical with the illustration in the Appendix to this chapter. Generally, data limitations preclude placing much confidence in quantification of interproject relationships, yet they clearly exist. Instead of trying to measure them separately, as was done above, a better strategy is to "bundle" highly complementary projects and contrast them with competitive projects similarly "bundled."

## Other Benefit Criteria

The effects (i.e., benefits) of a project in transportation may depend on the kind as well as the amount of investment made. There may in

---

40. For example, if project costs are A = 300, B = 350, C = 140, and D = 100, the maximum *NPV* is combination ACD, whose gross benefits are 920 and costs 540, for *NPV* = 380. The above example and numbers are taken from Kuhn, chap. 5, and Appendix B.

fact be different anticipated benefits, depending on whether Project A is a highway and Project B is a railway or a pipeline.

We have already noted that the distribution of the benefits and costs may be important in project appraisal and that the decision maker may want to apply distributive weights as a means of accounting for equity considerations. But the distribution of the benefits (or costs) may be crucial in another sense—it may influence the total results of the project. Indeed, the actual results of many projects, especially in poor countries or regions, deviate significantly from the anticipated results. Surprises, of one sort or another, abound in the ex post project evaluation literature.[41]

One reason for such surprises involves the responses of particular individuals or groups to the new economic opportunities created by a project. Such responses are obviously conditioned by the extent of the awareness that new opportunities exist and the attitudes and incentives of those who perceive the new opportunities. Improved access between a producing and a consuming region that reduces travel time and costs may induce producers to maintain the same production as before and reap benefits in the form of more leisure or higher profits. On the other hand, it may call forth more production and lower freight rates. The actual results may therefore differ sharply, depending on these alternative responses. Furthermore, there is abundant evidence that the responses depend in large part on which particular groups receive the benefits.

For example, social group A may have the reputation of being highly aggressive, willing and able to seize economic opportunity whenever and wherever it is perceived, while social group B may have a distinct aversion to such behavior and favor tradition and the quiet life. A project whose benefits largely accrue to A will probably show more impressive economic gains than if the benefits of the same project mainly accrue to B. Thus attitudes to economic change and indeed toward economic activity in general may be extremely important. They are often related to religious, cultural, and ethnic differences and hence raise delicate issues for the project analyst.[42]

However, there are some general inferences from the foregoing that merit inclusion in any outline of project appraisal that seeks to go beyond mere technique. Abstracting from attitudinal differences, whatever their source, the awareness of new economic potential created by the transport project is clearly important. In this sense, the kind of increase in transport capacity between any pair of nodes may influence

---

41. See, for example, A. O. Hirschman, *Development Projects Observed* (Washington, D.C.: The Brookings Institution, 1967); and Wilson et al., *The Impact of Highway Investment on Development*.

42. For a brief discussion of these issues, see Wilson et al., pp.192ff.

the response and hence the results. At one extreme is a pipeline connecting a supply source to an end user (refinery or electrical power plant). Whether such a pipeline is buried or above ground, it cannot have any impact on awareness of new opportunity along its right-of-way beyond that implicit in those who undertook the investment in the first place. Those along the right-of-way may be aware of its existence but they cannot use it. In fact, a pipeline is better viewed as part of the investment associated with the industry of which it is a part.

At the other extreme is a highway with unlimited access. Along its right-of-way, anyone can use it. Such a road permits use of relatively small and inexpensive units of capital (trucks, buses, cars) under independent ownership and allows small-scale, local entrepreneurs to enter the industry. There is little need for and less possibility of large-scale, remote, or alien ownership of trucking facilities than is the case with a railway or pipeline. The road therefore provides experience in management and organization that may be widely shared and diffused and readily grasped[43]; and the income so generated is likely to be localized and hence provide further stimulus to other local enterprises along the right-of-way.

The ability of trucks to transport small shipments more efficiently than other modes can is especially important to a relatively poor region, where trading is likely to be highly individualized and individual sales relatively small. The greater number of potential participants in the trucking industry implies a more competitive outcome. Thus cost reductions will be passed along to shippers to a greater extent than would be the case, say, of a single rail line under monopolistic remote control centered in the capital city.

Socially and culturally, road transport permits a higher degree of personal contact than trains that pass by, planes that fly overhead, or pipelines beneath the surface. "Trains go by and trucks stop—an essential difference when viewed as carriers of culture instead of freight."[44] The increased contact by truckers with other businesses may broaden horizons and induce entry into new fields. Hirschman even argues that the latitude for corruption in the trucking industry is less than for rail and hence, "any comparison of transport costs for rail and road that does not attempt to correct for likely differences in their levels of performance . . . will fail to do justice to the real advantages of road over rail transport in a corruption-ridden country."[45]

---

43. For example, repair and maintenance of vehicles is not technically difficult and can be learned quickly. See R. Farmer, "Inland Freight Transportation Pricing in Eastern Saudi Arabia," *The Journal of Industrial Economics*, July 1962. He notes that "the Saudis have easily taken to mechanical transport" (p.177).
44. Wilson et al., p.201.
45. Hirschman, p.109.

Thus, the technology of road transport has greater potential for positively influencing attitudes toward economic activity than do alternative modes. These important aspects are wholly ignored in the technically straightforward calculation of net present values or internal rates of return. Especially in poor countries or regions (e.g., Appalachia in the United States), such indirect effects may be more important than the direct effect deduced by the analytical apparatus of formal benefit-cost analysis with its single-minded stress on efficiency.[46] Hirschman notes some of the "surprises" to the decision maker in the difficulties following completion of a project and their (occasionally) equally surprising resolution. He develops what may be a general principle of the "Hiding Hand,"[47] which asserts that since the costs and results (benefits) of a particular project cannot be known with certainty in advance, the general underestimate of costs and overestimate of benefits may be *required* to initiate many projects that ultimately turn out to be successful. Sawyer, after examining projects undertaken in the early nineteenth century in the United States, concluded that the "miscalculation or sheer ignorance" of their costs was "crucial to getting an enterprise launched at all," especially with respect to transport projects and projects designed to open up new resources that were ultimately highly successful. "Had the total investment required been accurately and objectively known at the beginning, the project would not have been begun."[48]

Essentially the "hiding hand" is a way of inducing action through error. Such errors in prior project evaluation can, of course, lead to enormous economic waste (e.g., the British-French Concorde). It is reasonable to attempt to improve the estimates of benefits and costs and to make them as unbiased as humanly possible. However, it needs to be acknowledged that while overestimates of benefits and underestimates of costs can lead to disaster or white elephants, they can "occasionally serve to ward off another, less visible but nonetheless real, disaster: missed opportunity."[49]

It is not easy to take the kinds of considerations noted above into account. They are clearly not suitable for quantification. Yet in poor regions they may, in fact, turn out to be critical to the ultimate success of a project. To the extent that the prior systems analysis outlined in chapter 5 has considered them in the process of making traffic forecasts, the more straightforward analysis in terms of *NPV* or *IRR* may

---

46. See Wilson et al., chap. 8, for further elaboration.
47. Hirschman, pp.12–13.
48. J. E. Sawyer, "Entrepreneurial Error and Economic Growth," *Explorations in Entrepreneurial History*, May 1952, as quoted in Hirschman, p.16.
49. Hirschman, p.30.

suffice. But when issues of road vs. rail are involved, they need to be more explicitly examined. This, however, requires a degree of familiarity with the local situation, the people affected, their customs, attitudes, and institutional arrangements, which the typical analyst neither possesses nor has time to acquire.

Formal benefit-cost analysis should therefore be viewed as no more than a guide to action for the decision maker. It should not be viewed as giving cut-and-dried answers to either additional capacity requirements or modal choices. Judgment is needed not only at every point in the analysis but also in the ultimate decision because of the uncertainties and the inadequate data, as well as the indirect effects. Cost-benefit analysis is truly an art rather than a science. It can only assist the decision maker in rendering better transport investment decisions and thereby offset to some extent the excesses induced by the Grand Transportation Mystique.

# Appendix

### Illustration of Benefit-Cost Analysis for Highway Choice

Assume two nodes connected by 100 miles of narrow, winding, gravel road. A systems approach implies that the road will soon reach "capacity." All alternatives have been narrowed down to two: (1) pave the present highway to two lanes along the existing alignment and (2) pave to two lanes and realign so that total distance reduces to 80 miles. Engineering estimates of alternative (1) indicate two categories of $L$ and $K$ will be needed as follows:

$L_1$ (unskilled labor)   = 1,000 man-years @ Rs.100 (rupees) per mile
$L_2$ (skilled labor)   = 500 man-years @ Rs.200 per mile
$K_1$ (domestic "capital") = 10 units @ Rs.20,000 per mile
$K_2$ (imported "capital") = 20 units @ \$1,000 plus import duties of Rs.1,000 per unit per mile

If the official foreign exchange ratio is Rs.5 = \$1.00, then the rupee cost of the project per mile is $L_1$ = Rs.100,000, $L_2$ = Rs.100,000, $K_1$ = Rs.200,000, and $K_2$ = Rs.120,000, or a total of Rs.520,000 per mile. The analyst may wish to make certain adjustments in the form of shadow wage rates and foreign exchange. Suppose $MP_{L_1}$ = Rs.60, even though the money wage is Rs.100, and it takes Rs.7 of national resources to generate one dollar of foreign exchange, rather than the official rate of Rs.5 = \$1. We also know that import duties are to be deducted. With these adjustments, the opportunity cost of the project becomes Rs.500,000 per mile, or a total of Rs.50 million.

By similar estimates and adjustments, alternative (2) is deemed to cost Rs.700,000 per mile, or Rs.56 million for the 80-mile project. Construction time for both is estimated as one year. The costs of the projects may therefore be taken as Rs.50 and Rs.56 million, respectively, with which we must compare respective benefits.

Using the traditional consumers' surplus approach, we note that present two-way traffic ($ADT$) is as follows: passenger cars = 60 $ADT$, trucks = 200 *ADT,* buses = 40 *ADT.* For simplicity we assume only three vehicle types and a three-year time horizon after the construction period. Normal traffic growth in the region has been 20 percent each for cars and trucks and 10 percent for buses, and is expected to continue. According to the systems approach, additional traffic generated by the improvements will be 10 percent of normal traffic for trucks, 20 percent for buses, and 30 percent for cars. Traffic estimates are shown in the table below.

|  | *Trucks* | | *Buses* | | *Cars* | | |
|  | *Normal* | *Generated* | *Normal* | *Generated* | *Normal* | *Generated* | *Total* |
|---|---|---|---|---|---|---|---|
| Base Year ADT | 200 | | 40 | | 60 | | 300 |
| Base Year + 1 | 240 | 24 | 44 | 9 | 72 | 22 | 411 |
| Base Year + 2 | 288 | 29 | 49 | 10 | 86 | 26 | 489 |
| Base Year + 3 | 346 | 35 | 54 | 11 | 103 | 31 | 580 |

Cost differences per vehicle-mile between paved and gravel roads are estimated at Rs.3.0 for trucks, Rs.3.4 for buses, and Rs.0.7 for cars. Thus, the total benefits to normal traffic arising from reduced vehicle operating costs for the first year following paving of the highway for alternative (1) are:

240 trucks × 100 miles × 365 days × Rs.3 = Rs.26.3 million
44 buses  × 100 miles × 365 days × Rs.3.4 = Rs.5.5 million
72 cars   × 100 miles × 365 days × Rs.0.7 = Rs.1.8 million

Total    Rs.33.6 million

Note that we have assumed that each *ADT* travels the full 100 miles and that operations are continuous throughout the year. If actual travel is less than 100 miles per *ADT,* as seems likely, and if there are days in the year that the right-of-way is impassable because of, say, flooding, the amount of shipper savings will be reduced. For simplicity, we maintain the above assumptions.

By similar calculations, shipper savings during the second and third years after construction of alternative (1) are Rs.39.8 million and Rs.47.2 million, respectively. The benefits to generated traffic are similarly computed, but only half of them are counted, as the earlier analysis indicates. These are Rs.212 million, Rs.2.6 million, and Rs.3.0 million, respectively, for each of the three years following completion of the project. Other benefits include Rs.2.0 million per year for savings in maintenance costs of a paved road vis-à-vis a gravel road. Time savings will not be estimated for passenger travel or for consignees, although in principle they would and sometimes should be included.

Thus, the aggregate three-year benefit stream is Rs.37.8 million in the first year after construction, Rs.44.4 million in the second year, and Rs.52.2 million in the third year. If the properly estimated social rate of discount is 12 percent, the present value of this expected benefit stream is Rs.106.4 million. Since the cost is estimated at Rs.50 million, the benefits less costs ($B_1 - C_1$) equal Rs.56.4 million. Alternative (1) is clearly feasible.

How about alternative (2)? We have assumed that mileage will be reduced under the second alternative by 20 percent. Thus, given the simplifying assumptions above, vehicle operating cost savings will rise by 20 percent, as will annual maintenance savings. The benefits under alternative (2) can therefore be estimated as Rs.127.7 million, while the costs are Rs.56 million, or $B_2 - C_2 = $ Rs.71.7 million. Thus alternative (2) is preferable to alternative (1), as are its benefit-cost ratio and internal rate of return. There may be other advantages to alternative (2), such as fewer accidents with the decreased mileage driven. On the other hand, possible social dislocation associated with the realignment needs to be considered as an added cost of alternative (2).

In reality, of course, the problems are more formidable. If different modes are being compared (e.g., road vs. rail), far more attention needs to be placed on service differentials and operating cost differences.[1]

Nevertheless, the foregoing illustrates the major rule of project choice where the projects are substitutes for one another, namely, choose the one with the highest net benefits, $B_i - C_i$. In principle, there is no difference if the two alternatives consist of different modes. However, in these cases, especially in poor countries, the *kind* of investment (whether highway, rail, pipeline, waterway, air) may be instrumental in evoking different responses (see text).

---

1. A good illustration of the road-rail problem is given in P. Roberts and D. Dewees, *Economic Analysis for Transport Choice* (Lexington, Mass.: Heath Lexington Books, 1971), chaps. 2–8. Hans Adler has a series of illustrations like the above in *Economic Appraisal of Transportation Projects* (Bloomington: Indiana University Press, 1971), Part II. In fact, the above illustration is adapted from one of Adler's.

# Index

Act to Regulate Commerce (1887), 168, 171, 172, 207, 238, 261, 262, 263, 272
A-J-W effect, 187–91, 196–98, 204, 206, 227, 231
Alabama Midland Case (1896), 264
American Trucking Associations, 213, 270
AMTRAK, 153
appropriate user share: estimation of, 115–20
airline industry: quality of service, 43, 201–203; and technological change, 232; and deregulation, 252–53, 270

Bankruptcy Act, 266
Baumol-Bradford-Walters theorem, 151
barge transport, 177, 178, 179, 198, 207, 215, 216, 226, 228, 231, 253. See also inland waterway
benefit-cost analysis: for highways, 101; and efficient investment criteria, 280, 298, 301–15; constituents of, 295; national income approach to, 305–307; difficulties of, 315–17, 329; distribution of, 317–19; as a guide to action, 330; illustration of, 331–33. See also public investment criteria
Borts, George H., 86

capacity of modal infrastructures: rail, 295–96; highway, 296–97
C&O (Chesapeake and Ohio Railroad), 81, 82
Chow, Garland, 125–26, 127
Civil Aeronautics Board (CAB), 153, 187
Cobb-Douglas production function: 76–78, 247
commodity markets and freight rates, 7–14, 212, 244
ConRail, 265, 270
costs: concepts of, 58–60; difference be-

tween private and social, 60–61; variability of, 64; structure of, 66; measurement of, 67; of motor vehicles, 92–93; of highway maintenance, 93–95; of regulation, 175–76
cost functions: railroad, 72–91, 121, 133, 180; Griliches's rail, 73–76; motor carrier, 91–130, 133, 180; inland waterway, 130–31; oil pipelines, 131–32
cross-elasticity of demand: rail and truck, 14–21
cross-section analysis, 68–71, 78, 80, 86, 242

demand, elasticity of: for transportation, 3–9, 54–56; definition of, 7–8; for commodities, 8–13, 21–30; between rail and truck, 14–22, 44–54; for rail transport, 19–30; and elasticity of supply, 30–42; and quality of service, 42–54
density-based rate structure, 137–38
Department of Justice, 239
Department of Transportation (DOT), 83, 87, 88, 186, 256, 270
deregulation: consequences of, 250–56; and safety, 256–58
Due, J., 86n

earnings credit method. See highway cost allocation
economies of density, 84, 85, 86, 87, 90
economies of scale, 72–86, 151, 167; in railroading, 90, 142, 178; in trucking, 178, 258; summary of trucking studies of, 121–24; flaws in studies, 125–30; for inland waterways, 131, 142, 178; for oil pipelines, 132, 142, 178; classical situation of, 144; and monopolies, 174
efficient user charges: highway, 94, 102; problems of, 95–100